MONCKTON MILNES
The Years of Promise: 1809–1851

Sir F. Doyle. Mr R. M. Milnes. Lord Morpeth. Lord Galway. Mr R. P. Mil.
Lady Galway.   Mr Wyvill. Lord Glendg.

Scene at Fryston, Jany 1844.   Drawn by W. H. Leatham
                                                 from recollection.

THE LIBRARY AT FRYSTON, JANUARY 1844

James Pope - Hennessy

MONCKTON MILNES

The Years of Promise
1809—1851

CONSTABLE: LONDON

LONDON

PUBLISHED BY

Constable and Company Ltd.

10–12 ORANGE STREET, W.C.2

•

INDIA

Orient Longmans Ltd.

BOMBAY CALCUTTA MADRAS

•

CANADA

Longmans, Green and Company

TORONTO

First published 1949

Printed and bound in England by William Clowes and Sons Ltd
London and Beccles

0C0203234 6

TO
LADY CREWE

Contents

List of Illustrations

xi

List of Illustrations

Preface

This study of the youth and early middle-age of Richard Monckton Milnes, Lord Houghton, will be followed by a second book dealing with his life from 1851 until his death in 1885. A third volume containing a selection of hitherto unprinted letters to Lord Houghton from his friends will be published subsequently, since many of the letters are of great intrinsic interest, some of considerable literary merit and all of them illuminate from one angle or another the social life, the literature and the politics— English, French and German—of Western Europe in Lord Houghton's day.

Monckton Milnes (as his contemporaries usually called him) left no memoirs. In age he amiably resisted the persuasions of his family to write down an account of some of the events and people he had seen. This refusal to apply himself to the exacting task of reminiscence was in keeping with his temperament, for Monckton Milnes was easy-going and not given to harsh concentration. One squat volume, entitled *Monographs Social and Personal*, published by John Murray's when Lord Houghton was sixty-three (and mainly consisting of reprints of sketches of his contemporaries already published elsewhere) is the only formal comment on his era that he has left behind him. Besides these *Monographs*, which are written with delicacy and with a certain elaboration, Lord Houghton's printed works comprise five volumes of verse; the famous *Life, Letters and Literary Remains of John Keats*; a pamphlet on Puseyism, one on Ireland, one on the *Events of 1848*; some printed speeches; a few essays on social subjects; an introduction to an edition of Peacock; some contributions to the *Philobiblon Society's* papers; and a handful of articles on literary and political matters scattered through the serious periodicals of that time. Five years after Lord Houghton's death, at Vichy, in August 1885, there appeared in London the official two-volume *Life, Letters and Friendships of Richard Monckton Milnes, Lord Houghton* (Cassell & Co., 1890), by Sir Thomas Wemyss Reid. This comprehensive and scrupulous example of memorial biography records Milnes' development in chronological detail, but it was written before the passing of time had set Lord Houghton into any sort of perspective.

The chief source for Wemyss Reid's volumes and for the present

xiii

book is the very complete collection of Milnes' papers which he himself most carefully accumulated for his posterity. For reference purposes I have called these the 'Houghton Papers.' The Houghton Papers comprise many thousand letters, notes, invitations, verses, memoranda, pamphlets, bills, account-books, and visiting cards of the mid-nineteenth century; as well as the eighteen stout, leather-backed commonplace books into which Monckton Milnes crammed records of his friends' conversations, fragments of his own inmost thoughts, and any scraps of knowledge which he considered interesting or bizarre, comical or sinister. The whole collection of these papers, housed in twelve japanned-tin deed-boxes, was last examined by Wemyss Reid, who printed a part of the material in his book. While most thankfully acknowledging my debt to Wemyss Reid's work, I must make it clear that in every possible instance I have quoted direct from an original manuscript or letter rather than from the transcripts in his biography. Moreover, much of the material which seems of consequence to us to-day was not, for a variety of reasons, thought of value in 1890. I have deliberately set out to make as many direct quotations from letters and diaries as was possible, for I believe that it is only by such word-of-mouth methods that we can approach an understanding of the past.

It was during a conversation with Lord Houghton's only son, the Marquess of Crewe, one autumn evening in 1943, in the bookroom at Argyll House in Chelsea, that I put to him my tentative proposal to write his father's life. With his charming and habitual courtesy, Lord Crewe agreed that with the lapse of sixty years the time for some re-assessment of his father's career might now have come; and with that known generosity in all literary matters, which he had inherited from Lord Houghton, he implied that he would give me access to the papers I should need. The idea I was discussing with Lord Crewe in that and several other conversations about Lord Houghton was for a shorter study than this book has in the event turned out to be. The great and evident interest of much of the material preserved amongst the Houghton Papers has led me on, in the past three years, to try to resurrect more roundly the life and atmosphere of Lord Houghton's world.

Lord Crewe died in 1945, and so he has not seen the execution of a work which, written with his sanction, could never have been undertaken without his interest and his help. Very few people living at this moment can claim to have known Lord Houghton, perhaps none can now claim to have known him well; and it was thus invaluable to me to be able to discuss his life and character with his son. After the war Lady Crewe put into effect Lord Crewe's intentions with regard to this biography: placing at my disposal the boxes of the Houghton Papers, and giving me the freedom of the Fryston Library, a part of which is now in her possession at West Horsley Place. This statement of unvarnished facts suggests the sweeping scope and scale of the help accorded me by Lady Crewe. Nor has Lady Crewe even limited herself within the wide terms of such practical assistance, for throughout my work upon this book I have been persistently aided and buoyed up by her encouragement, her confidence, her judgement and her advice.

I wish also to record my very grateful thanks to the following persons for the various forms of help which they have given me in the course of my writing of this book:—Lord Houghton's granddaughter, the late Lady Annabel Crewe; Mr. Ralph Dutton, Miss Gwendolen Freeman, M. Maurice Gendron, the Earl of Ilchester, Mr. William Jackson of Harvard University, the late Earl of Lytton, M. Henri Martineau of Les Editions Divan, Mr. John S. Mayhew of Washington, Mr. Robin MacDouall, Miss Marion Manzies, Miss Constance Moore, Mr. Harold Nicolson, Mr. Derek Patmore, Professor Hyder E. Rollins, the Earl and Countess of Rosse, Mr. Michael Sadleir, the Marquess of Salisbury, Mr. John Sparrow, Mr. Paul Wallraf, Mrs. Gordon Waterfield, Mrs. Wignall, Mr. Carl Winter and Mrs. Woodham-Smith; as well as to my mother, Una Pope-Hennessy, and to my brother John for constant and constructive help. I have also had the benefit of the advice on style and punctuation of that eminent authority in both these matters, Sir Edward Marsh.

J. P.-H.

May 1949

Chapter One

1809   *1829*

I

I roamed about the courts last night quite late, and was struck with the contrast New Court presented to what it did a month ago. One solitary light appearing through the narrow casement, where thousands used to shine . . . that solitary light being in *your* room. [1]

Some days after his father's death young Augustus Fitzroy had come back to Cambridge alone. He wandered mournfully through the quadrangles of Trinity in the long June evenings, over the bridge that spans the river, on under the limes and the chestnut trees, the steeple of Coton church at the end of the vista.

It was the summer of 1828. Trinity was empty of undergraduates. The round grass plot in the new court which Dr. Wordsworth, the Master, had just added to the College was ragged with weeds. As he entered this court in the dusk Fitzroy had seen that two windows, on the first floor of a staircase to the left of the gateway tower, were lit up. The windows of this court were tall and, in theory, medieval. Like the ugly stucco walls in which they were set, the windows showed a sham quality, for their elaborate Gothic frames were made of cast iron. Officially styled the 'King's Court' in honour of the reigning monarch, George the Fourth, this addition to the college buildings was not regarded with any pride by the undergraduates of Trinity. It had been planned in 1823 with the object of reducing the number of Trinity men living on the loose in the town, and built with an economy which was thought shameful. To Augustus Fitzroy, however, Trinity New Court and most notably these two lighted windows in it aroused the happiest reflections. In these rooms, during term, kept Fitzroy's first and closest of Trinity friends. His name was Richard Monckton Milnes.

Writing next day a letter to his 'dear old Milnes,' Fitzroy told him that someone seemed to be living in his rooms in New Court. What a pity it was not Milnes himself, who was spending the vacation at Boulogne, that dubious place of residence for English families. With Cambridge evacuated by those clever friends ('Kembles and such') whose company Milnes evidently now preferred, Fitzroy thought he might have seen as much of him

---

[1] Letter from Augustus Fitzroy to R. M. Milnes, 18 June 1828.

this June as he had used to do some months ago. They had each come up to Trinity in 1827. Fitzroy had remained a Pensioner, while Milnes assumed the ample blue and silver gown of a Fellow-Commoner of the college.[1] Their immediate friendship, devoted on Fitzroy's side, tolerant on the part of Milnes, was not standing the strain of second-year developments any better than the majority of early undergraduate connections. Fitzroy, a serious and pious youth of seventeen, son of a Canon of Westminster and grandson of the Duke of Grafton, intended to take orders in the English Church. His attitude to life was more severe than that of Richard Milnes. 'I would hope that one year's sejour at Cambridge or in society had not eradicated all those good qualities inherent in your nature': this had become the tone of Fitzroy's letters to his friend. A few months later he announced, using the sentimental idiom of the day, that the thread which bound them together was 'within an inch of dissolution.' The friendship of two young hearts, free from the cold influence of the world, could never more be theirs. From the threshold of his rectory in Suffolk he looked back at Richard Milnes as 'a man who hourly prostrates himself before ambition.' 'I can not forget,' ran one solemn adjuration, 'that there is a want of consistency and principle, and the want of these must ever make the human heart at seasons faithless and changeable.' But you must not merely write Fitzroy down a prig as he stands there for a moment in the night in Trinity New Court, a sad boy with his face turned upwards to a lighted window, in the reign of George the Fourth.

II

Fitzroy was only the first of his contemporaries to condemn rather than to examine or to appreciate the sparkling, fitful personality of Richard Monckton Milnes. Fitzroy and his fellows were not entirely to blame. From his early youth Richard Milnes had made almost a profession of being misunderstood. 'Milnes is one of our aristocracy of intellect here,' Arthur Hallam wrote from Trinity in February 1829, 'a kind-hearted fellow as well as a very clever one, but vain and paradoxical.' 'The common charges, vanity and paradox, were preferred' reported another Trinity friend of a conversation about Milnes with a Dutch family in Naples. From the beginning to the end of his life Milnes was provocative and paradoxical. Developed in boyhood as a defence against his father's more bitter form of humour,

---

[1] *Admissions to Trinity College, Cambridge*, edited by W. Rouse Ball and J. A. Venn, vol. iv, 1801–1850 (Macmillan 1911), p. 283.

the habit of shocking and amusing, of pretending to treat flippantly subjects about which he and other people in fact felt deeply, grew on him. The smoky spiritual atmosphere of mid-nineteenth century England was not that in which this gift was likely to shine out. Few people bothered to penetrate beyond the surface.

Monckton Milnes was not a vain man. He was sensitive to the point of morbidity. He was, spasmodically, ambitious in a strict worldly sense; but he could not intrigue and was not grasping. In some ways a product of his age, he belonged by and large to some earlier, wittier and less upholstered period. Always respected for his kindness of heart and his patronage of letters, he was looked upon askance by many who did not know him and by some who did. Strange legends and stories gathered about his name in his lifetime, like the mists that rose on autumn mornings from the river Aire, to cling about the sloping gardens and the pillared portico of his house at Ferrybridge, in the West Riding of Yorkshire.

Ideally every biography should be the answer to a question. The question in the present case is, Who was Richard Monckton Milnes? It is a commonplace that you can hardly take up a volume of English nineteenth-century reminiscences without coming across his name. The indices to books of letters, of diaries, memoirs and biographies of that period yield a harvest of references to him, under M for Milnes or H for Houghton, the peerage Palmerston finally allotted to him in 1863. Many of these references are affectionate. Many of them are hostile. Most of them stimulate your curiosity. Like one of the more ubiquitous characters of Balzac, Milnes glides in and out of the studies and dining-rooms of his great contemporaries. He is most usually remembered to-day in certain specific roles: the man of whom Carlyle could speak no evil; the man Disraeli ridiculed and despised; the man who wanted to marry Florence Nightingale; who liberated the mind of the young Swinburne and saved innumerable lesser poets from starvation; and wrote the first published biography of Keats. You could compile a yet more indiscriminate list of Milnes' activities, and it was for his variety that he was mocked by some of his own countrymen. It took a young American to leave us what is perhaps the most just estimate of Milnes:

Monckton Milnes [we read in a passage of *The Education of Henry Adams*] was a social power in London, possibly greater than Londoners themselves quite understood, for in London Society as elsewhere, the dull and ignorant made a majority, and dull men always laughed at Monckton Milnes. . . . He himself affected social eccentricity, challenging ridicule with the indifference of one who knew himself to be the first wit in London and a maker of men —of a great many men. A word from him went far. An invitation to his breakfast table went farther. Behind his almost Falstaffian mask and laugh of Silenus, he carried a fine, broad and high intelligence which no one questioned. As a young man he had written verses which some readers thought poetry and which were certainly not altogether prose. Later in Parliament he made speeches, chiefly criticised as too good for the place and too high for the audience. Socially, he was one of the two or three men who went everywhere, knew everybody, talked of everything and had the ear of Ministers. . . . He was a voracious reader, a strong critic, an art connoisseur in certain directions, but above all he was a man of the world by profession and loved the contacts—perhaps the collisions—of society. Milnes [he concludes] was the goodnature of London; the Gargantuan type of its refinement and coarseness; the most universal figure of Mayfair.

In his opinions Milnes was always volatile, and often inconsistent.

About his views [Herbert Spencer wrote of Monckton Milnes in his *Autobiography* [1]] one gained but an undecided impression. Whether it was the effect of mental restlessness or whether it was the effect of readiness to listen to ideas of all kinds, however extreme, there seemed in him an unsettled state of opinion upon most things.

Spencer also records Milnes' 'constitutional love of excitement' and his inability 'to lead a quiet life.' Bearing these later verdicts in mind and comparing them with the more sage and solid outlook of Augustus Fitzroy and his friends, it is easy to understand that these sober-minded Cambridge youths found Milnes at the age of eighteen already wayward, unstable, and thoroughly unlike themselves.

III

The first comment on Richard Monckton Milnes at Cambridge occurs in the small pocket diary kept for nearly forty years of her married life by his mother,[2] Henrietta Milnes. After a journey into Wales during September 1827, the Milnes family had

---

[1] *Autobiography* (1904), vol. ii, p. 96. Spencer first met Milnes in 1851. 'There were exceptions, however, to his restlessness,' Spencer adds, '. . . His information about people and things was copious; and he abounded in anecdotes, which he narrated with an enjoyment that was infectious. Full of kindly feeling, too, he was . . . (and) genuinely desirous of aiding whatever he thought good.'

[2] The journal, which consists of two small octavo volumes bound in red leather with flaps like those of a bank pass-book, is written in a merry, easy style in Mrs. Milnes' sloping hand, but is not dated day by day. It is possible that these volumes were written up later in Mrs. Milnes' life from her own memories and from old diaries which she then destroyed.

4

returned to their house near Doncaster, driven up to London, seen the Thames Tunnel, and come down to Cambridge towards the close of October to see Richard installed at Trinity. The day after they arrived there his mother helped him to arrange his books in the alcove book-shelves of his room in New Court. She was then led by an old butler into a gallery behind the Hall, to watch him dine there for the first time. 'He seemed,' she noted, 'as much at home among all the dons as if he had been there for years.'

The solicitude with which Mr. and Mrs. Milnes settled their only son into his University life was due to the fact that he had been ill as a boy. His bad health had precluded his remaining at school, and although in his admission to Trinity Mr. Richardson of Ferry-bridge School, Yorkshire, was given as his master, he had in fact been educated at home by a tutor, working at English, Latin and Greek themes, mathematics and French in his father's house outside Doncaster, Thorne Hall. Thorne, which Mr. Milnes rented in 1817 since he found he could not live at Fryston (his family house at Ferrybridge), stood in only twenty-five acres of ground. This lay near the Fishlake and Sykehouse estates of the Milnes family, and it was to reclaim waste lands on these by 'scientific' farming that Mr. Milnes had gone there. His wife, partly brought up at the court of St. James's, where her father had been Comptroller to George the Third,[1] preferred metropolitan to Yorkshire life. She was always begging Mr. Milnes to shut up the house and go abroad 'for the children's sake.' Mr. Milnes thought otherwise. It was not until Richard was established at Cambridge that he closed Thorne and took his wife and his daughter, some books and his plate, to France and then to Italy for a visit of eight years. From her marriage until 1827 Mrs. Milnes was left to console herself with her flower-garden and her music; and it was in this way that Richard and his little sister Harriette passed a peaceful but not very stimulating childhood in the West Riding. That countryside, now so desolate and romantic, with its crumbling mansions, devastated parklands and abrupt mountains of slag, its factory chimneys and steep, grey mining villages, was then only in the earlier stages of industrialisation. A Proustian recollection of the smell of beech-leaves in the high park trees which he would climb to watch the deer was one of the few memories from this period which Richard cherished, and

---

[1] Mrs. Milnes' father, the 4th Viscount Galway, b. 1752 and d. 1810, was Comptroller from 1784 to 1787 and a Privy Councillor. He was usually drunk when addressing the House. In May 1792 Lord Auckland wrote from the Hague: 'Lord Galway has been here in a state of continued intoxication, which must soon put an end to him. His understanding (such as it was) is quite gone': *The Complete Peerage*, vol. v, p. 410.

it was doubtless during this time at Thorne that he contracted the pronounced distaste for all country pursuits which never after left him, and which was so marked in later years when he himself, inheriting his father's lands, became in his turn a Yorkshire squire. His calm boyhood, interrupted by one visit to the French Channel coast and a short tour of Scotland with a tutor, was thus literally confined within a family circle. Cambridge was his first essay at independent life. He had at his back neither the public-school experience of many of his Trinity friends nor the wider knowledge of the great world which Fitzroy, for example, would have imbibed from the ducal household at Euston.

No portrait or drawing of Milnes at Cambridge has survived, nor have we any distinct account of his physical appearance at this moment of his adolescence. Unlike his father, a tall man who had once been a very handsome one, Richard Milnes was short. He did not come much above the shoulders of a man of average height, and he filled up little space in a room. In later life he grew portly, and before the age of fifty he had developed a double chin; for the present, however, we must imagine him as small, slight and brown-haired—brown hair worn long and curling, with a glint Carlyle described as 'olive-blonde.' His forehead was broad and intellectual, but his jaw and mouth (described to me by one who knew him well as 'coarsely moulded' and 'preventing any claim to the accepted standard of good looks') contrasted strangely with it, suggesting a character in which intellect and sensuality might be in conflict. His nose was straight, his eyes blue-grey, his eyebrows fair, his glance open and direct. He was well but not luxuriously dressed. The amiable impression his appearance made on you was summed up by Alfred Tennyson, who passed him on entering Trinity for the first time in February 1828: 'That is a man I should like to know,' he said to himself; 'he looks the best-tempered fellow I ever saw.'

Milnes' own opinion of himself in his first term at Trinity is implicit in the half-humorous account which he sent home to Thorne Hall, in November 1827, of his meeting with the German phrenologist Spurzheim. In one of the long letters by which he kept his family informed of the details of his Cambridge life he told them that he had asked Dr. Spurzheim to dinner to meet his tutor and 'two or three quiet men.' After dinner the doctor began to feel the bumps on Richard's skull. He told him that he found him eminently benevolent and fond of music and poetry; wishing for approval, liking flattery and with a tendency to satire and ridicule. 'I need not tell anyone who knows me how true this is,' Milnes commented, before going on to another piece of German wisdom

6

less likely to be palatable at Thorne. Parents, declared Dr. Spurzheim, were responsible for all their children's faults and dispositions; Milnes' tutor, Connop Thirlwall, agreed. The reception given to this theory at Thorne Hall is not recorded, but it certainly needed no cranial expert to divine how sharply Richard Milnes' own personality was influenced by that of his father, Robert Pemberton Milnes. Mr. Milnes did not die until his son was in his fiftieth year. Throughout that long span of time his influence upon Richard's temperament was positive but not invariably constructive. Watchful and critical to excess, Mr. Milnes came to assume the role of a Greek chorus in the successive scenes of his son's career.

IV

Robert Pemberton Milnes was the elder of the two sons of Richard Slater Milnes, a rich cloth manufacturer of Wakefield. The family claimed that they were by origin small gentry from Derbyshire, and that in the reign of Charles the Second an ancestor who moved to Wakefield had entered the wool trade and obtained a monopoly in the cloth of the district. This monopoly lasted throughout the eighteenth century and its profits were augmented by such side interests as brick-kilns. It produced a considerable fortune, which was increased by a series of skilful commercial marriages. In religion the Milneses were Dissenters and in politics they were Whigs. Slater Milnes was Member for York from 1784 to 1802 and a financial supporter of Fox. He lived at Effingham House in Piccadilly, cutting a figure in the Whig world in the last decade of the eighteenth century. By his marriage with the daughter of a chapel-going Leeds merchant he came into possession of the old Strafford demesne, Great Houghton Hall, but he bought for himself an estate near Ferrybridge on the river Aire in the West Riding, a 'handsome square mansion' called Fryston Hall. Fryston had belonged to an acquaintance of Horace Walpole, and lay not far from Kippax, the long Gothicised house of Walpole's crony, Sir John Bland. Slater Milnes added an Italian front, with Ionic pediment and pilasters, to Fryston, and taking up residence there in 1790 he lived the full-blooded life of a political country gentleman (Stubbs painted him as a neat, red-coated figure riding to hounds in a Yorkshire landscape) until his sudden death in 1804 at the age of forty-five. At his death his two sons and seven daughters found that their father had left most of his money and both his estates to his widow for her lifetime. She continued to try to live at Fryston, managing the now impoverished lands.

Robert Pemberton Milnes was not quite twenty-one at his father's death. 'I idolised my father,' he wrote many years later, describing him as the handsomest of men and best of whist-players. Robert was already an effective young man, singularly handsome, something of a dandy, a very good rider, with an interest in politics and a passion for country life. He gambled a little, though fortunately less than his brother, Rodes Milnes, who had fallen in with the self-indulgent set that clustered round the Regent and who ended by ruining both his brother and himself. Politically, Robert Milnes was a Tory, claiming that he had been shocked out of the Whig party by the unpatriotic talk of the members of Brooks's club. In 1806 he became one of the two Members for the little borough of Pontefract on the edge of the Fryston estate, and within a year he had made a reputation as 'the brilliant political meteor of Bolton Row.' In the autumn of 1808 he married his neighbour Henrietta Monckton, a daughter of Lord Galway. In the following June a son was born. Christened Richard after his grandfather and Monckton after his mother's family, he was removed to the seaside at Scarborough with his mother as soon as she could travel.

During this visit to Scarborough in the summer of 1809 there occurred an incident which became a topic of speculation in London for some weeks, and which radically affected the life of Robert Milnes and thus indirectly that of his son. While Mrs. Milnes and her husband were at breakfast one August morning (she records in her journal) a King's Messenger drove up in a post-chaise with a dispatch from the Prime Minister, Perceval, offering Milnes the choice of a seat in the Cabinet either as Chancellor of the Exchequer or Secretary of War. Milnes was only twenty-six, and the offer was made on the strength of his able speaking in the House. The compliment was a great one. He immediately replied: 'Oh no. I will not accept either. With my temperament I should be dead in a year.' His wife knelt and begged him to take office, if only for their child's sake; he remained adamant, went up to London to refuse the offer, and shortly afterwards gave up his interest in politics and his Pontefract seat. He subsided into the local interest of the West Riding of Yorkshire and came seldom to London, where his name lingered for a few years as a legend; no longer the political meteor but 'Single-speech Milnes.'

This refusal of public office (which incidentally was the occasion of Palmerston's first admission to a Ministry) is an example of Mr. Milnes' talent for behaving in a way in which he was not expected to behave. The eccentricity of his reactions and the difficulty of predicting what they might be or how suddenly they might change became the ruling factor in his family's life, and

8

later gave sudden twists and jolts to his son's public career. Characterised by Disraeli as 'a Shandean squire, full of humour and affectation,' by Walter Savage Landor as 'wise and honourable' and by another witness as 'high-minded' and 'impressionable,' Robert Milnes may seem to us, in perspective, an attractive and unworldly figure. He had a healthy faith in the position of the country gentlemen of England—'an Order which no other sovereign but ours of England has, and which Kings and Princes have no conception of—its Supporters, the Horse and a Fox—my own, the Wheatsheaf, its Crest—its motto *Hospitality*.'

Though he never travelled without his set of Shakespeare and had himself written verses in imitation of his favourite poet, Prior, Mr. Milnes affected a contempt for the arts. In a short travel journal which he kept during a tour from Milan to Naples and back by Rome and Florence in 1831, he expressly stated in the first paragraph that

little will be said on Arts, Literature or Antiquities. I shall write what I hear and see, that at any future time I may go the tour again, without travelling. . . . If continued throughout the route, it will be a morning's reading. I do not intend it to be a book, for persons to buy.

This prim philistinism made his son's early and passionate interest in poetry and his reverence for artists most distasteful to Mr. Milnes. No doubt because of his own failure to make a great political career, Mr. Milnes was fiercely determined that Richard should achieve a position of power and influence in the House of Commons. To write poetry in imitation of Wordsworth, to read Shelley and Keats, seemed to him not only a waste of time but also a dangerous drawback in a political man. In his day the House of Commons had been composed of hard-bitten country gentlemen, not poets or novelists, and he could not foresee that the House of the eighteen-forties would contain men such as Bulwer-Lytton and Disraeli. Upon the romantic youths of Trinity, living in the shadow of the Byronic tradition, he turned the cold, clear eye of the eighteenth century.

My father was always trying to give me two educations at once [Richard Milnes wrote retrospectively in his commonplace book], one an education of ambition, vanity, emulation and progress . . . the other of independence, self-abnegation and the highest repose. He thus failed in making me either a successful politician or a contented philosopher.

The real affection between father and son cannot be questioned; the contrast in temperament is too significant to be ignored.

Richard would be saying [noted Mr. Milnes on viewing the Apennines] that the Apennines are looking at me with the heaviness of the eye of a girl in love, or some such touching simile; their molten shapes set me a thinking, that somebody must have held a hot shovel over all Italy.

By the length of his life and the force of his character Robert Pemberton Milnes can claim to become a chief personage in this book. He does not often emerge into the foreground, however, for he lived chiefly in Yorkshire (at Fryston or at Bawtry), endeavouring to salvage his family's finances (wrecked by the extravagance of his brother Rodes), selling land to the new railway companies, reading and criticising his son's speeches and pamphlets, playing piquet with a neighbour, and making caustic but diffuse comments on the politics of the day. It was in reaction against his prejudices and interests that his son's character developed. Where the father was strict, the son became tolerant; where the father was sternly logical, the son cultivated paradox and hyperbole, became sentimental and seemed frivolous. The influence of Mrs. Milnes, to which her son by his home education had been exposed for eighteen years, was a civilising one. Although a scrupulous wife and mother, Henrietta Monckton had retained throughout the long years at Thorne a zest for living which she afterwards deliciously indulged in Milan, in Venice and Florence and Rome in the early eighteen-thirties. For the fourth member of the family, his young sister Harriette, Richard Milnes felt an affection which was perhaps the deepest and most enduring of his life. When she married he was inconsolable, and in the London of the eighteen-fifties Mrs. Norton would still tease him by telling people that he cared more for Harriette than for any other woman; to which Miss Cissie Grote replied, 'What an unnatural brute.' The chief explanation of Richard Monckton Milnes' complicated psychology lies in these family relationships. Before returning to Cambridge, leaving Mr. and Mrs. Milnes and their daughter leading an uneventful life near Doncaster, it is germane to hear the opinion on Robert Milnes of that most penetrating of nineteenth-century psychologists, Thomas Carlyle. 'Your father,' said Carlyle in 1841 after a visit to Fryston, 'has many remarkable things about him, all loose and distracted. If they were only braced up and fibred together he would be a very distinguished man.'

V

Richard Monckton Milnes was sent to Trinity because his father had been entered for that college as a Fellow-Commoner in 1801 (though since Pemberton Milnes neither matriculated nor graduated,

there is some doubt that he ever resided there). By 1827
several changes had taken place at Trinity. There was first the
New Court, that visible symptom of the new regime which had
begun in 1820 when Christopher Wordsworth, an austere brother
of the poet and author of a long ecclesiastical biography, had
succeeded to the Mastership. In his own extreme old age, not
many weeks indeed before his death, Milnes (looking back across
the gulf of nearly sixty years) irreverently referred to Dr. Wordsworth as 'an old man . . . who had not recommended himself to
the undergraduate mind by any exhibition of geniality or especial
interest in our pursuits, our avocations or even our studies.' [1]   In
1822, a year before the Speaker of the House of Commons, acting
as proxy for George the Fourth, laid the foundation stone of the
New Court, Dr. Wordsworth had made an important change in the
administrative structure of the college by adding a third Tutor
to the two traditionally in charge of the undergraduates. There
was now 'Whewell's side,' 'Peacock's side' and 'Higman's side' at
Trinity—Milnes, Thackeray, Alfred and Charles Tennyson being,
for example, on Whewell's side, while Augustus Fitzroy, the
Lushington brothers and James Spedding were on Peacock's, and
Milnes' Irish friend Stafford O'Brien on Higman's. A feature
of Trinity life which Dr. Wordsworth left unchanged was the
detested chapel system, by which every undergraduate in the
college had to be in Chapel at seven o'clock in the morning.
This measure, largely a disciplinary one to ensure that self-indulgent
young men got up at a proper hour, was the subject of many
complaints and petitions, one of which Milnes drafted while still
among the youngest of the freshmen. Chapel was theoretically
followed by attendance at lectures from eight till ten, reading from
ten till two, relaxation such as calling on a friend or wandering to
glance over the prints at Deighton's bookshop before dinner at
three o'clock; vespers, tea and work from eight till midnight
bringing to a close this ideal day. This strict curriculum was not
adhered to by everyone. The richer members of Trinity filled in
time with breakfast parties (hams, fowls, pies, porter, champagne,
coffee and tobacco) from ten till one, wine parties about four o'clock
at which port, white wine and cherry brandy were consumed with
fresh fruit and French plums; and later parties beginning at seven
in the evening. This set did no work, read Colburn's latest novels
during lectures, and bothered little about preparing for a degree

---

[1] Address to the sixth annual meeting of the Wordsworth Society, 8 July 1885,
printed in *Some Writings and Speeches of Richard Monckton Milnes, Lord Houghton,
in the Last Year of his Life with a Notice in Memoriam by George Stovin Venables, Q.C.*
(Privately printed at the Chiswick Press, 1888.)   Lord Houghton died 11 August
1885.

(which was still to be obtained by means other than success in examination). It kept alive the loose traditions of unreformed, eighteenth-century Cambridge in the midst of the increasingly earnest nineteenth-century university. This was a set with which Milnes and his friends felt little sympathy.

I see you think the tenor of my last letter to my mother too gay, too flippant [he wrote to his father some months after his arrival at Cambridge]. In the amusements I frankly write of, and which you consider such a prostitution of time, is there one inconsistent with ten hours a day reading?

Although his Trinity friends thought him 'mirthful' and frivolous, Milnes was in fact engaged in working fairly hard, in making experiments in public speaking at the Union, and in trying generally to prepare himself for a future which did not at that moment seem very tempting. His father was now, by his family's standards, a poor man, for he had undertaken to pay the enormous gambling and racing debts of his brother Rodes, and he was slowly coming to the decision that he could no longer afford to live in England.

I seem now only to begin to feel the blight that has fallen on the hopes of my childhood [Richard wrote to him in December 1828]; it is an undefined regret, a sense of having lost a place in society— and to hear you call yourself exiled, exiled without almost a name, without a good cause, without even the miserable consciousness that you have enjoyed what you have lost . . . makes me very wretched. When I examine it I half find it a selfish and grovelling feeling, but it comes upon me when alone, and more still when I look round on those who have brighter courses before them.

With this check upon his natural exuberance, Milnes did not really enjoy his early Cambridge career. Trinity itself was magnificent in its aspect and its traditions: still, except for the new block of buildings, the Trinity of Byron's day—the Great Court, Neville's Court, the spacious library with its black and white flooring, its Gibbons incrustations, its solemn and elegant busts, and the great painted window, then scorned as ludicrous but now admired as much as the Reynolds windows in New College Chapel at Oxford. In the high, dim hall a charcoal fire burned, while the daylight came filtering through the oriel windows, illuminating a little the dark wainscoting and the waxed tables and the portraits of Newton and Dryden, of Cowley and Richard Bentley that hung along the walls. But for the daily life performed against this splendid architectural background, Milnes had little use. One day, he complained, seemed very like another. Even the air was insipid. It was only in retrospect that he romanticised his undergraduate career.

VI

As the decades of Victoria's reign rolled on there must have seemed much to romanticise in that distant, Georgian world of Trinity from 1827 to 1830—'the dawn-golden times' of Tennyson's *In Memoriam*. This great poem and the friendship it celebrated cast a lustre back over the time and place, making even the ugly New Court (where Hallam also kept in first-floor rooms) a haunt of legend; and turning Arthur Hallam himself into an idyllic figure. But, as Mr. Harold Nicolson has suggested in his analysis of Tennyson's Cambridge period, few of the fervent young men who composed the famous Trinity set centring round Arthur Hallam ever achieved permanent fame or became really eminent Victorians. Youthful promise, particularly undergraduate promise, merits posterity's attention only if it is fulfilled. Of the two most promising men at Trinity in Milnes' day one, Arthur Hallam, died at the age of twenty-two, leaving nothing behind him but a gleaming, gesturing phantom in the memories of his friends; the other, Thomas Sunderland, an orator of the first class, became insane at much the same age and disappeared from public view. Apart from Arthur Hallam and Charles, Frederick, and Alfred Tennyson, members of 'the Set' included Richard Chenevix Trench, a mild religious poet who ended up as Archbishop of Dublin; J. W. Blakesley, who achieved some anonymous publicity in later life as 'the Hertfordshire Incumbent' of *The Times*; James Spedding, who devoted a lifetime to the rehabilitation of Sir Francis Bacon ('gnawing on that bare bone', Venables, another member of the Set, called it: 'giving five-and-twenty years to a showy quack') ; Dean Merivale; and Kinglake, author of *Eothen* and prolix historian of the war in the Crimea. John Sterling and Charles Buller belonged to the preceding Cambridge generation; Thackeray and Edward FitzGerald, though contemporaries of the Hallam set, did not attract their notice.

There would be no point in trying to reconstruct the precise relationships of the members of this charmed circle to each other, to Hallam, its natural centre, and to Richard Monckton Milnes. Hallam, who came up to Trinity in June 1828 (when Alfred Tennyson had been there five months and Milnes nearly a year), was at first 'unjust' and stand-offish with Milnes. They later became friends; and for a few months of 1829 intimate friends. 'I am sorry I ever acted towards you with caprice,' wrote Hallam in July 1831; 'at the time I had reasons which seemed to justify my conduct but I intend to forget them, or to apply them differently.' It was to Hallam that Milnes addressed a jocular note from the basket of the balloon of Mr. Green the aeronaut, in which he ascended over Cambridge in May 1829; but he admitted to his sister that for the once he saw Hallam he would see O'Brien or some more entertaining friend twenty times. With Alfred Tennyson, and especially with his brother Frederick, he was on the pleasantest terms; 'Poor Fred Tennyson is sitting by me while I am writing. He took up your long letter and said "I have no one to write to me on such things."' The daily lives and friendships, studies and squabbles and enthusiasms of these Georgian undergraduates are not in themselves of any consequence: they become of interest only if they offer clues to the later development of some significant personality. The Cambridge days of Alfred Tennyson, which made so dynamic a change in his outlook and consequently in his poetry, conform to this requirement; those of Richard Monckton Milnes do not. Tennyson, an awkward and inhibited genius from a Fenland rectory, was liberated by his experiences at Cambridge and by the influence of Arthur Hallam. Milnes, already gay and self-possessed, reacted against his environment as surely as Tennyson submitted to it. In a sense his character was already formed, if this verb may be used of a character so free and fluid as his. Of all the young men surrounding Arthur Hallam, youths who gave themselves such solemn and serious airs and who planned to change the world in their generation, Tennyson and Milnes fulfilled their promise best. The notable gifts of men like Trench and Merivale were soon smothered in conventional Church of England careers ('have you seen Trench's new volume?' wrote Blakesley, himself an example of unfulfilled renown. 'Here we all think that the clergyman has swallowed up the poet. . . . We are most painfully disappointed'), whereas the qualities which made Milnes loved and a little distrusted by his Cambridge friends—the *engoûements* and the kaleidoscopic opinions, the vulnerability and the anxiety to be fascinated by whatever was new—merely became stronger and more marked as he grew older. They were not qualities which could carry him to eminence as a poet or a politician—but they made him into one of the most original creatures of the age.

VII

The two spheres of activity in which Milnes was anxious to perform at Cambridge were the Union Debating Society and the Apostles. To join the Union, which met in a low, stuffy room at the back of the Red Lion Inn—'cavernous, tavernous,' Milnes called it—you paid the annual sum of one gold sovereign. This fee entitled members to the use of the reading-room and its journals and gave them the opportunity of practising, before green baize tables loaded with tumblers and water decanters, those tricks and wiles of oratory with which they hoped subsequently to captivate the House of Commons and the country. Milnes began to speak in the Union almost as soon as he had settled into his rooms at Trinity. Throughout his life a nervous speaker, he perhaps acquired in the Cambridge Union the pompous and elaborate manner of public oratory which Disraeli cruelly ridiculed, and which formed such a contrast to his easy, natural and witty address in private conversation.

The 'Apostles,' on the other hand, was the most astringent and exclusive society in the University. Founded in 1820 as the Conversazione Society, with a rigid membership of twelve, it soon adopted the nickname given to it by the outside world. Membership of the Apostles was then, as now, a signal honour, and involved a kind of implicit responsibility for keeping up with fellow-members for the rest of one's life. Members met in each other's rooms to hear one of their number read some paper on a religious or philosophical topic, which was afterwards discussed. The Apostles of Milnes' day included Hallam and Alfred Tennyson, Trench, Spedding, Alford, Merivale and Sunderland. The Society was not without its private intrigues, and an undated note left by Thomas Sunderland in Milnes' rooms in New Court suggests that Milnes (who had only been elected after much earnest argument among the Apostles) did not always share the outlook of his fellow-members. Sunderland was anxious to get Kinglake made one of the elect:

I called on you today [he scribbled] to talk to you about securing Mr. Kinglake's election to the Apostles. I still think the best plan will be to say nothing about the matter to the other men till a day or two before our first meeting. Then I will ask them *separately* and as they will not have time to concert a rebellion en masse, I have no doubt we shall succeed perfectly. . . . We really must [he concludes] introduce someone among them who is not so vulgarly gregarious as the larger portion of our worthy brother Apostles.

Sunderland, whom Tennyson has described in the lines *A Character* as 'quiet, dispassionate and cold' with a 'lack-lustre dead-blue eye,' had a morbid horror of 'gregariousness.' Writing to tell Milnes that he could not go to Germany with him one summer, he described the delightful isolation of the Cumberland sea-coast on which he was living, alone and brooding on Robespierre and Saint-Just; the rocks along the coast earning his particular praise because, although in perfect harmony with one another, they never appeared in groups.

Alfred Tennyson's membership of the Apostles was later described by one of his fellow-members as lending a halo to the society in his day. Though dating from the period of Tennyson's great fame, this phrase no doubt reflects the feelings of the Apostles for the lank, sombre and leonine young poet from Lincolnshire. In the years just before and in those just following Arthur Hallam's death, old members of the Apostles writing to Milnes would give news of Alfred's progress. It is clear that they regarded him with a kind of humorous awe, though their respect had been a little shaken by the fiasco of his paper on ghosts, which he threw into the fire on the very evening on which the Apostles were assembling to hear him read it to them. Hallam was trying hard, both by conversation and by writing, to draw public attention to his friend's poetry, and Milnes took the initiative by placing the lines

> List'ning the lordly music flowing from
> The illimitable years—

on the title page of an essay on Homer which won him the English Essay prize for 1829 and which he thereupon had printed as a pamphlet. The general view of the Apostles was that Alfred was a genius, but a lazy one, and that he needed a good deal of explaining to English people in general. 'How can a man with such great natural strength of body live so indolently and be well?' Henry Lushington wrote to Milnes. 'The worst of Tennyson's poetry is that it is necessary to hear him read it before you can perceive the melody, at least for ninety-nine men out of a hundred,' wrote Blakesley in November 1830. The Apostles' interest in Tennyson and their sense of a species of responsibility towards him did not wane with the years.

Alfred Tennyson has been here with us for the last week. He is looking well and in good spirits: but complains of nervousness. How should he do otherwise, seeing that he smokes the strongest and most stinking tobacco out of a small blackened clay pipe on an average nine hours in every day?

The sense of Tennyson's indolence was not confined to the Apostles: 'Why will not Tennyson give up absurdities of every kind—the errors of his morbid, Germanised and smoke-sodden temperament; and set about writing like a man?' Aubrey de Vere, the younger brother of a Trinity friend, expostulated. 'It will never do writing a song one day and a sonnet a month after—he must write continuously and laboriously.' That Tennyson finally learned to write 'continuously and laboriously' is unfortunately proved by another apostolic letter, describing the poet at work on his *Idylls of the King*. Though written in 1856 this facetious letter is relevant here, since it exemplifies the Apostles' attitude to and their sustained interest in the success of the poet whom they had first brought to public notice.

The Laureate [Spedding began] cannot breakfast with anybody. The process of excretion (I speak spiritually) begins immediately after the last cup of tea; is accompanied with desire of solitude and tobacco; followed (when no disturbing cause interferes) with the production of some five and twenty lines of Idyll; which the slightest obstruction offered to the natural process shuts up for the day. I could not extract from him any alternative proposition: so I must leave you to seek him in his lair.

Modern commentators on *In Memoriam* and students of the Cambridge phase of Tennyson's life have written of the relationship with Arthur Hallam as though it were, in its day, unique. This is mistaken. The unique quality of the friendship lay squarely in the fact that one of the two friends was a major English poet, who has immortalised it in his finest series of lyrics. Seen in the perspective of Cambridge at that day, and particularly of the Trinity set to which they both belonged, the relationship falls into place as one among many such close mutual affections. The letters which Richard Milnes kept from this period of his life are filled with references to such things: 'Sir Jacob and I are inseparable, he is one of the dearest creatures I have ever seen. You would I am sure approve of our friendship, it is so unlike the routine of Cambridge arm-in-arms'; 'Garden and Monteith have not cooled at all'; 'Cavendish's brother is a charming creature and so well fitted for Fitzroy.' On Fitzroy's departure from Trinity in 1831, for instance, several of his friends were so affected that they burst into tears. It is clear that the atmosphere of Trinity at this moment was charged with emotion, which it happened to be the fashion to exploit, not to conceal. Their almost Elizabethan conception of romantic friendship forms the subject of a long letter to Milnes from Arthur Hallam, written in July 1831:

. . . I am not aware, my dear Milnes [wrote Hallam], that, in that lofty sense which you are accustomed to attach to the name of Friendship, we ever were or ever could be friends. What is more to the purpose, I never fancied that we could, nor intended to make you fancy it. That exalted sentiment I do not ridicule— God forbid—nor consider it as merely ideal: I have experienced it, and it thrills within me now—but not—pardon me, my dear Milnes, for speaking frankly—not for you. But the shades of sympathy are innumerable, and wretched indeed would be the condition of man, if sunshine never fell upon him save from the unclouded skies of a tropical summer.

Persuaded that Milnes had not received this letter, Hallam returned to the theme a month later,[1] protesting against

that *arrière pensée* of yours, as ingenious as unfounded, which makes you assume that because I have not towards you the more elevated & vehement species of attachment I am therefore incapable of it altogether, and by consequence, or rather by parity of reasoning, that my disinclination to a kind of phraseology, in which I used to indulge, is a proof of my having fallen away from all generous enthusiasm for the Good, the Beautiful and the True.

In this context the most intimate friendship which Milnes formed while at Cambridge is of some interest—both in itself and for the slanting light it casts upon the more famous Hallam-Tennyson relationship. It was with that now-forgotten but irresistibly charming character Stafford Augustus O'Brien.

VIII

O'Brien [wrote Richard Milnes to his parents in the early months of 1830] is fascination itself. . . . We sing duets together and I really think, if I was with him much longer, he would make me as good as himself.

Stafford Augustus O'Brien had come up to Trinity from Harrow in 1829, entering the college as a Pensioner in March of that year and becoming a Fellow-Commoner in October. His father, alleged to be the illegitimate son of a housemaid, was an Irish gentleman resident in north Northamptonshire, where he had inherited a family house called Blatherwycke Park. Stafford O'Brien himself was a boy of nineteen, effervescing with high spirits, with a talent for private theatricals and charades and a Southern Irish charm. While he talked he could never keep still —'O'Brien,' Milnes noted, 'goes through the series of attitudes of old Dresden.' He was deeply attached to his native land—

Ireland the only country that *might be* [as he called it, adding in elucidation] America will be, Italy has been, Belgium can't be, England (I suppose) is; but darling Ireland might be—what a delicious mixture of possible and uncertain is here.

Most of his short life (he died before he was fifty, after his return from a humanitarian tour of the Crimean battlefields) was passed in Ireland, where Milnes would visit him in his small house at Cratloe, on the banks of the Shannon near Limerick. His lightness

---

[1] MS. letter of Arthur Hallam, 22 August 1831. The earlier letter is undated but postmarked: Hastings 31 July 1831.

and wit and energy roused an immediate response in Milnes, whose
temperament, though at times similarly exuberant, was more subject
than O'Brien's to moods of pessimism and gloom. He introduced
O'Brien to Fitzroy (who subsequently married the boy's sister,
Angelina O'Brien, and was left a widower before he was thirty)
and to other friends, and generally made a great fuss of him.
During the vacations they wrote constantly to each other, and when
they had both left Cambridge for good they would arrange to meet
in Italy or Ireland or simply in London, or they would stay together
at Blatherwycke or Fryston, or at what O'Brien termed 'the lettered
towers' of Lord Northampton at Castle Ashby. O'Brien was in much
demand at such houses as Castle Ashby or Burghley, for he could
be relied on to be amusing, to arrange tableaux for Lady Exeter,
or to drive Lady Emmeline Drummond, three ponies abreast, in the
sledge.   His attitude to these houses and their inmates was salutary,
and his comments on 'the fine people' are curiously valid to-day.

The thing here [he would write to Milnes from some great house]
is getting vapid. The fine people are so very fine and my lord
and lady, most kind the twain, yet tremble at anything that should
go deeper than the surface, and seem to feel it a duty never to let
the talk run more than a minute on one subject unless that subject
be the movement or ailment of the fine people. . . . Stoics and
Epicureans, would to heaven they had a spice of Platonism.

His affection for Milnes was deep and genuine—'I have never seen
anyone at all like you, and I am quite provoked when I hear anyone
compared to you.' It was cordially returned. None of Milnes'
letters to O'Brien have been traced, though some mawkish verses
which Milnes wrote to him from Ferrara, but did not publish,
have survived. O'Brien was also the object of two of the poems
in Milnes' *Memorials of a Tour in Greece* (1833). In the exchange
of verses, and specifically of sonnets, between members of the
Hallam-Tennyson group there seems again some slight analogy
with the Elizabethans. 'Write a sonnet to me on the evening of
the 20th Septr.,' Hallam told Milnes, who was in Italy, in 1829:
'I will write one to you at the same time; between seven and eight,
if possible.' 'I will be candid enough to acknowledge that I
totally forgot my engagement respecting the Sonnet,' he told
Milnes in his next letter, 'at the time appointed, but in return you
must shew your courtesy by accepting of it thus late in the day.'
This letter contained a sonnet of Hallam's in which he urged
Milnes to return to England. A few weeks earlier Hallam had
written some other lines to Milnes—'a *chanson à boire*, written after
dinner, & addressed to you':

I'll pledge thee in this bloodred wine,
    Tho' thou art far away:
Heaven bless that honest heart of thine,
    And keep it from decay!

Thy tricksy spirit takes a pride
    In frolics quaint & elfish:
But never swerved from Honor's side,
    And ne'er did ought of selfish.

The sprightly doubt, the gay denial,
    The wit, like Greek fire running,
Which, wert thou for thy life on trial,
    Would never cease from funning

There be perhaps who think them vain:
    I've learned another lore:
And whether joy be mine, or pain,
    I like thee more & more.

Hallam, the three Tennysons, Milnes, Blakesley, Spedding, one or two others all wrote verses. Only O'Brien seems never to have composed a line.

The influence upon Milnes of his affection for O'Brien is hard to determine. 'Je n'ai jamais vu Milnes qu'engoué de quelqu'un ou de quelquechose,' Alexis de Tocqueville wrote in his *Souvenirs* (when describing him as 'épris de Madame Sand' in 1848), and indeed the series of his enthusiasms was almost numberless. But like other people who are vulnerable to each new excitement or fresh impact, Milnes was not in fact fundamentally affected by the advice or opinions of his friends. His friendship with O'Brien was in essence a youthful friendship. It was punctuated by the misunderstandings and complaints of immaturity, for as a friend Milnes was exacting as well as warm-hearted, as touchy as he was affectionate, at times as indolent as anxious to help. Later friends, such as Charles MacCarthy ('It is very naughty of you to think so ill of O'Brien, for I am sure he loves you') and Lord John Manners, were called in at times to rectify misunderstandings and patch up quarrels between the two. As they both grew older, the friendship tailed off, as such things will; but when O'Brien's public career came to a sudden and unhappy end in 1852 (he was Secretary to the Admiralty in Lord Derby's administration, and was among those dismissed for corruption during the 1852 election) Milnes came forward at once to help.[1] But Milnes' capacity for

---

[1] 'Lord Houghton is a good man to go to in trouble,' somebody once remarked. 'Yes,' replied W. E. Forster, 'but more than that he is a good man to go to in disgrace.'

taking trouble and his wish to help (responsible for such dissimilar
activities as his assistance of David Gray, his pushing of Swinburne,
and his foundation of reformatories for boys) were not yet in
evidence in his Cambridge days. O'Brien sometimes took it on
himself to remonstrate with his friend—'Often I am disquieted
about and sometimes cross with you,' he wrote on one occasion;
and on another, an August night at Blatherwycke, sitting in his
dressing-gown, he began a penetrating letter to Richard:

My very dear Milnes [he wrote], I have put out my candles and
was just going to bed, the stable clock had struck twelve when I
threw up the window to take one more look at the moon, as she
sunk behind an enormous elm—the light was just like it used to be
in Neville's Court when you disturbed its sanctity by gallopades
or singing as Doctor Luther sung and my thoughts wandered as they
very often do to you so I thought that I would at this stolen and
quiet hour write to you. However I will not be schoolgirlish,
although I could write very pretty things just now I am sure. . . .
It cannot be concealed that I am rather afraid of you. . . . I often
wonder what will be your future destiny and I think you are near
something very glorious but you will never reach it—I wish that it
were in my power to give you all the good I possess and which
you want, for I would willingly pull down my hut to build your
palace.

When Milnes had finally left Trinity and gone to join his parents
in Italy, Stafford O'Brien kept him regularly informed of the latest
pieces of college gossip: of how 'languidly extensive' and divided
the set had now become; how Hallam looked more and more
spiritual; how Lord Lansdowne's son, Kerry, was sinking from set
to set; that Arthur Buller's manners were 'almost fascinating';
that he thought the Apostles disliked him; that the number of
'secret diseases' in the University was said to be enormous. These
letters have an astonishing vitality. They explain Milnes' choice
of the nouns 'grace' and 'glitter' to describe Stafford O'Brien.

IX

Spiritually the life of these young men was a life lived in the
shadow of the Byronic tradition. That shadow was already
contracting and growing shorter.

It was then not only fashionable but almost indispensable for every
youth to be Byronic [Lord Houghton once explained when speaking
of these Trinity days].[1] Of course, though at Cambridge we had

---

[1] Address to the Wordsworth Society, 8 July 1885, *op. cit.*

not either the energy or perhaps the courage to be Corsairs or
Laras, yet nevertheless we enjoyed the poetry and especially the
later poetry of Lord Byron as something very cognate to our
dispositions and tempers, probably [he added reflectively] not the
best of either.

He went on to observe that in spite of the general recognition
of Byron he and his friends felt the urgent need of some poetry
which would satisfy their higher aspirations and elevate their minds.
In Keats and Shelley, both of them poets of youth who had been
spurned by the literary world, they found the ideal antidote to
the Byronic creed. They printed at their own expense an edition
of *Adonais*, from a copy brought back by Arthur Hallam from Pisa;
and Keats, whose first official biographer Monckton Milnes later
became, was assiduously studied, discussed and admired. Their
passionate propaganda for Keats and Shelley Lord Houghton
found in retrospect to be understandable; what seemed to him a
little strange, he said, on looking back, was that they should also
have developed so early and reverent an admiration for Wordsworth. Far better known than Shelley or Keats, Wordsworth
was still ridiculed by many people in the late eighteen-twenties.
Burns, who used equally simple language, but wrote of emotions
as unrestrained and interesting as Byron's own, was popular. But
Wordsworth, who not only used everyday expressions in his poetry,
but described everyday objects and incidents too, was not taken
seriously by the public. Here was an injustice almost as great as
that done to Shelley and Keats. Milnes and his friends took it up
with a vengeance; and so calm a witness as Macaulay later declared
that Wordsworth had never been so accepted and so established in
the minds of all who professed to care for poetry as he was at
Cambridge between the years 1830 and 1840.

Their motives for supporting Wordsworth were mixed: first, he
was a genius; then he was ill-thought of; next he was un-Byronic;
and last but most significantly he was morally elevating.

I rejoice to hear you are studying Wordsworth [Richard Trench
wrote to Milnes in July 1828]; he brings the mind to a sound and
healthy tone; do you not find him and Byron as the opposite ends
of a balance—as the one rises the other must necessarily sink—
you will cry out—here is some of his old abuse of Byron! I will
own . . . that from having worshipped false gods I am now an
iconoclast.

In November 1829 there was a debate in the Union upon the
contrasted merits of Byron and Wordsworth, Milnes speaking at
some length ('they tell me very fluently') and Hallam shortly.

In the voting Wordsworth gained a mere twenty-three votes; but this was merely the opening battle of a long campaign, and the defeated side consoled themselves by repeating Julius Hare's comment that their number was too large since there were not twenty-three men in the room worthy to be Wordsworthians. The comment is instructive, for in it we catch the echo of the Apostles' tone. It is always hard to fix upon the historical turning-points of taste, to decide when ideals change or at what moment the tide of fashion begins to ebb. That these gay and intelligent youths should prefer a poet because he brought their minds to a sound and healthy tone would have seemed ludicrous to Regency undergraduates. Within another thirty years such moral criteria had become the generally accepted standard of public taste in English verse. That Monckton Milnes should be a leader of these earnest propagandists may seem odd when we recall his later reputation and remember how much he was responsible for launching Swinburne upon the lotus-eating public of the eighteen-sixties. Yet he too was beginning to react against the artificiality of Byron's themes and treatment, and admired in Wordsworth both genius and some undefined quality which he and his friends vaguely called 'poetic feeling.' 'Passion, imagination, fancy, all were his, but not the one holy cement of poetic feeling to amalgamate and unify the whole'—so Milnes defined Byron's gifts while reading the first volume of the new Moore biography in January of 1830. His own poetry bore a permanently Wordsworthian stamp, though here and there in the little volumes Moxon published during the 'thirties and 'forties we find sonnets and lyrics of a wildly romantic quality. But the moral tone of Monckton Milnes' poetry remained, like that of Trench, unambiguously and irreproachably high.

The campaign against Byron and in favour of Shelley and Wordsworth was not confined to the precincts of Trinity or the dark, low-ceilinged meeting-room of the Cambridge Union.

I tried to convert the nicest woman on earth to Wordsworth, & failed!! [Arthur Hallam wrote to Milnes from Inveraray in July, 1829]. *En revanche* I made a convert to Shelley in the Glasgow steam-boat, & presented him with a copy of the *Adonais*, as a badge of proselytism.

Hallam was predisposed to like anyone who liked Shelley's work. On one occasion he wrote to Milnes in high excitement of 'an adorable creature, who wrote out all the *Revolt* with her own hands!!' and on another he told him that the vicar of Malvern, Dr. Card, was 'a *devoted Shelleyan.*' 'Shelley,' Dr. Card had remarked to Hallam, 'seems to have lived almost the life of a saint.' Dr. Card ('a trump, as you see,' wrote Hallam) had known Thomas Lovell Beddoes, who had first led him to discover Shelley's work, so in this instance Hallam was preaching to the converted. But he and the other Apostles were prepared to carry their war right into the enemy's camp. A story well-known to the Victorians, and recorded in different forms in a number of books of memories, tells how, on one snowy December day in 1829, Hallam, Milnes and the contemptuous Sunderland set off by coach across the countryside to Oxford to fight the cause of Shelley against Byron in the Oxford Union. Milnes had got Dr. Christopher Wordsworth to sanction the expedition by telling him only of the anti-Byronic aspect of the proposed debate, leaving the Master to assume that the Trinity men who were preparing to attack Byron's reputation at Oxford were advocating the claims of his own brother William, not those of the atheist Shelley. When they reached Oxford they found Manning and other leading young Oxonians awaiting them. The debate was not, from the Cambridge viewpoint, quite the success that could have been wished. To begin with, the three Trinity men were put off by the elegance and tidiness of the Oxford Union chambers, so unlike their own noisy room behind the Red Lion Inn. Then the Oxford young gentlemen seemed as elegant and unconcerned as their room, and lounged about the fireplace with provoking sang-froid. Worst of all, they alleged that they had never heard of Shelley, and one of them even pretended to think that the Cambridge contingent had come over to support the claims of Shenstone, and that the only line of this poet he could call to mind was one running: 'My banks are well furnished with bees.' The occasion was memorable for bringing together for the first time a number of men destined to mould the character of Victorian England. 'The man that *took* me most,' Milnes reported to his family, 'was the youngest Gladstone of Liverpool—I am sure a very superior person.'

X

Milnes left Cambridge in April 1830. He had been in poor spirits during his last months there, and the feeling that 'the thing is over, and for ever' was depressing. He told his mother that he bitterly minded leaving his Trinity acquaintances, since they were all the acquaintance he had anywhere. At the same time he did not over-rate the value of his Cambridge experiences or make the error of supposing that life at an English university is a good equipment for real life in the outside world.

I know nothing whatever of men [he wrote at this time to his father], and how should I? Unless a person falls in with my literary tastes I can have no companionship with him. I am at sea out of my own coterie.

In the degree examinations of the previous summer Milnes had suffered an attack of nerves, turned faint, and rushed from the examination room to his quarters in the New Court, where, throwing himself on his sofa, he burst into tears. It may have been this failure that determined him to take an unusual step on leaving Trinity. This was to attend the morning lectures of the University of London, as the new college in Gower Street, Bloomsbury, was hopefully styled by its supporters. Opened in 1827, the University College was scorned by Oxford and Cambridge, and it needed some moral courage for a Trinity man to go there. The poverty which now governed all his family's movements and had somewhat restricted his own Cambridge career led him to take a cheap lodging in Piccadilly, near the hospitable house of his mother's rich aunt Lady Smith. He would spend his mornings at the University or reading in his rooms, going by night to hear the debates of the House of Commons in St. Stephen's Hall, and returning through the gloomy streets in which the oil-lamps twinkled, and the watchmen cried the hours. In his *Reminiscences* Sir Francis Doyle has left a picture of London at this period, observing the great difference in the rate of living which absence of railways and expense of travel then made: 'you could not get more done by hurrying or fussing about,' and so time seemed of no importance. To Richard Milnes, not quite twenty-one, time did, however, seem of considerable importance; and his political ambitions, stimulated by these nightly visits to Westminster, made him feverish to enter the House himself. Radical in his literary judgements, he held in politics to a mild and nominal Conservatism, felt by his friends to sit ill on such a liberal mind, but which he did not officially shake off until 1846. There may have been a certain frank opportunism about this Tory faith, for his father had represented Pontefract (the seat Richard himself aimed at) in the Conservative interest; these were the days before the Reform Bill, and the support of the local squirearchy was more important than that of the Pontefract town electors. One of the reasons for Milnes' final political failure—his lack of any sincere party spirit—was already foreshadowed in his letters from Trinity, in one of which he prided himself on having no politics at all and judging every measure on its individual merits.

The weeks at London University were followed, according to Milnes' own project, by some months in Germany. His father had wished him to go to Paris to improve his French accent, but this Richard thought frivolous. He wanted to learn to study a subject more closely and completely than he had ever done at Cambridge, and he tried to fire his father's imagination by repeating his friends' descriptions of the young men at Heidelberg and Munich, with their depth of knowledge and their habits of 'studying everything, and everything well.' Trench and other Cambridge friends were planning to go in groups to various German universities, but Richard himself decided that he wanted to go alone to Bonn. His instinct for studying German philosophy in Germany was curiously right, for by so doing he was equipping himself to understand those spheres of German thought which so profoundly influenced the intellect of England in the following decades. His time in Bonn gave him, too, a sympathy with German ideas and aspirations which he kept for the rest of his life, and which explains his close friendship with men such as Varnhagen von Ense and the Bunsens. It also explains his attitude to the war of 1870, when he startled London society by entertaining the Prussian Minister and openly avowing his wish for the defeat of Napoleon the Third. Had he followed his father's advice and gone to polish up his French in Paris, Milnes would have seen the July Revolution, but he might have missed the opportunity for understanding that central fact of the foreign politics of his generation, the rise of German power in Europe.

When Mr. Milnes objected to his son's concentrating on German, Richard tried to reassure him by replying that he was not capable of concentrating on anything to the exclusion of all else: 'the only way to balance my life-boat of a mind is to let it go bounding on over every literary surge it meets with.' In the end Mr. Milnes gave way. In June of 1830 Richard Milnes left London for Brussels, and after passing by La Haye Sainte and its 'bone-grubbers' and looking at an unfinished Rubens at Cologne, he reached the gentle, placid town of Bonn beside the Rhine under a black sky and in a hurricane of rain.

Within a few days of his arrival news came of the death of George IV. Milnes' parliamentary aspirations burst into flame, and he wrote off post-haste to his father begging to be allowed to stand at the election which would ensue. He had all the neighbours behind him and it could cost only a thousand or fifteen hundred pounds. But Mr. Milnes, who was faced with the need to economise ever more stringently, told him to return to his German. His parliamentary prospects dwindled into the dim future, and he resigned himself to the idea of living out of England for some unpredictable number of years to come. He had already

sampled a life of exile in the summer of 1829, when he had been at
Boulogne and then gone to Paris with his parents, joining them again
in Lombardy after travelling through Switzerland alone. Mr.
and Mrs. Milnes and Harriette had now settled down in Milan.
The Milnes family were to remain in and about Italy until the year
1835.

Chapter Two

1829   1832

I

In the cold early spring of 1828, during Richard's first year at Trinity, Mr. and Mrs. Milnes and Harriette had paid a round of farewell visits to Milnes and Monckton relations at Fryston and at Serlby, had closed Thorne Hall and gazed their last for many years upon the fields and loose stone walls of the West Riding of Yorkshire. They had driven to London. They had taken, in mid-May, the Dover Road.

A contrary wind carried them to Calais, where they dined with Beau Brummell (sunk now into a passive and genteel senility) before pursuing their way along the coast to Boulogne. At Boulogne they found a society of English residents which was on the whole more respectable but also more amusing than they had been told it would be. They hired a roomy house in the *haute ville*, with a gallery that had windows opening on to the garden, engaged a cook named Cécile, and settled down for the summer. Richard, who came out to France for his vacations—rowing his mother and Harriette in a little boat off the coast or taking them to country fêtes in the outlying villages—raised strong objections to Boulogne. The town, an English debtors' refuge, had a very bad name among the youth of Cambridge. 'I dare hardly mention it,' he told his parents; 'Harvey gave me such a Bristol look when I said where I had been.' He learned, too, that his father was criticised for allowing Harriette to go about in Boulogne society before she had come out in London, and at his age such comment assumes an unnatural consequence. Although he later learned to run counter to public opinion, Richard Milnes kept always in his heart the acute sensibility to criticism normally symptomatic only of extreme youth.

A year amongst the English at Boulogne proved more than enough for Mr. Milnes. Determining to take a house in Paris, he set out with his family in June 1829, stopping at Chantilly on the way. In Paris they saw the ballet of *La Belle au Bois Dormant*, and persuaded Mrs. Opie [1] to inscribe her name in Mrs. Milnes' book. During

---

[1] Amelia Opie (1769–1853), the novelist and poet, who had become a Quaker in 1825, was the intimate friend of Mrs. Milnes' aunt Lady Cork, and widow of the painter John Opie (1761–1807), who had done a fine full-length portrait of Mrs. Milnes before her marriage. This portrait, which shows her to have been florid and merry-eyed, is now at Helperby Hall, Yorkshire. Mrs. Opie was often in Paris.

the first ten days in the French capital, and while Mrs. Milnes was busily enquiring as to the best means of furnishing a hired house there, her husband again changed his mind and decided that they were to live in Italy instead. Going straight to Geneva, they first saw the ranges of Mont Blanc upon a cloudless morning of high summer. Farther on, at Sécheron, they found the Vansittart family and so many other friends from the North of England that Mrs. Milnes declared it to be 'Yorkshire all over again.' Hastening to leave these last reminders of a more normal existence, they hurried on over the Simplon, which they crossed in their travelling carriage (Harriette, on the barouche seat, numbed with cold), and descended upon Italy into the laden orange-groves of Baveno, where they rowed along the lake to see the Borromeo palaces, with their painted ceilings, and where they heard much stale gossip of the notorious Princess of Wales. Pushing on to Milan they arrived for dinner at the Grande Bretagne hotel. They began next morning to hunt for an apartment, and soon took the handsomely-furnished floor of a palazzo, with a lofty gilded saloon and the added comfort of a warm bath. The sophistication and elegance of Milanese life was a contrast to the modest entertainments of expatriate society at Boulogne. Mr. Milnes had selected Milan because it was the nearest capital in Italy, one of the most accomplished, and 'beset by the fewest English.' There was also, for Harriette, the best musical school in the world, and she and her mother were soon enjoying the musical life of the city, which radiated outward from the Scala. For Richard there were the Ambrosiana Library and the Brera, as well as certain fashionable salons and the balls at the Viceregal Court, to which Mrs. Milnes, with her memories of the court of George the Third, insisted on getting the entrée. Moreover, for these three members of the family there was the perpetual recollection—implicit in the cavalcades of elegant equipages down the Corso, implicit in every sight and sound of this great European city and in the clear blue sky above it, against which the pinnacles of the Duomo showed so sharp and white—that this existence was an improvement upon the daily round at Thorne Hall, Doncaster. Even Mr. Milnes did not repine, or hanker overmuch after the chilly pleasures of a Yorkshire summer. 'When the Channel is once crossed,' he wrote at this time to his cousin Tom Bland of Kippax, 'and your forks and spoons with you, you don't lie awake at night thinking of Britain or the Badsworth.'

II

Milan was at this time under Austrian rule. Italy, and indeed the whole continent in which this insular Yorkshire family had chosen to reside, was still dominated by the measured decisions of the Congress of Vienna. The last conference of Metternich's system—a system from which England, under the guidance of Canning, was now speedily seceding—had been held at Verona seven years before. Northern Italy was occupied by eighty thousand Austrian troops. The Milneses had not been long in Milan before they noticed how many of their Italian friends were liable to arrest and confiscation of property. Their own servant, Donato, whom they had brought with them from Geneva, was arrested on the charge of talking treason and sent out of Lombardy under an escort after the apartment of his English employers had been ransacked for papers by the police. But throughout the Europe of Metternich and the restored Bourbons the traces of a great tradition lingered. At Boulogne the Milneses had stayed in a house once occupied by Napoleon (or, as Mrs. Milnes preferred to call him, Buonaparte), and there too they had been shown one of his hats. At all the villages along the road over the Simplon they had found preparations in progress for the reception of Marie Louise, crossing into Switzerland for the first time since the Emperor's abdication. Stopping by chance to change horses at the same place as the grand-ducal carriages, they had gazed with curiosity upon the grave, unanimated face of the ex-Empress, a ghost from the past to whom the village girls were bringing offerings of fresh fruit. In Milan itself the unfinished Arco della Pace stood dazzling white, the rough blocks strewn around its base looking, said Lady Blessington[1] (who had passed through the city a few months before the Milnes family reached it), like great fragments of alabaster: a monument begun by Napoleon to celebrate his victories, and now being completed to commemorate his defeat. The public gardens and the walk along the ramparts, where Harriette and Richard would wander in the evening, had been laid out by the Emperor's Viceroy, Eugène Beauharnais, who was popular and remembered, and had carried out many of Napoleon's own suggestions for beautifying Milan—the archducal palace which he had built, for instance, with its ceilings by Appiani, which Lady Blessington had also admired. Milan in 1828 had seemed to her splendid in the number of its palaces— Belgioioso, Serbelloni, Tezzoli, Casani, Litta and many more. It was not as good as Paris, although the turn-out and the clothes of the upper classes were copied from Parisian models. But it was spacious and clean, the opera house was well-aired and sumptuous, the Ambrosiana was interesting, the streets seemed stately and the people attentive and civil. Mrs. Milnes' reactions to Lombardy in 1829 were as favourable as those of Marguerite Blessington in

[1] In *The Idler in Italy*, two volumes of which appeared in 1839, the third in 1840.

1828. Her experience as a traveller was more limited, her com-, ments are less illuminating. After viewing the Iron Crown at Monza they had gone on to look at the Viceroy's palace there, and Mrs. Milnes records that this

struck me as being in the front what the house would have been at Serlby had Galway left it as it was and built over the sides which joined it to the wings : but then [she added] there is a raised entrance and pillars in the way of Basildon.

The only difficulty confronting Mr. Milnes when what he termed 'legislating' for a long stay in Italy was the question of Richard's future. 'Milan, Venice, Naples, Paris,' wrote this Yorkshire squire, 'there would I loiter four more years along the stream of time'; but what would suit him or suit Harriette would not do for a son whose political ambitions he was eager to foster. He declared it 'out of the case' for Richard to be permanently separated from his parents; yet it seemed almost equally wrong that he should live out of England for four solid years; and if he divided his time between his country and his family, Mr. Milnes reckoned, with a carefree sweep of exaggeration, that one-third of it would be spent on the road. Since the problem seemed insoluble, Mr. Milnes ceased worrying over it and turned instead to enjoyment of life at Milan, where he discovered they were as comfortable with four servants as they had been at Thorne Hall with eight.

III

Although Richard accompanied his mother and sister to the court ball given by the Viceroy to celebrate the marriage of the Queen of Hungary, and was himself amused to be asked to explain Cobbett, O'Connell and the state of English politics to the Archduke, he did not approve of frequenting the Austrian court. The occupation of northern Italy and the general effects of the Holy Alliance were distasteful to his tolerant mind. In July 1830, while at Bonn, he acclaimed the fall of the legitimate Bourbons with zest. On his way to Bonn he had stopped at Lille, where an old soldier of Napoleon, showing him over the citadel, had asked him if the English had a bed ready for Charles X, whom his subjects presently intended to send packing across the Channel.

How little I thought when I last wrote that I should be able to speak of so great an historical event as this French Revn . . . [he scribbled to his father at Milan]. Now we see for what it was Louis died and the Terrorists reigned—such a Revn as this could never have stood alone—it could only be the sum and corollary to that which had gone before.

He now looked forward to the liberation of Lombardy, for 'to no power is the shock so terrible as to Austria—every plank of the Imperial throne must quiver.' He envied his friend Augustus Fitzroy, who was actually in Paris witnessing these great events, while he, by his own insistence, was merely at the University of Bonn.

All the same, and in spite of persistent rainstorms and such major distractions as the English elections and the revolution in France, the three months at Bonn proved formative and profitable. Milnes took a small room, dined at the *table d'hôte*, and began making friends with the German students—such fine, free fellows with moustaches and big blue eyes, who wore their hair long, fought duels, drank Moselle wine, and sang divinely as they swaggered about the quiet streets of the old town on the Rhine bank, famous for its five-towered cathedral and the classical university buildings finished some twelve years before. The young Germans had the portraits of their mistresses painted upon their pipes, embraced each other in the street, and behaved with the general display of emotion which always attracted Richard Milnes. He would 'glide' with them down the waters of the Rhine under the stars, or walk out of the town of an evening along country roads and lanes bordered by the fireflies' flashing lamps. He read *Wilhelm Meister* and was introduced to Goethe's friend Frau Schopenhauer. In spite of the drinking and dancing during this warm, wet summer, the gay expeditions over the hills with a soldier's knapsack at his back, or by river to Bad Ems or the island of Nonnenwert beyond the Drachenfels, he worked hard, stimulated by the same atmosphere of application which Thomas Beddoes found so salutary at Goettingen University from 1825 to 1829: 'there is an appetite for learning,' had run Beddoes' analysis of German student life, 'a spirit of diligence, and withal a good-natured fellow-feeling wholly unparalleled in our old apoplectic and paralytic Almae Matres.'[1] Milnes attended the lectures of Niebuhr and August Wilhelm von Schlegel, describing the latter as just what he would have expected from the pet of Madame de Staël: a small, snobbish, ageing man with a wig which he would straighten from a mirror inside his snuffbox, credited by those who did not like him with putting rouge on his face.

But the aspect of German life which Richard Milnes found most sympathetic was the unrestrained and unaffected way in which the Germans showed what they were feeling—particularly the 'intense

---

[1] Letter from Beddoes to T. F. Kelsall, Goettingen, 4 December 1825 (*The Works of Thomas Lovell Beddoes*, edited by H. W. Donner, Oxford University Press, 1935).

domestic feeling' of reunions on the Rhine boats, when complete families might be seen publicly weeping. More than thirty years later Mrs. Carlyle was astonished to find Lord Houghton clasp her in his arms, kiss her and turn pale with emotion on her recovery from a severe illness, but this was in fact an incident characteristic of Milnes' nature. He was himself entirely aware of this amiable weakness.

I was thinking today [he once wrote from Fryston to a friend some seven years after his sojourn at Bonn] that the thing I was intended for by nature is a German woman. I have just that mixture of *häusliche Thätigkeit* and *Sentimentalität* that characterises that category of Nature. I think Goethe would have fallen in love with me, and I am not sure that Platen didn't. [1]

IV

Leaving Bonn at the beginning of September 1830, Richard Monckton Milnes, now twenty-one years old, proceeded to Milan, travelling slowly by way of Heidelberg and Augsburg, through the Tyrol to Verona. He found his family established in a large apartment which they had just taken in the Palazzo Arconati. At Christmas his father left them for six months, returning to Yorkshire to deal with his affairs, which were now even more entangled than before. Richard found Milanese society dull, the women beautiful but 'grossly ignorant,' the men too busy paying them court to develop their own mental faculties. His mother and Harriette were much involved in the world of music, and it was at this time that Mrs. Milnes made close friends with the singer Pasta, who came one day to consult her about the new Donizetti opera, *Anna Bolena*, then in rehearsal at the Scala. Madame Pasta asserted that she was discontented with her share in the partition of the last scene of the opera. 'You English,' she said, 'have so many beautiful airs which you sing among yourselves that I am sure you could help me.' Mrs. Milnes suggested, and sang, the popular English song of *Home, Sweet Home*, and Madame Pasta, sitting down to the piano, agreed that it would do. Donizetti adopted it, and sent a message of thanks to his Yorkshire acquaintances, who prided themselves that they had thus restored to Italy what had been by origin a Sicilian air. Richard, however, was bored by music. He disliked going 'a mile and a half' to the Scala twice a week, in rain or snow, and found that he could not talk at his ease in an opera box. Topics of conversation in the entr'actes at the opera house did not vary. He passed his time practising German with

[1] Letter to Charles MacCarthy of 15 October 1837.

Harriette's governess, reading English novels, writing poetry and trying his hand at a never-completed novel.

In the bright March weather of 1831 he left his mother and sister and, crossing Italy, paid his first visit to Venice. This first sight of Venice made a profound impression on him. He rated it the best resting-place for an intellectual and a poet that he had ever seen, and decided that he would return there at regular intervals throughout his life, at any rate every five years. This visit, and his later life at Venice (where his mother took a house in the winter of 1833, and again in 1834) produced some of Milnes' best verse, and the volume *Memorials of Many Scenes* published in 1838 contains a number of Venetian poems. Unlike Samuel Rogers, whose level eighteenth-century verses upon Venice are some of the least inspiring parts of that dull volume *Italy*, Milnes did succeed in conveying the Turneresque effects of a Venetian sunset, the 'golden haze of indistinct surprise' through which Venice first appears to a stranger:

> Transpierced, transfused, each densest mass
> Melts to as pure a glow
> As images on painted glass
> Or silken screens can show. . . .
>
> How mid the universal sheen
> Of marble amber-tinged,
> Like some enormous baldaquin
> Gay-chequered and deep-fringed,
> It stands in air and will not move,
> Upheld by magic power,—
> The dun-lead domes just caught above—
> Beside—the glooming Tower.

Architecturally, Milnes thought Venice much what Canaletto's paintings had led him to expect; but the splendour and decay of the whole city, its strange over-all melancholy combined with the intelligence of the conversation in the 'debris' of the Venetian society to which he was admitted, captivated him. He sent his father a letter to say how happy he was at Venice and to plead against going on at once to Rome, for which he had not yet prepared himself by reading. At the end of the letter he inserted some perfunctory views on the Reform Bill, then convulsing English politics and which his father supported while he himself opposed it. This political paragraph was perhaps a concession to Mr. Milnes, whose 'great ambition . . . on his son's behalf' was allied, we may recall (the words are those of Lord Houghton's first biographer), 'to a strong dislike of his literary tastes.'

34

Richard's time on the Rhine and in northern Italy had given free rein not merely to literary tastes but to literary practices as well. At Bonn he had written some agreeable poetry in a sad romantic vein: *On a Ruined Castle near the Rhine*, for instance, and *On the Jungfrau by Moonlight*, and he now composed verses on Venice and on Italy in which he openly contrasted

> The bland outbreathings of the midland sea,
> The aloe-fringed and myrtle-shadowed shore

with the 'cold ground' of England. When he printed, in 1838, a poem written in the year of his first visit to Venice and entitled *An Italian to Italy*, he explained that the northerner tends to underrate an Italian refugee's feelings for this southern land:

> 'What can *he* know of thee,
> Glorified Italy?'

We should weigh [he wrote in a footnote] in a just measure the physical differences between countries, where Life is worth living for its own sake, and those where all the excitement of social and political feelings is necessary to give zest and enjoyment to existence.

He was probably thinking of Yorkshire as he wrote those words. Throughout the rest of his life Richard Monckton Milnes hankered after the Mediterranean, hurrying off there whenever his responsibilities in London and the North would permit. By taking his family to Italy in 1829, Mr. Milnes had made inevitable just those developments of his son's character which he had been most anxious to discourage. Instead of an able young politician he had created an Italianate poet, instead of a parliamentary orator he had made a romantic who liked modish books of verse better than Hansard.

If you had only looked at the *Gem* [Richard wrote tartly to his father from Venice] you would have seen that I only sent for it because it contained some of Tennyson's finest poetry. Have you read the review of him in the Westminster?

In May 1831 Richard returned to England to take at Cambridge an honorary degree, the only course left open to him by his neurasthenic collapse during the examinations in 1830. He spent a few weeks in London, attending debates at the House and cultivating his few town acquaintances. His chief social supports during these early visits to the capital were his mother's various Monckton relations, outstanding among these Mrs. Milnes' aunt, old Lady Cork, who had been in her youth the friend of Johnson and Mrs. Thrale and had made a reputation in those far-off days as 'the lively Miss Monckton who used to have the finest bit of blue' at her house in Charles Street. Small, fat and fantastically dressed, with a fair skin and delicate lively features, Lady Cork still rose at six every morning and continued to dine out to within a few days of her death, at the age of ninety-four, in 1840. She was considered to be a kleptomaniac and had a habit of borrowing other people's carriages without asking their leave. She had first interested herself in her great-nephew in 1830, and when he finally came back from Italy and entered the House of Commons in 1837, she took some trouble to help him along in London society, telling him she thought him as wise as he was clever, and then qualifying this with a postscript: 'Doctor Johnson said never say a Gentleman is clever, a Carpenter may be clever.' 'I am very kind, but I always have some sinister design in it,' she once volunteered to a friend, explaining that she was helping some girl to get invitations in London since she had heard that her parents had a most comfortable country house; and she would certainly not have bothered with Richard Monckton Milnes had she not found him of good amusement value. As it was she welcomed him to her drawing-room in New Burlington Street, where the chairs were fastened to the floor to prevent people pushing them into formal circles, where she recited Pope, discouraged card-playing, and held forth generally 'in a strange kind of oracular tone' upon the London world of the previous century. Her rather predatory attitude to those she estimated 'lions' and her thirst for novelty show that blood was not the only bond that linked Lady Cork to her niece's son. They shared, to some extent, a point of view.

After this brief vision of life in London, Richard set off to Ireland, which he did not know and where his friends Eliot Warburton,[1] Richard Trench and Stafford O'Brien were severally awaiting him. From London to Liverpool he travelled on the railway, a novel method of locomotion which he judged gritty but safe: 'I cannot conceive a possible accident if you only sit still; for if the boiler was to burst it could not hurt those in the inside of the carriages.' It made you feel giddy if you looked at the ground. He told his mother that unless one slept all the way a long steam journey would be anything but pleasant.

[1] Bartholomew Elliott George Warburton, known as Eliot Warburton (1810–1852), came from Aughrim, County Galway, and had been a contemporary of Monckton Milnes at Cambridge—going first to Queen's College and then in 1830 to Trinity. He is remembered as the author of *The Crescent and the Cross* (dated 1845, but published 1844), one of the most lively and charming of all English travel books about the Near East, and for his tragic death in the *Amazon* steamboat disaster in January 1852. He was an intimate friend of Milnes, to whom he wrote frequently.

V

His heart charged with the emotions he had experienced at Venice, Milnes was in no mood to do Dublin justice. 'This city pleases me,' he wrote without enthusiasm of that sad and romantic capital, its staid classical buildings suffused by the misty northern light, the tang of peat-smoke saturating the air. The quiet squares and streets of brick compared ill with the great stone palaces of Venice crumbling over the canals, nor did the Liffey, with its hooped bridges and old cobbled quays, seem an interesting alternative to the Venetian lagoons at sunset. He seems to have written no poetry in Dublin city, though the Coleraine salmon leap and the caves of Cong, as well as the island of Valentia, to which he extracted an invitation from the Knight of Kerry, moved him to creditable verse. Before going to see Trench in Queen's County or the family of his Cambridge friend Vere de Vere,[1] Milnes returned to Dublin and then went up to Belfast to join Warburton.

After Milan and London, Dublin seemed to him empty. The city was still recovering from the final triumph of Catholic Emancipation, which had left many energetic and vociferous persons with no cause to uphold. The reign of Lord Anglesey as Lord Lieutenant (interrupted by his brief recall in 1829) was signalised by a series of unwontedly brilliant Dublin seasons. Sydney Lady Morgan, by then a writer of a European celebrity and easily the most famous woman in Dublin, had recently come back to Ireland after a journey through France undertaken with her husband 'in search of sensations of a more gracious nature than those presented by the condition of society at home.' This journey had resulted in her second book on France and another row with her publisher. Extremely short, voluble, combative and affected, with 'expressive' eyes placed crooked in her head, she had resumed her evening receptions in Kildare Street, and there she welcomed Richard Milnes as a young and distinguished English traveller, the nephew of her very old friend Lady Cork. Milnes had read some of Lady Morgan's works at Cambridge with admiration, and had even quoted at his father one of her more dogmatic dicta: 'They who would legislate for the world must live in the world.' He was quite ready to pay homage at Kildare Street. Lady Morgan treated him with her habitual coquetry, sending coy little notes to say 'You behaved *horribly yesterday*. Notwithstanding I sent to Mrs. d'Aguilar for a card for you,' lending him an otherwise unobtainable copy of her famous novel *O'Donnel* ('it is out of print, and as Colburn and I are at *war*, he won't give me another')

---

[1] Eldest son of Sir Aubrey de Vere (1788–1846) of Curragh Chase, County Limerick, and brother of Milnes' contemporary and friend Aubrey de Vere.

and asking him to come to her house to hear Paganini, then in Dublin for the three-day Musical Festival of August 1831, and fresh from his lucrative tour of England. Milnes' friendship with this vain and restless little woman lasted for many years, and when in 1839 she left Dublin for a small house in London near Hyde Park, he went regularly to see her, recording in his commonplace books some of the ridiculous stories to which she invariably gave rise. Meanwhile, when he left Dublin for Belfast he went armed with some notes of introduction from Lady Morgan, one of which, written to the principal of a college in Carlow and evidently left undelivered, is preserved among the Houghton Papers: 'You . . . brought Saint Dominic into fashion with me,' she wrote to this priest, after explaining that young Mr. Milnes was Lady Cork's nephew and a friend of hers; 'I have already lighted a taper at his shrine, and banished a picture of St. Francis from my Boudoir, tho' it was given me by Cardinal Fesche.' It must have needed all the persuasiveness of Nicholas Wiseman, with whom Milnes made close friends in the ensuing winter in Rome, to banish the impressions of Dublin Catholicism from his mind.

The travel journal which Milnes apparently kept during his journey in Ireland with Warburton has, unhappily, not survived. Warburton, who was a year his junior, had been at Trinity during his last term there. With Arthur Hallam, O'Brien and Fitzroy he had acted in a production of *Much Ado About Nothing*, for which Milnes, who played Beatrice, wrote an epilogue. Warburton, who came from County Galway and who began with the intention of studying law but ended as a roving writer, was as fond of Richard Milnes as some of his other Trinity contemporaries. He called Milnes too 'mercurial' and 'gifted' for friendship, but declared he always felt him to be 'more to me than anyone.' Throughout his short life, Eliot Warburton maintained the same sort of watchful or apprehensive affection for Milnes that O'Brien and other Trinity intimates also kept up. Like them he often complained of Milnes' neglect, but like them he felt a real love for him. Warburton shared, too, the Apostolic attitude to Alfred Tennyson—that irreverent awe with which they watched the slow growth of his sombre genius. Two months before the publication of the 1832 volume of Tennyson's poems Warburton copied out for Milnes the new poem, *The Lotos Eaters*. While appreciating the beauties of this poem, they were unable to resist an exchange of facetious letters upon the best methods of eating the lotus—Milnes suggesting a regular salad dressing, while Warburton insisted that they must be eaten raw like nasturtiums, insects and all, and that they tasted like the scent of hyacinths.

Aubrey de Vere, with whose poetry Milnes' own had certain affinities, early developed a clear and unswerving appreciation of Milnes' personality. Four years after Lord Houghton's death he was asked [1] to jot down his recollections of him. These recollections took the form of some general notes upon Milnes' character— emphasising his lack of solid ambition, his preference for intellectual excitement and novelty as against social distinction, his capacity for playing with the world without being seriously a man of the world, and the strength of his affections, which de Vere considered that most people underrated. He maintained that in his dead friend's view the worst woe of humanity was the loss of youth— about which Milnes wrote a once popular poem, *The Flight of Youth.* Added to these general notes, or rather prefacing them, de Vere set a calm and vivid account of his first meeting with Richard Monckton Milnes in Ireland, when he himself was only seventeen.

One evening of late summer, 1831, at about nine o'clock, as the family of Sir Aubrey de Vere were seated in the library of Curragh Chase, their house in a spacious deer-park in County Limerick, they heard the wheels of a post-chaise upon the gravel. Leaving the great debate on the Reform Bill which they were reading aloud to each other, the father with his sons and daughters went out on the terrace, which overlooked the lawn with its cedar trees, sloping down to a lake. Out of the post-chaise jumped a young man with a 'jaunty step and a vivacious intelligent face' who ran up the stone steps to the terrace and asked if the eldest son of the house, his Trinity friend, was at home. Taken into the house he was welcomed by the whole family and

in another half-hour we seemed to have leapt into an intimacy with the young traveller as close as if it had begun years before, so entirely easy and familiar was our guest in all his ways and so singularly unconventional in his manners.

So natural did they feel with him that they ventured to suggest resuming their family reading. Milnes replied that nothing could interest him more than the Reform Bill debate, but, typically, he

soon had had enough of the speeches, jumped up, lighted a bed-chamber candle, and began to coast round and round the room, examining the books with which its walls were lined. Now and then he laughed as a flight of parliamentary rhetoric reached his ears; but the books excited his attention far more. He took down many of them, perused their title-pages carefully, turned over a few of their leaves hastily, and replaced them. Having run rapidly

---

[1] By Wemyss Reid, who published them (Reid, vol. i, pp. 114–120).

through the lower shelves he got a chair and subjected the higher
to the same rapid inspection. . . . When we had all retired for the
night he took half a dozen volumes to his room, promising not to
read them in bed till daylight returned.

The next morning he convulsed the family by reading Dean
Swift's *Advice to Servants* aloud at breakfast until the tea grew cold,
and during his stay at Curragh he fascinated every member of the
family by his good nature and accomplishments, his knowledge
of foreign languages and foreign countries, his stories of great
men he had seen, and his artificial and incomprehensible Toryism.
He was then 'much devoted to German literature and in sympathy
with German philosophy,' more under the influence of Goethe
than of any other writer, and full of enthusiasm for Victor Hugo.
His portmanteau was crammed with books of poetry, many of
them books with which the de Veres were not familiar; and he thus
introduced them to Keats, Shelley, Landor and Tennyson as well
as to the prose works of Kenelm Digby and the brothers Hare.
The first bright entry of this instructive guest made an unforgettable
picture in young Aubrey's mind, and here again began a lasting
friendship. 'Aubrey de Vere,' Milnes once wrote of the Irish
poet, '. . . one of the most glorious creatures in this or any other
world.'

Having finished with Ireland, Richard set out for Rome, where
his family were now living. The tone of Richard's letters from
Ireland, a country to which his father referred in his stilted, old-
fashioned way as 'that Emerald which costs us so much in the setting,' had brought forth more criticism from Mr. Pemberton
Milnes. Why go and see people in great Irish houses, he asked.
You could see them in London. Richard 'should have informed
himself by an intercourse among the priests and the peasantry.'

VI

While Richard had been travelling in Ireland, his parents and
his sister had taken a leisurely tour down to Naples, and then up,
for the winter, to Rome. Mrs. Milnes notes that they reached the
Eternal City in October. 'We entered just as we ought by the
Coliseum and the aqueducts. Why was I so soon to lose the idea
of being in the Rome I had read of?' In the next sentence of her
journal she supplied the answer: 'The illusion was gone when we
took an apartment in the Piazza di Spagna and heard English
talked in the place.'

The Romans also took the view that the multitudes of English
visitors spoiled Rome. Seven years earlier Stendhal had noted

the profound hatred that the English provoked amongst the Roman working-classes, a sentiment that was only equalled by the scorn with which the aristocracy and the Roman bankers treated their wealthy but unwanted guests. Without the English, he reflected, the Romans would die of starvation, but no mere economic argument could reconcile the latter to overbearing English ways. 'Les Anglais,' he wrote in his essay, *Les Anglais à Rome*, published in November 1824,[1] 'croient qu'il leur est permis de se conduire en Italie comme ils n'oseraient pas se conduire à Londres'; and the result of English insolence was that the Romans avoided English contacts so far as was feasible. There was no real social liaison between the Roman families and the English visitors, even when (as often happened) they found themselves at the same reception and in the same chain of rooms.

We do not know how sensitive the Milneses were to this hostile atmosphere. Probably they were content to gyrate within the circle of strictly English hospitality, for Mrs. Milnes chiefly records fancy balls at Lady Coventry's and dinners with Cardinal Weld. She engaged a Roman maid named Clementina, and a hair-dresser for herself and Harriette who came to their house in his own carriage. Severn, the friend of Keats, was persuaded to design a 'correct and beautiful' Greek costume as Harriette's fancy dress. Daytime diversions consisted of sightseeing, walking in the Borghese and Doria-Parmufili Gardens, and driving to the outskirts of the city. Mr. Milnes declared that he was disappointed in everything but the aqueducts, insinuating that if everybody had his courage they would profess his contempt for half the temples and his disrespect for the Forum. At the beginning of the New Year, 1832, Richard arrived in Rome. He had come by Paris and Lyons, had his hair cropped short, read the new Scott novel *Count Robert of Paris* on the journey, and caught a malarial chill coming over the marshes from Cività Vecchia by night in the chaise and four of an Italian contessina who had been too afraid of the bandits to travel alone. The impact of Rome upon Richard was far more positive than it had been upon either of his parents: 'St. Peter's nearly knocked me down, the Vatican blinded me with the multitude of its treasures, and the Coliseum has a glory of ruin which must be grander than its first perfection.' Three aspects of Rome particularly fascinated him. It was his first revelation of the grandeur of the ancient world; it was his first experience of a really elegant cosmopolitan society, as different from Milan as Milan had been from Boulogne; and it was the

---

[1] *Pages d'Italie*, ed. Henry Martineau (Editions Le Divan, Paris, 1932), p. 216.

centre of Catholicism in its most alluring and spectacular form. The prestige of the Church, at its lowest ebb towards the close of the eighteenth century, had been restored by the misfortunes and the courage of Pope Pius VI, greatly increased by the able and holy pontificates of Leo XII and Pius VII, and was now under Gregory XVI crescent and impressive. At twenty-two Richard Milnes' religious views were indeterminate. Always susceptible, always open to persuasion, he contracted at Rome a pronounced but superficial fancy for the Roman Catholic Church.

The enticements of antiquity, first felt in Rome that winter and experienced again in April at Pompeii, partly inspired his six months' journey through Greece later the same year, which in turn gave rise to the first of his published volumes of verse. The second aspect of Rome, the society aspect, has not in itself much bearing upon the development of his character. Writing an article on Fryston for the newspaper *The World* in 1877, Isabel Burton, the wife of the explorer, repeated a story of Lord Houghton as a youth in Rome which sounds, to say the least of it, apocryphal. According to Lady Burton, the youthful Richard Monckton Milnes confided to a fashionable English lady in Rome that his one ambition was to scintillate in the society of the Eternal City. This admission apparently amused his confidante: 'she looked down at the young man, shy and sensitive, blushing and awkward, and informed him with a smile that he had better abandon the idea.' The point of the story, in so far as it has any, is that Lord Houghton encountered the same lady many years after in London, and seating himself on a stool at her feet, looked up at her and said, 'You see, Lady ——, I have carried out my idea in London, and with some success.' It is likely that the emphasis of this anecdote has shifted out of true. Sensitive he was born and sensitive he remained; but he was never diffident, awkward or shy. His intimate and self-confident manner was at first resented by society in the eighteen-forties. In these early Roman days it may have been boisterous as well. In the letters of his Catholic friend Delabarre Bodenham we catch sight of him striding back from Albano, 'a haystack of cane leaves' in his hat, chanting doggerel verses of his own composition and stopping Lord Northampton's carriage in the middle of the road. It was more likely these high spirits (and the kind of impertinence that led him to offend Lady Coventry by asking her if she had ever read Gulliver's Travels), which made him a shade unwelcome in the English world at Rome. The glimpses we can still catch of this almost obstreperous gaiety seem to contrast abruptly with the calm and silence of those Roman streets. 'This great cloister,' Richard called it, 'the ghost of a city'; a parallel to Stendhal's comment 'tout est tranquille à

Rome comme dans un village.' In this tranquil atmosphere it was inevitable that his mind should turn from the ruins of ancient Rome to that other *raison-d'être* of the Eternal City: the Roman Catholic religion.

Richard Milnes was one of those human beings whose opinions are formed and changed by purely personal factors. Abstract ideas and clear intellectual processes influenced him little. All his life he was pulled back and forth by private enthusiasms and emotional reactions. His attitudes to life at Cambridge and at Bonn had been emotional attitudes. So it continued. In Lombardy and in the Rhineland he had seen Roman Catholicism at its best, in Ireland he had seen it at its worst. In none of these countries had it particularly affected him. In Rome, on the other hand, a set of new and personal contacts led him to examine the Church closely. Aubrey de Vere has stated that Milnes once told him he too would have become a convert to Catholicism in these early days had it not been 'for the uprising of a Catholic school inside the Church of England.' De Vere, who regarded Milnes as a vague if reverent theist, did not consider this an accurate account. To a man convinced that Catholicism was right and Protestantism wrong the activities of Doctor Pusey and his friends would not constitute a valid reason for remaining within the Church of England's fold. Milnes may himself have thought this reason he gave de Vere the true one; but it is more likely that he was never a convinced Christian (in later life he would jokingly call himself a 'Puseyite sceptic'), and that like many other of his intellectual equals and contemporaries he preferred to shelve his doubts and continue to practise the religion of his class in England— represented at the very gates of his Yorkshire home by the little, low church of Ferry Fryston, in the vault of which his body now lies. That he was tempted towards Catholicism at all may seem odd when we recollect that his paternal grandfather and grandmother were strict chapel-going Methodists.[1] The florid streak in his character will, however, account for this aspect; a streak inherited from his mother, whose immediate ancestry contained Portuguese and Jewish blood. Such an heredity could in part explain his religious tendencies at this period. For a more immediate cause we need not look far, however; no farther, indeed, than the high-walled garden of the Collegio Inglese in the Via di Monserrato in Rome.

---

[1] Milnes told Henry Reeve in February 1856 that his family were such strict Unitarian Dissenters that he had never been into a church till he was twenty (*Memoirs of the Life & Correspondence of Henry Reeve*, by J. Knox Laughton, Longmans, 1898, vol. i, p. 360). This was, of course, a typical exaggeration.

VII

The English College, closed since French soldiers had pillaged it and defaced the tombs in 1798, had reopened in 1818, one more symptom of the reviving confidence of the Catholic Church. It had been founded for English pilgrims in the fourteenth century. The monument of Christopher Bainbridge, Cardinal Archbishop of York, the envoy of Henry VIII, who was poisoned at Rome in the pontificate of Leo X, stood in the cloister.   In the college hall hung portraits of the Catholic martyrs of Elizabeth's reign.   John Milton had been a guest here in 1638 and Crashaw two years later.   For more than two centuries an isolated cell of English expatriates, the College was beginning in the eighteen-twenties and thirties to show some positive signs of life.   The students, under the direction of their youthful and learned Rector, Doctor Wiseman, were now doing more than praying for the conversion of England; they were preparing to take part in it.   Several notable conversions of English people in Rome had already taken place, and these, together with such phenomena as the visit in 1833 of Newman and Hurrell Froude, seemed to justify the new optimism now pulsing within these chilly medieval walls.   Many of the non-Catholic English visitors in Rome were intrigued by the activities of the English collegians and attentive to the erudite literary conversation of their Rector.   A few chosen Englishmen would even be invited to eat in the refectory of the College, and were surprised to find that modern novels (Walter Scott, for example) were read aloud during the meals.   Among young non-Catholics who frequented the English College Richard Milnes was prominent.   The link between his family and the English Catholics in Rome was, appropriately, his father's old acquaintanceship with Cardinal Weld.   This elderly Catholic squire from Dorsetshire, who had taken orders on the death of his wife, was the kind of man Mr. Milnes could readily comprehend.   He was neither exotic nor ethereal.   He had as background the routine experience of an ordinary English country gentleman and he had undergone the normal processes of marriage and parenthood.   With Mrs. Milnes he was gallant, sending her a water-colour sketch of Terracina (where they had met him on their way from Naples) with a flattering message about his attachment to the place in which he had first spoken to her and a genial reminder that though the sketch was a poor one she would hardly find another cardinal to do a better.   It was Cardinal Weld, Lord Houghton remembered in after years, who had first taken him to the English College and introduced him, in that restful and romantic atmosphere,[1] to Nicholas Wiseman.

Wiseman was only seven years older than Richard Milnes, but he had already been in charge of the English College since the age of twenty-six. He was tall and pale, grave and even a little pompous in his manner, humorous and a visionary. He had made his reputation as an oriental scholar and a linguist, but now, after some years of extreme spiritual suffering, he was emerging as a preacher and was beginning to concentrate all his attention upon the recovery of England for the Catholic Church. His feeling for his faith was Spanish in its splendour (he had been born in Seville, of an Irish father), and even his subsequent experiences of the revived Catholic Church in what Manning called 'the chill and utilitarianism of modern England' did not dim his magnificent conceptions. He loved Rome and its countryside with a scholarly passion. The summer evenings at the villa of the English College at Monte Porzio were the happiest recollections of a not altogether satisfying career. On his deathbed in the London of the eighteen-sixties his mind turned back towards Italy: 'I can see the colour of the chestnut trees,' he was heard to murmur, 'and Camaldoli and the top of Tusculum.'

In his book of recollections, *Monographs*, Lord Houghton included an essay upon Wiseman in which he reflects upon these Roman days. In it he mentions that he was 'brought into frequent relations' with the rector of the English College because he formed a ' lasting friendship' with one of the students, a kinsman of Wiseman, called Charles MacCarthy. 'If the story of that friendship could be written in full,' states Wemyss Reid in his official *Life* of Milnes, 'the reader would perhaps know more of the true nature of the man than he could do if he had met Milnes at a hundred dinner-parties.' The basis for this comment seems simply to be that the friendship of Milnes and MacCarthy continued intimate until the death of the latter in 1864, and survived a severe variety of ups and downs. Some ten years after they had first met, Charles Mac-Carthy, who had abandoned his vocation and was wandering aimlessly about Europe, developed money trouble in an acute form. The details are fortunately lost, but it would seem to have been his own fault. Milnes came sturdily to his help, arranged and guaranteed various loans, and chose the brisk Victorian solution of shipping MacCarthy off to be collector of customs on Turk's Island

---

[1] 'We have seen all we could . . . of the English College,' wrote Robert Monteith in a letter to Milnes from Rome dated 6 July 1835; 'we found it so quiet and cool, so mild & kindly—just as before so now in the long noiseless summertime. I thank you Milnes for taking me to that house.'

in the Bahamas. Here, amid the mildew and the mosquitoes, the young man languished, writing Richard Milnes long, importunate letters pleading for release, reading cases of French novels which came to him from Milnes' London bookseller, hoarding his small stipend, and receiving occasional replies from 26 Pall Mall urging him to stick it out. Ultimately MacCarthy became Governor of Ceylon. The success of his colonial career was certainly due to Monckton Milnes, but the interest of this friendship (which is the best-documented relationship in Milnes' career, a great bundle of MacCarthy's letters surviving, interleaved with Milnes' replies) is that it gives us one more crib by which to construe Milnes' character. Like O'Brien and Warburton at Cambridge, Mac-Carthy submitted at Rome to the full fascination of Milnes' personality, a personality then at its best in intimacy though later noted for the diffusion of a general, room-filling warmth. Like those earlier friends, MacCarthy would complain of 'levity and disregard,' express fears that Milnes was becoming hard, try to break off the friendship in pompous irritation, and then submit to the charm 'all over again. In 1842 he could write of their first meeting ten years before: 'from that time to this you have been the chief person in my life, the friend and brother and confessor, the end and aim of all my thoughts and actions and hopes.' Milnes could unquestionably be very endearing when he bothered to be so, and before the switching beam of his attention had gone from one person to the next. Side by side the friends would pace the walks of the English College garden, Charles MacCarthy in his long student's robes, Richard Milnes in his well-cut English suit. Together they would speculate upon literature and painting and religion in the Roman sunlight. At this period of his life, in MacCarthy's phrase, Milnes liked 'to bask and loiter in pleasant fancies.'

Although these intimacies did not really bring Milnes to the brink of the Roman Catholic Church, they did arouse his interest in religion. His apprehension of spiritual values was always sharp, even after his lyrical gift had been extinguished in the course of a sociable and not ascetic middle-age. Like many of his thoughtful contemporaries he was beset by religious doubts, and a friend to whom he unveiled these in 1834 wrote to reprimand him for busying himself 'with systems and doubts and differences between Christians.' He was told he approached 'God's mysteries with the profane touch of the logical understanding' and thought that he could be 'wafted into a haven of rest by your sense of beauty.' He was urged to thrust back these intellectual complications and follow 'gifted friends' such as F. D. Maurice into a blind, unthinking faith in the

Anglican Church.   That he was unable and unwilling to take this
advice is apparent, and was indeed to be expected from a young man
of his intelligence.   In a further letter the same confidant, Thomas
Dyke Acland, tried to dispel the fear that obsessed Milnes during
his religious moments: the fear that 'an abiding sense of (God's)
presence would entirely absorb' all his faculties.

VIII

A severe contrast to the Collegio Inglese and its atmosphere of
humane and pervasive Catholicism was provided by another milieu
much frequented by Richard Monckton Milnes in this first Roman
winter—the Palazzo Caffarelli, on the Palatine Hill.   Here, in a
set of spacious apartments along the second floor, with great
windows flung open upon an airy garden filled with cypresses and
tubs of orange trees (an unrivalled prospect of all Rome beyond),
there lived the family of that most inflexible of Prussian Protestants,
Hans Christian von Bunsen.   Emissary of the court of Berlin to
the Vatican for many years, Bunsen passed his time in Rome in
negotiations with the Pope, in biblical and archaeological researches,
in attempts to decipher the Etruscan alphabet, and in keeping the
German community up to the mark by simple Teutonic festivals
round a sparkling family tree at Christmas-time or by ostentatiously
celebrating the tercentenary of Luther's break with the Church.
His linguistic studies—he was alleged to have declared that the best
way of learning new languages was to study six or seven at once—
had already brought him some fame, and by the time he was made
a Chevalier and appointed Prussian Minister in London in 1839
he had become a scholar of European repute.

When Richard Milnes first met him in Rome, Bunsen was forty.
He was growing burly and his hair was turning sparse and grey.
His expression was as 'angelic' as ever, but his face (thin, alabaster
white and glowing with enthusiasm in his youth) was now becoming
round and pink; in another ten years it seemed to Carlyle 'a red
face large as the shield of Fingal.'   His chief happiness was to instruct
and improve those about him, but these didactic habits were by some
people found tedious.   In Rome he had slowly fallen in love with
a Welsh girl, Fanny Waddington, had married her and bred a
family.   His wife's nationality together with his own colloquial
command of English made the household at the Palazzo Caffarelli
a natural centre of gravitation for serious-minded English persons
in Rome.   Milnes owed his introduction into this high-thinking
circle to his old friend and Trinity tutor Connop Thirlwall, who
thanked Bunsen in December 1832 for the indulgence he had shown

to his young friend—'whose character I think you have rightly interpreted.' The nature of this interpretation is not recorded, but the tone of notes received by Milnes from the Palazzo Caffarelli (and which accompanied loaned books upon the intricacies of German theology) implies that the Prussian scholar deprecated Milnes' over-eager curiosity. Richard's own attitude to Bunsen was one of chilled respect. George Bunsen, the Chevalier's more warm-blooded son, has stated that Milnes learned to 'look up to and revere' his father in Rome—'without ever (and this lasted through life) feeling entirely at his ease in his presence.' His friendship with the Bunsens, extended to the whole family and carried on over the years, gave new emphasis to the pro-German sympathies he had contracted at Bonn. It occasioned a long winter sojourn in the Prussian capital in 1845, but it also and indirectly opened up to him a safe path into the mazes of French politics. His evenings at the Palazzo Caffarelli were in fact responsible for his later intimate knowledge of the political and literary world of Paris and for many of his French friendships, amongst them those with Guizot and with Montalembert.

In life itself, and still more in biography, which is life laid flat upon a table for others to peruse, the chain, the casual links of circumstance are of a special interest. Personal contacts no doubt do form the scaffolding of a public career, but their importance should not be over-rated. Monckton Milnes' failure in public life can be traced to two major misconceptions: he placed an excessive reliance on the value of the merely personal relationships which he had easily established with French and German as well as with English statesmen; and he did not discern that a gift for making friends with foreigners, useful in diplomacy, is of rather less than no advantage in English home politics. Because in the eighteen-forties he could correspond with Guizot or go and chat at the Tuileries with Louis-Philippe; because he knew Bunsen and Alexander von Humboldt and the court of Berlin; because he could visit Madrid or hob-nob with Italian exiles and Polish patriots, he judged that first Peel and then Palmerston had a clear duty to give him public office. This profound confusion of the realities of public life with those of private life (combined perhaps with a reputation for paradox and indiscretion) shipwrecked his father's plans and his own political ambitions. To the end of his days he believed that a youth spent in Italy, Germany and Greece had given him an unusual understanding of the European scene. In many ways he was right. This did not mean that any English Prime Minister would necessarily think him so.

Meanwhile it is of interest to note that his intimacy with the

Prussian family in the Palazzo Caffarelli led to another connection spiritually remote from the Bunsen orbit. In the early spring of 1832 three remarkable Frenchmen had together come to Rome. The eldest of these three, the Abbé de la Mennais, who had refused a cardinal's hat from Gregory XVI, was a tiny, fanatical priest, learned, well-known and consumptive. With him came his two collaborators in the notorious project represented by the newspaper *l'Avenir*, and which aimed at a spiritual regeneration of the Catholic Church in France by means of a total separation of Church and State. The policy of la Mennais and his two young followers, Comte Charles de Montalembert and A. F. Rio, with its implication that the Church in France was not all it should be, had earned the hostility of the French bishops; and the three friends had now come hopefully to Rome to obtain a direct judgement from the Pope upon their policies. The Pope kept them for some weeks in suspense and gave no judgement; although he later issued the famous condemnation which drove Lamennais (as he afterwards called himself) out of the Church and then on into open infidelity, and caused the orthodox Montalembert much chagrin. The least remembered but most engaging of these three men was Rio, a gay and quixotic young Breton who was then preparing his great work, *L'Art Chrétien*, the fruit of his Italian journeyings. Rio, whom Gladstone thought the most striking Frenchman he ever saw, had made friends with Fanny Bunsen, happy to find at last an opportunity for investigating his belief that the Bretons and the Welsh were by origin the same nation. She would sing the songs of Wales to him in the great saloon of the Palazzo Caffarelli, and it was here that he met the young English poet, Richard Milnes, with whom he contracted a firm and instantaneous friendship. He in turn introduced Milnes to Montalembert. This too was a success: 'so French in his emotions and so English in his thoughts,' wrote Lord Houghton after Montalembert's death, recalling how he and the three Frenchmen would visit Wiseman at the English College, when 'the conversation of the decorous seminary' would become 'as bright and coloured as that of the gayest Paris drawing-room.' Even the Lutheran household of the Bunsens took him back, by a loop-line, into the heart of the Catholic Church.

Tired of waiting for a Papal judgement, Rio and Montalembert left Rome in April for Naples, on foot. Milnes had preceded them to Naples by some days, and had been swept into the life of that noisy city, passing his time with Augustus Craven ('the only fine man I ever liked') and with the family of Ferronayes, one of whose daughters subsequently married Craven and was author of that nostalgic but over-sweet book of pious reminiscence

Récit d'une Soeur. Mr. and Mrs. Milnes and Harriette had gone north. Richard wrote to tell his mother that though he was liking Naples a 'teasing' episode prevented his seeing as much of Rio and Montalembert as he had intended. The young Frenchmen spent most of their time in the company of a Scottish family named Malcolm, the Malcolms' invalid daughter Lady Campbell and her husband Sir Alexander. Gossips in Rome had felt it their duty to hint to 'that stupid Sir Alex' that Richard Milnes had fallen in love with his wife. Sir Alexander found this easy to believe; he infected his parents-in-law, and possibly his wife as well, with his conviction. As a result (Richard complained) he was excluded from all the Malcolms' jaunts and invitations—no more picnics, no carriage excursions to Pompeii, no musical evenings with Rio, Montalembert and Lady Campbell. Though his letter to Mrs. Milnes implicitly denied it, Richard may in fact have conceived a passive, formal admiration for this lady, who was elegant, ethereal and ill. When Lady Campbell died a few years later, he wrote an elegy on her untimely death:

> Before the tranquil beauty of her face
> I bowed in spirit, thinking that she were
> A suffering Angel, whom the special grace
> Of God intrusted to our pious care,
> That we might learn from her
> The art to minister
> To heavenly beings in seraphic air.

Further verses praised Lady Campbell's 'blue-veined eyelids,' low voice, quiet gaiety and 'lightly-pliant mind.' But in these years any occasion, and above all a melancholy one, stirred Richard Milnes to write a poem, and it would be unwise in us to be as credulous as Lady Campbell's jealous husband. It seems likely that Richard Monckton Milnes, like many Englishmen of his class, was never capable of passionate love. When still a bachelor of nearly forty, anxious to marry Florence Nightingale, Milnes confided his diffident emotions to a friend. This friend was a woman— S. T. Coleridge's daughter—and she (of course) repeated these confidences. 'Mrs Sara Coleridge told us,' wrote a friend of Miss Nightingale's, 'his confession to her was that he wished to be in love and could not.'[1] Yet Milnes was not impervious to feminine beauty, at any rate in his youth. '. . . Eminent beauty loses its hold upon one with lengthening life—at least I find it so,' he wrote

---

[1] Letter of Fanny Allen to her niece Emma Darwin, 26 December 1847, printed in *A Century of Family Letters: Emma Darwin* (ed. H. Lichfield 1913), vol. i, p. 113.

to MacCarthy in 1844, of another girl whom he was rumoured to admire; 'she is most beautiful, but I don't know that she has any other charm, and I get her out of my head without much difficulty.' These are not the accents of romantic passion. Richard Milnes' romanticism was confined to landscape and to literature. His personal relationships were too numerous and distracting to allow him the avid lonely concentration that great love requires.

Thus separated from Rio and Montalembert, Milnes was forced back upon the residents of Naples for company. Chief among these was his distant cousin Sir William Gell, the famous archaeologist, traveller and historian, then between fifty and sixty years old, who lived at the Villa Gellia and acted 'as a sort of classic Consul of the place.' In his volume *Monographs*, published in 1876, Milnes wrote of Sir William Gell as belonging 'to that class of scholarly dilettanti which will soon be a subject for archaeology in English society.' He described the contrast between Gell's dry style in his *History of the Morea* and his cheerful, jocular manner in daily life, and recalled how the old man would be carried in a palanquin through the ruins of Pompeii, cracking such jokes with the donkey-boys that they sometimes let his litter fall from laughing. Also in Naples Milnes met the fiercest opponent of the romantic school— the little bespectacled Count Platen, who was then writing his last play, *Die Liga von Cambrai*, and who died in Italy three years later, at the age of thirty-nine. The personality of Platen, an avowed homosexual, at first disappointed Milnes, who had regarded him as 'the mightiest' of German poets after Goethe. But after the initial disillusion they struck up an acquaintanceship, and Milnes translated at least one, and perhaps more, of Platen's poems—his hexameters, *Antiques*, inspired by the sight of Roman statuary in an Italian museum:

Free! let us free,—throw open the doors, lay open the presses,
Here in the dark and the dust is it seemly for *us* to be dwelling?
What we, and where we have been, oh! remember, and give us
    your pity.
Once, this rare old vase was the pride of the gardens of Egypt,
And Cleopatra herself bade her courtiers fill it with myrtle:—
This so daintily carved,—this duplicate layer of onyx,
On thy finger, Antinous, rested, a jewel unvalued—
Thine, thou beautiful boy, too soon sped away to thy heaven.

The translation appeared in Milnes' first book of prose and verse, *Memorials of a Tour in Greece*, published by Moxon in 1833.

Chapter Three

1832   1835

The gusto of Sir William Gell, the fervour of Count Platen, helped to make real to Richard Milnes the civilisation of the ancient world, which had formed the humdrum study of what he still called in this connection 'a very painful boyhood.' That January he had been overcome by his first sight of the Coliseum; and now the brittle by-streets of Pompeii confirmed his interest in antiquity and brought a new actuality to his early memories of learning Latin with his father at Thorne Hall, of Greek themes copied out for Mr. Binns, the tutor, on lined paper, of the more thorough and professional scholarship of Trinity. And so when he met his Cambridge contemporary Christopher Wordsworth in Naples that April, and found he was about to embark on a lengthy tour of Greece, Richard was readily persuaded to ask his parents' leave to join the party. He told his father that the journey could not cost more than £150, and that it was to be undertaken in the company of Christopher Wordsworth, his friends Robertson and Grey, and a couple of frugally minded German *literati*. Their plan was to cross the Adriatic from Otranto to Corfu; to sail down the Ionian Islands—under British occupation since 1815—visiting Ithaca and Leucas, to cross over to the Morea from Zante, and to work their way north-eastwards into Attica, with Athens as their goal. One of Wordsworth's aims in this journey was to trace out the line of the ditch of Sparta, and though Mr. Milnes wrote omnisciently to Richard that this could take but a fortnight, they hoped to make it last for several weeks. Mr. and Mrs. Milnes (and little Harriette, who was also consulted) gave Richard the permission. He went up from Naples to Rome. On 7 July 1832 he started out for Greece.

To Wordsworth and to Robertson—Grey had decided to remain in Italy—the archaeological aspect of their journey was the all-important one. For Milnes, on the other hand, Greece held a variety of appeals. He was quite prepared to help Wordsworth identify the great ditch of Sparta or to make his guess at the precise position of the Dodona oracle, but he was also concerned with Mediterranean politics and hypnotised by the legend of Lord Byron. It was not eight years since Byron's death of fever at Missolonghi.

The War of Greek Independence, which had begun with the revolt
in the Morea in April 1821, and had been rendered spectacular to
English people by the death of Byron in 1824 and the battle of
Navarino in 1827, was now officially over. By the Protocol of
February 1830, the Powers, afraid of Russian influence, had
recognised Greece as an independent state and had offered the
position of sovereign prince of Greece to Leopold of Coburg.
Leopold had accepted the job in February and resigned it in May.
Meanwhile, the terms of the Protocol, which stringently limited
Greek territory, had been rejected by the Greek President and
dictator Capo d'Istria, who had been Foreign Minister to the Czar
Alexander I; but in October 1831 Capo d'Istria had been assassi-
nated, and Greece had subsided into a state of anarchy. The
Powers quickly drew up another Protocol, by which Greek territory
was extended to a northern line from Arta on the west coast to
Volo on the east. They had this time offered the crown to seven-
teen-year-old Otho of Bavaria. The offer was accepted by Otho's
father, and Greece was now awaiting the arrival of its new king.[1]
It was during this turbulent interregnum that Milnes and his party
chose to go to Greece. They found the communities of shepherds
and mountaineers of which the Greek nation was composed in a
state of suspense. In his *Athens and Attica* [2] Wordsworth (who spoke
Greek well) relates how he and Milnes had been questioned by a
group of peasants at the bridge of Euripus about the imminent
arrival of their king. 'They congratulated themselves on their
recent liberation,' Wordsworth recorded, 'on their being, as they
style themselves, Independent Hellenes, and no longer slaves of
Turkey.' Milnes, who was young enough to believe in progress,
felt convinced that the advent of King Otho would transform the
character of modern Greece. He wrote comfortably of the 'culp-
able negligence of the allied powers in delaying the Bavarian troops
and regency—there is no doubt' (he continued with all the smugness
of the ill-informed) 'that the moment a regular constitutional
Government arrives, everything will fall into its right place with
wonderful rapidity.'

The conflict between his political pretensions and his literary
temperament, which was to confuse, indeed to mar, the whole of
Milnes' adult career, was already evident during this visit to Greece.
It comes out clearly in the book of prose and verse which he published

---

[1] Otho landed at Nauplia, with an army of Bavarian officials and soldiers,
in January 1833; he accepted a liberal constitution in 1844; and was deposed
in 1862.
[2] *Athens and Attica: Journal of a Residence There*, by the Rev. Christopher Wordsworth, M.A. John Murray, 1836.

on his return to London.[1] Nineteen pieces of verse are interspersed with slabs of descriptive and often didactic prose; the eulogy of some idyllic myrtle grove will tail off into a pompous disquisition on the price of raisins or the crimes of Capo d'Istria. The verse included the translation of Platen's *Antiques* as well as a number of pieces directly inspired by the places Milnes was seeing—the lines *On a Grotto and Warm Spring at the Head of the Gulf of Lepanto,* for instance, which began:

> Within this grot did Amphitrite,
> Willing a beauteous shore to bless,
> Expose the full unshaded light
> Of all her ocean queenliness.

The most popular verses in the volume were the *Lines Expressive of the State of Feeling Excited by the Consciousness of Being in a Classic Country:*

> Oh, blessed, blessed be the Eld,
> Its echoes and its shades,—
> The tone that from all time outswelled,
> The light that never fades;—
> The silver-pinioned memories,
> The symbol and the tale,—
> The soul-enchaséd melodies
> Of merriment and bale.

When Alfred Tennyson heard that Milnes was going to publish his poems on Greece, he wrote that he hoped there would be 'much glowing description and little mysticism' in the book. 'Your gay and airy mind,' wrote Tennyson, 'must have caught as many colours from the landskip you moved thro', as a flying soap-bubble.'[2]

A comparison of Milnes' *Memorials* with Wordsworth's *Athens and Attica,* and with the sumptuous *Greece: Pictorial, Descriptive and Historical* which Wordsworth produced in 1839,[3] suggests that Milnes and his chief companion were of very different casts of mind. *Athens and Attica* and *Greece* are filled with exact and scholarly information; easily written; threaded through with a strand of wry humour. They show every evidence of hard work. *Memorials,* as

---

[1] *Memorials of a Tour in Some Parts of Greece: Chiefly Poetical,* by Richard Monckton Milnes. Edward Moxon, Dover Street, 1833. It was dedicated to Henry Hallam in memory of his son Arthur, and had a quotation from Shelley on the title-page.

[2] MS. letter from Alfred Tennyson, postmark of 3 December 1833.

[3] This fine volume, illustrated with 350 engravings on wood and 28 on steel by Copley Fielding, Hervé, Meissonier, Sargent, etc., was published by William S. Orr and Co., Paternoster Row, in 1839 and re-issued in 1840, went through seven editions by 1882, and was translated into French.

I have indicated, is a slight and ill co-ordinated little book which some of Milnes' friends urged him not to publish. Christopher Wordsworth was nearly two years older than Monckton Milnes; that is to say, he was almost twenty-five. He was the third and youngest son of the Master of Trinity (himself the youngest brother of the poet William Wordsworth) by his Quaker wife, and he was already a fellow of and an assistant-tutor at his father's college. He later became Headmaster of Harrow, and ended Bishop of Lincoln, by Disraeli's patronage. Christopher Wordsworth was known for his clarity of mind, for his quickness and courtesy, for his untiring capacity for work, and for a tendency to sarcasm which, as a bishop, he rigidly restrained. Milnes told his father, before they started for Greece, that he thought Wordsworth was unique. He said he liked him better every day. But in the tiny manuscript journal from which Milnes afterwards wrote up the prose passages of his *Memorials* there are hints that Wordsworth's seriousness could pall.

Wordsworth [Milnes wrote to his mother from Athens] never believes he has gloated long enough on any antiquity whatever, and loves an old wall with a passion more intense than that with which any of Rio's Italian heroines burnt for their unseen lovers.

Although they had equipped themselves with all the right books—including Pouqueville and Gell [1]—Wordsworth was perpetually lamenting that he had not brought with him Palmerius' *Graeciae Descriptio* (published in 1673); and though Wordsworth succeeded in identifying a number of important sites—including that of Dodona—Milnes discovered that he had 'an extraordinary lack of the organ of locality.' Wordsworth would sometimes crack a joke—saying for instance that Milnes' new fangled india-rubber boots were 'rubbing out the roads'—but he seems on the whole to have been a severe travelling-companion. After Milnes' return to Italy in December 1832 Wordsworth and Robertson remained in Greece some weeks. They were robbed, and Wordsworth stabbed in the neck, on their way back to Athens in February 1833. Robertson, Wordsworth and the remaining German (one had proved so disagreeable that they left him in the Ionian Islands) were more thorough archaeologists than Milnes, who was always anxious to press on to Athens and its potential gaieties.

You must remember [he wrote to Mrs. Milnes and Harriette, when he had finally reached that ravaged capital] that the will of one person in a party of four can have no weight and that it is

[1] Pouqueville's *Voyage dans la Grèce*, Paris 1820; Gell's *Itinerary of Greece*, 1819. They found Gell full of errors.

equally impossible in such a country as this to separate yourself from the others, or to persuade them to fall in with the plan you prefer.

II

The four travellers were held up at the very outset of their journey. When they reached the Ionian Islands they learned that it was not yet safe to travel through the Morea and that they must reach Athens by some other route.

The political state of the Morea is at this moment the most terrible [Richard wrote from the town of Zante to his young aunt Caroline at Hastings]; I have the hills of its coast in clear view from the window where I am writing, but I suppose you might as well put a pistol to your head as attempt to walk five miles into the country. The whole is in the hands of certain predatory chieftains, who have armed the population for their own purposes, and now these peasant armies, after having done nothing since Capo d'Istria's death but rob and murder one another, are driven by actual starvation to every possible mode of pillage and outrage.

My darling Jetty [he wrote to his sister on the same day, 25 August]; You must think you will never get a letter from *real* Greece and that I am going to live in these islands, but you will excuse us being so slow when I tell you that we have found out that this is the *very earliest* we could go on any further on account of the malaria and now we are obliged to go quite back to the North to be quite safe.

They were faced with the alternatives of sailing straight to Athens, or of returning up the coast to the Turkish provinces and coming down upon the new Greek frontier from the north. They chose the Turkish provinces, since it would give them the chance of seeing Moslem life.

In the Ionian Islands Milnes had been intrigued by the sharp contrasts between 'Englishism' and Orientalism. At Corfu, where he was charmed by the flowering myrtles in the groves of olive trees, by the quantities of arbutus and of smilax, by the fountains playing at sunset under a 'deep orange and very pale lilac' sky, he made friends with the English garrison, but he was pained to find that Greeks were not accepted in the English society of the island. At Zante, a town with arcades which Wordsworth found 'dark and dwarfish' and where streets had Venetian names which recalled an earlier but equally alien rule, they met Thiersch, the tutor of the young King of Greece, on his way back to Bavaria. On another occasion Milnes spoke with a man who had actually seen Lord Byron on Ithaca, and said that he had been much beloved.

When at length, in early September, they got away from the islands of the Ionian Sea, they started on horseback for the Turkish city of Janina, which they entered one evening in 'thick moonlight.' For some days they rode slowly on across Greece to the coast of the Gulf of Salonika, journeying through the classical vale of Tempe in full view of Mounts Pelion and Ossa. Turkish civilisation aroused Milnes' curiosity and even his respect:

Turkey and the Turks [he told his mother] are a miracle to look at and think about. You are in quite a new world—that these solemn idle people, never working, never reading, never thinking, should have jumped from their sofas upon their horses and conquered a quarter of the world seems impossible, but perhaps the most interesting light in which they can be regarded is as a dying nation.

Though the moonlight in Janina had been bright enough to reveal the 'forks' on which criminals were impaled alive, and which were plainly visible from the inn window, Milnes liked the Turks. He regretted to find that many of their old customs—particularly the wearing of the great folded white or green turbans—were being superseded by habits from the West. Sometimes the travellers were entertained to dinner by Turkish pashas—eating burned almonds and mutton rolls, clinking glasses of strong liqueurs with their hosts—and sometimes they slept in Turkish houses or on the floor of some rustic hovel with the Greek or Turkish family, the asses, dogs and fowls grouped with them round a central fire. When they reached the town of Volo on the Gulf of Volo they were entertained by the Turkish governor, Ibrahim Aga, at a great dinner which ended in a performance by dancing boys who were dressed as Turkish women, and danced to the music of a fife, a fiddle, some tambourines, and a human voice singing a 'sharp drawling song.' Behind these dancers a buffoon clad in fur and skins mimicked their movements, and the English travellers happily recognised a survival of 'the old Satyrick clown.' But the dance became increasingly 'lascivious and violent' and ended with the Turkish guests getting thoroughly involved with the Greek dancing boys. Milnes, who had had too much to eat, said he dropped off to sleep.

Leaving the lovely vale of Tempe with the river Pineus running through its midst, the travellers came out upon the vast uncultivated plain of Thessaly, which they traversed for a succession of days. The pass of Thermopylae disappointed Milnes; Marathon seemed 'not very striking—a desert plain on the sea surrounded with low hills and equally barren'; only the island of Negroponte, the ancient Euboea, surpassed his highest expectations by its beauty.

But though many of the famous sites did not come up to his hopes, a thousand natural details moved Milnes deeply. In his notebook he jotted down descriptions of the 'immense plateau tapestried with wild vines,' of the oleanders, arbutus and wild palms, of the shingly, narrow valley of some river fringed by a few fine oaks. He gazed on Mount Olympus through a grove of white mulberries, and at twilight watched the planet Venus rise above the cone of that Mountain of the Immortals. He waded half-naked in the mud off the coast of Trachini and saw the wild geese sailing mournfully by. In some of the ruined temples they found walnut trees planted by the shepherds to give shade. And always they would carefully examine the broken blocks of marble half-hidden by the smilax, reconstruct and copy down and interpret the fragmentary inscriptions, make notes about the figures in the bas-reliefs. Under Wordsworth's guidance Milnes developed a temporary interest in these relics, filling his little pocket-book with scrawled sketches. Wordsworth one day remarked that the colours of the Greek autumnal woods seemed those of flowers, not trees; but Milnes was always conscious of the pure, fierce beauties of the Grecian landscape, the bays and headlands, the pine-clad solemn hills, bathed in atmosphere he described as 'mother-of-pearl.' He watched the scintillations of colour in the wide Greek skies, noting down change after change as it occurred: the sunset at Glyky with its 'clear rose, light saffron and olive tints'; the sunset at Rachly 'burning-gold and roseate . . . contemporaneous with a light blue moonlight.' After one rain-storm the sky was filled with grey and green-grey banks of cloud, beneath which the lightning flashed and glimmered white, while at the same time, in another part of the sky, tones which ranged through the spectrum from dark blue to 'deepest orange-red' were glowing.

They reached Athens on 13 October, 1832, at night.

III

In 1832 Athens bore the aspect, to-day all too familiar throughout Europe, of a capital city utterly devastated by war. Milnes and his companions entered the city by a gateway still guarded by the Turkish police. They rode on for a mile through streets of derelict houses in the darkness, the Acropolis 'just traceable in outline' on their left. The modern town of Athens was a desolate forest of charred ruins. It had been burnt out during the revolution, and save for a handful of painted wooden houses and an inn, it had not been rebuilt.

Out of this confused mass [Richard Milnes wrote to his mother and sister] the few remains of antiquity rise with a solemnity and perfectness that makes them look much more like the unfinished edifices of a new city than the remains of an old one.

Like all those who visit Athens for the first time, Milnes was taken aback to find how small the Acropolis and its temples looked by daylight. They wandered round the ruined town next morning. Even the ugly town clock, which Lord Elgin, adding insult to injury, had given the city to atone for his removal of the Elgin marbles, had been destroyed. Milnes, who felt passionately against Lord Elgin ('It would be difficult to add anything to the obloquy with which the spoliation of the Parthenon, by Lord Elgin, has been met all over the world,' he wrote in *Memorials of a Tour in Greece*), was glad to be told of the nemesis which had overtaken the English collector's chief agent, Signor Lusieri. Lusieri, who was so unpopular with his fellow-townsmen that he had to barricade himself into his house, had died suddenly of a broken blood-vessel. When his neighbours battered down the door, they found him lying dead in a pool of blood. Upon his chest was crouched a great black cat. It was sucking up his blood.

Despite the wrecked state of Athens, Milnes was delighted to have reached it. The primitive life they had been leading in north Greece, which had seemed so romantic at first, had not been comfortable. 'The rough travelling, amusing enough for two or three days,' he told his mother, 'is rather boring in the long run, but one is driven to think a good deal in self-defence.' But now, in Athens, he could indulge his two great pleasures: talking and meeting new people. A small, haphazard and very heterogeneous society was assembled in the Greek capital, awaiting as impatiently as the peasants of Euripus the delayed arrival of the king. There was General Church, the Liberator of Greece, whom Milnes found 'solemn, rather quixotic-looking'; there were American missionaries; there was young Lady Franklin, the second wife of Sir John Franklin, who had already made his name by Arctic exploration, and who was now commanding the *Rainbow* frigate off the coast of Greece. Lady Franklin was an amusing, enterprising young person, who made long and dangerous journeys accompanied only by an English servant girl, and had ridden from Constantinople to Vienna. Milnes also met Madame Pittachi, an 'unhappy fine looking woman,' who was the sister of Mrs. Teresa Black, the Maid of Athens. He was told that Byron had said of the Maid that 'if she had been high-born, and if she had been rich, she was pretty enough to marry, but in love as I was I knew what I was about.' He learned, too, how much the Macri family (Teresa's parents)

had disliked Lord Byron, who had lodged, with Trelawny, in their
house. These last pieces of gossip—fragments of the Byronic legend
—he got from the most interesting and apparently the most loquacious of his new Athenian friends, George Finlay, the friend of
Byron and the historian of Greece, who was at this time in his
thirty-third year.

When Byron had first seen George Finlay, at Cephalonia in
November 1823, he had affected to think him Shelley's ghost.
Milnes, who had never seen Shelley and could not judge of this
resemblance, thought Mr. Finlay looked like Augustus Hare.[1]
Finlay was then resident in Athens, with the intention of buying
an estate in Attica and farming it. He had come to Greece in a
wave of enthusiasm during the War of Independence, and though
he had returned again to Scotland for a short period he could not
long resist his love for Greece. He told Milnes, always an eager
listener, many stories of the War—of Capo d'Istria's political ruth-
lessness, of Odysseus' suspicious nature and love of beauty, of the
splendid character of his friend Frank Abney Hastings, a British
naval officer who had died at Missolonghi, and whom Finlay
thought a greater figure than Lord Byron—in fact 'the greatest man
the Greeks had.' He told Milnes that Byron had said 'nobody
could know what Shelley was but one who knew him well' and
that 'Trelawny would be a good fellow if he could spell and speak
the truth.' He described Byron's 'bodily activity and moral
indolence,' his 'unintelligible dandyism of expression' and his
capacity for being actuated by the impression of the moment. On
one occasion, Finlay related, Lord Byron had been much aroused
and had cried out that he would go to Corinth whether the Turks
were there or no; he had written a Song of Corinth, he said, and
'this was something, and people would read it with stronger feelings
if the author had died there.' Byron had then, according to
Finlay, 'stopped short and blushed as if caught in a crime.' Finlay
also repeated that Byron was convinced he would die in 1824, his
thirty-seventh year, since this had been predicted by an old Scots-
woman many years before.[2] He told him, too, how sensitive Byron
had been over the criticism of *Don Juan*, when Hookham Frere
had said the quarto edition of the poem was too bawdy for the

---

[1] Not the author of *Memorials of a Quiet Life*, but his less famous young uncle
the brother of Julius Hare and joint author with him of *Guesses at Truth* (1827)
who died suddenly at Rome in 1834.

[2] Finlay's story of the influence of this prophecy on Byron's mind was told by
him to Dr. Julius Millingen (1800–1878), who published it in his memoirs. It is
confirmed in Finlay's autobiographical sketch, written at the request of the
President of Harvard University in 1861 and prefixed to the seven-volume edition
of Finlay's life-work, *The History of Greece, B.C. 146 to A.D. 1864* (Clarendon
Press, 1877).

table and too big for the pocket. On the whole, Byron did not emerge from Finlay's anecdotes as a very romantic figure. It may have been Finlay who told Milnes the poet always carried a contraceptive in his waistcoat pocket.[1]

After some weeks in Athens, Milnes set off, apparently without his late companions, for Napoli di Romagna, which he found to be more like a fort than a town and situated on a not particularly fine bay. 'Wretched time of it here,' he scrawled in his notebook; and proceeded onwards to Vostitza, where he found the *Rainbow* frigate and its captain, Sir John Franklin, the husband of his Athens acquaintance. 'Talked with Sir J. Franklin in Rainbow,' he noted; 'degradation of the British flag.' Sir John, a bluff and business-like sailor, offered Milnes a berth as far as Patras; but he was not the man to like undergraduate poets.

I cannot say Mr. Milnes particularly pleased me [he wrote to Lady Franklin at Athens[2]]. He appeared to me to be one of those young travellers who, from a hasty passage through Greece, have drawn conclusions which the longer residents and better informed persons know not to be correct. . . . His exalted idea of the Greeks of the present day was much shaken by hearing and seeing what is passing in this neighbourhood. . . . I brought him from Vostitza to Patras in this ship, and then procured him a passage in an Austrian brig of war to Corfu, so that he tumbled upon his legs. He spoke of having seen you daily at Athens and of spending every evening in the society where you are, though I did not imagine he was a person after your taste.

Milnes found that the Austrian brig which took him to Corfu had several friends of friends of his aboard, as well as a young nephew of Sir John Franklin's who reminded him of Stafford O'Brien. Also on board was 'a poor Polish doctor' whom Milnes seems to have entertained with his German songs. From Corfu Milnes made his way back to Italy, reaching Venice (where his mother and Harriette were living) a day or two before Christmas 1832. It was midwinter when he re-crossed the Adriatic. As he looked his last at the Ionian Islands, which he was not to see again for ten years, he watched another sunset: 'sweet sunset,' he noted, 'sun behind a flaccid cloud like a golden fleece—the Greek pale violet *after-sky*. Outline of the islands lovelier than ever.'

[1] Commonplace book, 1839–40.
[2] Letter of autumn 1832, printed without date in H. D. Traill's *Life of Sir John Franklin, R.N.* (John Murray 1896), p. 192. Another letter of February 1833, not printed by Traill, describes the attack on Wordsworth and Robertson by robbers near Delphi, two months after Milnes had left Greece.

IV

While Richard Milnes was ambling along the dusty mule-tracks of Thessaly, his mother and Harriette had decided on a private expedition of their own. Mr. Milnes had suddenly got some news about his money affairs which seemed good. He hurried off over the Alps, leaving his wife and daughter to wait for him in Milan. Left to their own devices, they became bored. The court of Milan had now taken up the custom of going to Venice for the Carnival, which meant that the Opera went there too. Mrs. Milnes easily persuaded herself it would be good for Harriette if they followed suit. 'I decided to go to Venice if Harriette liked it,' she wrote in her journal, 'and she was much pleased at the thoughts of it.' At the end of October they left Milan, travelling *voiturier* but with such quantities of luggage that rude passers-by shouted after them, 'Ecco una casa intiera!' The roads were desolate and they feared robbers; but they arrived successfully at Venice and began to look for an apartment. The Contessa Albrizzi, whom they had known at Milan, sent her son to help them, and on his advice they rented a very small house, 'hardly large enough to tie a dog in.' Mrs. Milnes found the use of the gondola awkward at first, especially getting into it backwards in full court dress; but she and Harriette soon acclimatised themselves to Venice, visiting the islands and the glass-works, watching the pigeons feeding on the Piazza, drinking 'the most excellent coffee in Europe' and going to dances and conversaziones which might last till any hour of the morning. On their first evening out in Venice, Mrs. Milnes was introduced to a Conte Capo d'Istria, a brother of the dead dictator. When she told him that she had a son travelling in Greece, he replied that he hoped he would come home safely, since the country was infested with desperate brigands and there was nothing to eat. Richard would be lucky, he added, if he got an egg a day. Anxiety about Richard's journey was the only disturbing factor in their gay and happy Venetian life.

Mrs. Milnes and her daughter were made free of seven Venetian houses. In two of these rival salons were held—those of the Contessa Albrizzi and the Contessa Benzoni. Byron, with whom the Benzoni had been in love in 1819, had called her 'a kind of Venetian Lady Melbourne,' and had been fascinated by the fact that she had had a child by her half-brother. It was at her house, Mrs. Milnes learned, that he had first met Teresa Guiccioli.[1] Byron had complained that the conversation of the Venetian salons

---

[1] Byron had first seen the Guiccioli at Mme Albrizzi's, but was first presented to her in April 1819 at Mme Benzoni's.

had 'none of that snip-snap . . . which makes half the talk of
Paris and London'; but to Mrs. Milnes and Harriette it formed a
welcome contrast to conversation in the West Riding or at the
York hunt ball.   At Madame Albrizzi's they 'met all the Litterati,'
for in literary matters this lady 'really shone.'   She had been the
friend of Canova and of Alfieri, of Foscari and the Abbate Morelli;
and in her prime she had been called the 'Madame de Staël of
Italy.'   Mrs. Milnes found out that the Albrizzi was a Greek, and
had been married three times, the first time at the age of twelve.
She was now getting old; Mr. Milnes (who came to Venice in 1834)
wrote with characteristic exaggeration to his Yorkshire cousin that
Madame Albrizzi, 'like Macbeth's witches, has had this midnight
revelry these eighty years.'   The Benzoni, on the other hand, was
not an intellectual person, but she charmed Mrs. Milnes by telling
her tales of Englishmen who had fallen hopelessly in love with her,
and had remained that way for the rest of their lives.   It was clear
to Mrs. Milnes and Harriette that the Benzoni, however absurd
she might seem now, had once been a figure of high romance.
Was it not to her that the Venetian composer Perruchini had written
his famous song, *Biondina in Gondoletta*?

During the two months of waiting for Richard to turn up from
Greece, both mother and daughter were having a great success
with the Venetians.   After a nervous debut, which ended in a
triumph (the men in the audience 'knocking their little canes on
their hats and calling out'), Harriette was often asked to sing to
their new friends, while her mother accompanied her on the piano.
Unlike her brother Richard, who only spoke low-class Italian,
Harriette had now perfected her Italian accent and pronunciation.
Her audience would cry out in raptures that she could not be English
—'è la nuoestra Enrichetta' they would cry.   Harriette's greatest
success was when she was singing one evening at the Baroness
Westylar's.   A large scorpion began creeping down the wall behind
her.   Mrs. Milnes, at the piano, noticed that everybody in the
room had risen to their feet and were silently pointing at the wall.
Harriette, who had not noticed the scorpion, now observed it, and
put it in her pocket-handkerchief.   When she had finished her
song, she threw the insect out of the window.   The Venetians
screamed in unison and loudly declared that 'only the *Milnes*' child
could have done such a thing.'

A day or two before Christmas 1832, Richard joined his mother
and sister in Venice.   He had a bundle of new poems in his portmanteau, and the night after he arrived he sat over the fire in what
he called 'the wee drawing-room' and read Harriette *The Lay of
the Humble*, a poem in twenty-three stanzas which she said she had

no wish to hear. It became one of his most popular poems, for it was elevating and morally sound:

> I have no comeliness of frame,
> No pleasant range of feature;
> I'm feeble, as when first I came
> To earth, a weeping creature;
> My voice is low whene'er I speak,
> And singing faint my song;
> But though thus cast among the weak,
> I envy not the strong.

Richard too had a great success with the Venetians. His cordial manner pleased them as much as it displeased most English people, and they enjoyed his singing of duets and of *buffo* songs. 'I see it would be perfectly impossible to go out nowhere here,' he wrote to his father after his arrival; 'the only thing is to limit it as much as possible.' The letters from his father which he had found at Venice were depressing, almost despairing. The optimism with which Mr. Milnes had set off for England had proved wholly unjustified, for he found that instead of being better his finances were now infinitely worse owing to further entanglements of his brother Rodes. He sent Richard a melancholy report on this situation. His son tried to make the best of it: 'let us pass the next years of our existence unknowing and unknown, making our very poverty a source of our intellectual well-being through keeping us out of the noise and calls of general society,' he wrote. Mr. Milnes had bitterly reproached himself for being unable to set Richard off at once on a political career.

If you ever regret [wrote Richard] that our own sad fortunes put off to an infinite distance all your Parliamentary projects for me, it is some consolation to remember that in the present state of the political world, with my political feelings, even with a hundredfold my ability, my career could never be anything but one of ambitious pleasure. There is disgrace on the very threshold to come in as a nominee of the Duke of Newcastle (which I was really vexed to see you envied Gladstone).[1]

V

At Venice, Richard passed his time between escorting Harriette and their mother to parties, and writing up his Grecian notes into a publishable form. In June 1833 Mrs. Milnes and Harriette set

---

[1] In December 1832 W. E. Gladstone had been returned as one of the members for Newark. Although this was the first reformed Parliament, Newark was a nomination borough which the Act had spared. Gladstone got the seat through the Duke of Newcastle, father of Sir John Gladstone's friend Lord Lincoln.

off for Berne, where they had arranged to meet Mr. Milnes on his
way back from England. They travelled *voiturier* to Milan (where
they had left their own carriage) in conditions of terrible heat.

We kept taking off one thing after another [wrote Mrs. Milnes].
Our Italian maid Mariette sat opposite to us fanning herself with
all her might and singing one Milanese song after another which
helped pass the time when the heat was so excessive. How extraordinary it is she said that you rich English people (for they fancy
everybody rich that comes from England) should put yourselves
to this inconvenience when you can be cool and comfortable in
your own country.

The amiable Venetians were sad to see them go, and one of
Mrs. Milnes' friends gave her a bust of the Duc de Reichstadt as
a parting gift. Meanwhile, Richard had decided to make a little
tour to Pisa and Florence with a young couple whom he had
lately met—the Comte and Comtesse Adolphe de Circourt.

Richard's mother called the Circourts 'clever and agreeable
people.' They were much more than that. At thirty-one
Adolphe de Circourt, who had a profile like Dante and knew the
entire *Divina Commedia* by heart, was already one of the most
profound scholars of his generation—'*mappemonde vivante des con-
naissances humaines*,' wrote Lamartine, '*homme où tout était tête*.'
Circourt wrote voluminously throughout his life, but published
nothing but review articles; leaving behind him a great mass of
manuscript comment upon the history of Europe at every epoch,
including a number of memoirs on the French statesmen of his own
time. By turns petulant and gay, Circourt was a man very much
to Richard Milnes' taste. His conversation offered glistening
stores of information that must have dazzled Richard's magpie
mind. In that summer of 1833 when he and his wife asked Milnes
to come with them on a carriage tour of northern Italy, with the
illuminations at Pisa as their final objective, Circourt had been
travelling about Italy on an extended honeymoon for nearly two
years. The eldest son of a returned émigré belonging to an old
Lorraine family, Adolphe de Circourt had been brought up in the
strict *bien-pensant* royalist society of Besançon—not unlike that of
Nancy described by Stendhal in *Lucien Leuwen*. He later frequented
the same circles in Paris, salons such as that of Madame de la
Tour du Pin-Montauban in which he first met his young Russian
wife. He had resigned his post at the ministry of foreign affairs
shortly before the Revolution of July, and on the flight of Charles X
he had felt in duty bound to leave France. He retired, with other
refugees of the July Revolution, to Geneva, where he married
Mademoiselle Anastasie de Klustine. After a visit to France in

1831 the couple had left for Italy, and had been there ever since. As travelling companions they were far more amusing than Wordsworth and Robertson and the German student in Greece. Each of them approached Italy from a different point of view: '*Circourt*,' wrote an old friend,[1] '*savait l'Italie d'un bout à l'autre et ne la connaissait pas, sa femme la connaissait et ne la savait peut-être qu'imparfaitement.*' They both belonged to that cultivated, easy-mannered international society which was wandering freely about Europe in the years after the Congress of Vienna, and which Milnes preferred to all others. At Florence, where they took him from Pisa, the Circourts had many connections—the Comte through his devoted friend Lamartine, who had been attached to the French legation there from 1825 to 1828, the Comtesse through the letters of Bonstetten to members of the little Tuscan court.

Madame de Circourt, who later established one of the most famous and eclectic salons of mid-nineteenth-century Paris, was as remarkable a character as her husband. In the erudite society of Geneva, living still upon memories of Coppet, she had won the affectionate admiration of two old and celebrated men—Bonstetten and Sismondi, who now addressed to her letters which they would earlier have written to Madame de Souza and Madame de Staël. '*Allez dans le monde, mais ne toilettez pas trop*,' Bonstetten had written to her when she set off for Italy after her marriage. '*Cette vie est le vol d'Icare: ayez soin de vos ailes.*' In the Circourts Milnes must have recognised a perfect combination of elegance and fashion with unworldliness, of scholarship with gaiety, of outward frivolity with deep inward piety. In Venice, two months before, he had been overcome by an adolescent mood of self-contempt.

I will tell you candidly that I think your judgement of yourself much too hard [MacCarthy had written in March 1833, in reply to some subjective epistle of Richard's], I do not by any means believe in that frivolity of mind of which you accuse yourself . . . I should say that you would end in some great passion either of love or of generous ambition which will give you that steadiness of purpose, that concentration of all your powers into one burning-point which is all you want, and for which I think you have all the seeds and elements in your mental constitution.

His friendship with the Circourts, which lasted until their deaths,[2]

---

[1] Colonel Huber-Saladin, who edited the memorial volume *Le Comte de Circourt, Son Temps, Ses Ecrits: Madame de Circourt, Son Salon, Ses Correspondances* printed for distribution amongst the Circourts' friends in 1881 (Paris, Imprimerie de A. Quantin, 7, Rue Saint-Benoit, 1881). A copy of this book was sent to Lord Houghton.

[2] Madame de Circourt died, lamented by Sainte-Beuve and all her circle, in 1863. Her last note to Milnes is dated 1862 and speaks of '*ma vieille et fidèle amitié.*'

may have been good for Milnes in his current mood of self-doubt and depression, but the immense scholarship of the Count was not a quality which he could emulate. In 1833 Milnes was chiefly in need of literary encouragement. This he found at Florence, and in a positive, almost an exaggerated, form.

VI

Just as Mrs. Milnes and Harriette were leaving Milan (where they had broken their journey to Berne) they received the agitating news that Richard had fallen ill of malaria at Florence. He had got overheated watching the Pisa *luminari* and had driven out in an open carriage immediately after it. 'I longed to turn the horses' heads that way,' wrote his mother in her journal, 'but I was expecting to meet Mr. M. at Berne from England.' It was a relief to her to learn that Richard was in the hands of an English doctor, and that instead of lying exposed to the haphazard comforts of a Florentine hotel he was being cared for in an English villa at Fiesole.

Mr. Landor [she read in her son's first letter] was kind enough to ask me to come and stay at his beautiful villa as long as I liked, and here I have been a week. . . . I have my books, and Mr. Landor's delightful conversation, and my whole day to myself, and a carriage at my orders whenever I want to drive out.

He had 'tumbled upon his legs' again.

Richard Monckton Milnes owed his introduction to the Landor family to his tutor, Julius Hare. Walter Savage Landor, a tall, white-haired, stately man in his late fifties, with an agreeable presence and old-fashioned manners camouflaging a violent temper, had been in Italy since 1815 and at Fiesole since 1829. These years at the Villa Gherardesca, where he lived with his plump wife, Julia, his four children, his dog and his cats, formed a brief and peaceful interlude in Landor's fiery career.

He was living [wrote Lord Houghton in a reminiscence of his own stay at the villa in 1833 [1]] in a more than ordinary tranquillity, and having vented his rage against all kings and constituted authorities in his writings, he submitted with common decorum to the ordinances of government and society. But the demon of discord was too strong within him, and ere a few years had lapsed he was once more in England.

The Villa Gherardesca, three miles out of Florence in the gentle

---

[1] Review of Forster's biography of Landor (1869), republished in *Monographs* (1873).

Tuscan hills, was set back behind an iron entrance gate, 'nestling,' wrote Dickens in 1845, 'amid olive trees and vines.' The main front faced north. Above the door was a row of five tall windows, and over the centre windows another storey was set upon the house-top like a tower. The roadway up to the house was steep and in summer dusty and hot; but the two gardens of the villa—in one of which a fountain was always playing—were cool and scented and filled with cypresses and mimosas, lemon and orange trees, roses, lilacs, myrtles and laurustinus. Many of these trees and flowers had been planted at Landor's direction. From his bedroom window Richard Milnes would look down on Landor bending over his flowers 'with a sort of worship,' and would notice that he seldom touched them. Within the front door was a high-vaulted hall, with lofty rooms opening to left and right, and another room through each of these again. Upstairs were four main bedrooms, in one of which Milnes lay listless with his fever, while the night-ingales sang in the nearby woods. The whole room was scented with the perfume of tuberoses and mignonette, which came drifting up from the flower-beds thirty feet below the open window. The rooms of the Villa Gherardesca were bare of furniture—which Landor scornfully termed 'carpentry'—and were without mirrors, objects he equally disliked; but the white-plastered walls were encrusted with Italian primitives in heavy gilded frames. Many of these pictures were fakes, or at any rate were not painted by the artists to whom Landor self-confidently attributed them. But, as Milnes pointed out in his memoir, Landor was one of the first Englishmen to collect Italian primitive art at a time when Guido and Carlo Dolci were still generally admired. Milnes believed that, among 'some pretenders,' Landor did possess genuine examples of the work of Ghirlandajo and Masaccio, Benozzo Gozzoli and Fra Angelico. While staying at the Villa, he wrote a poem upon this collection of pictures, addressing it to little Walter Landor, a solemn boy of nine and whimsically attributing the child's calm nature to the influence of these pictures on his mind. One stanza will suffice:

> Is it not that within thee, as a shrine,
>   The power of incommunicable Art
> Is working out its ministry divine,
>   Silently moulding thy all-virgin heart
> To its own solemn ends? Thus dost thou wear
> That priestly aspect, that religious air.

Little Walter's father was enthusiastic about these verses. 'They show,' he said, 'you have been in Greece after being in Germany.'

Seated on the terrace and gazing out towards Vallombrosa, Milnes would spend evenings polishing and correcting the manuscript of his Greek tour, while the sun sank behind the vine-covered hills. The example, and still more the encouragement, of so eminent a poet as Landor confirmed his wish to publish his own poems, whether his father liked it or no. 'Landor,' he wrote to Mr. Milnes (then negotiating with lawyers and his brother's creditors over the Yorkshire estates), 'approves some part that I have shown him and he approves few things.' But when Landor did approve, he did it wholeheartedly. He told Milnes to read Trelawny's *Adventures of a Younger Son* because there had been nothing like it since the Iliad. A few years later he wrote in reply to a letter of Milnes' about Robert Landor's tragedies[1]: 'You are right about my brother's tragedies . . . I swear to you no man but Shakespeare has written three such tragedies. His versification is the best for the drama that ever was constructed.' Landor treated Milnes' work in the same headlong way. 'A great deal of rattling on the part of Landor,' we read in Henry Crabb Robinson's diary for 20 May 1838, 'who maintained . . . that Milnes is the greatest poet now living in England.'

Milnes himself found much to like and even to emulate in his host. He noted that 'the diligent exercise of composition had been useful to his temperament,' and admired Landor's powers of conversation, which 'equalled, if not surpassed, all that has been related of the table-talk of men eminent for social speech' and which alternated with 'a laughter so pantomimic, yet so genial, rising out of a momentary silence into peals so cumulative and sonorous, that all contradiction and possible affront were merged for ever.' 'Landor's words fall like stalactites,' he wrote in a notebook some five years after the visit to Fiesole; and, again, 'Landor's mind is a web of the finest silk and horsehair.' 'The domesticity' of the Villa Gherardesca in this halcyon period of Landor's life 'though not cheerful, was not angry.'

I have no ailments [Landor told Milnes], but why should I? I have eaten well-prepared food; I have drunk light subacid wines and three glasses instead of ten; I have liked modest better than immodest women, and I have never tried to make a shilling in the world.

But the influence of Landor on Milnes' impressionable mind was by no means the most important effect of this sojourn at Fiesole.

[1] Robert Eyres Landor (1781–1869), youngest brother of W. S. Landor, was the author of *Count Arezzi* (1823), which was mistaken for a work of Byron's, and of other forgotten tragedies.

It was during these summer weeks at the Villa Gherardesca that Richard Monckton Milnes first met and made friends with Charles Brown, 'a retired Russia merchant, with whose name I was already familiar as the generous protector and devoted friend of the Poet Keats.' Milnes' passionate interest in Keats, dating from his first days at Cambridge, was as strong as ever. In Rome he had cross-examined Severn for memories and anecdotes about his friend; and now at Fiesole he found Landor to be one of Keats' fiercest champions.[1] Charles Armitage Brown told Milnes that he had collected as many of the scattered papers of the poet as he could lay his hands upon, and intended to publish these on his return to England. The rest of the story is well known: how Brown prepared, but did not publish, a biographical memoir of his friend,[2] and how, on leaving for New Zealand in 1841, he gave this memoir and all his other papers relating to the poet into the keeping of Monckton Milnes, with the injunction that he should write and publish the first English biography of Keats. Brown had devoted much anxious thought to this choice of a biographer. 'Mr. Milnes is a poet himself,' he wrote to Severn in March 1841,[3] 'an admirer of Keats and, in my mind, better able to sit in judgement on a selection for publication than any other man I know.'

A chill caught driving in an open carriage at Pisa thus led directly to the publication of that concise and sensitively written study, the *Life, Letters, and Literary Remains of John Keats*, 'edited' by Richard Monckton Milnes and published in two small volumes by Edward Moxon of Dover Street in 1848.

VII

When he was well enough to travel, Richard Milnes left Tuscany and made his way to Switzerland. At Berne he found his mother and his sister peacefully installed in a very large chalet, to which they had moved from the hotel recommended to them by Anastasie de Circourt. Mr. Milnes, whom they had been expecting by every diligence for the last few weeks, arrived at the same moment as his son, one of them walking in at the front door and the other at

---

[1] There is no reason whatever to accept Hall Caine's tale that Landor deterred Milnes from writing a life of Shelley and told him to write the life of 'a' young fellow named Keats (who) died at Rome a while ago.' (See *Keats and the Victorians*, by G. H. Ford (Yale University Press, 1944), p. 69, where this foolish story seems to be accepted.)

[2] Brown's *Life of Keats* was published by the Oxford University Press in 1937 (edited with an Introduction and Notes by D. H. Bodurtha and W. B. Pope). The MS. was then in the possession of the Marquess of Crewe, but is now in the Houghton Library at Harvard.

[3] Brown's *Life of Keats*, p. 22.

the back. 'Well!' cried Richard; 'this is indeed quite fit for a
romance!' He had not seen his father for a year, and the reunited
family now settled down for some weeks of one another's company.
A cousin from Yorkshire and some Cambridge friends of Richard's
passed through Berne, spending a few days and nights at the chalet.
Switzerland was full of English travellers. Not long before her
son's arrival Mrs. Milnes had been surprised by a call from 'a
young man . . . whom I had never seen' who announced himself
as Richard's friend Stafford O'Brien, and spent the evening at the
chalet. Separations had not diminished O'Brien's feeling for
Milnes:

My dearest Richard [he wrote from the Falcon Inn at Berne,
on 2 August 1833], I have had the greatest pleasure in making the
acquaintance of your mother and sister—and I scarcely know how
to tell you how happy every tone and look made me that at all
sounded or looked like you.

O'Brien was on his way to Rome, Richard on his way back to
London. By one of his sudden, incalculable decisions Mr. Milnes
had arranged that Richard should return to England with him,
while Mrs. Milnes and Harriette took the carriage back to Milan
and then went off again to Venice, where the two men would join
them later in the winter.

As Richard and his father were leaving Berne on the first stage
of their journey home they received 'the melancholy intelligence of
the sudden death of Richard's friend Arthur Hallam,' which had
occurred in Vienna on 15 September. (Arthur Hallam was twenty-
two.) Richard, who was deeply shocked at the news, embodied
his feelings in a short elegy, which he later published in *Poems of
Many Years* (1838). The opening stanza ran:

> I'm not where I was yesterday,
> Though my home be still the same,
> For I have lost the veriest friend
> Whom ever a friend could name;
> I'm not where I was yesterday,
> Though change there be little to see,
> For a part of myself has lapsed away
> From Time to Eternity.

He also wrote to Arthur's father, Henry Hallam, who replied
from Clifton on 6 November 1833:

Nothing is so gratifying to me as to hear his praises—& in truth
he was no common light in this world—Were he not mine by the
closest tie, I should still say, that he was the noblest and most
remarkable character I have ever known. . . . You have been

misinformed as to the place of his intended interment. It will not
be in London, but among his maternal family some miles from here.
I have as yet no tidings that his remains have been put on board
a ship at Trieste, & I do not expect to see the last rites performed
till some time next month.

One of Richard's objects in returning to London in the autumn
of 1833 had been to arrange for the printing and publication of his
Memorials of a Tour in Greece. He went to Edward Moxon of Dover
Street, an enterprising young man who had set up his own publishing house with Samuel Rogers' aid some three years before.
Moxon had printed Hallam's famous essay on Tennyson in the
short-lived *Englishman's Magazine* in 1831, and he had published
a small volume of Alfred Tennyson's poetry at the end of the year
1832. It was natural that under the circumstances Milnes should
wish to link Arthur Hallam's name with his own first-published
work. This he achieved by dedicating the *Memorials* to Henry
Hallam, as

an open testimony to the affectionate admiration with which I
regarded one, whom I loved with the truth of early friendship, and
you with a parent's passion . . . I hold his kind words and earnest
admonitions in the best part of my heart, I have his noble and
tender letters by my side, and I feel secure from any charge of
presumption in thus addressing you, under the shield of his sacred
memory.

Thus launched, *Memorials of a Tour in Greece* achieved a modest
success, not selling at what Milnes called a 'vulgar rate' and being
purchased chiefly by the author's personal friends. Writing from
Trinity about the *Memorials*, Milnes' tutor, Connop Thirlwall,
accused him of being too sentimental about Greece, of being
occasionally inaccurate, artificial and over-imaginative.

I have read it with a great deal of pleasure [he wrote], and even
of instruction—for it contains much that is interesting to one who,
like myself, is condemned to frame an image of Greece out of the
fragments in which its form is reflected by various senses and minds.
But I am conscious that no small share of my enjoyment has been
owing to my knowledge of the author, and that without this introduction many things might have appeared to me in a different
light.

Unlike the big bundles of letters from Milnes' other Cambridge
friends which have survived, Hallam's correspondence with him
(the 'noble and tender letters' of the preface to *Memorials*) now
consists of nine letters only. It is possible, though not altogether
likely, that there once were more. Hallam was not really intimate

with Milnes for any length of time at Trinity, and did not relish Richard's rather exaggerated reverence for him.

Your notion of what I have been, & what I ought to be, is so hopelessly different from my own, and your idea of Religion is so unlike anything I am accustomed to call by that name, that we have hardly an inch of common ground to start from,' [Hallam wrote to Milnes in May 1832, in a long letter in which he accused him of trying to 'compensate for the absence of love for God' by a love of Truth and Beauty.]

Back in 1829 he had, for a period, made Milnes the confidant of all his hopes and fears—hopes of his own 'poetical faculty' ('it hums now in my heart: God grant me, if I am to have a Poet's destiny, at least a Poet's power!' he wrote in August 1829), and fears of going mad, and of turning atheist.

In my fits of gloom I so often look death, & insanity in the face, that the impulse to leave some trace of my existence on this bulk of atoms gathers strength with the warning that I must be brief. . . . I feel day by day that it is only in the pure atmosphere of Feeling (the word is not that which I need, but I have no better at the moment) I shall find ultimate peace of mind. What are thoughts and opinions? Cher ami, devices to grow cold. . . . Let us have one aim, while this incurable somnambulism we call Life is upon us [wrote this precocious boy of eighteen], To become the most *purely*, the most *thoroughly*, the most *excitingly*, the most *permanently* benevolent that endeavour can make us. . . .

This period of exchanged confidences did not endure. By the spring of 1832 Hallam's opinion of Milnes had turned full cycle, and he thought him as full of errors and 'nonsense' as when they had first met at Trinity in 1828. He was particularly sharp upon Milnes' religious vagaries. 'If the gospel is right,' he wrote to him in May of the year before his own death, 'you are momentously wrong.'

Milnes was not able to attend Hallam's funeral at Clevedon in Somersetshire in the first week of January 1834, for he was awaited by his family at Venice. During this English interlude his aunts and his grandmother had been agreeably impressed by his character. 'I never saw him better,' one of the aunts wrote to Mrs. Milnes, 'and my mother is so delighted to receive him unchanged in heart and temper, not tainted by the corruption of the world.'

VIII

Left alone together in Switzerland, Mrs. Milnes and Harriette had made a private expedition down Lac Leman to Geneva, where they had been thrilled to be shown the Contessa Guiccioli, 'very

décolletée', at the *table d'hôte* of their hotel.   They had then hurried
back to Milan and across to Venice, which drew them like a magnet.
This time they took a far larger apartment in a 'fine palazzo,'
with a hall one hundred and ten feet long, a music room, a drawing-
room, a dining-room all down one side of it, and a range of bedrooms opening off the other.   The palace had belonged to an English
lady who had 'had her gardener educated' and had left him her
fortune.   It was the gardener who now leased the palace to
Mrs. Milnes.

Richard and his father travelled together over the Simplon in
December, with snow up to the carriage windows.   At Milan they
had an argument as to whether Richard should come straight on
with Mr. Milnes to Venice or go down to Rome, where O'Brien
was waiting for him.   The fact that he had with him O'Brien's
regimental smallclothes decided the issue in favour of Rome: 'so
mysterious are the springs of human nature', was Mr. Milnes'
comment.   Mr. Milnes went on to Venice alone.   Here he found
himself swept into the vortex of Venetian life, for his wife and
daughter were determined to show him off to all their friends:
'When we got him into the Gondola he thought there would be
no end to it.   When we entered the various rooms they all called
"E veramente Ricardo!   E sempre Ricardo!"'   Although he
pretended to find that the land side of the palazzo his wife had
taken was 'not dignified'—'you could not get up it in a carriage,
you could not have got up it in a wheelbarrow'—and that the butter
tasted of onions and tallow, Mr. Milnes adored Venice.   He wrote
to his cousin Tom Bland at Kippax of the masked crowds, the
bands of music, the gondolas gliding off into the night from the
steps of the Opera, of all 'these un-English modes, these contrasts
to life at Kippax.'   As he walked or floated in a gondola past the
'glorious churches' and palaces, he could not resist making comparisons between these splendid scenes and 'Kippax street and Fryston village.'   There seemed no reason why their Italian exile
should ever end.

Mrs. Milnes had been eagerly awaiting her husband's arrival so
that she could carry out a project on which she and Harriette had
set their hearts.   This was to give a ball.   Although the ball had
to take place in Richard's absence, they all judged it a startling
success.   Twelve dozen bottles of champagne were consumed, an
elaborate figure-dance designed by Mrs. Milnes was performed,
and the dancing lasted until half-past nine the next morning.
When Richard arrived in Venice, in February or March 1834,
there were more entertainments at the Milnes' palazzo and they
introduced the wondering Venetians to the English pastime of

tableaux vivants: 'their curiosity was great to know what we were going to do, seeing a large Saloon in darkness.' Harriette, Richard, an English Miss Ingram and two or three Italians enacted the 'Wounded Greek,' the 'Gamesters,' 'Abraham and Hagar,' and 'Saint Mark.' 'It all went off wonderfully well to the great delight of our friends.'

Milnes had remained in Rome for the carnival of February 1834, which, owing to a Papal indulgence, was a singularly brilliant one, and a great contrast to that of the previous year.

. . . People pelted one another with sugar and lime most assiduously for five whole days [he wrote to one of his aunts]. . . . And there was plenty of masking foolery; for instance, I paid visits and walked about in white muslin and a blue satin toque.

The Irish poet and mathematician George Darley, who was in Rome at the same time, has left a description of the crowds at the Carnival of 1834:

Nothing was strange but a rational creature. Here stood a bear whispering soft nonsense into a lady's bonnet; there, a German with whiskers brought over his back like pigtails, dishevelled mane, and ravine of teeth, unconsciously looking the ogre. This carriage was driven by a fat cook-maid—that loaded with three powdered baboons by way of footmen—t'other filled with half-a-dozen Grand Turks or Indian squaws. Now the Senator (Prince Orsini) drove up in his gilt coach . . . now six whole troopers rode down at a high trot, fire in their eyes, and flaming swords in their hands, to announce, as they gallantly cleared the streets, that the ponies might canter to the Capitol. [1]

Darley, a tall, shy, stammering and melancholic man with a streak of genius, seems to have met Milnes for the first time during this winter of 1834 at Rome. As ardent an Elizabethan as Beddoes, Darley is now remembered only as the author of *Nepenthe* and *Sylvia* and for his edition of Beaumont and Fletcher. At the time Milnes first made friends with him he was writing regularly on Italian art for the *Athenaeum*. He was also a shrewd literary critic but particularly disliked William Wordsworth's poetry and the 'leek and go-cart school' to which Milnes belonged.

Why invert the rules of creation and pronounce only the mean magnificent, while you consider the lofty beneath your notice? [he

---

[1] From *The Life and Letters of George Darley, Poet and Critic*, by Claude Colleer Abbott (Oxford University Press, 1928), p. 108. Mr. Abbott prints the majority of Darley's letters to Monckton Milnes (shown to him by Lord Crewe) in this comprehensive study.

asked Milnes in a letter of March 1836]. . . . There is no reason
that humble nature as well as exalted should not have its poet.
But as a *system* it can never succeed. It will only draw the spine
out of poetry and leave it draggling. Do take a course of intellectual
tonics against the Wordsworth rabies.

He told Milnes that on the subject of poetry they must be 'ever in
amicable opposition, like the lion and the unicorn.' Darley was
at this time forty years old, but he was prematurely aged in appearance, and suffered from bouts of acrid despair such as that in
which he poured his soul out to Milnes in a letter from Paris
postmarked October 1834.

You know my theory of the hereafter [he wrote in this letter],
that it will be a mere sublimation of this life, and that each of us
will be in it but the eternal child of his own individual nature.
What can *I* then gain by a future Life but an everlasting occasion
to make myself miserable? What should I lose by annihilation
but perpetual self-crucifixion? . . . Lord! Lord! that the heart
can be in such a foul fester, so becrawled & beslimed with the
deadliest worm & yet not eaten out at once! Ugh! that it should
hang for years in one's bosom still putting forth clusters of polypes
& flowering at every point like a lump of coral by the discharge
of its own corruptions. How am I rambling?—rambling, rambling,
yet never leaving the one centre, myself.

Darley's biographer has suggested that the 'despondent' tone of
Darley's letter to Monckton Milnes arises from the 'abundant
riches of his friend—in youth, talents and prospects' in contrast
to Darley's own life. This may be true: but it is also certain that
Darley responded to the peculiar, softening spell which Milnes
exerted over harsh or complicated characters. Richard Monckton
Milnes had a very pronounced gift for getting on best with people
whom the world in general found too violent, too rebellious, too
stern, or too original for easy companionship. It was this gift
which brought him the friendship and confidence of George Darley,
the affection of Landor, the tenderness with which he was treated
by Alfred Tennyson. It later brought him the 'unmixed regard
and friendship' of Thomas Carlyle. Milnes kept throughout his
life an affinity to genius and a reverence for it which James Anthony
Froude declared to be 'truer and deeper' than that of most of his
contemporaries. It was this sensibility, not vulgar curiosity or
a 'feline' anxiety to corrupt, that led him twenty years later to take
such pains with the drunken and boyish Swinburne. It was this
affinity, and the delicate sense of duty deriving from it, that led
him to prepare his *Life* of Keats.

IX

For the summer of 1834 the Milnes family took a house on the Brenta. In the autumn Richard travelled to Munich and the Salzkammergut. He and his parents had now been living out of England for nearly eight years, and much though they enjoyed Italy they had a natural longing to go home. Richard was already twenty-five. Harriette too was growing up. It was time to return to Yorkshire and to London, and an improvement in Mr. Milnes' financial position made this now feasible. 'I need not say with what pleasure my mother and Harriette look forward to the possibility of passing some months of this year in England,' Richard wrote to his aunt in February 1835, 'how earnestly they look forward to embracing you all again.' They were then living in a dull and gloomy house in Florence, going sometimes to the Tuscan court, but on the whole leading retired lives. 'You may live and die as domestically and in as thick an atmosphere of in-difference as in London,' Richard wrote of Florence during this stay. The late spring of 1835 was passed on the Brenta, but by the autumn definite plans for the family's return to England had been laid. They left Italy by way of the Tyrolese Alps, and wènt on to Lake Constance (where Mr. Milnes suddenly announced that he would like to build a house) and to Zurich. Here Richard and his father seem to have left Mrs. Milnes and Harriette, perhaps going on ahead to get everything ready for them. The two ladies drifted about Switzerland for a few weeks, and then set out for Paris. Anxious to get their letters at the Poste Restante as soon as possible, they decided to drive fast across France.

It was fine clear weather when we left Nancy [wrote Mrs. Milnes in one of the last vivid and unpunctuated passages of her foreign travel journal] and rather frosty and when we had proceeded a few postes we decided if at dusk we did not feel ourselves fatigued to go on travelling all night as by that means we calculated we should reach Paris the second day in time to get our letters out of the Post office and we felt impatient for news from England. . . . It was about eight when we arrived (at Bar-le-Duc) and (partook) of a *petit souper très bien servi* and bought some *confiture de groseilles* for which the town is famous. . . . We then ordered the horses, lit our little lamp which we hung between the windows and made our-selves as comfortable as we could for the night. . . . It was a beautiful clear moonlight night and there appeared no end to the length of the road before us. We looked out behind at our trunk now and then, and the light of the moon cheered us so we felt no fear. . . . We got to Chalons at seven in the morning and they gave us some *café au lait* in the carriage and excellent rolls. . . . We

stopped about 7 o'clock at Meaux where we had had accommoda-
tion. . . . We started early the next morning in order to arrive in
good time at Paris, but unfortunately just as we arrived at a village
before Bondi, we felt the carriage knock from side to side in a most
unusual manner, and having succeeded in stopping the Postboy
who was going full tilt, we found that the axle tree was broken in
two.

After a row with the village blacksmith over the price he charged
for mending the axle tree, they clattered into Paris that night.
The two ladies spent a few days at the Hôtel de Bruxelles in the
Rue Richelieu, and on 13 November stepped aboard the packet
at Boulogne.   After a quick but rough passage they landed in
Dover, went to the hotel, and found themselves 'stirring a coal fire
and listening to the people talking English around us for the first
time for eight years.'
    Italy was now a memory.   Before them lay London—and the
West Riding.

Chapter Four

I

Upon reaching London that November evening of 1835, Harriette and her mother found Richard waiting for them in the rooms he had taken at Hawkins' Hotel in Albemarle Street. They found, too, a letter announcing the not unexpected death of the Dowager Lady Galway, Mrs. Milnes' aged and dislikable stepmother, who was also a first cousin of her husband. By her death Robert Milnes inherited a pink brick house with a pond before it at Bawtry, on the borders of Nottinghamshire and the West Riding, and a sum of eleven thousand pounds. The death of his own mother soon after put him in possession of the Fryston house and lands near Ferrybridge, but gave him at the same time the moral responsibility for looking after his three maiden sisters, the Misses Louisa, Jane and Caroline Milnes, who were nearer his son's age than his own, and who became henceforth a permanent factor in the family life.

After two weeks at Hawkins' Hotel, Richard, his sister and his mother set off in a new carriage for the North. Welcomed with raptures at Serlby, the great Palladian house of the Moncktons in Nottinghamshire, they went on to Fryston, which had stood empty for ten years. Here they received a body of persons described by Mrs. Milnes as 'twenty-five of our most intimate friends,' gave an impromptu dinner and a tenants' ball and then returned to pass the rest of the winter at Bawtry. The Milnes parents were, on the whole, enchanted to be back where they belonged. Harriette settled easily down into the role of a country belle, though her acquirements were now vastly superior to those of other Yorkshire girls. She was taller than her brother, and unlike Richard she was beautiful. She wore her hair in braids and had large blue eyes described by one admirer as 'mooney.' From her father she had inherited a sharp wit and a satirical turn of speech. Three Yorkshire winters and two London seasons successfully blotted out from Harriette's mind any nostalgia for Italy—for the Milanese ramparts in the sunset, the Venetian lagoons, the pale, romantic youths who had found her so charming. In 1838 she married

her mother's fox-hunting nephew the sixth Lord Galway,[1] and
became châtelaine of Serlby. Her brother, who worshipped her,
was distressed by her marriage, and probably never cared much
for 'Galway.' Like his aunt (who was now also his mother-in-law)
Lord Galway had foreign blood,[2] but in his case it seems
to have given his character neither eccentricity nor charm. He
may be seen standing in the water-colour sketch of Fryston
library, which forms the frontispiece of this book. Lord Galway
was a conventional young man, a staunch Conservative, fond of
practical jokes, and always prepared to support his father-in-law's
views against those of Richard Milnes.

While Harriette was cheerfully surrendering to the West Riding
atmosphere, Richard stood out against it alone. His first letter to
MacCarthy that autumn was 'filled with regrets and longings
after Italy.'

The Milnes' life in Yorkshire after their return from the Continent in 1835 was on quite a different scale from their previous
penurious existence at Thorne Hall. Instead of doing experi-
mental farming from a small rented house, Mr. Milnes was now
owner of two houses and estates, one of them a possession of some
consequence. In spite of his gloomy forebodings, he had been
able to save Fryston Hall at the nadir of his family's finances a
few years back, but he now affected an anxiety to get rid of either
Fryston or Bawtry—'I care little,' he wrote, 'which.' As a matter
of fact he sold neither. Richard, who lacked the childhood memories
his father had of Fryston and had not Mr. Milnes' acute compre-
hension of the standards of life and hospitality which the world
still demanded of an English country gentleman, was not deeply
concerned whether Fryston went or not. When its sale seemed
inevitable in 1831, he had been more disturbed over the fate of
his grandfather's small library—fat, calf-bound volumes of speeches
and trials, tracts, English poets, letter-writers such as Horace
Walpole—than at the prospect of losing his patrimony. Fryston
gave him a kind of right to stand for Parliament for the borough of
Pontefract, but apart from this it was then of no importance to
him. Honest men, he wrote cheerfully to his father, would think
none the worse of them 'for having lost a large house with four

---

[1] 1805–1876, educated at Harrow and Christ Church; sat as Tory M.P. for
East Retford 1841–1876; Lord-in-Waiting March 1852 to January 1853. He
m. Henrietta Eliza Milnes on 25 April 1838 at St. George's, Hanover Square;
their son, the 7th Viscount, was born 18 November 1844.

[2] The grandmother of Mrs. Milnes and of her brother the 5th Lord Galway
was Elizabeth da Costa Villa Real, daughter of the Portuguese Jewess Kitty da
Costa. Their mother was a Miss Mathew, a connection of the West Indian
family of Byam of Antigua.

FRYSTON HALL, FERRYBRIDGE, FROM THE PARK

pillars before it.' Later, in Milnes' own hands, Fryston Hall became one of the most famous country-houses in Victorian England, but he never loved it. It was finally sold by his son, the late Lord Crewe, in the present century and has been pulled down. No study of Milnes' life would be complete without some detailed consideration of Fryston; for, whatever he may have thought about it as a young man, this big square house in Yorkshire, with its white portico and its four white pillars, its marshy parkland filled with drifting sheep, the prospects from its windows stained by factory smoke, became the main and permanent *décor* against which Richard Monckton Milnes lived and aged.

II

At Ferrybridge the Great North Road crosses the River Aire. Below the bridge, beside the road, upon the Castleford bank of the river, rise the blind brick walls and the sturdy chimneys of the biggest power-station in the North of England. Close to the power-station, forlorn and miniature in contrast with it, stands a grimy church. St. Andrew's, Ferry Fryston, has a Norman doorway and a little Gothic tower. It was founded in the twelfth century, but has been rigorously restored, partly in flint. The River Aire (still a highway for the laden, slow coal barges) [1] here spreads lazily outwards across the meadows of Ferry Fryston and Water Fryston, saturating the reedy grassland and making a marsh in the graveyard of the church. Hemmed in by willow-trees and bulrushes, with a few black yews sprouting amongst the tall tombstones (which are ogival, and look as thin and brittle as biscuits and lean crookedly this way or that), St. Andrew's is not easy to reach. A path of cinders strewn along a dyke takes you over the soggy ground, between fences of wire. Behind the church other wires show criss-cross and rectilinear against the sky: wires from the telegraph poles of the nearby railway, wires from the power-station roofs strung high across the churchyard, and making St. Andrew's seem a church in a cage. Inside, the church is simple and whitewashed. A brass tablet just above the pulpit commemorates Robert Pemberton Milnes.

The pathway over the marsh and into the graveyard branches right from the road to Fryston Hall. This road is now in the final stages of disruption. Worn and hummocked, it runs between

---

[1] In the nineteenth century the River Aire (which drains the Leeds–Bradford area) was literally an open sewer. Today the West Riding rivers have been reclaimed by the West Riding Rivers Board (founded in 1894), but in Milnes' time the Aire, which ran below the Fryston garden, stank.

flooded fields, the lines of leaning telegraph posts between it and the river, upon the farther bank of which the houses of Brotherton show half a mile away. Take a car with good springs and go down this road: you reach at length an unpretentious entrance gate, with a yellow lodge house sitting beside it. The lodge was ornamented in the eighteen-eighties, when some armorial heraldry and coroneted initials were added to it, but the thread of smoke from the mock-Tudor chimney-pot and the scarlet geraniums along the window-sill show that it is lived in now. Through the gate and on up the drive to the Hall, the country seems to open out. It becomes undulating, but stark. On either hand lies parkland gone to waste, grass rank with tares and dandelions and stained with pit-dust. Dotted everywhere about this barren landscape are the stumps and roots of great park trees, which have been felled—the old oaks and the beech trees which, with the thorn thickets, were rated the chief beauty of Fryston Park. The muddy road winds on, over hill over dale, towards the crest of a low rise upon which a line of buildings shows light against a background of dark evergreens. On getting nearer you find that this line of buildings is the front of the old stables of Fryston Hall. Four high stone gateposts are set in a row before the stables, each post capped in eighteenth-century exuberance by a great stone wheatsheaf with heavy harvest ears, the Milnes family crest. Behind the stables and the evergreens are a farm road and a few cottages, the hamlet of Water Fryston. Some hundred yards to the right of the stables, a raw patch of earth, raised like a stage above the level of the fields, marks the site of Fryston Hall. Only the cellars remain of the Milnes' house at Fryston, for the rest has been taken down and carted off to Airedale, where the stones are now incorporated in a Baptist church. The site of the house is fenced in with rusted barbed wire; its surface is covered with a litter of broken pots and bottles, fragments of tile, brick and shard, pieces of chalk and sandstone. But if you climb under the wire and stand on this rubbish heap, you can look out across the park and the river to the distant horizon, with its turrets of factory smoke. This was the view from the long windows of the library at Fryston and from the windows of the great bedroom above it which Carlyle occupied in the spring of 1841. It was of this view that Carlyle was thinking when he wrote to his host some months later:

It is almost strange to myself how memorable Fryston, with its porches, parks and all the environment of it far and wide, now dwells with me. . . . Good old Yorkshire—a kind of embellished Scotland. Rivers rushing seaward with their ancient voice . . . airy hilltops, with outlook over wide fruitful expanses; and ever in the distance some Leeds, some Wakefield sending up its great black smoke coulisse, its great black banner which announces, 'Behold, O Squire, I too am here!'

Fryston Hall was some twelve miles from Wakefield, where the Milnes family had originally made their fortune, but only five or six from the mining town of Castleford and from Pontefract, the electoral borough which lay upon the rim of their estate. Like so many of the towns and villages of the North of England, Pontefract played a notable part in English medieval history, and has since, save for a brief Cromwellian episode, subsided into a state of provincial peace. But North of England towns such as Barnard Castle or Pontefract still show signs of their ancient consequence. At Pontefract you may see the remains of the castle in which Richard the Second was killed, and just outside the town limits is St. Thomas's Hill, where the great Earl of Lancaster, the sworn enemy of Gaveston, was beheaded in 1322. In March 1822, five hundred years almost to a day after this execution, workmen trenching for liquorice beds on the Milnes' land in Spital Hardwick, close by St. Thomas's Hill, struck their spades against a stone object. A huge stone coffin was unearthed, containing a skeleton with its skull between its knees and a boulder where the head should be. Assuming this skeleton to be the miracle-working body of Thomas of Lancaster, which had been lost at the dissolution of Monckhill Monastery during the Reformation, Mrs. Slater Milnes had the bones encased in lead and then in wood, and the body put back into the stone coffin in which it had been found. This was then placed in the gardens at Fryston Hall 'with a triangular bit to lift out of the lid, so that religious persons may look in.' A macabre relic of the historic past of the West Riding, the coffin remained throughout Richard Monckton Milnes' lifetime in a shrubbery near the house, where the pine trees cast a shade upon it, and where in high summer the tang of rhododendron leaves was sweetened by the heavy scent of stocks in the great flower-borders that fringed the lawn.

During the reign of Queen Victoria, and owing to the hospitable activities of Monckton Milnes, Fryston Hall acquired a more than local fame. Here, in a part of Yorkshire suddenly made very accessible to Londoners by the coming of the railway through Knottingley and Castleford, Milnes would entertain his acquaintances and friends. The great majority of these were literary or political persons, and most of them were either already celebrated or likely to become so. English or foreign, married or solitary, young or old, most people who became Lord Houghton's friends sooner or later found themselves stepping down from the train at Knottingley Station, where the carriage from Fryston would meet them and take them back through the beechwoods and larches to the big white house on the hill overlooking the River Aire. Here, on the top of the steps leading to the front door, Milnes would be waiting, 'his brown hair flowing carelessly from his broad forehead, his blue eyes beaming with gladness at the arrival of his friends . . . both hands extended.'[1] The arrival would be followed by tea in the library, a long room walled by bookshelves and containing chairs of padded and buttoned scarlet leather. Sometimes there would be twenty guests staying at Fryston; sometimes, as Henry Adams found, only three; sometimes (Swinburne for instance) a single intimate. Those who ridiculed Lord Houghton declared he would do anything or see anybody rather than be left in Yorkshire alone; though contradicting themselves in their next sentence by suggesting that no one who was not already famous could gain admittance to Fryston. Other people, with a surer basis in fact, would whisper about the collections of erotic literature which, like the sets of sermons, tracts and criminal trials and the books on current politics and on magic, formed an integral part of the library Houghton assembled for himself at Fryston. He would jocularly refer to his house as 'Aphrodisiopolis.'

In spite of its owner's special interests, Fryston was never in any way sinister or mysterious. The distinguished Swinburne scholar Monsieur Georges Lafourcade gives a highly coloured account of Fryston in his work *La Jeunesse de Swinburne*.[2] This learned Frenchman interprets Lord Houghton's house as a kind of sadic temple, '*l'auberge des rencontres étranges*' and '*perdu dans le Yorkshire humide*.' Fryston was unique among northern English country-houses only because its master was an intellectual and a cosmopolitan. It was not in itself an especially remote or especially remarkable house: but it was lived in for fifty years by a very anomalous character, a Yorkshire landowner who hated the land and country pursuits, preferred London to the West Riding, and Paris and Italy to both of these.

---

[1] This quotation, and a part of the description, are taken from the anonymous article 'Celebrities at Home, No. XLIV. Lord Houghton at Fryston Hall,' which appeared in *The World* for 20 June 1877. The article was written by Isabel Burton, wife of the explorer, and much re-written in proof by Edmund Yates. *The World* had already published an article on Houghton in their series *Portraits in Oil* (No. XLVI, by Escott) on 9 June 1875; and in August 1883, at the very end of Lord Houghton's life, published an attack on him in one of its *Letters to Eminent Persons*.

[2] *La Jeunesse de Swinburne* (1837–1867), by Georges Lafourcade: Publications de la Faculté des Lettres de L'Université de Strasbourg (published here by the Oxford University Press, 1928, two volumes).

III

Though he did not become master of Fryston until his father's death in 1858 (when he himself was middle-aged), Richard Milnes used the house as if it were his own while his parents still lived. Within ten years of the Milnes' return to England railways had become a part of every-day existence, but even before this, Fryston had been more accessible than numerous more isolated Yorkshire houses. Far from being *perdu dans le Yorkshire humide*, Fryston had at its gates one of the major coaching-stations of the North. The inns at Ferrybridge were many and famous, and at the height of the stage-coach boom at the end of the eighteenth century as many as thirty public vehicles and a great procession of private carriages passed over the bridge every day. Indeed, it was probably because of this proximity to the Great North Road that Richard's grandfather, who liked London life, had bought it from Walpole's friend Charles Crowle. At the time of this purchase, effected just before the French Revolution, Fryston was a rambling and irregular block of a house standing high above the river bank. Slater Milnes imposed a superficial unity upon the conglomerate architectural features of the old house by erecting a new front, with four grand Ionic pillars carrying an Ionic pediment, refacing the whole building with slabs of white stone, and adding a pillared porch over the steps to the front door. The Ionic columns on the front of the house rose to the height of the two main stories, and had long windows in between them; a glass door between the centre pair of pillars gave egress from the first-floor drawing-room to a little balcony or terrace, from which two flights of steps curved down to a gravel drive. All along the top of the house a balustrade was constructed. The effect of these additions was to increase the dignified appearance of the house, to make it look noble, expensive and clean. Here and there above the new pediment and the balustrade peeped out the chimney-stacks and the angular, irrelevant roofs of the old hall.

Inside, the house showed more definite signs of age and of an irregularity which had defied reconstruction. Above the big dining-room was a lofty, cavernous bedroom, forty-five feet long, and hung with dim brownish portraits of Stuart royalties. The library had a floor of stone flags, though elsewhere lay fine flowered English carpets, that in the drawing-room being black and pink and white. The furniture was like that of all English houses of the day—Chippendale tables and bookcases with glass fronts and with mahogany urns above them, chairs upholstered in padded brown or scarlet leather, curtains of brocade and of chintz, screens with miniatures pinned to them, heavy table-cloths edged with fringe. As the decades passed, more strictly Victorian articles were introduced—octagonal stools from India inlaid in mother-of-pearl, ottomans with flounces, firescreens worked in wool, library-steps covered with stuffed plush and brass nails. Milnes himself was not remarkable for visual sense, and though he finally married a woman of highly cultivated taste and sensibility, it is unlikely that she was able to do much to transform the accumulations of objects at Fryston, nor was she perhaps allowed much latitude of choice.

Mrs. Milnes would wish [runs a note written (and doubtless also inspired) by her husband] that in framing the picture which she left with Mr. Hogarth, the words *The Angel of Death* in gothic letters should be inserted or attached to the frame.

The pictures at Fryston were mostly inherited family portraits, many of them of great beauty: two tall, full-length Romneys of Milnes men, a Hoppner, two Reynoldses, a little Turner landscape, a Stubbs of Slater Milnes on horseback, and a fine, prosperous-looking Opie of Richard's mother, standing in a pale satin dress beside a clump of giant sunflowers. The most noticeable feature of the inside of the house, however, was the quantity of books. Bookcases clung to every wall, lined the passages and some of the bedrooms, were found in cupboards and on landings. The main bookroom was panelled with cedar-wood, and the shelves in it encroached to the very edges of the mantelpiece, over which hung a conversation picture of Samuel Rogers talking to Mrs. Norton. The house was run with an informality unusual even in an English country house, but the outward paraphernalia of living at Fryston was the same as in other houses of the day—large fires, comfortable chairs, a profusion of good food and drink combined with bedroom draughts, stone passages, baize doors and hip-baths. 'Almost all country-houses are pleasant,' wrote an old Cambridge friend of Richard Milnes in 1862, 'but few are as pleasant as Fryston.'

IV

However lukewarm Richard's feelings might be about day-to-day country life, there were many aspects of it which thrust themselves upon his notice. His father's traditions; his own future responsibilities; a swarm of healthy cousins from the northern dales and the country round Wakefield—all these acted as reminders that he could not afford merely to languish after Italy. When in the 1837 election he became one of the members for Pontefract his ties with the neighbourhood became both more intimate and less evitable.

In the decade of the eighteen-forties, when both of his parents were beginning to look and to feel rather old, the neighbours turned to Richard to sustain the reputation for originality and liberal hospitality which his father and his uncle Rodes had kept up during the period of the Napoleonic wars. Mr. Milnes, his hair now turning white, was still a thin, spry, handsome man, though less talkative and more crotchety than in his youth; Mrs. Milnes, who in the days Opie had painted her was a bright-eyed, ample lady with brown hair and a mischievous smile, looked gaunt and ill. Both were as popular with their friends and neighbours as they had ever been, but the point of view towards life adopted by their son was less understood and less welcome. Rodes and Robert Milnes had been immensely dashing in their youth. Yorkshire people who remembered them then drew unkind comparisons between their straightforward, acceptable charm and the more complicated, more intellectual character of Richard Monckton Milnes, a young man who said he could not shoot because of an astigmatism, and found some equally convincing reason to avoid a hard day out with the Badsworth.

I am inclined to think the next generation, however cultivated, has not a spark of the originality that formed the charm of the two brothers, the Father and Uncle [ran a typical neighbourly comment on the Milneses]. Poor Rodes told me he thought his Nephew the first young man in England!!! I am sorry I have not met Robert of late. I hear he is quite as cheerful, as original, and as charming as of old. I met the son at Doncaster last meeting— when he said to me, with his easy manner, 'Is Mrs. Damer with you?' I replied that she was not—when he added, 'Oh, I am sorry she is not for we then could have asked you to Fryston.' I thought of Robert and of Rodes and of the olden time.[1]

It was this easy manner that raised a hedge of prejudice against him during Richard's first few years back in England. And it was resented in London as well as in the West Riding. It was disliked at Holland House and Lansdowne House almost as much as at Ledstone or Kippax, at Womersley or at Byram.

V

Having survived their first Yorkshire winter for eight years, Mrs. Milnes and Harriette drove down to London in the early spring of 1836 to face the more exacting gaieties of a London season. Richard and his father had preceded them, hiring (with O'Brien's help) Lady Kilmaine's corner house at the junction of

---

[1] Undated, unsigned page from a letter (? from a Colonel Damer) found loose amongst the Houghton Papers.

South Street and Park Lane. The economies he had made by moving his family to the Continent (where they had lived for a round sum of a little more than a thousand pounds a year) and the legacy from Lady Galway gave Mr. Milnes some money in hand, part of which he spent on the task of launching his son and daughter upon the London world. The house in South Street cost eight hundred pounds for one season, and the Milneses gave frequent dinner and breakfast parties. 'We had as much gaiety as we desired,' Mrs. Milnes noted reflectively in her diary; 'Society here,' she added, 'is attended with so much fatigue I was glad when the season came to a close.' Enervated by their years in Milan, Venice and Rome, the family were not entirely prepared for the brisk pace which London Society liked to keep. It was the last full season of the reign of William the Fourth. Politically it was the period of Reform, and socially it was one of transition. In the eighteen-thirties royal domesticity was represented by the clutch of Fitzclarence bastards, and the tone of London Society, which could tolerate such a scandal as the Melbourne-Norton trial, was not high. The 'thirties were a frivolous and exuberant period, sentimental and full of artifice. In literature its products included *Contarini Fleming* and *Venetia*, Bulwer's historical novel of *Rienzi*, Lady Blessington's silk-bound Keepsakes; in painting Landseer was already much admired; for architecture we need think only of Barry's elaborate designs for the new Palace of Westminster. There is something about the reign of William the Fourth which inexorable chronological fact alone prevents one from calling *fin-de-siècle*.

Since the windows of Lady Kilmaine's house in South Street looked out into Hyde Park, the Milnes family could daily watch, when they did not wish to take part in, the cavalcade of broughams and carriages and curricles, elegant and highly varnished vehicles with spinning yellow wheels and modish grooms, which passed up and down beneath the chestnut trees. Contemporary writers could make even the familiar Park appear unreal and romantic: Disraeli wrote of the dusty chestnuts as being 'in silver bloom'— 'the pink may has flushed the thorns' runs his description of the Park in springtime, 'and banks of sloping turf are radiant with plots of gorgeous flowers . . . the water glitters in the sun and the air is fragrant with that smell which only can be found in metropolitan mignonette!' On the occasion of a royal review of troops in the Park this spring (one of the king's last public appearances) the Milneses gave a breakfast-party for forty people. This form of morning entertainment was then fashionable. It startled American visitors, who saw in it yet one more proof that the English upper class was relentless in its pursuit of pleasure. The moralising novelist Lady Chatterton notes in her diary for these years that breakfast parties made each day of the London season seem like two. A cousin of the Milnes family, Lady Chatterton used to meet Richard and his mother frequently, at breakfast with Rogers or elsewhere. She was a great admirer of young Milnes' 'kind-hearted trustfulness and pleasant counteractions of the least touches of ill-nature.' Mrs. Milnes really preferred seeing people in her own house: 'what I enjoyed most were our dinner-parties,' she recorded in her journal, 'which were principally composed of my son's friends, some of them very agreeable and literary, amongst others Wordsworth the poet and Samuel Rogers Esq.'

This revelation of London life excited Richard. Hitherto the victim of circumstances obliged by his father's poverty to wander about the Continent, he was at last back in his own country and among his own equals and contemporaries. But he had now to face up to making a career. His father's wishes and his own darting interest in public affairs, as well as a harmless youthful vanity, made him want to strike out at once into political life. So far as a seat in the House went, little could be done until the ageing king should die. Since political reputation was still partly made in certain drawing-rooms and clubrooms of London, the most Richard could hope for during 1836 was to leave his mark in these circles and to foster a vague reputation for 'promise.' Gregarious, warm-hearted and fond of conversation and gossip, Milnes was not, in our sense, a snob; but he found it interesting as well as natural and useful to be on easy terms with persons of importance. In 1836 English society was a heavily ramified fortress. Young men without title or position found it hard to gain admittance to the inmost wards. Most people in London had forgotten Richard's father and his early parliamentary success. The Monckton relations, a tribe resolutely headed by old Lady Cork, were of more practical value to an ambitious young man than the faded celebrity of his father and grandfather in the already distant era of the French wars. Cambridge friendships—with Kerry, Lord Lansdowne's eldest son, for instance—gained Milnes the entrée to a few of the great houses, but in some of these his ebullience and self-confidence aroused a stern and frigid opposition. Unflattering nicknames were attached to Richard Milnes—'London Assurance' they called him, 'the Cool of the Evening,' and (later, after Victoria's accession), 'In-I-go Jones.' In these first days in London he was chiefly accepted as a young poet. He cultivated literary friendships, giving to Tom Moore, Southey and Wordsworth the eager admiration which had won Landor's heart in Florence three years before. Yet, though able at length to pay personal homage to the literary idols of his earliest youth, he refused to take even the great poets too seriously: 'Wordsworth looks to me like a benevolent wolf' he noted in his commonplace book.

In the memoirs of A. F. Rio,[1] the young Breton with whom Richard had made passionate friends at Rome, we learn that after Milnes' election to the House of Commons in 1837 he would affect to take his own literary and poetical reputation very lightly. This affectation of frivolity gave offence, in its turn, but in a new quarter, and to an old man with the sharpest tongue in London. Samuel Rogers, says Rio, was the last man in the world to pardon Milnes 'cette espèce de dédain.' Rogers took it quite personally: 'Il y voyait une insulte.' On the more public stage of London Richard Milnes was already committing just those disarming errors of taste, judgement and behaviour which had so disturbed his more thoughtful friends at Cambridge and in Rome.

VI

In after years Monckton Milnes was accused of trying to rival and even to eclipse Samuel Rogers as a literary host. There was no temperament in London less like his own. Together with Lady Cork, who had chattered to Dr. Johnson, and the sisters Mary and Agnes Berry, who had been loved by Horace Walpole, Samuel Rogers was a survival from the period before 1789.

There always seems something patriarchal in relation to ourselves in persons who have lived to the present generation from before the French Revolution [Lord Houghton has written in his memoir of the Berrys]. That deluge has left a strait behind it, separating the historical worlds, and those who have been on the other side of it seem to have enjoyed a double life. Miss Berry's youth witnessed the great century of common sense and chief era of the liberation of the human mind . . . she was the living tradition of a world of shattered hopes, dispersed illusions and drifted philosophies.

The same was true of Samuel Rogers, though in a far less positive or vital way. While the Misses Berry remained simple, spontaneous and amiably fashionable to the end of their long lives, Rogers, with his white face, sparse white hair and white eyebrows, his venomous tongue, kind heart and suave, asexual manner, seemed sometimes like a living corpse. 'How can you go and dine with Rogers this hot weather? He has been dead these thirty-two

---

[1] These interesting memoirs were published in Paris in 1873, in two volumes, under the title *Epilogue à l'Art Chrètien.* 'Your name is repeatedly mentioned as well as my obligations to you during my London *heigh days* from the year 1838 to '40,' wrote Rio to Lord Houghton in English, in a letter of 17 April 1872 or '73. He regretted, in this letter, that he had been unable to consult Houghton upon the manuscript of the memoirs.

years and cannot be expected to keep' and 'Rogers is no *living* poet' are samples of the sort of spite which his own asperity inspired. Milnes heard that when Rogers told Sydney Smith that a 'little wren at Paestum had looked at him with a curious eye,' the Canon had commented, 'Why, I wonder? If it had been a carrion crow, one could have understood it.' Such cruel humour is characteristic of London society in any epoch, but Rogers certainly gave as good as he got. Mrs. Norton, whose hectic letters and novels contain odd splashes of good writing, described him in a letter to Hayward as a man in whom tastes preponderated over passions:

He was the very embodiment of quiet, from his voice to the last harmonious little picture that hung in his hushed room, and a curious figure he seemed—an elegant, pale watch-tower, showing for ever what a quiet port literature and the fine arts might offer, in an age of 'progress,' when everyone is tossing, struggling, wrecking and foundering on a sea of commercial speculation or political adventure; when people fight over pictures, and if a man does buy a Raphael, it is with the burning desire to prove it is a Raphael rather than to point it out with a slow white finger to his breakfasting friends.

But it was into just that turmoil of political adventure that Richard Monckton Milnes was longing to plunge. He did not at all want a quiet port. He was straining his eyes towards the high seas of success.

Although the lay-out of Milnes' *Memorials of a Tour in Greece* may possibly have been imitated from the alternation of poetry and prose in Rogers' *Italy*, Milnes did not and could not admire Rogers' work; and Rogers demanded admiration. Although they shared a passion for meeting people and making new friends, they were deeply dissimilar. In contrast to Samuel Rogers, so brittle, so sarcastic, Richard Monckton Milnes seemed especially warm-blooded and mercurial. Their friendship was confined to break-fast-table civilities, and soon even these were remitted. 'Old Rogers lives and goes on breakfasting, but is a good deal estranged from me,' Milnes wrote in February 1844; 'I rather think he is the loser by it.' 'Rogers has been here, very cross and very much petted,' he wrote from Woburn five years later, when Rogers, then nearly ninety, had broken his thigh; 'he stumps about most wonderfully, and has lately had the gratification of the deaths of several old people younger than himself.' But after Rogers' death in December 1855, Milnes would say that he was the very last friend to whom Rogers had spoken. He had found him watching the sunset from the dining-room window of his house overlooking the Green Park. The old man had continued gazing silently at the sky for some moments after the sun had disappeared, 'with a look of intense hope on his face' and then, turning to Milnes, he had cried out: '. . . I too must go very soon and pass through a momentary darkness; but the sun will rise again, and so shall I!'[1]

Rogers was the only poet of Milnes' widening acquaintanceship who did not help him in an enterprise which took up a certain amount of his time that summer. This enterprise was the editing of *The Tribute*,[2] a miscellany published by subscription for the benefit of the old clergyman poet Smedley, and intended to contain unprinted verses by the leading as well as the lesser poets of the day. *The Tribute* had been initiated by Lord Northampton, a literary peer with a generous heart. He was the nominal editor, but the real work was done by Bernard Barton, 'the Quaker Poet,' and young Monckton Milnes. Lord Northampton was much offended when Milnes suggested he should read a set of the proofs. Although people promised poems and money readily enough, there was the usual difficulty in keeping most of the contributors up to the mark. By the time *The Tribute* appeared in the late summer of 1837 (having taken eighteen months to incubate) Smedley was dead and his widow busy publishing her own memorial volume. *The Tribute* was just the kind of project in which Milnes, with his good nature and his persistence, could help. It also brought him into close contact with Lord Northampton (whom he had known slightly at Rome) and involved visits to Castle Ashby, where he would meet his old friend and Northampton's neighbour, Stafford O'Brien. Wordsworth sent a poem and so did Landor, two of the Tennysons, Aubrey de Vere, George Darley, Miss Strickland, Lord John Russell and many others of now inferior fame. The volume has escaped oblivion by reason of Alfred Tennyson's contribution to it. Badgered by Milnes, and in spite of the prolonged and silent melancholy caused by Hallam's death, he sent in the verses beginning:

> Oh that 'twere possible,
> After long grief and pain
> To find the arms of my true love
> Round me once again.

[1] This story was told by Milnes to Lady Chatterton and printed in the posthumous *Memoirs of Georgiana, Lady Chatterton*, edited by her second husband, E. H. Dering (Hurst & Blackett, 1878).

[2] *The Tribute: A Collection of Miscellaneous Unpublished Poems*, by Various Authors. Edited by Lord Northampton (London: John Murray, Albemarle Street, and Henry Lindsell, Wimpole Street, 1837). It was a stout octavo volume of 422 pp., containing one hundred and thirty-one sonnets, songs, stanzas, epitaphs, complaints, paraphrases, addresses, lines, etc. It had a large subscription list headed by the Queen.

Had it not been for Milnes' nagging, these verses, which later formed the nucleus of his great poem *Maud*, might not have been written at all.

Dear Milnes, I have *not* been forgetful [Tennyson wrote]; these two poems have been causing me infinite bother to get them into shape; one I cannot send: it is too raw, but as I have made the other double its former size, I hope it will do. I vow to Heaven I never will have to do with these books again—so never ask me.

Even this solitary contribution in the place of two which he had promised had been the occasion of a row. Milnes had promised Lord Northampton a poem by Tennyson before he had asked 'dear old Alfred' himself. Tennyson then refused to send in anything to *The Tribute*. He called Keepsakes edited by members of the aristocracy 'vapid books,' and added that 'to write for people with prefixes to their names is to milk he-goats; there is neither honour nor profit.' Milnes lost his temper. He wrote an angry letter. Tennyson met this with good humour, denied the charge of 'insolent irony' and said that Milnes had addressed him in terms applicable only to Lytton Bulwer. Had he been writing to a nervous, morbidly irritable man, down in the world and oppressed by fortune and the reviews, Tennyson declared that he would have chosen his words more tactfully;

but that you, who seem at least to take the world as it comes, to doff it and let it pass—that you, a man every way prosperous and talented—should have taken pet at my unhappy badinage made me lay down my pipe and stare at the fire for *ten* minutes, till the stranger fluttered up the chimney.

With Landor, who submitted a *Recollection of Lines by Madame de Genlis*, Milnes had better luck, for though the verses themselves are formal and lifeless, Landor was overpoweringly amiable about the project.

My contributions to poetry [he wrote from Clifton, where he was now living] are utterly worthless. I seldom keep anything— what I do keep I send to Lady Blessington, having told her long ago that I would never publish anything before she had judged whether it were worth a place in any of her publications. I am sure however she will more easily pardon me than you will the sending of such verses as you see on the other side. . . . Mine will inevitably be the worst in the volume. Lest you should think I am affecting modesty, I will dash down that idea, and tell you plainly that all the poetry of all the writers in it, usque quoque, is not worth my death of Clytemnestra, which I wrote in an hour.

Aubrey de Vere, always a good friend, told Milnes that he had seen a copy of *The Tribute* in which Landor had scrawled a note that Milnes' own ballad was 'the best thing in it.'

The quality of contributions to this charitable miscellany was, in fact, as mediocre as was to be expectd. Trench told Milnes that except for himself and Tennyson everyone had sent 'the poorest or nearly the poorest, things they had by them.' Trench was mistaken: for he overlooked the two loveliest poems in the book, *The Mermen Ringers* and *Her Own Epitaph*, submitted to Milnes in the elegant archaic handwriting of George Darley. Darley was now back in England. He had quickly responded to Milnes' appeal.

Lord N. of course enlisted you . . . for his kindhearted project [he wrote to Milnes in November 1836],—it is the sole description of charity to which I can contribute & will do so with the greatest pleasure. Alack! for the power to put my hand into a richer scrapbook than mine, & bestow something more than a halfpenny ballad. Indeed I don't know what to send—all my *scraps* are either as long as a lawyer's brief or as little attractive. Something 'popular' you say—bless your five wits I could never write anything popular in my life! . . .

Darley liked Tennyson's poetry as much as he hated Wordsworth's. He told Milnes that he had seen 'a pearly little keepsake song' of Tennyson's recently: 'I caught a glimpse of the lustrous little thing in the Annual dunghill which Lady Emily Somebody scrapes together—and crowed, being a better judge of jewels than corn.' 'Is he a catherine-wheel of splendid emanations?' he asked, in a letter refusing an invitation to meet Tennyson at Fryston.

How I envy you the power of communing with such minds!—envy you what I could never enjoy. . . . But what can T. have to drown him in the slough of despond, as you tell me, if he retain the free use of his faculties? . . . Is he in the flames, furies, & tortures, agonies and excoriations of the 'tender passion'? Let him think of me—my heart is in the grave—I have been luckless in every hope, expectancy, & ambition—my way of life has always been in the gloom, & is now in the shadow of death—I have 'browsed upon wormwood'—must henceforth earn my bread in the bloody sweat of my brow—without a prospect before me but a slide into my tomb made slippery with the same. . . . Ah *caro mio!* we sons of poetry & poverty are all joint-heirs to the crown of thorns, & we must only take off its sharpness by entwining it with all the roses we can. There's a sprig of my poetic philosophy—he is welcome to a cutting, it will shoot anywhere.

Although they resumed in London the friendship they had begun at Rome, Milnes could never persuade Darley to come to see him

if he had any company; the shy stammer and morbid temperament
of the Irish poet entirely prevented his taking any part in ordinary
sociable life.

In the same year, 1836, Richard Milnes paid a second visit to
Ireland, staying at Cratloe, near Limerick, with O'Brien and his
father. While on his way to this house in one of the 'national cars'
and listening to the rhythmic hoof-beats of the horses in the twilight,
Milnes composed the jingling verses beginning:

> I wandered by the brook-side,
> I wandered by the mill,—
> I could not hear the brook flow,
> The noisy wheel was still;
> There was no burr of grasshopper,
> Nor chirp of any bird,
> But the beating of my own heart
> Was all the sound I heard.

When he reached Cratloe he scribbled down the song on a piece of
paper in his bedroom, and trotted downstairs to read it to the family
before dinner. The O'Briens' verdict was unanimous: they
declared it was too poor to print, and had better be burnt
at once. Milnes ignored their warnings, published the poem and
allowed it to be set to music. It swiftly became one of the most
popular songs of that era. It was sung in the dingy streets of London
and beside the Mississippi's yellow banks. It was sung in drawing-
rooms, it was sung in music halls. Today the song has merely
a nostalgic or pathetic ring about it. Yet the rhythm of the metre
(and the perpetual refrain: 'But the beating of my own heart:
Was all the sound I heard') echoes something other than the brisk
hoofbeats on the Irish country road. We can catch in it the
impatient, pulsing tempo of Richard Monckton Milnes' own life—
a hasty, urgent, hither-and-thither rate of living: the throb of
youth, ambition, enquiry, enterprise.

VII

Richard Milnes' second season in London, that of 1837, was
marred by the severe illness of Harriette. He was forced to pass
the spring and early summer in Yorkshire, where he kept himself
alert by reading the new books—Carlyle's *French Revolution*, Miss
Martineau on the United States, Browning's play *Strafford*, *Lyra
Apostolica*, Maurice's *Kingdom of Christ*. He was also planning how
to furnish the rooms which he had now taken at 26 Pall Mall.
One of them was to contain a series of chalk portraits of his closest

friends. These rooms (in which he lived until his marriage in 1851) were over a tailor's shop on the opposite side of the street to the Reform Club, and not far from that club and from the Travellers' and the Athenaeum. Here he lived in bachelor comfort, keeping a manservant and a carriage. The bow-windows of the front rooms looked down into Pall Mall, upon the passing carriages and the pedestrians: an Ackermann scene.

In June 1837 William IV died at last. Princess Victoria was proclaimed Queen. Parliament was dissolved. The parties went to the country. When the new Parliament, in which the Tories still preponderated, met for the first time in November Richard Monckton Milnes was among the new members. His election as one of the representatives for Pontefract gave the greatest satisfaction to his family and to himself. His father had presented him to the electors of Pontefract as 'an uncompromising Tory,' a phrase which was interpreted to mean an uncompromising Protestant as well. Although the great Reform Bill was now five years old, money still changed hands during elections in such country towns as Pontefract. Sir Culling Eardley Smith, who had polled five hundred and fifty votes at the 1834 election in Pontefract, took a stand against the practice of paying head-money in 1837. He declared in a petition that his supporters had dropped to one hundred and twenty-four, and he gave the price of votes at Pontefract as three guineas for a single vote and six for a double. This question of bribery at Pontefract came up again in the course of the next years. It proved an awkward ghost to lay.

Whatever the actual circumstances of his election, most of Richard Milnes' friends weighed in with congratulations and advice. A few, like Landor, remonstrated:

What in the name of goodness can *you* be doing in that place so justly called the House of Commons? A place in which there are not twenty wise men nor ten honest ones. Of the ten, I must allow, if indeed there be that number, your party has six—but then you yourself must stand for five.

Julius Hare wrote from Hurstmonceux vicarage to congratulate his old pupil: 'though I hardly know whether it is a matter of congratulation to get into such a sea of turbid inactivity, into such a flatulent chaos as our great Talkee is now.' From Paris Charles MacCarthy, as anxious and as deeply affectionate as ever, sent a solemn letter of encouragement.

Few men, I should think [he wrote], have begun their careers under a happier star. With all your powers fresh and youthful and germinating still . . . at the opening too of a new era when old parties seem to be going to pieces, and old prejudices exploding on all sides, you are just in the very spring-tide of success.

Richard, he declared, had nothing to do but spread his sail. MacCarthy was gentle and unworldly. He was ill, he was far away and he knew nothing at all about English politics. Milnes, on the other hand, now knew enough of the world to realise that to succeed in politics he must do more than spread his sail. He knew that he would have to tack constantly. And for this purpose he must judge with accuracy the direction of the prevailing winds.

Chapter Five

1837   1840

I

A few days before Christmas 1838 (when the new reign and the new parliament were already more than one year old) the Conservatives of the West Riding gave a banquet in Pontefract Town Hall. The dinner was dignified by the presence of Lord Mexborough, the local Tory bigwig, and of the mayor of Pontefract. Two young members of Parliament were also prominent: Mr. Milnes Gaskell, the member for Wenlock, and his cousin Mr. Monckton Milnes, the Conservative member for Pontefract. A gang of glee-singers from Leeds kept up the merriment of the evening by singing glees after each toast, their songs ranging from the solemn *Hail, Star of Brunswick* (after the toast to Queen Adelaide) to more plebeian airs such as *With a Jolly Full Bottle* and *Life's a Bumper*. A myriad toasts were drunk—the Queen, the Queen Dowager, the Duke-of-Wellington-and-the-Conservative-Peers, Sir-Robert-Peel-and-the-Conservative-members-of-the-House-of-Commons, Church-and-State, the Conservative member for Pontefract. It was a genial and a gratifying evening. 'One of those feasts of reason and flows of soul, which the wise, and great, and good of all ages have delighted to join in' ran the modest description in the local Tory newspaper.

The Conservative member for Pontefract, at that moment nearing twenty-nine years of age, was congratulated for carrying an old head on young shoulders. Without overt distaste he listened to a speech describing him in adulatory terms. 'A most effulgent, and most brilliant and most luminous star on the political horizon'; a youth who would tread in the footsteps of Sir Robert Peel and prove a shining ornament to his country. Proposing the toast, Mr. Robert Smith declared that every drop of his blood thrilled in his veins at the mention of the name of Richard Monckton Milnes, Esquire. Such compliments were a convention on a provincial occasion of this kind and they came late in the evening, when Mr. Smith and the company were flushed with the food and drink provided by the proprietor of the Red Lion Inn; but they were, all the same, directly inspired by the very lengthy speech in which Milnes had just replied to the toast to Sir Robert Peel.

In his speech Milnes had spoken of the House of Commons as ruled by the Conservatives from the Opposition bench, praised Sir Robert Peel in terms of veneration, and declared himself dead against the secret ballot and in grave fear of mob rule in England. The second of his speeches, in answer to the toast of his own health, explained why he had lately voted against a motion to improve the lot of the West Indian negroes, and reminded his audience that he had defended singlehanded the good name of the Pontefract electors against the calumnies of Sir Culling Eardley Smith.[1] Both speeches teemed with allusion and hyperbole and both were impregnated by a tone of lofty seriousness. To a large extent this style was the style of the period. It was appropriate and expected, but in this case it was almost unduly complicated. Clauses lay enmeshed in clauses. Antitheses were tangled up with oratorical questions, and periods jostled one another as they came crowding from the wide mouth of this plump little dark-haired young gentleman. Did Sir Robert Peel, he asked, harbour in his heart one feeling of natural indignation? One feeling of pardonable resentment? *No!* Lord Melbourne he obliquely described as 'the preceptor of the inexperience of the royal mind.' 'Speaking with the deference which becomes a subject,' Monckton Milnes went on, 'we cannot but feel that the royal mind, in after years, may take its colour from the impressions which are made upon it in the present days of blooming youth.'

It would be unfair to single out too many of these phrases, but it is likely that these two speeches are fairly typical examples of Milnes' public and parliamentary manner. 'He never caught the House of Commons tone,' Disraeli noted in an acidulated memorandum upon Monckton Milnes, found amongst the papers at Beaconsfield and published by his biographers [2] in 1914. 'Too easy and familiar in Society, the moment he was on his legs in St. Stephens he was nervous, took refuge in pomposity and had no flow; a most elaborate style and always recalling his words.' Disraeli, who was not an unprejudiced witness and who dismissed 'Dicky' as 'one of the most insignificant members of the House of Commons,' attributed Milnes'

---

[1] Sir Culling Eardley Eardley (1805–1863), who dropped the surname of Smith in 1847, was a well-known religious philanthropist of the mid-Victorian era. He had been a member for Pontefract in the 1830 Parliament, had not sought re-election in 1831, but had contested the seat as a 'purity' candidate in 1837. In February 1838 he presented a petition to the House of Commons alleging gross bribery at Pontefract during the 1837 election. Milnes had defended himself against the petition in the House.

[2] Moneypenny and Buckle: *Life of Benjamin Disraeli, Earl of Beaconsfield*, vol. iii (John Murray, 1914), p. 51. The purpose of Disraeli's memorandum is not clear. It seems to have been inspired by some notes Disraeli was making on the genesis of *Tancred* and other novels.

failure to his physical appearance as well as to his nervousness and pomposity. Describing Milnes' face as 'like a Herculaneum mask or a countenance cut out of an orange' and as 'irresistibly comic,' he says that when speaking Milnes produced 'the effect of some celebrated droll . . . and before he had proceeded five minutes, though he might be descanting on the wrongs of Poland or the rights of Italy, there was sure to be a laugh.'

Monckton Milnes [he wrote elsewhere in his description] was a good-natured fellow and not naturally bad-hearted; he was highly instructed and very clever. But he was always ridiculous—from an insane vanity . . . accompanied by a degree of envy which made him unamiable. . . . His passion [he concludes] was office. He wanted to sit on the Treasury Bench with folded arms, and to be a man of business.

Disraeli's biographer considered this note, which was written reminiscently during the eighteen-sixties, as too harsh: the contempt of one man of letters who had gone in for politics and made a success of it for another who had tried it and failed. But there was more to it than that.

Milnes' approach to public speaking was altogether too literary. In the notebooks which he now began to keep with regularity (and which show that he was as sedulous and prodigious a reader as Gladstone and the other young men of those conscientious days) he would write down phrases and sentences on current topics (Canada, for instance, or the ballot, or Lord Auckland) and tick these off as he made use of them, transferring the remainder to pages headed 'Loose bricks not used in the House.' This was an almost fatal habit for a man who aimed at making fluent speeches. In the same early notebook he recorded a saying of his idol, Peel: 'I have always found a young man speak well in inverse proportion to his premeditation.' In his first utterance in the House, the night after the fiasco of Disraeli's speech on Lord John Russell, he had acted on Peel's advice and made what he himself called in a letter to MacCarthy 'an earnest, almost passionate remonstrance against something that had just been let fall and lasting about five minutes.' This had seemed successful. Stafford O'Brien, who was anxiously listening in the public gallery, was relieved by the speech: 'utterly devoid of anything like mannerism or Milnesism' was his moderate praise. In the same letter to MacCarthy Milnes had described how Disraeli had 'nearly killed the House' by his famous first speech. He adds that Peel 'quite screamed with laughter'—a statement which does not tally with Disraeli's own account of his failure in a letter to his sister. About Milnes' slight effort Sir Robert was distinctly agreeable: 'Just the right thing,' he said. From this moment dated Milnes' notorious admiration for Sir Robert Peel.

II

Disraeli, his friend George Smythe, and other members of the House of Commons who ridiculed or disliked Monckton Milnes always accused him of toadying first Peel and next (after Peel's eclipse in 1846 over the Corn Laws) Lord Palmerston and Lady Palmerston. There is no question that Milnes wanted office and he probably thought (as others have thought before or since) that to be on good terms with the leader of your party was the best way of getting it. At the same time, he may have admired Peel's talents as earnestly as other young Tories: 'You told me once with great seriousness, "Peel was a man of *real talent*," a great man,' wrote Carlyle to Milnes in December 1841. With Milnes admiration quickly became exaggerated, perfervent and public. He had not been in the House many weeks before Peel asked him to dine with a small party: 'He was more genial than I should have thought possible, and told stories out of school with good grace—one or two decidedly bawdy.' But Peel was in some ways a difficult man to feel enthusiastic about:

His high austere character [in the words of Justin McCarthy] made him respected by opponents as well as by friends. He had not perhaps many intimate friends. His temperament was cold, or at least its heat was self-contained. . . . He was by nature a reserved and shy man, in whose manners shyness took the form of pompousness and coldness. Something might be said of him like that which Richter said of Schiller: he was to strangers stony, and like a precipice from which it was their instinct to spring back.

The letters from Peel to his ardent young admirer have exactly this chill but rather stately note; but Milnes was not easy to freeze or to repel. He would constantly seek Peel's advice, sometimes upon rather frivolous subjects. He had for some reason a romantic anxiety that Queen Victoria's coronation should be as splendid and sumptuous as that of George IV (King William having cut the expenditure at his own crowning from £240,000 to £30,000) and he wished to put a motion to this effect before the House. Peel replied patiently, suggesting that the subject was suited to a question rather than a motion:

If the opinion be generally entertained, in favour of a full-sized Coronation—it will have its due influence. If it be not—a division would in my opinion be unwise. My own impression is that considering the state of the Revenue you would not find universal support among the Conservative Party. Considering too that the proper function of the House of Commons is to inculcate Economy rather than Expense. . . .

The letter tailed off politely in an implied reproof. To the calm and frigid intellect of Peel, the voluble, fussy, and emotional Monckton Milnes must have seemed one of the oddest phenomena of the new House of Commons—fully as odd as the perfumed Disraeli, with his mannerisms and his ringlets, and far, far removed in spirit from the solemn young Gladstone.

I had 5½ minutes talk with Gladstone about you at Glasgow in a strain you would somehow have liked [wrote Robert Monteith [1] to Milnes from the British Hotel at Edinburgh on 16 April 1837], though it was not all honey. I believe you are a being that requires sympathy more than admiration & on the whole I think you get a very gratifying share of both.

'Look at life through the purple veil of the grape!' Milnes wrote hopefully in his commonplace book at this epoch: 'May we live as by the side of a grave and looking in' was William Gladstone's aspiration in his journal for March 1837.

The first House of Commons of Queen Victoria's reign differed little in political complexion from the last House of Commons of William IV. The advantage remained with the Tories, who began at this epoch to use the name 'Conservative,' following a lead given by Wilson Croker in an article for the *Quarterly Review*. The Tory renaissance dated from a few years earlier. At the dissolution of 1831 there had been some fifty Tory members in the House of Commons; in 1835 this number had increased to 300 and by 1837 to 315. The Whig Government of Lord Melbourne commanded a total of 342 votes in the House, but this was made up with malcontent Irish and radical groups. Peel's difficulties in keeping the Tories from splitting into opposed groups were prodigious; his problems at this time have been described by John Morley as hardly less than those of Melbourne, the Prime Minister, and of Lord John Russell themselves. Peel was by far

---

[1] Robert Monteith, the son of Henry Monteith of Carstairs, went up to Trinity in 1828. He was the cousin and inseparable companion of the theologian Francis Garden (1810–1884), who belonged to the set of R. C. Trench, F. D. Maurice and Sterling at the University, became for a time a 'Newmanite,' and ended up as sub-dean of the Chapel Royal. Monteith seems to have done nothing with his life, but evidently thoroughly enjoyed it, and was not too much under Garden's influence: 'I am very happy today,' he wrote to Milnes in September 1839; 'I have resisted a very irresistible adultery—thank God—I only fear I shall reward myself now by yielding.' He was always an intimate friend of Milnes, lectured him on his character and generally made fun of him in an affectionate way.

the most eloquent and brilliant speaker then in the House. He spoke strongly and with dignity, without passion but in a way that touched 'the very core of the House of Commons. (His speeches) told of the feelings and inspirations of Parliament as the ballad-music of a country tells of its scenery and its national sentiments.' There was a distinct literary element in the House of 1837—Grote, the historian of Greece, who sat for the City of London, Edward Lytton Bulwer, Benjamin Disraeli, Charles Buller and the dilettante Lord Morpeth, as well as Sir William Molesworth and Richard Monckton Milnes. Palmerston, who although he had been many years in office had so far made no real impression on the country or even on the House, was Foreign Secretary in Melbourne's cabinet, while Lord John Russell was the Whig leader of the House. The Irish National party was represented by O'Connell and by Sheil.

It does not take long for a man to find his place in the House of Commons, or more properly for his fellow-members to con-sign him to it. Richard Milnes remained a Member for Pon-tefract (for the first nine years a Tory member, for the next seventeen a Whig) from 1837 till Palmerston gave him a barony in 1863. During these twenty-six years he often amused the House and sometimes surprised it. He did some good by a judicious and disinterested support of several humanitarian measures. But he never attained office and he was never taken seriously. Except for one moment of disillusion in 1843, when he wanted to throw up his seat and try for a place in the Paris Embassy, he took his position as an M.P. with an amiable dignity. His attendance at the House brought a feeling of actuality to his daily life. It kept him in touch with political changes. It gave him a front row in the stalls, though he never succeeded in clambering over the footlights and up on to the stage. To understand the balance of his life correctly, it is essential to keep his connexion with Parliament in mind—to picture him going down to the House day after day during sessions, either in his silk-upholstered carriage or by foot down the Duke of York's steps, across the end of St. James's Park and into Church House, Westminster, where the House of Commons was sitting during the building of Barry's Palace of Westminster.

III

In the spring of 1838, which followed one of the coldest winters ever recorded ('Murphy's winter' with the Thames frozen over from Oxford to London), Harriette Milnes was married to her cousin. To Richard the marriage was a harsh blow. He doted upon his sister with an exclusive affection which he never gave to any other woman. MacCarthy, who, goaded by spasms from gallstones, was becoming increasingly querulous and subjective, wrote to say he had heard that Milnes was in very low spirits, looked a different man and 'would never recover from the marriage of your sister.' The friendship with MacCarthy was anyway getting into a tiresome phase—a few months later he wrote, gratuitously, to protest against 'all those cold, ungenial formulas of people whom you haunt in London.' Milnes was, in fact, now well embarked upon his London career.

A long sitting and conversation with Mr. Rogers after the Milnes' marriage breakfast [wrote Gladstone in his diary for 25 April 1838]. He spoke unfavourably of Bulwer; well of Milnes' verses; said his father wished them not to be published, because such authorship and its repute would clash with the parliamentary career of his son. Mr. Rogers thought a great author would undoubtedly stand better in parliament for being such; but that otherwise the additament of authorship, unless on germane subjects, would be a hindrance. He quoted Swift on women. . . . He has a good and tender opinion of them; but went nearly the length of Maurice (when mentioned to him) that they had not that specific faculty of understanding which lies beneath the reason.

Mrs. Milnes, who (let us hope) had not overheard these slurs upon feminine intellect, noted in her own diary that the marriage had taken place on St. Mark's day—'the patron saint,' as Mr. Milnes had remarked, 'of Harriette's much-loved Venice.' 'A wedding is always solemn and affecting,' Mrs. Milnes continued in characteristic vein,

even when such bright prospects as now attend it, in the union of two beings so amiable that we have every reason to look forward through the blessing of God to every happiness for them which can exist in this world! After a few days we returned to Fryston.

The discussion of Milnes' poetry by Samuel Rogers and Gladstone was no doubt caused by the simultaneous appearance of two volumes of his verse. These successors to the Grecian pieces of five years before were entitled *Memorials of a Residence on the Continent* and *Poems of Many Years*. Privately printed in 1838 for circulation amongst the poet's friends, they were published and put on sale later the same year. The twin volumes were well and prominently reviewed, praised for 'the equable tone of sound, unaffected sensibility which pervades them,' but declared to be out of keeping with the times. Quoting *The Flight of Youth*, with its melancholy little metre:

Yes, he must have gone away,
In his guise of every day,
In his common dress, the same
Perfect face and perfect frame

.   .   .   .

In your hands be borne the bloom
Whose long petals once and only
Look from their pale-leavéd tomb
In the midnight lonely;
Let the nightshade's beaded coral
Fall in melancholy moral
Your wan brows around,
While in very scorn ye fling
The amaranth upon the ground
As an unbelievéd thing.

The Sun suggested that twenty years earlier these lines would have excited general attention—'but the present age has no great relish for pure, abstract poetry; it is essentially practical and utilitarian in its predilections. . . . Mr. Milnes . . . cannot hope to be extensively read.' The majority of Milnes' poems were probably too slight and too personal to become popular at that epoch, and there was in any case only a limited demand for poetry. Milnes noted a story of Murray the publisher speaking to a lady novelist of the moment: 'You think, ma'am, that the public don't like poetry. You're wrong, ma'am. They hate it.'

Extensively read or not, these two small, neat octavo volumes achieved a *succès d'estime*. They were bound in the dark cloth with a white label habitual to the Dover Street publishing house of Edward Moxon, the young publisher who had produced *Memorials of a Tour in Greece* in 1833 and who had lately put out a six-volume edition of Wordsworth, as well as the famous illustrated issue of Samuel Rogers' *Poems* and a reprint of his *Italy* with the Turner plates. Milnes sent copies to all his friends and most of his acquaintances, and received in return compliments which ranged from the vociferous and exaggerated enthusiasm of Landor to the restrained and frosty congratulations of Lord Jeffrey and Sir Robert Peel. One admirer whom he did not know, and whose opinion is thus entirely unbiassed, was very much 'affected' (as she put it in the jargon of the day) by his poem *The Lay of the Humble*: as she lay on her couch in Wimpole Street, Miss Elizabeth Barrett read it and thought it 'exquisite.' In 1843 she confessed to R. H. Horne that she was disappointed by Milnes' later poetry. This seemed by comparison with his earlier work to lack fire and imagination. He had become 'didactic.' Someone had told her, too, that

The Lay of the Humble was not original. 'Taken from the German, I think they said it was. Do you know? I wish I knew. It is very beautiful in any case.'

Between them the two volumes contained nearly everything that Milnes had so far written. All the Greek poems reappeared in *Memorials of Many Scenes*, together with a set of mellifluous, nostalgic sonnets and other poems written during the years in Italy, and recalling the halcyon days at Venice and Naples, at Florence and Rome. The weeks at Bonn University also found their memorial amongst the many scenes, as well as poems written during his Irish journeys, a meditation on the Madeleine which Arthur Hallam had admired, and some rather tasteless jingles about Frome and other places in England. *Poems of Many Years* were arranged sectionally: *The Book of Youth, The Book of Friendship, The Book of Love, The Book of Reflection* and *The Book of Sorrow*. Amongst these *Books* were several poems which were especially admired: *The Flight of Youth*, in particular, *The Lay of the Humble, Shadows, The Long Ago*. Scattered throughout the two volumes there are passages showing real sensibility. These lie embedded in much that is stilted, conventional and commonplace. Milnes' lyrical gift faded as he grew older. He was never a hard worker and it is likely that he did little polishing of his poems when he had got them down on paper. In his old age Lord Houghton once said that a few of the things he had written deserved to live. That estimate is about right.

IV

One of the notes which Milnes received acknowledging the gift of his two books of poems was written on gilt-edged paper, in an untidy cursive hand. It came from Gore House. 'Dear Sir, Accept my best thanks for the two charming books,' wrote Lady Blessington. 'Our excellent friend Mr. Landor left me to-day for Bath.' She ended by begging him for a contribution to one of her Books of Beauty and asking him to come any evening he liked to Gore House. Milnes complied with both requests. He became a regular contributor to her Annuals and an habitué of the house and garden in Kensington Gore. 'Let me thank you for the poems! They are charming and so full of freshness that they will perfume my book like violets,' Lady Blessington would write, or sending him an unfinished plate of 'the pretty Mrs. Gordon Campbell' she would add coaxingly: 'I have selected for you the most admired of my Beauties because I know you will render her justice.'

Lady Blessington was at this time forty-nine years old. She had moved to Gore House from Seamore Place in the spring of 1836, and was now entering the lavish and harassing final phase of her life. Madden, her biographer, records that he noticed a change in her manner as she settled down to the role of the *salonnière* of this country-house in Kensington. He had already observed a distinct development during the twelve years he had known her—when he left her at Naples in 1824 she had been enchanting, carefree and irresistibly charming; three years later in Rome he had found her more literary, more authoritative; another five years and she had seemed saddened; and now, at Gore House in the late eighteen-thirties, she was sparkling but didactic, rather feverishly brilliant and at the same time desperate from worry. To keep up the tone of intellectual brilliance combined with high fashion (a mixture that drew the cleverest men of the day to her green damask drawing-room) was a perpetual and even agonising strain. It involved a good deal of insincere flattery of acquaintances, but, as Forster points out in his *Life of Landor*, the most fascinating of all Lady Blessington's attributes was a plain but rare one: an exceptionally true and affectionate heart. After her death Landor wrote the poignant lament:

> Ah! Marguerite, with you are gone
> The light and life of Kensington.
>
> . . . . .
>
> Can all the world to *me* atone
> For losing you and you alone,
> Or for that yearly summons—*Come*
> *While your two lilacs are in bloom?*

Landor took the habit of passing part of each spring at Gore House, where he would wander in the garden in the morning sunshine, talking to Lady Blessington (who rose very early) and sniffing at the two lilac trees—one white, one 'dim purple'— which grew below the terrace. It was he who brought Milnes into the Blessington orbit. In May 1836 he wrote to him to say how loath he was to venture down into London from this leafy refuge: 'The moment I leave the gates of this house, I feel as a badger would do turned out of a bag in Cheapside.' The atmosphere of Gore House, where conversation was easy and informal, but the surroundings sumptuous and even grand, must have exactly suited Richard Milnes. Lady Blessington, now stout, her smooth, benign full face swathed in a kind of wimple, would guide the conversations (aided and supported by Count d'Orsay) from the great armchair in which she liked to sit. The Gore House company, almost exclusively male, was more distinguished than any she had entertained in Seamore Place.

And just as her company and her ambience accorded well with Milnes' tastes, so his talents and position were of the kind that she found most sympathetic. Both of them had manners which were rated over-demonstrative in the cold, conventional world of the *haut ton*; both of them had kind hearts and a passion for unpopular causes and people. Their friendship had a solid basis in the similarity of their temperaments. D'Orsay too liked Milnes, and supported him at his more awkward breakfast parties. In June of 1839, in response to Milnes' request, Count d'Orsay drew his profile.

Psychologically the d'Orsay profile portraits of the men of that day are not very subtle or instructive. The most famous is his portrait of the old Duke of Wellington. Most of the men he drew were shown in flat profile, looking to their right and seated in a chair. The drawing of Milnes, which is in pencil, with a faint rose-pink blush upon the cheek and greyish eyes, shows a thoughtful, clear-sighted young man with a straight nose, a high forehead, a clumsy chin and an underlip very slightly protruded. The eyebrow is a little arched. Milnes' hair is long and curling. At the back it reaches to his coat collar; at the side the lobe of his ear just shows; and over the forehead the locks of hair seem looped back, and fall curling above a side-whisker which reaches to his cravat. He wears the high-gilled, stiffened shirt-collar then in fashion, with a satin stock wound round it, and a frilled shirt-front. The coat-collar is wide, and high behind—a modified version of the humped redingotes of the Regency. At this moment of his life, and for the next eight or nine years, Milnes was noticeably well-dressed. His great friend Mrs. Grote[1] ('the origin of the word grotesque'), wife of the historian and one of the Radical hostesses of the day, was sometimes commissioned to get him shirts and shirt-fronts in Paris. In April 1844 (five years after the date of this particular portrait) she told him that she had got him 'chemises lovely to behold. Miss Coutts must look another way or yield'—a reference to the great banking heiress whom Milnes, in common with every other youngish man of that day, was urged by friends and family to marry. She got him 'plain Puritan shirts' as well as 'Elégantes': 'if you wish I will yield you up two more Paris fronts, which is the last effort I can make to give you a start this season.'

Probably Milnes, like Dickens, submitted to the influence of

---

[1] Harriet Grote (1792–1878), wife of George Grote the historian of Greece and Philosophical Radical Member of Parliament, was one of the most remarkable Englishwomen of the last century. Her biography of her husband stands high in the list of great English biographies; and she was a woman of outstanding intelligence and wit. In the late 'thirties she became, and remained, one of Milnes' most staunch friends and supporters. The Houghton Papers contain many highly entertaining letters from Mrs. Grote.

RICHARD MONCKTON MILNES IN 1839

d'Orsay in his clothes, though the result was less noticeable and less vulgar than Dickens' imitations of 'Cupid's' cuffs and curls. He certainly found d'Orsay co-operative over the social muddles which he was apt to make:

Cher Mills, [d'Orsay wrote after some forgotten incident at Covent Garden] Je pense que Chesterfield avec ses sentiments de féodalité mal digérées, s'est figuré que vous l'aviez traité en bagatelle dans sa loge . . . c'est la seule manière dont je puis expliquer qu'il se soit offusqué si pompeusement. Je lui expliquerai ce que vous désirez.

In the self-conscious world of aristocratic London society, Milnes was still in need of loyal friends.

V

At much about the same time as his entry into the Gore House set, Richard Milnes began another intimate friendship (it was certainly no more) with a woman who was younger than Lady Blessington, and quite as much discussed. This was Milnes' near contemporary in age, Caroline Norton.

'Monckton Milnes would be a delightful match for Mrs. Norton, if he could only be pathetic,' Lady Blessington once said. The adjective was used in their sense and not in ours. A 'pathetic' person was then one who aroused sympathy in others. In the spring of 1838 Caroline Norton was only turning thirty, but she already had more than enough to be unhappy about. One of the three marvellously handsome Sheridan sisters, she had been involved by her husband in an odious public scandal with the Prime Minister, Lord Melbourne, during the season of 1836. Though cleared in the legal action brought by George Norton, she was still separated from her children and cold-shouldered by half London. Caroline Norton was a lush, sombre, heaving beauty of the type that Lewis was then painting in his oriental water-colours. She was literary, highly intelligent, over-excitable, and as sharp-tongued as her sisters Lady Seymour and Mrs. Blackwood (better known to posterity by their later titles of Duchess of Somerset and Lady Dufferin). Like Lady Blessington, she had a quality of Irish impulsiveness that appealed directly to Monckton Milnes. Then, besides, he would have pitied her, for he was a tender-hearted and imaginative man.

Milnes' French friend Rio, for whose benefit both he and Samuel Rogers would collect and show off their literary friends, met

Mrs. Norton at one of Rogers' breakfasts in the summer of 1838. Rio, whose serious Breton charm was singularly difficult to resist,[1] had been deeply disappointed by the last two lions he had met with Rogers: Thomas Campbell, whom he judged an old-fashioned 'christophobe' of the school of Voltaire, and Tom Moore, who had been drunk. Rogers promised him that he would counterbalance this disappointment. He would introduce him to Poetry herself. On the appointed day Rio arrived at St. James's Place, and found assembled a company which included his friend Milnes. He was galvanised by the beauty and the profound melancholy of a young woman who remained silent throughout the meal: this must be 'the Muse' herself. 'Cette autre Niobé, torturée comme l'ancienne par les angoisses maternelles, n'était autre que Mrs. Norton.' After the meal, when Rio, at Milnes' kindly instigation, had told of a boyhood episode of his own in 1815—described a few years later in his little book *Une Petite Chouannerie Bretonne*—Mrs. Norton completed the conquest her silence had begun by rising and advancing with outstretched hand. 'Sir,' she said, 'I have one favour to ask of you. Come to dine with me next Tuesday so that you may meet my sisters, Lady Seymour and Lady Dufferin.' The effect of these few simple and polite words was electrifying. When it became known that Mrs. Norton herself proposed to write a poem about the *petite chouannerie* (in which Rio and a few loyalist boys had fought Napoleonic troops and suffered casualties), Milnes, Tom Moore, Kenyon and Landor hurriedly followed suit. Mrs. Norton, Landor, Milnes and 'le vénèrable Wordsworth' kept their promise.

One of the few jokes about Monckton Milnes which have retained some currency is the name that Mrs. Norton is supposed to have given him: 'The Bird of Paradox.' As it happens, she did nothing of the sort, for the nickname was invented by their common friend William Stirling of Keir. But though this particular joke was not Caroline Norton's, she had all the Sheridan wit. Milnes jotted down a good many of her remarks and a good number of stories about her in his early commonplace books. 'The saddest moment for me,' she once said to him (she was much courted and admired) 'is when a man seems uneasy at being left alone with me, when his voice lowers and he draws his chair nearer—I know I am about to lose a friend I love, to get a lover I do not want.' She told Milnes

---

[1] Rio won many friends during his visits to England. 'How grateful I feel to God for the pleasure I have enjoyed for the last fortnight,' Milnes' cousin Miss Charlotte Williams-Wynn wrote in her scrapbook in June 1841. 'I was introduced to Mr. Rio on the 9th, and . . . I saw him practically every day. His conversation was to me like some church bell.' (*Memorials of C. Williams-Wynn*, edited by Her Sister, Longmans, 1877, pp. 9–10.)

that Lady Harriet d'Orsay had called her lovers sick nasturtiums that required to be supported on sticks—

they knock at your door and fatigued with that exertion rest on the stairs—when they enter you rush forward pushing an armchair or sofa into which they fall—repose for an hour and then you ring for the servant to take them away.

She told him, too, that her publisher, Colburn, had urged her to 'devote her talents to the fashionable vices of the day and he would pay her what she chose—no romances or imaginative things,' and that a maid who had sinned (as it was then called) had burst into tears and cried: 'it's all very well for you fine ladies with your books, but *we* have nothing but love to amuse *us*.' She laughed at everything, including herself and her mean-minded husband, who was always speaking of the great expense the suit he had brought against Melbourne had put him to—'just as if it was a foolish luxury I had indulged in.'

Mrs. Norton was voluble and indiscreet, with the thoughtless, enchanting freedom of the Sheridan family. She said she was sure that her brother-in-law Blackwood looked on each of her books as an illegitimate child—'as a thing wrong in itself to produce but only excused by the frailties of human nature.' But she was also a woman of strong affections. Throughout her uneasy life she remained a devoted and encouraging friend of Richard Monckton Milnes. Like him she often spoke without thinking of the effect her words would produce. Like him she was paradoxical and flamboyant and demonstrative. Like him she was gregarious and adored Society, though when she was tired and discouraged she would refer to the life of a woman of the world as a 'treadmill.' She shared with Milnes a sharp perception of real human values:

Nelly's vanity [she once said to him of Lady Dufferin] is to have all the room exclaim: 'What a pretty woman!' Mine is that the two or three persons I care about should turn round and cry: 'Here she comes!'

VI

Milnes' life in London during this period (1836 to 1840, let us say) was not entirely filled with politics, poetry and the society of amiable and pretty women such as Mrs. Norton; nor were little notes on diminutive sheets of scented paper, with the affected words 'Dear Poet' immediately beneath the embossed monogram, the only letters that arrived at No. 26 Pall Mall. Milnes' physical and mental resistance must have been very great to sustain the lazy

turmoil of the House of Commons, the mannered gaiety of fashionable drawing-rooms, and the high thinking and taut conversation
of such serious-minded friends as John Sterling and Thomas Carlyle,
with both of whom he became intimate at about this time.

However much amusement he got out of darting about in London
society, Monckton Milnes always maintained an intellectual equilibrium. 'A little ice-fall makes a great noise in the mountains,
as a little intellect in high society,' he noted, after two London
seasons. The elegance of the phrase need not make its sincerity
suspect.

The worst part of common society [he observed more simply in
1839] is its unimpressiveness if long continued. The music that
makes the young thrill and tremble is merely agreeable to you—
the splendour that dances in their dreams afterward is to you a
show very well performed.

He recorded, too, a remark made to him by the Bishop of
London: 'The higher classes in England,' the Bishop had said,
'have the Athenian appetite for calumny.' In the same year Milnes
wrote at some length in his notebook of the sense of unreality which
haunted him in the 'great societies of the world'—a sense of the
'phantasmal nature of those present and of my relations to them,
an impression that both I and they are parts of a phantasmagoria,
in which *I*' (he adds) 'have the superiority of seeing through the
delusion.' This qualification carries the hint of the observer, the
man who watches but cannot act. He was, now and throughout
life, liable to moods—the moods inevitable to any man of sensibility
who is tempted to try to live in the desiccating atmosphere of a
beau monde.

Milnes' record of his feeling of the phantasmal nature of the
world finds a curious echo in the 'kind of ghostly astonishment'
which Logan Pearsall Smith has described as the habitual state of
mind of Thomas Carlyle.[1] Pearsall Smith drew attention to Carlyle's
persistent use of such words as spectracalities, spectre-chimeras, to
his picture of himself as 'a spectre moving amid spectres.' Was this
consciousness of the unreality of the material world one of the links
that now suddenly bound Milnes to Carlyle?

The precise year in which Milnes first met Carlyle is not certain.
His boon friend Charles Buller, who had been Carlyle's pupil, may
have introduced them in 1838 or '39, while a note from Spedding,
dated 1837, discusses means of getting together an audience for

---

[1] See *The Rembrandt of English Prose* in Logan Pearsall Smith's volume of essays
Reperusals and Re-collections (Constable & Co., 1936).

Carlyle's first course of lectures in that year. Milnes had read *The French Revolution* and his admiration for Carlyle was quite as authentic as, and far more plausible than, his admiration for Peel: 'Carlyle's writings make on me the impression of the sound of a single hatchet in the aboriginal forests of North America.' The conversation of Carlyle proved as original as his writings, though it was often so gloomy that Milnes called it 'cinerous.' The little lined pages of Milnes' commonplace books were soon black with prophetic excerpts from the monologues at Cheyne Row. 'The immense advantage of our time over twenty-five years ago in point of seriousness—no Castlereagh would do now—the world is something to us it was not to him,' for example. It seems peculiar that the world should have seemed something to Milnes that it also seemed to Carlyle, but in spite of apparently antipathetic characteristics and ways of living, they made fast friends. Underneath the 'nonsense' and the 'twaddle' of which Arthur Hallam used to accuse him, Milnes concealed an intelligent mind, and this was fully appreciated by Carlyle. He liked Milnes' manner, too, for it formed such a contrast to his own moroseness and irascibility; he called him 'bland-smiling,' in a letter which he wrote to Emerson in 1840:

A most bland-smiling, semi-quizzical, affectionate, high-bred, Italianised little man, who has long olive-blonde hair, a dimple, next to no chin, and flings his arm around your neck when he addresses you in public society![1]

Warped by neurosis and bad health, Carlyle's character had in it a power of intense affection and a great need for sympathy. A part of this affection he concentrated on Richard Monckton Milnes: 'Where in the wide earth are you? . . .' he wrote to him in November 1841; 'those kind laughing eyes, what scene do they now look on; what mortals hear that half-serious, half-quizzing, wholly-friendly voice?' Most people reacted to Carlyle with awe, some of them (Miss Jewsbury, for example) with terror. Milnes had an entirely different approach—he teased Carlyle. He would 'defend all manner of people and principles' (wrote W. E. Forster) 'in order to provoke Carlyle to abuse them,' behaving at times like 'a naughty boy rubbing a fierce cat's tail backwards and getting in between furious growls and fiery sparks.' It may have been this provocative attitude, this wish to force Carlyle to perform, that inspired a rather tart remark about Milnes made by Carlyle in old age. Asked by a young admirer whether Milnes had not been a

---

[1] Wemyss Reid, p. x.

familiar friend of his in his early days in London, the Sage of Chelsea replied: 'Yes. He looked at you out of the boxes.'[1]

Although Carlyle said he approved of Milnes' cheerful contentment with his reputation as 'a saloon celebrity poet,' he thought he had genuine literary talent. In the early spring of 1841 he convinced himself from internal evidence that Mrs. Gore's extremely amusing anonymous novel of fashionable life *Cecil the Coxcomb* was written by Milnes. He sent Milnes a letter to ask if his conjecture was right, and added an admonitory word:

I know not whether I should counsel the said Milnes to be more austere and 'serious' [he wrote], probably not. I will counsel him to be *sincere* and ever more sincere, in his own province; and to consider that there is a gift in him, which may either be reported in Heaven's Treasury for evermore, or squandered in Mayfair in a few seasons.

VII

Other sober-minded people besides Carlyle were prepared to take Milnes at more than his face value. Henry Crabb Robinson, a man of good sense but not a very interesting personality, first met Monckton Milnes in January 1838. He thought his conversation stimulating, and, despite the inevitable spate of paradoxes, he judged him 'a thinker.' Milnes called on him a fortnight later and they talked pleasantly of German literature. Crabb Robinson was pleased by *Memorials of Many Scenes*, which he thought should 'certainly fix his reputation as a poet,' but considered it a pity that Milnes 'has contrived to get a character for foppery and arrogance.' Robinson was not put off or even disturbed by the reputation of his new friend—'he will get over this' was his sane and only comment. He breakfasted with Milnes from time to time or met him at Rogers', and always recorded these occasions as agreeable.

This was, in most directions, a successful period in Milnes' life. In spite of what Carlyle called his 'blarney and quiz' and his 'terrible perversities,' he was already a figure of a certain consequence in the literary world. At the end of 1838, for instance, his aid was enlisted by Spedding and Carlyle in their project for founding the London Library. He was asked to get Lord Northampton, Rogers and other people of influence interested in the scheme, which resulted in the creation of that inestimably useful institution. Milnes was now becoming a man of whom something was expected.

[1] The admirer was Francis Espinasse, a minor journalist, in whose *Literary Recollections and Sketches* (Hodder & Stoughton, 1893) are several pages devoted to Milnes' friendship with Carlyle. Espinasse states (p. 77) that Carlyle appreciated Milnes' 'sunny humanities,' but once described him as 'going about talking the most palpable nonsense.'

Carlyle urged him to write a novel of contemporary life—'an emblematic picture of English society as it is? Done in prose with the spirit of a poet, what a book were that!'

In the winter of 1839 Milnes published in *The London and Westminster Review* a long critical article on a number of books by Emerson, whose essays were published in England in the following year. This article, the earliest English appreciation of Emerson in print, was a result of Milnes' intimacy with the American visitor Charles Sumner. Milnes deals sympathetically with American thought, while giving frank attention to the weakness he detected in the American system of life: that in the United States then (as now) it was almost disreputable to be 'poor and retired,' that Americans liked living in swarms and travelling in droves, and that the whole country was still 'a home for genius of hand, and a desert for genius of head.' Milnes was always extremely well liked by Americans, who had on the whole a thin time in Victorian London, where it was fashionable to ridicule them, sometimes to their faces. In the article on Emerson (which elicited a letter of friendly, stilted thanks from Concord) Milnes attacked those who laughed at the American way of writing. Too much nonsense had been talked about it, he declared; it was a language not yet matured and it was 'too much to expect that the development of *their* mind should exactly square itself with *our* form of expression.' He explained that many American phrases were in reality Elizabethan: 'we should, in fine, read every American book as if it were the produce of another age of English literature than our own, without any thought of worse or better.' This kind of tolerance, singularly rare in the vituperative world of English letters, was one of Milnes' most disarming attributes.

Although his poems and the Emerson article contained signs of talent, Milnes did no literary work of lasting value during the years 1836 to 1840. Nor is this in the least surprising, for the life he was leading was hardly calculated to aid creative or even critical work. He was here, there and everywhere: dining with Miss Agnes and Miss Mary Berry, dancing at Lansdowne House, attending a garden-party at the Duke of Devonshire's at Chiswick, helping his old aunt Lady Cork—'Corky is in great form,' he wrote irreverently to Harriette in August 1838—listening to Dickens' explanations of his row with his publisher Bentley, laughing at Theodore Hook's jokes about the Lytton Bulwers[1]—always on the move, always talking, laughing, spouting paradoxes; and eating and drinking. By May 1839, when he was not yet thirty, he was suffering badly from the

---

[1] E.g. 'Sir Lytton Bulwer the greatest bitch of the two'; or 'Bulwer—a nose in curls' (Commonplace book, 1839–40).

gout, which never left him alone for the remainder of his life. The resistance to his personality remained strong in some quarters of London society, but by now he had his friends and even his admirers. He had houses which he frequented and others to which he would not think of going. He had learned his way about that close, compact London world with some sureness, and could exhibit it to Americans, such as Sumner, or to old friends from Paris or Italy. He gave rein to his passion for novelty and for notoriety. It was about this time that his sister, Harriette Galway, confessed she was relieved that some contemporary murderer had not been reprieved, since otherwise Richard would have had him to breakfast the next morning.

During these first four years of fevered London life, Milnes got more and more letters of complaint from neglected friends such as Eliot Warburton and MacCarthy. Stafford O'Brien too upbraided him for no longer keeping to his promises. 'I thought your manner getting hard in London,' he wrote in April 1839, 'and like folks who have got their gottens by struggling.' 'Tell me,' he wrote again (this time in January 1840), 'what you are chiefly struggling after now or whether, as I hope, you are beginning to live like a gentleman and consider yourself to have made your fortune.' Like Carlyle, O'Brien warned Milnes of the dangers of Mayfair. Nothing could be more ephemeral, he wrote, than the pleasures of the world; he compared them to a perennial disappointment he remembered from his own Northamptonshire childhood, when he and his brother as little boys would run out into the December garden to collect the freshly fallen snow in a bowl. 'It was all very well when we left it, white and overflowing,' he recollected, 'but when we came back and it was melted, how little there used to be and that little how dirty.'

Most of Milnes' time between 1836 and 1840 was spent either in London consolidating his position or in Yorkshire recuperating from this process. In the very late summer of 1838 (after the specially exhausting Coronation season, with its spectacular balls and routs) he travelled down to Bagnières de Bigorre in the Pyrenees with his friend James Colville, driving through the Vendée and the Charente in a green chariot, in the drizzling rain. At Bagnières he sprained his ankle dancing the cachucha down a mountainside. In the autumn he returned to Yorkshire.

VIII

In the late summer of 1839 Milnes journeyed up to Scotland for the celebrated fiasco of the Eglinton Tournament, where he watched Caroline Norton's sister, Lady Seymour, perform her part as Queen

of Beauty in a downpour of Ayrshire rain. His friend Robert
Monteith had offered to take a cabin for him on one of the many
yachts—the *Amethyst*, the *Orion* and so on—which lay moored off
the little port of Irvine ('five yards from Eglinton') for the occasion,
but Milnes had made his own arrangements. Monteith had refused
to go to 'the Eglintonian mummery'—'the Torment (as they call
it in Ayrshire)'—but was anxious to show Richard as much of
the country as he could.

Where shall we go in Scotland? [he wrote to him from Carstairs
in September 1839, in a burst of true Highland hospitality]
Ld Belhavens, Douglas', Montrose's, Mr Forbes', Howe Drum-
monds, Houstons, Blackburns, my cousins at Winton, the Colvilles,
Kirkman Finlays', Colquhouns, Sir A. Campbell's, Gibson Craigs,
Carmichael's, Kinlochs, Hunter Blairs' . . .? I wonder how you
will do in Scotland [he added more thoughtfully]; —you must not
be flippant or flashy or eccentric or clever or poetical or *anything*—
mind that. Lie fallow in a state of calm negation—& you will
bear such a crop of Milneseed when you return as will delight
yourself & some of your friends & all your enemies.

Milnes spent two months going from castle to castle in the
North, and ended up in Edinburgh on his way to the Lakes.

Do you want to know what people say of you in Edbg? [Mon-
teith demanded in another letter (of 30 January 1840)]. Jeffrey
stands up for you—scarcely Madame. Sir T. D. Lauder utterly
irreverential & mendaciously anecdotical. The Lord Advocate
deeply hostile. The Gibson Craigs far from a proper state of mind.
Lady Belhaven very favourable, but not at all surprised at the
severe verdicts of others.

Milnes found this amiable letter when he returned to 26 Pall
Mall in February; and even here Monteith was not prepared to
let him alone:

Well, you are established once more at the sign of the Black
Heart [he continued mockingly]. Cards are leaving you like a
snow shower—& many similar flakes are crystallizing round the
dingy mirror of the front parlour. The foolish pomposity of the
Carlton is in full operation—& all goes on as heretofore—Balls,
dinners, gossip of marrying & giving in marriage—while Chartism
like the day of Judgement waits like a thief in the night, or a gun-
powder plot, to send it all rocket high into thin air. 'The pillared
palace of Rank & Wealth is too heavy for the squalid mud bank
on which its built' as Robert Monteith says. . . .

There was much more along these lines. It is not surprising
that the two had squabbled slightly during their journey through
the North.

Coming back to Yorkshire via the English Lakes, Milnes passed some days in Wordsworth's company, but to judge from the dicta of the old poet which Milnes scribbled down, the conversations at Rydal Mount were not memorable. 'I like the stone walls of the Lake country that carry the feeling of *property* so high among the hills' is a typical example. It may have been on this occasion that Milnes observed Wordsworth's facetious habit of referring to his ageing wife as 'my old phantom.'

One result of his journey to Scotland was a passionate love-poem entitled *Love and Nature*, which Lady Blessington snapped up for *Heath's Book of Beauty* for 1840. It is impossible to judge how much —if any—of these verses are based on some actual emotional experience on a 'highland tarn.' The poet describes kissing his love in a boat upon the Scottish lake, while a pallid sun shines through the mist:

> Still as an island stood our ship,
> The waters gave no sound;
> But when I touched thy quivering lip,
> I felt the world go round.
>
> We seemed the only sentient things
> Upon that silent sea:
> Our hearts the only living springs
> Of all that yet could be!

The tone of the poem is artificial, though this is no valid reason for supposing he did not have some flirtation in Scotland. 'I am not in love,' he had written to MacCarthy in one of his now rare letters to him eighteen months before, 'for if I was, I should not be so cross and nervous.'

IX

We have no descriptions from which to recreate the rooms Monckton Milnes inhabited at No. 26 Pall Mall; the building is demolished now. We know only from Disraeli that there was an alcove with a bow-window, in which he and Louis Napoleon could speak privately without being overheard by the rest of the company. From Milnes himself we know that the rooms were expensive (at times he thought of giving them up) and that one of them was decorated with the chalk portrait-drawings of his closest friends. The rest must be mere surmise: the books and high bookcases, the heavy stuff curtains, the comfortable bachelor furnishings, the litter of papers and letters in baskets, the mahogany tables, the pipes, the deep, high armchairs. It is a pity we know so little, for his London life radiated from these rooms for fourteen years, and it would be interesting to watch him in them. The confined and crowded space of the temporary House of Commons is more familiar and easier to picture. So too are the shadowy gardens of Gore House and Holland House; and the chilly, ill-lit residence of the Thomas Carlyles in Cheyne Row, now preserved as a museum. We can still stand on the very threshold that Milnes, with his light, dapper step, would cross on some sunny morning more than a hundred years ago, when he had brought his horse down to Chelsea to ride by Carlyle's side, discussing Goethe and Schiller, about the country lanes; but we can get no clear conception of what the inhabited house then looked to him. Milnes himself probably thought little about London as a place to live in. It was already a grimy city, and like his other contemporaries he accepted it. He observed, in 1841, that the London buildings looked so well by moonlight because the smoky parts coincided with and deepened the shadows, 'bringing out the light parts in high relief.'

A general impression of London at just this moment can be found in Guizot's book of recollections: *An Embassy to the Court of St. James in 1840*.[1] Sent over by Louis-Philippe to negotiate a settlement of the Near Eastern question, which was bringing England and France to the edge of war, the new ambassador (who had never been in England) entered London in his carriage as the light was failing over the Georgian squares one evening of February 1840. As he passed along the streets, nothing of note attracted his eye. The public buildings, the shops and private houses all seemed small and monotonous and, after Paris, meanly ornamented. Columns were everywhere—large and small columns, pilasters, statuettes, 'embellishments of all kinds.' But the extent of the city impressed him: 'London conveys the idea of unlimited space, filled with men incessantly and silently displaying their activity and their power.' The façades of the houses were neat and new, and he liked the width of the pavements, the effect of the large panes of glass, of the iron palings and the knockers on the doors. London had 'an air of careful attention.' An air, he concluded, that almost counterbalanced the absence of good taste.'

The general bad taste of London life was often criticised by strangers. Posterity has given an undue glamour to such figures as Lady Blessington and Mrs. Norton, who though beautiful in their prime led lives that were always embittered and sometimes downright tawdry. A few of the finest-looking of the great ladies and

---

[1] This London volume of Guizot's *Memoirs* was translated and published on its own by Richard Bentley in 1862.

their daughters must indeed have seemed supernaturally beautiful, diaphanous beings at the Lansdowne House or Buckingham House balls. But the women of London Society, though rich and leisured, were overdressed by Parisian standards. Twenty years later the American Henry Adams disliked Englishwomen for seeming dowdy and bespangled with too many clumsy family jewels. Men's clothes too were becoming less spectacular; the dandies of the Regency were dead or ageing, and to the general public Disraeli and d'Orsay were almost figures of ridicule, but there was no austerity about the ballrooms or the Park carriages in 1838 or 1840.

Not all of Richard Monckton Milnes' life was spent in London. The family at Fryston and Bawtry, the relatives at Kippax and Serlby, the noisy town electors of Pontefract, the voluble dissenters, were always present over his shoulder. His London friends saw only a well-dressed, vivacious young poet or a hopeful romantic politician, lolling in the Gore House salon while Liszt played the piano or being attentive to Lady Peel in Whitehall Gardens. They knew he was Member for Pontefract and came from Yorkshire, but they did not bother about the importance of this connexion in his personal life. Letters of Yorkshire gossip from his mother and of political judgements from his father, letters from the aunts Louisa, Jane and Caroline, and from his sister Harriette; letters, too, from his Pontefract constituents, protesting, suggesting, petitioning, flowed into the rooms at 26 Pall Mall. With the letters came hampers, lovingly packed by Mrs. Milnes, containing game-pies and plovers' eggs and 'household bread.' Peaches and strawberries from the Fryston strawberry-beds came too when they were in season, and he would send boxes of these round in his carriage to Caroline Norton or some other friend.

These letters and these hampers must have been comforting at times. It was a brittle and even a lonely career upon which Milnes had now deliberately embarked, and in fact he proved too warm-hearted and enthusiastic to achieve real renown in the frosty worlds of fashion and of politics. 'This existence,' he wrote down in his little crimson-leather commonplace book for 1840, 'is melancholy with all its splendours. A life of immense acquaintance, without friendship and without love.'

Chapter Six

1840

I

'Society is unhinged by her majesty's marriage,' Charles Dickens wrote in February 1840 to Landor,[1] then grumbling away in his house at Bath. Dickens himself was indeed unhinged by this great event, or at any rate in a state of high excitement about it. Accepting his first invitation to breakfast at 26 Pall Mall on 7 February, three days before the royal wedding (and by a coincidence his own twenty-eighth birthday), he took the opportunity to send to Richard Monckton Milnes transcriptions of the songs being sung (he said) in the London streets:

> So let 'em say, whate'er they may
> Or do whate'er they can;
> Prince Hallbert he will always be
> My own dear Fancy man.

These and other verses were coupled with an extemporised conversation about 'Saxe-Humbug' and 'Go-to-Her' in the vein of Sam Weller, but rather coarser than the young novelist's reading public might have relished. Dickens' jokes were mild in comparison with the examples of club wit (mostly turning upon the Queen's virginity) which Milnes was himself inscribing—some words indicated by a modest dash—in his daybook; and not in his daybook only.

You peril my reputation [wrote Robert Monteith from Carstairs in February]. I receive notelets from you containing the last indecencies on the subject of Royal venery; I burn with chaste and loyal indignation, shout with laughter & end with showing the documents right & left. . . . How different our own simple provincial spirit! How sincere was the mighty bonfire I raised on a hill top—how spontaneous the gush of ale & porter which it cost 9 men's toil to distribute, how cordial the vibrations of the catgut to which 800 people danced & reeled like Baal worshippers round the blazing summit, how keen the aspiration of the up-flung rockets! How our poor villagers lit their windows—every pane

[1] *The Letters of Charles Dickens*, edited by Walter Dexter (Nonesuch Press, 1938), vol. ii, No. 248.

in a glow! While you representatives of an enthusiastic people
with your hearts shrivelled with meanness & envy & hate & com-
petition & debauchery could only make bawdy charades on this
solemn sowing of a new Royal tree. Do you mean to insinuate
he has dared to touch her? . . . You M.P.s must know better of
course—we never thought anything could have happened so soon.

Milnes was one of the few public men of that time who did
not allow the contemporary sentimentality about royal personages
to queer his views. By 1840 the demure tone of the new reign
was becoming noticeable. Admiration for its morality was
succeeding the ridicule and hatred which George IV had brought
down upon the throne and which had been violently revived
by the case of Lady Flora Hastings. There were not many people
to whom Carlyle could say, as he said to Milnes in 1844, that
he found the Queen 'much too infatuated a phenomenon for my
mind to dwell upon: those two dumpling faces in all the shop
windows make one sick in the street.' Milnes himself, who had
no patience with cant, remained aloof and critical. When the
whole nation was mourning the Prince Consort in 1862, and the
campaign to present him to posterity as a sanctified Maecenas was
already in full swing, Milnes wrote to George Bunsen (the son of
his old friend the Chevalier) in Germany:

There is a very true feeling of regret among all politicians for
Prince Albert's death. It is they who will be the real sufferers:
he did very little for Art, or Science or Literature (notwithstanding
all the puff) but he was of inestimable value as an intermediary
person between Ministers and our excellent but not clever Queen.

When Guizot dined at Windsor [1] a month after the Queen's
marriage he found the pattern of domestic royal life already set;
a pattern with which the reminiscences of several ladies-in-waiting
have made us only too familiar. The Queen sat upon a sofa before
a round table, sewing. Prince Albert played chess. Conversation
was 'neither animated nor interesting,' and Guizot was left to
carry on a flagging duologue with Lady Palmerston. He noticed
that over the three doors to the drawing-room were three portraits—
Fénelon, Peter the Great, and Anne Hyde. Intrigued by this
incongruous collection, he asked the reason for the arrangement.
Nobody had noticed it before. Nobody could tell him why they
were there. He suggested that it was because they were paintings
of the same size. Everyone agreed that might be so.
As soon as the new French ambassador had settled into Hertford
House, Manchester Square, a fine house (though with a gravel

[1] Guizot, *op. cit.*

courtyard and a dank garden) which was then being used as the French Embassy, mounds of notes and visiting cards began to pile up. Amongst these notes was a letter from Rio, introducing his distinguished friend, the poet and Conservative member of Parliament, Mr. Monckton Milnes. Milnes had written to Rio to claim this introduction, and had been warned not to be pained if he found Guizot's manners cold—'they are so to everyone, even to Louis Philippe' wrote Rio. Whether Milnes did find the ambassador's reception uncordial we do not know. He was well accustomed to the frigid manner of Sir Robert Peel and in any case he had enough conversational warmth himself to do for two people. Milnes was never deterred by the coldness, shyness or formality of the eminent.

The acquaintance with Guizot, which began in this way in the spring of 1840, developed into a genuine, even a rather close friendship. It was especially valuable to Milnes during the next five or six years. Guizot, like himself a Conservative (his father had been guillotined during the Terror), was at this time fifty-three. He was a small, alert man with a stern and bony face. Guizot and Thiers were the two greatest names in the politics of the July Monarchy. They had co-operated for the first time in the Cabinet of 1832, and Guizot had now been sent to England by Louis-Philippe to counterbalance Russian influence in London. England, under Palmerston's truculent guidance, was supporting Turkey, while France stood by Mahomet Ali. During this summer Guizot and Palmerston succeeded in fixing up an agreement, the Convention of London, which deprived Mahomet Ali of everything but Egypt and returned Syria to the Porte. Even so, a near-war situation—or, in Milnes' realistic view, a *paix armée*— persisted between England and France right on into the summer of the next year, when Guizot and Louis-Philippe managed to end it with the signature of the Treaty of London in July 1841. Throughout 1840 and early 1841 the Whig Government was slowly disintegrating, while the Opposition led by Peel gathered resolution and energy day by day. Palmerston believed war with France to be sooner or later unavoidable, whereas Peel shared with Guizot the view that this would be the worst possible calamity for both countries. In October 1840, Guizot was recalled to Paris to become Foreign Minister (and, on Soult's retirement, Prime Minister) in Louis Philippe's new Cabinet. For the next eight years he was the dominating personality in French politics—incorruptible, commanding, high-minded, severe. In the Revolution of 1848 he escaped across the Channel and stayed in England one year. He then retired to live on his lands at Val Richer, an Augustine monastery near Lisieux in Normandy. Monckton Milnes stayed at Val Richer in August 1857 and again in 1866. He described it (in a letter to his wife written during his first visit) as

quite a country-house, with a well-kept garden, and a good deal of land about. . . . It was an old abbey which M. Guizot bought for an old song, and gutted entirely, except a long gallery (now full of books), into which all the rooms open, and which has given me the notion of putting book-cases in the gallery at the top of the stairs at Fryston.

In Normandy and in Paris Guizot led a life of quiet scholarship, in the midst of his family, until his death twenty-six years later in 1874. He never once complained of his eclipse or strove to get back into power, but for all his purity and earnestness of purpose he was as much abused as any other French politician. 'Pray don't look upon me as a friend and supporter of Guizot, if it is him you mean by "that good and pure man,"' Charles de Montalembert wrote to Milnes in November 1840; 'we call him *l'austère intriguant.*' 'Monsieur Guizot me fait toujours l'effet d'un mauvais prêtre,' said Tocqueville to Milnes in Paris that same winter. 'Comme Robespierre était le meilleur des mauvais gens, Monsieur Guizot est le pire entre les bons gens,' he was told by Sainte-Beuve.

Upon the French question of 1840–41 (as upon most other problems just then) Milnes was an eager supporter of Peel and opponent of Palmerston. 'A war between France and England is in fact the great civil contest of civilisation itself,' he reflected, 'the fratricidal duel of the two favourite sons of Providence.' When Guizot had gone back to France in October 1840, Milnes began to send him letters on English politics. Often accused by his old Cambridge friends of being a lazy correspondent, Milnes was at his best writing long surveys of the political scene for foreign statesmen. From Guizot he received lengthy and informative replies. Guizot liked Milnes extremely; it was not only an official and practical friendship, though Milnes undoubtedly thought the connexion useful—he had now fixed on the Under-Secretaryship for Foreign Affairs as his political goal. Guizot too found it a help to receive astute reports upon the state of House of Commons feeling from someone who knew what he was talking about—for Milnes was bound in the end to hear everything that was going on in ministerial or opposition circles. Refusing an invitation to Fryston in September 1840, on the grounds that the situation was too delicate for him to be able to leave London, Guizot wrote in dejection of the *mauvaises passions* now unleashed in England as in France. The prime role of any government, he said, should be to discourage these.

Mon cher Milnes, soyez en sûr, le premier devoir, la première habileté des hommes qui gouvernent, c'est de bien mesurer la valeur des questions, l'importance des choses, et de ne pas mettre dans l'enjeu mille fois plus que ne peut valoir le gain de la partie. C'est là la faute énorme qu'a faite en ceci Lord Palmerston.

If he could get away from London, he would go to his family in · Normandy:

Car, voyez-vous, la famille, la maison de la famille, les affections et les interêts de la famille, c'est là ce qui nous entoure et nous protége quand nous naissons, quand nous mourrons; c'est là le refuge sûr et doux auquel il faut toujours regarder et tenir dans toutes les vicissitudes de la vie.

Milnes' friendship with the French statesman was based on terms as simple as these. People in general, he observed, gave little license to Peel and Guizot, whereas they were quite ready to accept or applaud the tergiversations of Thiers and Palmerston. 'Grave and dogmatic' men like the two former statesmen were expected to be undeviatingly consistent. Milnes, who was never himself in any danger of being grave or dogmatic or consistent, had all the same a capacity for getting on with those who were so. He was not daunted by their austere attitude to life. In later years Guizot was always anxious to take any amount of trouble for friends of Richard Monckton Milnes when they were in Paris. It was, he said, the least return he could make for all Milnes' kindness to him in London in the summer months of 1840.

II

The season of 1840 was unfortunate for the Milnes family. On the 22nd of April in that year, Mr. and Mrs. Milnes set off from Fryston on their way to London, where they intended to stay till June. They spent one night at Manchester ('a bad Inn, a bad dinner, and a bad bed, and all dear!' Mrs. Milnes recorded in the journal, which had now reached its second volume). They rose early next morning and went by rail to Birmingham, posting thence to Cheltenham Spa, where Richard joined them for a few days. After Richard's return to London they made an expedition on the 1st of May, with the Galways, to Malvern. And at Malvern they agreed to mount the hills to see the famous view across the orchards of Herefordshire to the Black Mountains. Harriette and her mother were carried up the hill in chairs. Lord Galway rode a donkey. Mr. Milnes rode a pony.

I seemed to have a sort of presentiment about it [Mrs. Milnes observed afterwards]. . . . I was the first and shall never forget it. No pen can write or words express my feelings! I saw Mr. Milnes riding up the hill on the grass and called out to him to beg he would keep the path. I had hardly done so when he arrived at the top, the ground fell in, the horse could not recover itself and threw Mr. Milnes and fell back upon him. Oh what an awful moment!

She and Harriette rushed down to get a surgeon ('I know not how Harriette and I ran from top to bottom of that steep hill in our agony'). Mr. Milnes was moved into a first-floor room of the inn. Richard was sent for. His father had decided to die.

Mr. Milnes did not die. After being heavily bled, given lavish doses of morphine, and placed in a 'water-bed,' he slowly improved. By midsummer he could hobble about on crutches, but although he lived another eighteen years he was never the same man again. For the rest of his life he was subject to spasms, headaches and long bouts of intense lethargy and melancholia, interrupted by periods in which he would seem as spry and caustic as before. Henceforth his physical and mental vagaries were now a cause of perpetual concern to his family.

III

On coming back from Malvern, satisfied that his father was not at death's door, Milnes resumed a life of busy sociability. On the last day of May he formed one of a company assembled at Gore House to hear Lady Blessington's latest protégé, Franz Liszt. The actor Macready, who made a note of this evening in his diary,[1] thought Liszt the most marvellous pianist he had ever heard ('I do not know when I have been so excited'), but Milnes seems to have been more intrigued by the rumour that 'Litzt,' as he called him, had already 'killed' two London pianofortes under him. The presence of Liszt at Gore House was in itself an example of Lady Blessington's determination as well as of her charm. The young pianist had reached London on the 7th of May; by the 9th his success was as great as that of Paganini in 1831; on the 13th he refused to be presented to Lady Blessington, about whom very disagreeable things were being said in Paris. On the 15th d'Orsay called to invite him to Gore House; he found this singular, but concluded that 'they' had heard he did not wish to know them. Two days later he had been there, Lady Blessington had said 'Quel dommage de mettre un pareil homme au piano,' and her

---

[1] *Diaries of W. C. Macready*, edited by William Toynbee (Chapman & Hall, 1912), vol. ii, pp. 63–4.

conquest was complete. From then on, for the rest of his stay in
London, Liszt was perpetually in and out of the house at Kensington.[1] Lady Blessington told him he looked like Bonaparte but
also like Lord Byron, while d'Orsay drew his portrait 'for publication.' The united technique of this couple was irresistible. They
used a combination of charm and iron-clad impudence against
which the disapproval of staid London society was powerless.
The technique used on Liszt had already been practised, in a
lesser degree, upon Milnes over his 1838 volume of poems. In
April 1838 Crabb Robinson confessed that he was gratified to
think Milnes had refused to send his new poems to Lady Blessington (whom at that moment he scarcely knew).[2] A month
later, and Milnes had done so, and become, as we have seen,
an habitué of the sumptuous drawing-room at Gore House.

Though Richard Milnes was always ready to go to mondain
concerts or recitals like that of Liszt, and was a person to whom
foreign musicians such as Hector Berlioz were recommended when
they first visited London,[3] he was not particularly musical. In
Milan, egged on by ennui and by the influence of his mother and
sister, both of whom had well-trained voices and a passionate
interest in opera, he had gone fairly regularly to a box at the Scala.
No doubt he went at times to Covent Garden or the Paris Opera.
But musically he was a philistine and in his younger days he was
quite as happy singing himself, for he had a good baritone voice.
He would sing in Yorkshire country-houses after dinner, choosing
the sentimental songs then popular—*I am married to a mermaid at the
bottom of the sea* or his own *Beating of my own heart* and *The Old
Manorial Hall.*

In May 1840 Richard's great-aunt, old Lady Cork, died. He
sometimes said that he intended writing a sketch of the character
and reminiscences of this astonishing nonagenarian, but for this,
as for many of his other literary projects (a memoir of George
Darley, for example), he lacked both energy and concentration.
Few Victorians could have left pithier verdicts than Milnes on
their contemporaries, but his poetry and occasional articles such
as that on Emerson took up all the time that he did not spend
reading, speaking in Parliament, dealing with constituents, or
just talking his life away in the drawing-rooms and the clubs.

[1] *Correspondance de Liszt et de Madame d'Agoult* (Bernard Grasset, 1934).
[2] *H. C. Robinson on Books and their Writers*, edited by Edith J. Morley (J. M.
Dent & Sons, 1938), vol. ii, p. 549.
[3] A letter of 19 June (? 1848) from Paul Grimblot begs Milnes to interest
himself in Berlioz' forthcoming concert in the Hanover Square Rooms, and explains
that Berlioz, being a genius, often has no *savoir-faire* and if left to himself would
starve.

In June of this year a fourth volume of his verse appeared, with the title *Poetry for the People*.[1] It was chiefly composed of pieces already published in the magazines. Despite its title it was not markedly democratic in character.

I think it ought to be entitled *Poetry for the World* instead of *for the People* [wrote Lady Blessington on 30 June], as it addresses itself to every mind, ay and heart too, that has a spark of intelligence in the one or goodness in the other. . . . Accept my congratulations on this new leaf to your wreath of bays.

At this moment Milnes was much taken up with the fashionable craze of mesmerism.[2] This interest, with its combination of novelty and sensationalism, was exactly the kind of thing to catch his attention and even to hold it for a few weeks. At the beginning of July he submitted himself to an experience then very usual to Londoners: he went to see a man hanged.

IV

'The greatest poet in the House of Commons came here yesterday morning at half-past three, and we drove together in his famous fly . . . to Newgate to see Courvoisier killed,' Thackeray wrote to a friend on 7 July 1840.[3] The experience of seeing Lord William Russell's murderer hanged before an audience of forty thousand people proved too much for Thackeray's sensibilities. For two weeks afterwards he kept brooding upon the young Frenchman's face, and the thought of what he had witnessed lay as heavily upon his conscience, he said, as cold plum-pudding on the stomach. To 'work it off' he settled down to write an article on the hanging. This paper, published in Fraser's Magazine for August, under the heading *Going to See a Man Hanged*, describes the scene in lurid detail.

Thackeray's essay [4] opens with a statement that Milnes (called 'X——' throughout) had suggested the expedition, a fact borne out by Thackeray's note of acceptance from Coram Street: 'Dear Milnes, I shall be very glad to make one at the hanging and shall expect you here.' The essay explains that Milnes had voted for

[1] *Poetry for the People, and other Poems*, by Richard Monckton Milnes (London: Edward Moxon, Dover Street, 1840).

[2] A letter in *Mrs. Brookfield and Her Circle*, by C. & F. Brookfield (Pitman, 1906), vol. i, p. 47, refers to Milnes' passion for mesmerism. He wrote a comic poem on Alexis the Mesmerist entitled *Mesmerism in London*, a manuscript of which is in the possession of Mr. John S. Mayfield of Washington, who has kindly supplied me with a photostatic copy.

[3] Letter from Thackeray to Mrs. Proctor, *Letters & Private Papers of W. M. Thackeray*, ed. Gordon N. Ray (Oxford University Press, 1945), vol. i, p. 454.

[4] Reprinted among Thackeray's *Sketches and Travels in London* and bound up with *The Book of Snobs* in the Smith Elder uniform edition of his works.

William Ewart's motion for the abolition of capital punishment,[1] and was anxious to gauge the effect of a public hanging upon the public mind. Thackeray refused to sit up the night before the hanging; he went to bed and tried to sleep normally, but by the time Milnes and one or two friends arrived at half-past three in the morning he had hardly succeeded in sleeping at all. Milnes and his companions had been at their club, and they arrived in high spirits to eat cold fowl in Thackeray's lodgings and to drink a cup of coffee followed by sherry and soda water. At four they set off for Snow Hill in Milnes' carriage, which was newly upholstered in a fawn-coloured silk. As the carriage (one of its occupants puffing a cigar) rattled through the sleeping streets, the dawn broke over London, over the cool clean streets and the leafy trees in the trim squares. There was dew on the grass in Gray's Inn and the window-panes of the old brick houses there reflected the sunrise as a sheet of flame. As the carriage turned into Holborn they came upon sudden signs of activity. The keepers of the gin-shops were taking down their shutters, and squalid, silent crowds were flocking out of the pubs and on towards Newgate, their shadows (Thackeray writes) showing blue and elongated on the pavements behind them as they shuffled eastward into the rays of the rising sun. As Milnes' carriage neared the prison he and his companions felt 'a dumb electric shock': for there before them stood the great black gallows jutting up in the morning air. Getting out of the fly they elbowed their way into the crowd, a 'gentle, good-humoured crowd,' and stood talking and listening for the next four hours. The windows of all the neighbouring houses had been hired out for the occasion. All the roads and pavements were densely thronged. Standing there watching and waiting, Thackeray was impressed by the greasy, dissolute, faded air of most of the young people—chiefly members of the criminal classes—all about him. This was the real London underworld, he reflected, an underworld contrasting most sharply with Dickens' idealised portrait-types, such as Nancy, the thief's mistress. Boz, he said in his article, did not dare tell this truth. Thackeray's descriptions of some of the characters in the crowd are far closer to the brilliant, sordid realism of Arthur Morrison than they are to Dickens' and Cruikshank's more acceptably comic or pathetic interpretations of poverty and vice.

Towards eight o'clock the sheriffs' carriages, gleaming in the sunshine, lumbered into view. As the clock struck eight Courvoisier was

---

[1] William Ewart (1798–1869), advanced liberal and free-trader, by whose efforts hanging in chains was abolished (1834) and capital punishment restricted (1837). In 1840 and later years he unsuccessfully proposed the abolition of capital punishment, in which Milnes supported him.

led on to the scaffold. Watching each hideous detail as the executioner pulled a black nightcap over the young man's face, Thackeray confesses that he then shut his eyes. But nothing could obliterate from his mind the savage horror of what he had seen, the mingled curiosity and indifference of the crowd, the expression on the murderer's pale features. 'I feel myself ashamed,' he wrote boldly in *Fraser's*, 'at the brutal curiosity which took me to that brutal sight.'

Milnes' reaction to this experience may or may not have been the same as Thackeray's. For all his delicacy of feeling Milnes had a toughness which protected him from any too vivid appreciation of horror. He was essentially a lover of sensation. He had not yet developed the coarseness which Henry Adams, Richard Burton and others noted (and rather admired) in him in the late eighteen-fifties and sixties; but even at this earlier epoch he was already collecting autographs and woodcuts of Courvoisier, of Calcraft the common hangman, and of other notorieties connected with crime or its punishment. In after years the Fryston library contained an enormous quantity of criminal trials—far more than the usual complement of a country-house library of the day. Amongst these ranks of well-bound books on murder were a series of brown-paper scrap-albums with the letters and relics of particularly odious criminals pasted in, accompanied by newspaper accounts of their careers. In Monckton Milnes, as in many other reformers, a desire to correct or alleviate some form of crime or of injustice was coupled with a fascinated interest in its actual commission. Thus his wish to abolish the death penalty did not prevent his indulging his bizarre taste for hangmen's autographs, and his later zeal for boys' reformatories went hand in hand with an interest in flogging and a collector's attitude to books on school punishments. There was nothing secretive about Milnes' attitude to these matters. On Sunday mornings at Fryston he would sometimes amuse himself by watching his guests recoil before a piece of the dried skin of a notorious murderer, which he kept pressed between the pages of some appropriate book.

Thackeray's humane article and Milnes' continued activities against public hanging made no immediate impression on London. In 1849 Dickens, who had 'considerable experience of executions,' [1] wrote his famous letter to *The Times* in which he described the 'wickedness and levity' of the crowd which had gone to see Mr. and Mrs. Manning hanged. At length, in 1868, a law was passed providing for the private or intramural execution of condemned criminals.

[1] *Charles Dickens*, by Una Pope-Hennessy (Chatto and Windus, 1945).

V

In September 1840 Richard rejoined his family at Fryston, after
a tour of visits in the south-west, which included staying with Henry
Hallam, the father of his dead friend Arthur, and with Sydney
Smith and his wife at Combe-Florey in the shady vale of Taunton.
The Sydney Smiths lived in a pretty vicarage, with a wrought-iron
balcony and a walled garden with fruit-trees in it and circular
flower-beds, and rustic hoops and arches over which rambler roses
trailed. From Combe-Florey Milnes went on to the splendours of
Stowe, where he met the Queen Dowager Adelaide. He saw her
again a few days later at Alton Towers. The autumn passed
normally in a series of balls at York, an expedition to Hull to hear
an oratorio, and the coming and going of guests at Fryston. The
visit to Sydney Smith, whose famous wit he greatly admired,
recording numberless examples of it in his notebooks, was a triumph
for Milnes' perseverance. He had long suspected that the rector of
Combe-Florey was the originator of some of the taunting nicknames
by which he himself had first been known in London. The conviction did not perish during his stay in Somerset, where he had invited
himself. Some months afterwards he sent Sydney Smith an irritated
letter accusing him of inventing these unpleasing names. Sydney
Smith's answer was a masterpiece of urbanity and common sense.

Never lose your good temper, which is one of your best qualities
[he wrote], and which has carried you hitherto safely through your
startling eccentricities. If you turn cross and touchy you are a
lost man. . . . The names . . . are, I give you my word, not
mine. They are of no sort of importance; they are safety valves,
and if you could by paying sixpence get rid of them you had
better keep your money.

The Yorkshire autumn which followed his visits in the West may
have proved altogether too authentic for Richard. At any rate he determined that so soon as Parliament rose in November he would set off
for Paris, stay there some weeks and, relying on the friendships he had
formed with Montalembert, Rio and Guizot (now Foreign Minister),
burrow his way as far as he could into the warrens of French political,
literary and social life. By September 1840 it was obvious that the
Melbourne Government was doomed. A Tory Ministry under Peel
must come in during 1841. Now Peel would need an Under-Secretary of State for Foreign Affairs—and whom could he find more
suitable than his ardent and travelled young friend and admirer, the
Tory member for Pontefract? These were undoubtedly the arguments that led Richard, after a slight havering induced by the fear of
an outbreak of war, to board the Channel packet in the first days of
December 1840 and to take, at Boulogne, the diligence for Paris.

I

The Boulogne diligence, a ponderous vehicle loaded with passengers, its roof piled high with luggage, took twenty-five hours to cover the distance between Boulogne and Paris. It entered the capital by the Faubourg St. Denis in the early morning, passing beside but not beneath the high stone gateway of the Porte St. Denis (decorated with the solemn carved allegories dating from the reign of Louis Quatorze), and clattered on down the Rue de Bourbon Villeneuve, harness jingling, postilions screeching, till it rumbled to a standstill in the coaching-yard at the bottom of the Rue St. Eustache. In this yard, which was in a continual turmoil from the arrival and departure of coaches to the provinces, a bevy of hotel servants waited to swoop upon the English travellers. Thackeray, who described the arrival of the Boulogne diligence in his *Paris Sketchbook* (1839–40), writes of the raucous cries of the hotel touts, and pauses to indicate the merits of the chief Parisian hotels. If you could not speak one syllable of French, liked clean rooms, an English breakfast of boiled eggs and grilled ham, profuse but lukewarm dinners, and a society composed of English undergraduates, young English merchants out on a lark, clergymen's widows, lawyers' clerks, officers of dragoons and Lord Brougham he advised the Hôtel Meurice. If you preferred the best *table d'hôte* in the city, but heavy bills, the Hôtel des Princes. Among other possible hotels he listed the Mirabeau, Lawson's and the Hôtel de Lille. Richard Milnes, who had always stayed at the Meurice with his family as a youth, chose it again. On each of his many visits to Paris during the remainder of his life he stayed there too, so that the shallow arcades of the Rue de Rivoli and the lime-tree tops in the Tuileries Gardens across the street came to represent Paris in his mind. Thackeray wrote that you could get a decent room at the Meurice for three francs a day. Milnes took one (or perhaps a suite) at eight. His bill for the seven weeks of his stay, which included breakfast, the frequent hire of a cabriolet, wood for the open fire, seventy-two bottles of seltzer water and a good many messengers sent hither and thither—to Galignani, to Guerlain, to the Ministère des Affaires Etrangères, or to get seats at the Opera—came to nearly 1,500 francs.

Milnes reached the Hôtel Meurice on the morning of 8 December, sent round a note to Guizot at his office, and settled down to make the most of his visit.   Guizot replied the same morning, warmly, and inviting him to dine the next evening but one.   Milnes, however, was made aware of the acid hostility which Palmerston's handling of the Near East question had aroused in France.   Montalembert had written to assure him that there was no immediate danger of war, but he added the warning that they were all 'dreadfully exasperated' against England. Mrs. Grote, who knew Paris well, had refused point-blank to give him any introductions at this moment.

I do solemnly assure you that I should have need of all the influence I possess, among the French, to procure for *myself* a tolerably courteous reception at the present juncture. . . . I know you like agitated waters and therefore marvel not that you select this time as a time for mingling in the society of our neighbours, but I fear your character of M.P. and Tory together is not well calculated to propitiate the women, under existing circs, and at *Paris* the women are no cyphers. . . . I have letters from French persons which afflict me sorely.   I see no pleasure will henceforth attend any visit of mine to Paris.   The good feeling between us is, I fear me, annihilated.

She ended a long letter by a half-promise to arrange for him to meet George Sand.   Milnes had selected a stimulating rather than an auspicious moment in which to embark upon Parisian life.

Thackeray, who had passed a good deal of time in Paris without getting either to like or understand the French, and who persisted in writing of them in tones of adolescent ridicule, was declaring at this time that there was only one thing for the English to remember while in France—'that they hate us.'   Thackeray, who was as English in temperament as he was in appearance, detested French manners as much as he despised French literature—or at any rate the contemporary French novelists such as Balzac and Madame Sand.   He was living in this winter of 1840 in the Faubourg du Roule, to be near the *maison de santé* in which his young wife was confined.   Milnes was kind-hearted, and it may have been Thackeray's anxiety over Isabella that now made him, for the first time, appreciate 'Dicky Milnes.'[1]   He found Milnes 'amazingly

[1] Thackeray's opinion of Monckton Milnes fluctuated. The anonymous writer of a hostile sketch of Lord Houghton in *Truth* (in a series called *Anecdotal Photographs*) in October 1882 wrote: 'Thackeray in his cruel moods sometimes called his Lordship a Miss Nancy, and said that nothing irritated him more than to see him strive to get into the orbit of a very great man.   The author of *Vanity Fair* used sometimes to amuse himself at those convivial meetings at "the Deanery," which he attended once a month, in sketching the lions of the day as they would, he imagined, appear (should they live so long) a quarter of a century later.   He chose to give Monckton Milnes the make-up of an old Polonius.   In his more genial moods he liked him vastly.'

clever,' he wrote, simple, affectionate and 'eager to do good offices.' He did not 'talk big' and even if he was affecting 'to take an extraordinary degree of interest in the person before him, why it's a good affectation at any rate, and better than the common cursed indifference.' Milnes introduced Thackeray (who was making an effort to forget his wife's condition) to a charming young married Irishwoman from Norfolk, whose freshness and enthusiasm delighted him. With Thackeray, Milnes witnessed the second funeral of Napoleon in the Invalides, a ceremony for which the streets of Paris were brilliantly decked with banners, with gilt imperial eagles and with plaster goddesses in lines. Thackeray described the funeral in a newspaper article, and Milnes composed a stirring ballad of eleven stanzas:

All nature is stiff in the chill of the air,
The sun looks around with a smile of despair;
'Tis a day of delusion, of glitter and gloom,
As brilliant as glory, as cold as the tomb.

The pageant is passing—the multitude sways—
Awaiting, pursuing, the line with its gaze,
With the tramp of battalions, the tremor of drums
And the grave exultation of trumpets he comes.

It passes! what passes? He comes! who is He?
Is it Joy too profound to be uttered in glee?
Oh, no! it is Death, the Dethroner of old,
Now folded in purple and girded with gold!

It is Death, who enjoys the magnificent car,
It is Death, whom the warriors have brought from afar,
It is Death, to whom thousands have knelt on the shore,
And·sainted the bark and the treasure it bore.

From legion to legion the watchword is sped—
'Long life to the Emperor—life to the dead!'
The prayer is accomplished—his ashes remain
'Mid the people he loved, on the banks of the Seine.

In dominions of Thought that no traitor can reach,
Through the kingdoms of Fancy, the regions of Speech,
O'er the world of Emotions, Napoleon shall reign
'Mid the people he loved, by the banks of the Seine.

It was only a quarter of a century since Waterloo, but English sentiment about Napoleon was already changing. In another fifteen years Queen Victoria herself led the little Prince of Wales to pay homage at the tomb of 'Buonaparte' in the Invalides.

Milnes and Thackeray went together to see the youthful actress
Rachel (then in the second year of her startling fame) in the new
French version of Schiller's *Marie Stuart*. With F. O. Ward, an
English journalist (a disciple of the socialist Charles Fourier and a
lifelong friend of Monckton Milnes), and with one or two more
compatriots they formed a little 'set' centring round the Meurice.
'I passed by Meurice's, and it occurred to me that we had a pleasant
time altogether,' Ward wrote from Paris in 1850, reminding Milnes
of that damp but gay Parisian winter then ten years past.

In spite of the sweeping reconstructions carried out in Paris
under Napoleon III, it is easier to imagine the appearance of
Paris in 1840 than it is to picture London at the same period.
In 1840 Montmartre was still a village with a ragged row of
windmills against the skyline; there were hooded booths down
both sides of the Pont Neuf; the Opera, which had been built
in 1821, was in the Rue Le Peletier, a glassed-in passageway
leading to the salle from the stuccoed façade; Notre Dame was
masked at its western end by the old Hôtel-Dieu; a monstrous sus-
pension bridge, the Pont Louis-Philippe, straddled the river at one
point. To enter Paris from the country you had to pass the
barrières, at which everything you possessed was scrutinised by
customs officials wearing green uniforms, and where there was
always a jam of country-carts and peasants' baskets and mail-
coaches and post-chaises. But in its essential aspects Paris was the
same then as it is to-day—the sinking sun blazed in the same way
through the Arc de l'Etoile, and was mirrored in the same way in
the glittering windows of the palace of the Louvre. The fountains
shimmered in the Place de la Concorde. The Chevaux de Marly
pranced in the clear morning light. The steep, garlanded
dome of the Invalides stood out against the afternoon sky. The
Seine lapped at the stone *quais*. The chestnuts and the elms and
lime-trees (dripping rain from their bare branches that wet December) lined the Champs Elysées and the nineteen boulevards.

The precarious political situation was having, in that winter of
1840, one visible effect on Paris. Fortifications were being rapidly
thrown up, but no one would confess to Milnes their precise purpose. Guizot told him that their great value was that the Parisians
would never need to use them. Montalembert pointed out that
they were being built in a typically democratic manner, by cutting
down the trees of the Bois de Boulogne. A cabby sadly told him
that the Government were destroying the Bois—'et détruire, c'est
toujours joli.' The king, Louis-Philippe, explained that there had
always been and would always be in Paris a party strong enough
if supported by a foreign army to overthrow any Government.

This, he said, the fortification of Paris would prevent. The King and Guizot were together striving to maintain a policy of friendship with England which was deeply unpopular, and was the object of perpetual attacks in the Chambers and in the press. The work of Lord Granville, who had been at the head of the British Embassy in the Rue du Faubourg St. Honoré since 1824, was now highly complicated. The Granvilles were well established in Parisian life, and though there were always people waiting to criticise the Embassy (Montalembert complained to Milnes, for instance, that on a wet night his *fiacre* was not allowed to drive into the muddy Embassy courtyard), their entertainments were crowded and fashionable. Milnes dined, as a matter of course, at the Embassy and found Lady Granville's conversation sprightly: 'There is nothing so disagreeable as the type without the qualities,' she declared to him, 'a person with an open countenance that is not frank, or with a merry look who is dull.' One fancies that in Monckton Milnes she was not disappointed. His good-humour and his vivacity were famously apparent in his face.

One Paris activity of Milnes' which neither Lady Granville nor her husband would have approved was his custom of sending home letters to the leader of the English opposition, Peel. In these letters he transmitted, directly and *en clair*, messages to Peel from the King of the French and his Foreign Minister.

Tell Sir Robert Peel [the King told Milnes on one occasion] that I place all confidence in his declaration of the importance of the French alliance . . . and that I trust he can prevent any of his friends from injuring my position and that of my ministry.

'My ministry depends for its existence on the conduct of England,' Guizot chimed in. They both begged Milnes to emphasise to Peel (who they knew must soon succeed Melbourne as the head of the Government) that they dared take no steps towards disarmament. Milnes reported that Guizot was incredibly unpopular and the King quite distracted between his own love of peace and his conviction that his throne depended on popular faith in his nationalist tendencies. But if a Ministry urged him to war with England, Louis-Philippe told Milnes, he would break them or be broken by them. In one of his letters to Peel Milnes thoughtfully enclosed a plan of the Paris forts, which he had somehow obtained. Sir Robert replied in a friendly but distinctly non-committal manner.

I would have replied to your letters [he wrote at the end of January] but for two reasons—first the hazard of committing to the Post Office observations on such important and delicate subjects as those which you treated of, and secondly the possibility that you might have left Paris before my letter should arrive there.

The implied reproof in fact reached Milnes in London, to which he had returned after being delayed at Boulogne by a heavy storm. From Boulogne he sent a note to Guizot explaining that he could not be present at the moving of the Address, as he had hoped to be, but that he had sent Peel a full report of all that Guizot and the King had said.

II

In one of his *Paris Sketches* Thackeray made the point that it was impossible to get to know French people well. However often you saw your French acquaintances, you never got any more intimate with them. This may have been true for Thackeray himself, for his approach to the French was jovial, insular and impertinent. For Milnes, with his eagerness and alertness and his un-English ways, the case was different. He already had several good friends in Paris. Montalembert, now a friend of nine years' standing, was anxious to repay the hospitality Milnes had often shown him in London. At that moment in the throes of house-moving, he was lodging in a room in the Rue St. Dominique; but he took Milnes about, to the Lamartines' Saturdays, to Thiers' evening receptions, to dine quietly with Rio at the Hôtel des Ministres in the Rue de l'Université. With Lamartine Milnes struck up an acquaintance-ship based on what the French poet grandiloquently called the confraternity of poetry and the confraternity of the tribune. By another of his new friends he was taken to see the Raphaels, Veroneses and Zurbarans in the collection of Aguado, and it was during this winter that he first met George Sand, though his friendship with her came eight years later. Everywhere he went he found the French criticising their government, their politicians and each other. Madame Sand made in his presence an elaborate joke about the marches played at Napoleon's funeral. Montalem-bert told him that the presence of Louis-Philippe on the throne was like putting up a grocer and his family to be shot at. Lamennais (no longer a priest) said that the French were now engaged on a terrible experiment—to find the best method by which a Government could murder a people. Milnes was not dazzled by this golden shower of French wit. He discerned the serious situation behind the discontent and the badinage, and he came away from his first visit to Paris impressed by the intensity and the 'gravity' of the young Frenchmen he had met.

This impression was largely due to one new friend he made that winter—Alexis de Tocqueville. Tocqueville was at this time thirty-five. In appearance he was dark-haired and sensitive, with a delicate oval face and a grave, steady gaze. He had published *Democracy in America* in 1835, and four years later he was elected deputy for his local town in Normandy, Valognes. For ten years after his election he was entirely swallowed up in political life, which ended with his four-month period of office as Minister of Foreign Affairs after the fall of the July Monarchy in 1848. He has been described as remote, exact, and astringent, with an underflow of melancholy in his character and 'a strange desolated sense of the extinction of his class.'[1] His class was that of the country gentry, and all his affections gathered round the old granite château at Tocqueville, near Cherbourg, with its solid tower, its dovecote and its rooms dating from the reign of Louis Douze. Milnes, who stayed with him there in later years, referred to the tranquillity of that life in Normandy in an article on his friend in a *Quarterly*[2] of 1861, when Tocqueville had been dead two years. He tells how he would walk with Tocqueville through the lanes of the Cotentin, as lush as those of Devonshire, the orchard trees shining with apples, in the squally, gloomy Norman weather; or they would make excursions to the sea-coast: to La Hogue or Barfleur or to the lighthouse at Gatteville. How well Milnes understood Tocqueville's pre-eminent importance as a thinker and historian it is not easy to judge, for the article deals chiefly with his personality and political career. Lord Acton has compared the position of Tocqueville in France to that of Burke in England, and a more recent student of Tocqueville has called him the Prophet of the Mass Age.[3] One of his most significant contributions to historical thought was his theory that the Revolution of 1789 was still in progress, and would continue for many decades. In his *Souvenirs*, written in 1850 after his political eclipse and fully published for the first time in 1942, he predicted that Western Europe would one day be swamped by Russia. In these *Souvenirs*, which are in a sense his political testament, he mercilessly surveyed the men he had known during his years of public life. In tone this little book is chilling and bitter. Few of his friends were spared.

[1] See the illuminating chapter on Tocqueville in David Mathew's *Acton, the Formative Years* (Eyre and Spottiswoode, 1946).

[2] The article took the form of a review of the English edition of Tocqueville's letters: *Memoir, Letters, and Remains of Alexis de Tocqueville, Translated from the French by the Translator of Napoleon's Correspondence with King Joseph* (London, 1861). It was republished in Lord Houghton's *Monographs Social and Personal* (John Murray, 1873).

[3] J. P. Mayer: *Prophet of the Mass Age, a Study of Alexis de Tocqueville.*

About Milnes, to whom he was at that very moment writing letters of affectionate warmth, he is not altogether kind.

Milnes [we read] était un garçon d'esprit qui faisait et ce qui est plus rare, qui disait beaucoup de bêtises. Combien ai-je vu de ces figures dans ma vie dont on peut affirmer que les deux profils ne se ressemblent pas : hommes d'esprit d'un côté, et sots de l'autre.

In his *Quarterly* article Milnes admitted that some people might accuse Tocqueville of poverty of spirit and narrowness of perception; but he declared that his friend's greatest attribute was 'the singular unity of purpose pervading his whole moral and intellectual being.' Milnes may have first met Tocqueville in London in 1837, but it was not till the Paris winter of 1840 that he got to know him well. Tocqueville immediately treated him with exceptional courtesy, sending him books on the workings of the French constitution, taking him to see Barrot, or presenting him to the Comte de Tracy and his English wife. As soon as he had met Milnes in Paris Tocqueville wrote to say that he wished to do everything he could to make his stay useful and agreeable—both for his own sake and because he was convinced that the sole remaining chance of peace between England and France was to get to understand each other. But there was little about Milnes which Tocqueville, logical and aloof, could understand. He did not relish the paradoxes or like the enthusiasms; after all, it was he who wrote 'je n'ai jamais vu Milnes qu'engoué de quelqu'un ou de quelquechose.'

III

On his return from Paris, Milnes remained in London until Easter, when he went north. On this occasion he did not travel alone, for he had persuaded Thomas Carlyle (whose *Hero Worship* was then in corrected proof) to take a holiday from London and come to spend two weeks in the West Riding. Carlyle's visit to Fryston is well-documented by the long, descriptive letters he sent his wife. With his aid you are enabled to get inside that lost house for one moment and to look about you.

The new railway to the West Riding went through Derby. Here the travellers rested for the night. They had shared a carriage with Sir Robert Peel's son, who was on his way to Tamworth, Milnes read the *Oxford Tracts* all the way up in the train, arguing and talking 'in the smartest manner,' and Carlyle, gazing out at the fresh April fields and the clusters of cottages in the unspoilt countryside, had illegally smoked cigars. At Derby they sat up late in the travellers' room of the Royal Hotel, Milnes reading a tragedy of Landor's at one side of the table while Carlyle wrote to Jane at the other. Across the room two bagmen dined and talked. Overhead the gas jets blazed relentlessly.

The next day they reached their destination in the early afternoon, got out of the carriage two miles short of Fryston Hall, and walked thither by a short cut through the woods and over green and red fields which reminded Carlyle of Scotland and were bordered by unclipped hawthorn hedges in pink bud. As they drew near Fryston, standing amidst its ragged woods and rough wide park, Carlyle saw the figures of old ladies at the windows; in the hall Richard's mother, 'a tall ancient woman, apparently of weak health, of motherly kind heart, of old-fashioned stately politeness—a prepossessing woman' welcomed them at the drawing-room door. Carlyle won her heart at once by pointing to the smoking chimney-stacks of Fryston: 'these are indeed the wind-pipes of hospitality,' he said.

To Mrs. Milnes and to the three maiden aunts he was 'Mr. Carlyle, the Author,' one of Richard's odd literary friends. The eldest of the aunts, Louisa Milnes, had refused to listen to Carlyle's translation of *Wilhelm Meister* being read aloud at Fryston: 'a book about nothing but play-acting men and child-bearing women,' she had crisply remarked. But they all laid themselves out to be agreeable to their opinionated and insomniac guest. Richard's father spent much time alone in the library, smoking and ruminating, 'shrunken up, I daresay,' Carlyle speculated, 'in innumerable whims and half-diseased thoughts, though full of good nature. I like him very much.' It was explained to him that Mr. Milnes was greatly altered since the accident at Malvern, and he noticed that his flashes of wit and intelligence were interspersed with 'flashes of silence.' Harriette Galway, who came with her husband for two days of Carlyle's visit, seemed to him particularly sympathetic, 'decidedly worth something,' witty and with a sense of laughter. She sang and played, talked with Carlyle of German and Italian books she was reading, looked 'really beautiful' with her large blue eyes and her hair braided beneath a lace cap. She was petted by her family, teasingly addressed as 'ladyship' ('Will Ladyship have fowl?'), but seemed to survive the fussing and attention unspoiled. Lord Galway was dismissed as 'a furious everlasting hunter of foxes, but *good* to all other things and men.'

Carlyle was disturbed by the size of his bedroom, which he thought forty-five feet long, very high and wide, and filled with 'ancient, dead-looking portraits.' Four vast windows looked down into the silent garden, with its rhododendrons, stone coffin and cypress trees. He had little experience of English upper-class life, and he was vexed to find that the Milnes family dined at eight and breakfasted at half-past ten, when the post was handed round very publicly by a footman in red livery with a salver (Carlyle would smuggle his wife's letters out into the garden to read in privacy). Although he liked his hosts and was amused by them, he thought a country-house existence a great waste of time.

I never lived before in such an element of 'much ado about *almost* Nothing'; life occupied altogether in getting itself lived; troops of flunkeys bustling and becking at all times, the meat-jack creaking and playing all day . . . and such champagning, claretting and witty conversationing. *Ach Gott!* I would sooner be a ditcher than spend my life so.

He found, too, that he was expected to play the lion and allow himself to be provoked by Richard for the benefit of the local society. All the same the visit to Fryston increased his affection for his host. One day they rode over together to Wakefield, and Carlyle told Milnes he thought the picturesque 'a mere bore' and infinitely preferred simple hedges and fields. Milnes agreed that fundamentally he did so too. For the rest of the ride, as they galloped and trotted along the lanes, Milnes talked gaily about Puseyism, aristocracy, crypto-Catholicism and other unallied subjects. 'I like Richard better and better—a most goodhumoured, kind, cheery-hearted fellow, with plenty of savoir-faire in him too,' Carlyle told his wife. He was especially pleased by Richard's reply to the question 'Do you like Spenser's *Faery Queen?*': 'Is it as a public question that you ask me or as a private confidential one?' When the carriage rolled off from the doors of Fryston at eleven o'clock one April morning, taking Milnes and his guest to the station, Carlyle carried away with him warm memories of his stay. In the winter of that year he and Jane were travelling back to London by the Darlington railway. Suddenly as he looked out of the carriage window, in the moonlight, Carlyle saw that they were passing Castleford. He pointed out to Jane the woods of Fryston and the 'white *gazebo* under the gleam of the stars.'

IV

Begun in 1833, the series of Oxford *Tracts for the Times*, some of which Milnes was diligently studying in the railway carriage to Doncaster, came to a sudden stop in the year 1841. 'From the end of 1841 I was on my deathbed as regards my membership of the Anglican church,' wrote Newman in his *Apologia Pro Vita Sua*; for it was in that year that he had published his *Tract Ninety* (asserting that the Thirty-nine Articles did not oppose Catholic teaching and only partially opposed Roman dogma), had seen it condemned by his bishop and by the heads of houses, and had consequently suspended the production of any further Oxford Tracts. Richard Monckton Milnes was one of those who had been watching with a sympathetic eye the growth of that splendid and earnest regenerative movement within the English Church. He had admired Hurrell Froude's letters and notes, when these were published in 1837. He had been impressed by Pusey and by Newman. The emphasis on ritual and on the aesthetic aspect of religious observances appealed to him; and though not himself officially a Puseyite, he became furious at the attitude of the Church authorities towards *Tract Ninety*. He determined to publish something himself in the Tractarians' defence. For the booklet which he wrote, and which appeared soon after the withdrawal of Tract Ninety, he chose the short but provocative title— *One Tract More*.[1]

Most thinking persons in England had read one or more of the Oxford Tracts. Many people regarded it as a duty to read the whole series; though for those with a great deal to do it was proving almost too numerous—'I am very much in arrear with the Tracts,' wrote Sir Robert Peel to Milnes in June 1841. The *Tracts* had worried many people besides the Bishop of Oxford and the heads of houses; and the audacity with which 'an undistinguished and unconnected layman'—Milnes' own phrase—now took up what the Church authorities had denounced was almost sensational. More surprising still was the quality of *One Tract More*. Lord Jeffrey (hardly a lenient critic) called it 'the most masterly and admirable pamphlet of modern times'[2]; some years later Kinglake wrote of it as Milnes' best work. William Copeland, a distinguished Puseyite of that time, said it epitomised the whole movement:

you could not do better than take it as the key to the history of what we were doing then [he remarked in 1883[3]]; Lord Houghton

---

[1] *One Tract More or the System Illustrated by 'The Tracts for the Times' Externally Regarded*: by A Layman (London: printed for J. G. F. & J. Rivington, St. Paul's Churchyard, and Waterloo Place, Pall Mall, 1841). Although this tract made such an impression, apparently went into a second edition and was said by Milnes to be having 'a regular and quiet sale,' I have only been able to trace one example of it, that in the British Museum (a small octavo, bound in stiff purple boards with a white label; 89 pages; 2s. 6d.).

[2] In a letter to Lord Monteagle quoted in one from Aubrey de Vere to Milnes, dated 29 September (probably 1841).

[3] Letter from Copeland's nephew, the Rev. W. C. Borlase, November 1883. William Copeland (1804–1885) was a scholar of Trinity College, Oxford; he served as rector of Farnham, Essex, from 1849 until his death.

was one of those who were deeply interested in the Movement, and looked on from the outside, and treated us with respect and sympathy, and appreciated us and saw the historical connection between us and the past, while others could not or would not take the trouble to understand us.

Newman himself admired the Tract, and writes of it favourably in the *Apologia*.

The style of *One Tract More* is simple and persuasive. Its arguments are not tortuous, and the use of paradox (which makes others of Milnes' pamphlets seem frivolous) is cut down to a minimum. Starting from the premiss that the interest in 'Puseyism' was now widespread and no longer limited to 'theological schools' or 'ecclesiastical circles,' Milnes went on to point out that no unbiased essay on the subject existed.

There are not wanting [he wrote in his first few pages] able expositions of these principles nor vigorous attacks nor energetic replies; yet a fair criticism, presupposing no opinion, and implicating no doctrines, and simply inquiring into the true meaning of the matter, its relations to the past, its connexion with the present, and its tendencies for the future, may not readily be found, and it is the intention of the following pages in some degree to supply this deficiency.

He moved on to develop and analyse the theories of the relationship of Church to State which had been held in Europe both before and after the Reformation, and discussed the disadvantages of Roman Catholicism, Puritanism and ordinary Protestantism with an admirable detachment. There was much throughout the book to annoy bigots on all sides: he defended the Papal Infallibility as logical and even necessary under certain circumstances; he declared that in England the alleged pre-Reformation worship of stone and wooden images had merely been replaced by an equally ignorant worship of the words of the Bible; he wrote of the English Reformation as caused by the lusts of Henry VIII, by the rapacity of the Henrican nobility and by 'a sad intertexture of good and bad motives,' while admitting that the No-Popery feeling in England had 'twisted its roots into the crevices of many wrongs'; he defended Puseyism as having re-introduced religious fervour into the withering Anglican church, and boldly declared that it could not lead its followers into Roman Catholicism: a statement which in two years' time seemed ludicrously wrong. 'There have *not* been conversions from Puseyism to Romanism,' he wrote, 'while there have been conversions, and numerous ones, to Romanism from ultra-Protestantism.' But in general this little Tract is remarkable for its lucidity as well as for its entire lack of prejudice in any direction.

Amongst those who wrote to congratulate the author of *One Tract More* was William Gladstone.

I read your little book after my wife's party last night with great delight and warm admiration [he wrote in a letter dated Whit-Tuesday of 1841]; so much so that I would *not* write to thank you for it until I had this afternoon enjoyed an opportunity of looking over it again in cool blood to see that I might speak plain truth to you.

He praised the 'felicity' of Milnes' reasoning, 'the most profound appreciations and the strictest adherence to truth,' which he found throughout the book. He discussed, but rejected

a mean feeling, which happily is also a painful one, apt to find its way into the mind, when, after long struggles with one's own weakness and impotence for the mastering of a subject, one discovers that another person has by a quicker and a less toilsome ascent reached a more commanding point of view. I wish [Gladstone concluded] this were the alpha and not the omega of a series.

One Tract More forms the best single instance of Monckton Milnes' real capacity for thought and extreme adroitness of mind. But it did him no good with his dour Dissenting constituents. Milnes was the least calculating of men. He had written and published *One Tract More* as a protest against injustice and without thinking of the consequences to his political career.

V

On 4 June 1841 Melbourne's government fell at last. Its whole structure had been subsiding under a crushing weight of criticism for many months: it had involved the country in war with China and in an invasion of Afghanistan; it had earned the simultaneous enmity of France, Canada and the United States. England was discredited abroad and at home disrupted by anti-corn law and Chartist agitation. 'Deficits had become as annual as the harvest.' Working-class conditions were ghastly and getting quickly worse. The immediate cause of the Whig defeat in June was a no-confidence vote moved by Peel himself over the Government's proposals for averting the impending deficit for the financial year 1841–42. Although Peel's motion was only carried by a majority of one, Ministers dissolved and went to the country.

The Election generally will be a very severe one [Milnes wrote in a confidential note to Guizot], the changes on both sides very

numerous; and more members retiring altogether from Parliament
than have ever been known. . . . I do not think it impossible we
may return two conservatives for the West Riding.

His own election was not opposed, but he told Charles MacCarthy
that he looked forward with little pleasure to the new Parliament,
expecting it to be full of 'stupid violence and blind party spirit.'
The new Parliament met in August, and the Whigs found themselves in a minority of more than ninety. They were defeated on
an amendment to the Address and immediately resigned. Sir Robert
Peel now formed the famous Ministry which endured till 1846 and
which repealed the Corn Laws. It was described by Gladstone as
a perfectly organised administration.

Since the year 1832 Peel had set himself to create a new and
active Conservatism. From being mere defenders of the constitution the party had, under his guidance, taken up the cause of social
reform, and though it has been asserted that the reforming energy
was in the times rather than the Ministry, a number of important
reforms were passed in Peel's five years of office. In 1841 the
Conservative party included seven men who had been or were
destined to be Prime Ministers and five future Viceroys of India;
yet all these men looked to Peel to formulate their policy. The
new Cabinet consisted of fifteen members, with Lord Aberdeen as
Palmerston's successor at the Foreign Office. 'The two most
striking characteristics of the Government are no doubt its regard
for former official service and its observance of aristocratic connection,' Milnes told Guizot in a further exposition of the political
situation, in the late summer of 1841:

all the men who took the risks of office with Sir Robert Peel
in 1835 are amply rewarded. . . . Peel has now got so strong a
gripe of the aristocracy that he must either drag them along with
him in his advance or perish in the attempt.

He went on to explain that Peel had kept the distribution of offices
in his own hands, and he suggested that Guizot might therefore be
surprised that Milnes himself occupied no place. He said he felt
he had no right to complain, since Peel had retained the only really
enviable position—that of Under-Secretary for Foreign Affairs:[1]

I cannot help thinking [he added] that he might have trusted
to my discretion, but it is possible that Lord Aberdeen may have

---

[1] 'Further, the position of foreign affairs was so critical that it was arranged
that Peel should fulfil in the House of Commons the duties of an under-secretary
in that respect,' *Dictionary of National Biography*, vol. xv. The real Under-Secretary,
Lord Canning, was, like the Foreign Secretary himself, a member of the House
of Lords.

made some objection owing both to my known liberal inclinations in foreign matters and to the circumstance that a nephew of his Lordship's was very anxious to get the appointment.

Sir Robert Peel would not lose any support he could give him, Milnes added, though 'I cannot help wishing that he had been enabled to give his administration a more popular character.'

Though he could write thus reasonably and cheerfully of his disappointment, the fact that Peel gave him no job depressed Milnes terribly. He was now thirty-two, and he had been four years in Parliament. His friends and, worse still, his acquaintances had expected that he would get office in Peel's administration. 'I hear you are to be a Lord of the Treasury,' a fellow M.P. wrote in a letter of congratulation during August, while Mrs. Buller, the mother of his friends Arthur and Charles Buller, hurriedly wrote to offer him at a low price 'a very handsome and complete official dress' made for one of her sons to take to Canada but not worn more than twice.[1] It was bitter and exacerbating to be so publicly passed over; but for the moment his loyalty to Peel, though jarred, was not badly shaken. And it was always possible that the Prime Minister, for all his great physical powers, which enabled him to work for sixteen hours a day and to keep every subject of consequence under his own eye, might decide to surrender the Under-Secretary-ship. It was an unpleasing situation, but there was no reason to despair. If his father's health had been better, Richard would have discreetly withdrawn to the Continent, but Mr. Milnes remained ailing and unpredictable, and Richard spent the summer and autumn with his parents in the West Riding. It was the first big disappointment of his political career, and with his volatile temperament Milnes was easily cast down. Peel's indifference to his merits began to canker all his life and even his non-political activities. Here was the first suspicion that he could be a failure. The dangers Stafford O'Brien had foreseen at Cambridge a decade ago took on a shadow of reality: 'I think you are near something very glorious but you will never reach it.' In this mood of despair he turned to Mrs. Norton for encouragement; an undated letter from that warm-hearted woman evidently belongs to this period of his life.

Do not believe [wrote Mrs. Norton earnestly] that you and your poetry are not properly valued—all men have their enemies, and their discouraged hours (which are *spiritual* enemies) but in the

---

[1] 'I suppose you will be a Lord of the Treasury or a Police magistrate,' wrote the irrepressible Robert Monteith, from Scotland on 15 July; 'or a Commissioner to enquire into the state of game in the West Highlands or Poet Laureate or something or other under Peel?'

main, you must admit, that to be favourably known by your talents in your own country, and very many others, is a proof that your talents *have* been and will be, power to you, over men—(and over women, too, if you think that worth while). I wish I was a clever man, for then my opinion would be better worth having, but being only an intelligent woman, I can but reiterate that to me, it appears you have as fair a share of celebrity and esteem and . . . personal affection as any man of your age (for after all at your age a career is only at its outset) can boast. . . . What you still want in your career is a decided and active employment—when you have that you will be happy, and cease to be restless; and that will come with some turn of the political wheel.

For the forty-four remaining years of Monckton Milnes' existence the political wheel turned round and round and round, but by none of those revolutions did it bring him any decided or active employment.

It would be disproportionate to say that with his failure to get office from the Conservatives of 1841 the iron entered Milnes' amiable soul. There was nothing so dramatic as that. But for the next five years he was haunted by an obstreperous little doubt: would he ever get office from a Tory Government? This doubt influenced his subsequent defection to the Whigs. Milnes was not a time-server. Beneath his paradoxes and attitudes he was an intelligent, humane, good and liberal man. He was not yet radical in his views, but he was not Conservative either: 'it is certainly much *easier*,' he wrote in 1841, 'to be a pure-minded and unselfish liberal than Tory.' But his natural liberalism, his unease inside the Tory fold, was certainly reinforced by the fact that the Conservative leaders increasingly ignored his talents. Wit, he observed, was the last thing to make any impression in the House: 'the House will laugh at anything except wit.' Although he had not the prevision of Tocqueville he was more and more concerned at the horrifying conditions being created by the industrial revolution. His commonplace books for these years—1840, 1841 and 1842 —are filled with his reflections upon the hideous lives led by the working-classes in the great cities of England: 'the manufacture of pauperism,' he observed, 'will always increase with other manufactures . . . machines which throw thousands out of work are a means of idleness and the use of factory-children is a civilised slave-trade.' When he did at length openly join the Liberal Party, in 1846, he hoped again for office. Once more he was disappointed.

The major fact about Milnes' political failure is that he himself minded it a very great deal. When his old friend Lord Ashburton died in Paris in 1864, Milnes (or, as he had just become, Lord

Houghton) was passing April quietly at Hyères. There, amongst the lemon-groves and the silvering olive-trees of a Mediterranean spring, he sought out the parallels between his own career and that of Lord Ashburton. 'I had much in common with him,' he wrote to Lady Houghton, 'mainly the failure in public life, which he bore with a dignity and manliness I have never assumed, but which he felt quite as acutely.'

A new and corroding element of uncertainty and disillusion had entered his life in that summer of 1841.

VI

After his own unopposed election for Pontefract, Milnes remained at Fryston, awaiting a visit from Thackeray, who was over in England for a few weeks. Thackeray, at that time still no more than a clever journalist with a small but distinct reputation, a tall, round-faced personage with a ridiculous little nose, arrived at Fryston with his friend Frederick Pollock, a young lawyer. It is Pollock, not Thackeray, who has left a glimpse of Fryston that summer of 1841; a mere snapshot or still like an early Fox Talbot photograph.[1] He and Thackeray had come down to Fryston from York. Getting out in the park they strolled up between the trees in the July afternoon, towards the square, white house. As they neared it, they saw two figures standing outside the front door in the sunshine—their friend Richard Milnes and his spare, elderly father, who was wearing a dressing-gown and smoking a cigar. Mr. Milnes welcomed his guests by handing a cigar to each of them. 'You may smoke anywhere in this house,' he said, 'in your bedrooms if you please; and Mrs. Milnes does not mind it in her drawing-room. Only you must not smoke in Richard's room, for he doesn't like it.' Here we can catch an echo of that simplicity and charming hospitality which made Mr. Milnes' country neighbours love him. There had never been any nonsense about him, and his house reflected his practical temperament. 'Fryston,' said Thackeray, as he left a week later, 'combines the freedom of the tavern with the elegance of the château.'

With this click of the camera's eye the mists close in once more over Fryston, blotting it out until some later visitor—Henry Adams or Isabel Burton, for example—dispels them for us again. For the present it remains a blind façade: the large white house with four pillars before it which Milnes had laughed about as a boy at Cambridge.

[1] *Personal Remembrances of Sir Frederick Pollock, Sometime Queen's Remembrancer,* vol. i (Macmillan, 1887).

RICHARD MONCKTON MILNES IN 1845

Unhappily, Milnes' life in Pall Mall, and all the flurry and wit of his conversation, which was now beginning to gain a definite reputation for brilliance, is almost equally remote. Wit and charm are the first things to be forgotten and the most difficult of all attributes to recreate. Sir Henry Taylor complained in his auto-biography that no justice had ever been done in print to his caustic friend the first Lady Ashburton; Monckton Milnes' essay on her in his *Monographs*, although it listed a number of her *bons mots*, gave no idea, according to Taylor, of what she was really like when she was alive. In the same way the jaded reading public of the eighteen-nineties were deeply disappointed with Wemyss Reid's biography of Monckton Milnes, for they had expected to find in it the flavour and fascination of his wit. It was not only what he said but the way in which he said it that enchanted and amused people; and this is precisely the aspect of Milnes that we can never quite get to know. Intonation, smile, laughter, manner and expression are gone. By 1841 the renown of his jokes was spreading; and he carried on into the later decades of Victoria's reign that species of rather Regency flippancy which made Sydney Smith so sought out. One of Milnes' later friends, Lady St. Helier,[1] noticed that 'nothing annoyed him so much as when anybody interrupted him, which was a rare occurrence, for . . . it was difficult to do anything but listen,' and already, in the early eighteen-forties, O'Brien would chaff him for his habit of saying 'But . . .' or 'The . . .' whenever there was a silence at his table; O'Brien called it putting in a *caveat* to prevent anyone else speaking first. Milnes' jokes, though sharp, were not often ill-intentioned: 'You are not mischievous, only malignant,' Roebuck, the noisy radical lawyer and Member of Parliament,[2] told him at this time. Milnes jotted down what he considered his own best witticisms, but, denuded of his inflections and their atmosphere, they do not always seem funny today.

Throughout 1841 and 1842 Milnes was reading as voraciously as ever. While keeping up with the new novels he was also reading contemporary theology, philosophy and politics; and at the same time going back to Dryden, Cowley and Swift. His method of reading was infinitely painstaking: he would copy out whole paragraphs from such a work as Herman Merivale's *Lectures on Colonisation* (published in 1841) or Newman on Justification. Miss Elizabeth Rigby, who later married the painter Eastlake and became a distinguished figure in the world of Victorian painting,

---

[1] Whose recollections, *Memories of Fifty Years*, were published in 1909. She was the wife of the judge, Francis Jeune, Lord St. Helier (1843–1905).

[2] John Arthur Roebuck (1801–1879) was a barrister, a Q.C. and a man of violent views; he sat in the House of Commons as M.P. for Bath and later for Sheffield; he was an acquaintance rather than a friend of Monckton Milnes.

produced her travel-book *A Residence on the Shores of the Baltic* in 1841. This book and its authoress seem to have impressed Monckton Milnes mightily.[1] His restless thirst for travel had not been quenched by six wintry weeks in Paris. He was reading at the same time Malcolm's *History of Persia*, a book then twenty years old but full of the anecdotes and travellers' tales which Milnes loved. He was also reading some more Goethe, the newest novels of Balzac and George Sand, and the latest philosophical work of his old friend Lamennais. Most of these books must have come up for discussion at his breakfast table at one time or other during these two years, sharing the floor with quotations from Emerson, stories of the supernatural (such as the prophetic dreams of the wife of Archdeacon Manning), Miss Berry's habit of reading an ode of Horace after a party to compose her mind for sleep, the U.S. slave trade, the drunkenness of Lady Downshire, or speculations upon the will of the reprobate Lord Hertford, who had died at Dorchester House in the spring of 1842.

VII

During 1842 Milnes was much involved in the efforts then made to pass a Copyright Bill protecting author's rights. He spoke in favour of a bill introduced by Mahon [2] in April, a long speech very fully reported in the newspapers and for which Lady Blessington declared that he should be voted a piece of plate. One other question of principle interested him also at this moment: the

---

[1] Some of his friends were not equally impressed: 'I hope Elzth. Rigby has ruined her influence by this article on German women,' wrote Miss Harriet Martineau in a fury to Milnes on 9 February 1844. 'It has made people take steps to show the Germans that we do not abound in Rigbys,—that she may be taken as a single specimen of English authoress, if not of Engh. woman. I knew she wd. not be long in revealing herself, &, to be sure, she has done it. Nature seems to make odd blunders sometimes. Bulwer is a woman of genius got by mistake into a man's form, & E. Rigby is a Quarterly reviewer wrongly incarnated, in like manner.'

[2] Philip Henry Stanhope (1805–1875), styled Viscount Mahon until 1855, when he succeeded to the earldom of Stanhope, was Tory M.P. for Hertford 1835–1852 and procured the passing of a bill amending the copyright law in 1842. In January 1842 Milnes had thought of bringing in a copyright bill himself (see his note to Gladstone of 17 January 1842, printed in Reid, vol. i, p. 276), but when he found Mahon was doing so he confined himself to supporting this. In the debate on the Bill, 6 April 1842, Milnes achieved great distinction by his vehement attack on Wakley, who had opposed the measure, and in doing so had vulgarly made fun of Wordsworth. Wakley's point that the interest of the public was more important than and in opposition to that of authors was held by a number of other people, including, oddly, Milnes' friend Mrs. Grote, who wrote to him that she did not wish to see authors placed in a 'privileged' position.

perennial problem of political corruption. It was generally conceded that 'a million of money' had been spent in contested constituencies in the election of 1841, and few people in that zealous epoch felt that this was entirely right. In the spring of 1842 a thin pamphlet on the subject emerged from the printing press of Ollier, at 59 Pall Mall. Discreetly entitled *Thoughts on Purity of Election by a Member of Parliament*, it set out in the space of thirty-one pages to prove first that bribery was an essential element in any political election and secondly that it was positively beneficial. It soon became commonly known that this pamphlet was written by the member for Pontefract.

The author of *Thoughts* began by blandly analysing the meaning of the popular phrase 'purity of election.' He built up with care the imaginary figure of the perfect, well-informed, impartial voter and then pointed out that this figure had no existence in fact. Everyone voted at an election, he argued, for one reason only: because they believed that some benefit would accrue to themselves or their own interests from the policy of the favoured candidate. Now what earthly difference was there between the expectation of some distant benefit by legislation and the realisation of an immediate benefit by the acceptance of a crackling ten-pound note? Shifting his ground a little, he then suggested that if the last election had been so expensive, this must mean that people were harder to bribe, i.e. more virtuous; thus bribery elevated the moral character. Then, too, it was nothing but a tangible evidence of amiability on the candidate's part: what were the electioneering hand-shake, the unwonted familiarity with tenants, the affectation of interest in electors' family troubles, 'the confusion of ranks' at an election, if not a milder form of bribery? And freely contested elections had already reduced, and would reduce much further, the quality of the House of Commons; for contested elections were 'a very painful ordeal to reflective individuals.' What was needed was not less bribery, Milnes declared, but a very great deal more.

The newspapers were divided upon the merits of this publication. A Tory newspaper found it 'short and sensible,' while a more liberal journal wrote bluntly that Mr. Milnes thought better than he reasoned and to this fault added a great love of paradox.

You may be always quite sure [ran this notice] that if there be any one form, or any one phraseology, more calculated than all others to shock and bewilder the world, that form and that phraseology Mr. Milnes will adopt in preference to all others.

Yet it was just these shocks that that padded, urbane Victorian society needed. Milnes had often delivered them in conversation.

Now for the first time he did so in print. Far more interesting than the flimsy sophistry about bribery are the thrusts and lunges that he makes at contemporary values. He speaks sharply of the upper classes' ignorance of working-class 'conditions, wants, wishes and notions' and attacks the general assumption 'that there is an all-but-indissoluble connection between riches and respectability . . . the law regards it as penal to be utterly poor.' Without a similar background of experience and solely by the exercise of his own imagination, Milnes had come to feel as strongly as Dickens himself about the state of the English poor. He realised perfectly well that the society he enjoyed most—the long drawing-room at Bath House, the evenings at Lady Londonderry's, the Hollands' cypress-shaded lawns—were insecurely and immorally based upon the suffering of the working class. The delicious leisured world of money and beauty was moored like some luxurious, luminous barge upon waters that were dark and deep and might at any moment heave treacherously up and swamp them all. Milnes was at this time beginning his vast collection of books, pamphlets and manuscripts about the French Revolution. The fate of French society in 1789 was often in his mind. Meanwhile in England the Chartist and Corn Law agitations were getting into full swing. How much he was influenced in his unorthodox views of society by the conversations and writing of Carlyle (whose *Chartism* had come out three years earlier) one can only guess. He was certainly more likely to listen to him than to his own father on such questions. In 1842 Mr. Milnes was writing comfortably from Fryston that no matter how defective the wheat crop might prove distress was so general that public consumption would probably diminish even below this deficiency.

VIII

One of the most distressed sections of the community that spring was the weavers of Spitalfields. To aid the weavers, to amuse the Queen and, perhaps, to alleviate the decorous routine of court functions, Prince Albert had devised a State Fancy Ball. This entertainment, which took place at Buckingham Palace on 12 May 1842, was the first of a series of royal *bals costumés* given over the next few years. It was medieval in character and nominally related to the reign of Edward III, who was represented by the Prince, while Queen Victoria appeared as Philippa of Hainault. The selection of guests for the ball gave rise to anxiety and jealousy. Costumes were prepared with a Teutonic exactitude, and the Queen, who did not like being bothered about clothes, found herself 'quite bewildered' several weeks before the day of the ball: 'so many silks and drawings and crowns and God knows what to look at that I . . . am quite *confuse*,' she wrote to her uncle Leopold. Many rather idiotic jokes were current about the costumes: 'Mr. and Mrs. Gally Knight go to the Ball as remains of Saracenic architecture,' Milnes told his aunt Caroline, after describing his own dress as 'grave and simple—dark green cloth and amber satin and squirrel fur are the components of it—Macready promises it shall be unpretending, effective and becoming.' Thus modestly clothed, Milnes was proposing to impersonate the poet Chaucer, a choice over which a number of people raised their eyebrows. Wordsworth, who was seventy-five and irritated at the idea of being ordered to a State Fancy Ball, declared that if Monckton Milnes went as Chaucer there was nothing for him to do but to go as Monckton Milnes. Macready, then manager of Drury Lane, found himself swamped with requests for advice on medieval dress. Lytton Bulwer spent the morning with him fitting costumes, and finally selected that of Ruthven. Lord Normanby, Lord Douro and his brother Lord Charles Wellesley clamoured for armour. Colonel Buckley, six foot three inches tall, expected to find a suit to fit him ready made. Milnes paid Macready four separate visits over the 'long-waisted' Chaucer dress (with shoes to match made by Macready's character shoe-maker in St. James's Street), but the actor seems to have minded his persistence far less than the miscellaneous importunities of the Duke of Wellington's sons. Macready sometimes dined or breakfasted with Milnes, and probably felt that he was treated as a friend, not patronised as a person from the stage. 'I am glad,' he noted in his diary, recording the discussions on the Chaucer dress, 'of the power of showing Milnes civility.'

The Fancy Ball and the publicity and ridiculous chagrins connected with it gave Milnes and Charles Buller the opportunity to perpetrate a famous *jeu d'esprit*. Relations with France were still awkward, and Milnes and Buller took it into their heads to compose an imaginary debate in the French Chamber of Deputies and send it to the *Morning Chronicle*, in which it duly appeared. The occasion of the debate was given as a question by some deputy as to whether Monsieur de St. Aulaire, Guizot's successor as French Ambassador in London, was right to go to a ball celebrating the medieval victories of England over France. The oratorical style of each of the best-known French statesmen was parodied in turn. Rhetorical questions abounded—was the Ambassador going barefoot with his subordinates to the Palace, halters round their necks? Milnes imitated, amongst others, his friend Tocqueville and the poet Lamartine. Nothing, he made one of his statesmen say, was done for pleasure in England; everything had some sinister purpose behind it:

the aristocracy which prohibits amusement to the common people . . . never amuses itself; and when its haughty nobles and stiff *ladys* meet in their sombre 'at homes,' it is not for that interchange of bulletins of their gloomy atmosphere which the English call conversation; it is not to display their hideous dresses.

The debate closed with a statement by Guizot (Buller) that Lord Aberdeen had given most satisfactory explanations, that the Queen of England was endeavouring to educate her people by a series of archaeological entertainments, and that in deference to French susceptibilities Monsieur de St. Aulaire would go dressed as Joan of Arc. Intended as a political squib, this elaborate concoction became in Lord Houghton's own words 'a successful hoax.'

It seems incredible [he wrote years afterwards] that . . . it was discussed with gravity in the clubs; and, at the ball itself, Sir Robert Peel told me, with great satisfaction, that Sir James Graham had rushed into his room in Whitehall Gardens with the paper in his hand, exclaiming 'There is the devil to pay in France about this foolish ball.'

The provincial press in England reported the supposed debate with fury; the *Sémaphore de Marseille* translated it into French; the *Commerce* protested against the taste of allowing anyone to represent Joan of Arc, while other French newspapers formally denied that her armour had really been sent across the Channel for the French Ambassador to wear.

These manifestations of Milnes' gaiety were now greatly admired in London. His affability and his good humour, as well as his real originality of mind, had won through; and though a few personages like the old Lady Stanley of Alderley still professed themselves 'utterly disgusted with Mr. Milnes,'[1] most people were much amused by his sallies.

---

[1] 'Your mother has been utterly disgusted with Mr. Milnes who staid at Hurstmonceaux all the time they were there,' wrote Mrs. Edward Stanley to her husband in August 1844: *The Ladies of Alderley*, ed. Nancy Mitford (Chapman & Hall, 1938), p. 98. It is possible to surmise various ways in which Milnes may have offended old Lady Stanley during this visit to Julius Hare at his vicarage; readers of Miss Mitford's book will recall that this was not, in any case, a difficult feat. It is of more significance that in May 1843 Milnes was blackballed by the Travellers' Club, for which he had been proposed by Sidney Herbert in February 1840: he was told that at the election there had been a strong cabal against him, but that he had 'been blackballed in good company—with Landseer —The Travellers will have neither poetry nor painting,' wrote Colville,

I am retiring from business as a diner-out [wrote Sydney Smith in September 1843 to a London friend of his], but I recommend to your attention as a rising wit, Mr. Milnes, whose misfortune I believe it is not to be known to you.

Mrs. Grote, writing of a visit to the Molesworths at Pencarrow in Cornwall in this same year 1843, describes the liveliness of the conversation there: 'Mr. Milnes, often foremost to begin, like a "Bandillero" in the arena, shaking his paradoxical propositions in the faces of his doughty companions, and irritating their logical faculty to the verge of asperity.'[1]   His reputation was growing, and nearly forty years after the State Ball hoax, in the autumn of the year 1889, the ageing Parthenope, Lady Verney (sister of Florence Nightingale), liked to recall the stir this joke had made.   She and Milnes had found themselves at the same dinner-party a few days before the ball, and the bogus debate had come up for discussion. Everybody turned to Milnes in admiration: 'That was your wickedness, Milnes,' they cried, and later, when other anonymous skits were published, she heard people saying to him: 'I suppose you wrote that, Milnes.'   From being a little cold-shouldered by London society he was now treated with a special indulgence which Lady Verney thought had had 'an extremely spoiling effect,' preventing 'his making his mark in political life, as he ought to have done.' And then he was so many-sided, she reflected.   Her mother, Mrs. Nightingale, had once asked Henriette Guizot to meet him, 'as you know Mr. Milnes.'   'Quel Monsieur Milnes?' the statesman's sister had brightly asked.   'Est-ce que c'est Monsieur Milnes le poète, ou Monsieur Milnes le philanthrope, ou Monsieur Milnes l'homme politique et orateur, ou l'homme de société?   Il y en a tant.'[2]

IX

Milnes' collaboration with Charles Buller in the State Ball hoax was but one single, public instance of the complementary way in which these two often acted.   Charles Buller was three years older than Monckton Milnes, and must have seemed twice as tall; he was a burly giant of a young man, genial and talkative, his blithe face scarred by an accident in childhood which had also broken the

---

[1] The visit to Pencarrow is described in that charming book *The Personal Life of George Grote*, by Mrs. Grote (John Murray, 1873), p. 155.
[2] Dictated letter from Lady Verney to Harriette, Lady Galway, dated 26 September 1889.   'Parthe' Nightingale was an old friend and admirer of Milnes, whose paradoxes she especially relished.   When she asked him why he had left his *Patience of the Poor* out of his collected verse, he replied that the patience of the rich was just as great and that he had not wished to be invidious.

bridge of his nose. They had been acquainted since Cambridge, though there Milnes had been more intimate with Buller's brother Arthur, a handsome, boisterous youth despised by the grave Apostles for indulging in what one of them contemptuously called 'half-crown copulation.' On one occasion in those distant Trinity days Arthur Buller had had to apologise to Milnes for addressing him as 'son of a bitch' in a letter which had been accidentally read by Richard's mother, and on another he had written jocularly to explain why he thought he was with child. But now it was Charles whom Richard saw most frequently, and they were making, in certain circles, a sort of joint reputation for wit. Both Milnes and Buller were members of the 1841 Parliament (though on opposing sides of the House) and both belonged to the same clubs. They had the same set of friends in London and met at the same breakfast and dinner-parties and in the same country-houses. They also shared a sense of humour. Their dinner-table duologues and repartees enjoyed so much celebrity in London that they would sometimes rehearse these in the afternoons at their clubs, so as not to let each other or the company down. Buller was a thoughtful and able politician, whose career was threatened by a flippancy of manner very similar to Milnes' own. Like Milnes he was accused of 'levity'—that very mid-Victorian sin—and was widely misunderstood.

A propos to Politics [wrote Mrs. Grote to Milnes in a note dated 6 May (and probably belonging to the year 1842)], after you left me yesterday I had a long confabulation of nearly 2 hours with Chas. Buller, during wh. not a single joke passed between us!! You know how long & intimately I have known him, but you do *not* know how much good advice I have addressed to him. . . . However, with that untiring zeal for *the good of mankind* which has so long made a dupe of your humble servant, I made a hearty effort yesterday to awaken my clever & amiable friend to a sense of his real & becoming vocation; upbraiding him, with kindness, for all the *shocking* mistakes, as to taste and propriety, wh. he has been committing since Parlt. met. . . . In fact, Buller only wants the stimulus of grave & responsible duties to be a very useful and superior public servant. Wanting this, he strays driftless whithersoever his varied and undirected gifts of mind allure him, feeding on contemptible flatteries, & ephemeral triumphs, 'capering in Lady's chambers' (qu: *Salons?*) & in fact leading a life wh. vexes his true admirers.

Besides being an able politician, even a potential statesman, Charles Buller was a very good lawyer. He and his brother Arthur were the sons of a Cornish gentleman who had spent his life in the Indian service and had married a Calcutta beauty. Mrs. Buller figures frequently in Froude's biography of Carlyle, since Carlyle was at one time tutor to the two Buller boys. She was a kindly, faded, quick-witted Anglo-Indian lady, and she had stretched her originality so far as to adopt her son's bastard daughter (an unpleasant girl Thackeray kept in mind when creating his character of Becky Sharp). Carlyle's influence had left deep marks on Charles Buller's opinions, though the pupil's admiration for his former tutor was occasionally tempered by doubts.

The Carlyles are here [he wrote to Milnes one day, from the Barings' house near Alverstoke], and I think he is going the way of all flesh into extravagance and cant. His great business is working every truth which he ever taught into the shape of a paradox or falsehood. He is a prophet without a mission, holding no belief and promising no deliverance.

Buller was a violent reformer, and chief author of the famous 1838 report on Canada which goes under Lord Durham's name. His political judgement was good, sounder and less emotional than that of Milnes. In these early eighteen-forties he distrusted Peel.

I do not see why you need exaggerate so much as to say that Peel is in a position of greater practical power than Pitt or Walpole [he wrote to him after the 1841 election]; but I agree with you in thinking that this is one in which a bold and wise statesman might wield a great and safe power. But he is neither bold nor wise. . . . I have never seen him called on to originate a course of action or to bear the responsibilities of power, without seeing him break down under his task and break up the party which he led. . . .

In five years' time Milnes had himself come round to Buller's view of Peel, though for different and more personal reasons.

Milnes' friendship with Charles Buller, which was well established by 1842, ended only with Buller's sudden and early death, after a minor operation, in the autumn of 1848. Carlyle, who blamed the death on the surgeon's use of chloroform (then a novelty), was deeply shaken by it, and so was Monckton Milnes. The person in London who minded it most was Lady Harriet Baring, whose husband had that year succeeded to his father's title as Lord Ashburton.

To all of us his death is a sore loss [Carlyle wrote to her in a long letter of which she seems to have allowed Milnes to make a copy], not to any living creature, I think, could it seem a gain. . . . But to *you*, dear Friend—alas, it is a loss which I fear none of us can ever repair! In his own form he was by far the brightest soul in your circle—or indeed in all the world I know of. A great blank indeed to you, and who can console you? . . . All pious thoughts be near you, dear lady!

Lady Harriet Baring is now only remembered as the great lady of whom Mrs. Carlyle was jealous. It would indeed console Jane Carlyle to know how utterly her own fame has eclipsed that of Lady Harriet with posterity. In her lifetime Lady Harriet ruled half London—'the greatest lady of rank I ever saw,' Carlyle called her, 'with the soul of a princess and captainess had there been any career possible for her but that fashionable one.' Milnes was the only one of Lady Ashburton's closest friends to write a memoir of her after her death, and even this essay, which was studded with her witticisms, seemed lifeless to others who had known her well. Milnes realised how quickly she would be forgotten:

how are the social celebrities of any time to live even here beyond the shifting scene in which they have played their part? [he writes in his opening paragraph] . . . But I am here desirous to continue the recollection of a lady whose sphere of action was limited in extent and in duration; and whose peculiar characteristics rather impeded than promoted her position in an order of society where any strong individuality is both rare and unwelcome.

Lady Harriet Baring was the most brilliant conversationalist of any woman in London (Princess Lieven once said it would be well worth taking tickets to hear her talk), and could compensate thus, as well as by an extravagant chic in clothes, for her lack of beauty. In Mr. Bingham Baring, the son and heir of the millionaire Lord Ashburton by his Pennsylvanian wife, she had an intelligent, diffident but doting husband, who allowed her to do what she liked and who could afford to fulfil her slightest whim. She could travel across Europe with a retinue of carriages and servants whenever she pleased. In London she had apartments in Bath House. In the country she could choose between The Grange, Lord Ashburton's great classical palace in Hampshire, her husband's Surrey villa at Addiscombe and their house beside the sea at Alverstoke opposite the Isle of Wight. When the coming of the railways opened up the Highlands, the Barings hastened to construct a Barryesque lodge at the head of Loch Luichart, a lodge with a tower at one end and perched high above the lake amongst birch-woods and mountain burns.

Long before the first Lord Ashburton's death, Lady Harriet had begun to make Bath House and The Grange centres of the most glittering and sharp-tongued society in England. The Grange was a perpetual tumult of arriving and departing guests, of footmen and ladies' maids and long, complicated meals. It lay amidst deep beech-woods, traversed by twenty miles of rides, overlooking the River Itchen. In appearance it is still one of the strangest

houses in England: a greyish, 'topheavy Parthenon,' a huge cube
with a Greek portico and pediment on each of its four faces, four
wide terraces and four sweeping flights of stone steps.   It had been
built to designs by Wilkins (the architect of Trinity New Court and
of part of King's College), in 1809, and incorporated an old house
connected with Inigo Jones.   Intended to look like a Greek temple,
it rather resembled a square, sugared wedding-cake of monstrous
proportions.   Its position on the river-bank was rather lonely, and
outwardly there was nothing cosy about The Grange.   Addiscombe,
near Croydon, was a less ostentatious establishment, but it too was
the scene of perpetual and celebrated entertainments.   Alverstoke,
which Charles Buller called the most enjoyable winter residence
north of the Alps, was hedged in by evergreens, but from the
windows was a prospect of shingle beaches, of the sea dotted with
sailing-boats, the Isle of Wight in the distance.

'Wealth in abundance, ruled over by grace in abundance' was
Carlyle's definition of life at The Grange, at Bath House, at Addiscombe and Alverstoke.   To Mrs. Carlyle, Lady Harriet had at
first sight seemed like a 'heathen goddess': the cleverest woman,
she later admitted, that she had ever seen, but so autocratic;
so humoured and spoiled by her position as to be 'entangled
in cobwebs'; quite remote from real life; content to be merely
'the most graceful and amusing woman of her time.'   The great
luncheon parties and dinner parties with Cabinet Ministers and
Whig and Tory magnates, with Samuel Rogers and Lady Holland
and Lord Lansdowne and the Howicks, with such social make-
weights as Greville and Poodle Byng thrown in, fascinated but
rather repelled Carlyle.   Their conversation came more naturally
to Milnes than to the Scottish farmer's son; but Carlyle several
times implied that Milnes was different from the rest.   He found
that Milnes' presence in a house filled with the Barings' friends
could save his own sanity.   Carlyle admired the ease of the
aristocracy, the lightness and leisureliness which their breeding
gave them.   Their 'art in speech' impressed him, the skill with
which they flitted from one topic to another, avoiding all discussion
and all sincerity, playing at conversation as though they were
dancing an intricate minuet.   Milnes recognised the Barings'
world as 'more iconoclastic of all literary and political reputations'
than any other he knew, but he went back to it again and again.

Intellectual work was actively discouraged among the habitués of
Bath House.   The premium was on talk, not on literary production
or the writing of poetry.   'I like idleness,' Lady Harriet said to
Milnes one day, 'an Indian god on a lotus leaf or a ploughboy on a
gate.'   She said she needed no books in her houses, because 'a few

of my friends write and the rest never open a book: none *read*.'
Often and often she would summon Milnes 'Grangewards' or to
dine and sleep at Addiscombe, sending one of her little notes which
Froude has called 'terse, clear and peremptory, rather like the
commands of a sovereign than the easy communications of friendship.'

Among the possessions which Lord Houghton bequeathed to his
son is a very large, ugly chalk drawing of Lady Harriet's head by
Samuel Laurence. 'The best-looking ugly woman ever seen,'
Milnes noted soon after he first became acquainted with her.
'C. Buller,' he recorded a few months later, 'Lady H. B. and
Thackeray must all be children of one hidden, powerful, broken-
nosed individual.' The inner ring of her close friends, which
included Carlyle, Monckton Milnes and Charles Buller, contained
very few women, for she much preferred the society of intelligent
men. Charles Buller was probably her most intimate friend; he
treated her as his 'divinity,' and their relationship and resemblance
led to his being nicknamed 'Lord Harriet'. No slightest im-
propriety was permitted at her table, and the conversations of
herself and her friends were marked by a conscious strictness
termed by Milnes 'restraint of tone.' Lady Harriet's special gift
was the rare and winning one of dramatising everyday incidents
and making 'high comedy out of daily life.' She was subject to
'electric' transitions of mood, and loved to score off those she had
defeated: 'I do not mind being knocked down,' Milnes reports one
victim as saying, 'but I can't stand being danced upon afterwards.'
Even when ill, she remained, in Carlyle's words, 'brisk as a huntress'
and always ready to make fun of herself, or her conversations with
her doctor; of the Queen, the Carlyles, the Baring clan, or anything
that came to hand. Repeating that someone had confided in her
that his son was deaf, she explained that 'we could do no more than
say that we preferred the deaf people to all others, except the dumb.'

Milnes' friendship with her grew gradually. At first he found
her disconcerting: 'Lady Htte. Baring's charming sense when
tête-à-tête, her odious frivolity when a third person enters,' he
observed in 1840. But soon he was completely won over by her,
and touchy though he could be he seems not to have minded her
teasing. When speaking to him one day of what might happen in
twenty years' time she concluded 'what does it matter? I shall be
dead and you will be living in the country, too fat to be moved up
to town.' 'You'd better not go on saying that Peel sees nothing
in you, because I have such a habit of deference to him that I
perhaps must think the same,' was another of her sallies. But she
was genuinely fond of Milnes: she addressed him as 'poet,' wrote

him long conversational letters from Paris or Spa, and told him he
could not look unhappy—'I have seen you grave and dignified,
but never unhappy.' She and her husband and their friends and
their houses became from now on a part of the background of his
existence.[1] They represented wealth, aristocracy and what O'Brien
would have called the hard London world in its most seductive
but not necessarily most heartless form. Carlyle had warned him
of squandering his talents in Mayfair. It was not a warning he
was ready to heed.

In the memoir of Lady Harriet Baring [2] Lord Houghton printed
a great number of her *bons mots*. His notebooks contain a great
many more. It is doubtful whether he was really doing her a
service by this process of stenography, for though he chose the most
harmless remarks for publication, he had recorded some rather
silly as well as rather unagreeable things. 'Friendship, no doubt,
has great advantages—you know a man so much better and can
laugh at him so much more'; 'I like animals the best of all things,
Frenchmen next as being most like them'; 'Active hate is very
disagreeable—not so to hate naturally as comes to me.'

And then, just as we are about to judge her, she seems
to speak out to us: for amongst all the chips and pieces of Lady
Harriet's conversation which Monckton Milnes wrote down, comes
one evidently intended for our ears. 'What a horrid injustice it is,'
Lady Harriet exclaimed, one day in the year 1848, 'what a horrid
injustice it is to be judged by what one *says*. As I and Milnes
know.'

---

[1] A charming impromptu tribute to the society at the Grange was paid by
Milnes in the following verses, scribbled into the copy of his volume of Eastern
poems, *Palm Leaves*, which he gave to Lady Harriet's mother-in-law in 1844:

> Wander East or wander West
> Wander where you may
> Ever sweeter comes the rest
> From the weary way:
> Happiest he who ends his range
> In the circle of 'the Grange.'

> Take a leaf and write on it
> Thanks that still on earth
> Grecian Art and Gallic Wit
> Blend with English worth:
> Palm-Leaves are a poor exchange
> For the friendship of 'the Grange.'

[2] Published in his *Monographs, Social and Personal* (John Murray, 1873).

Chapter Eight

1842   1843

I

A longing for a change in atmosphere made Richard Milnes decide in the late summer of 1842 to set out on a journey to Constantinople and to Cairo. Ever since his visit to Greece in 1832 he had felt curiosity about the Near East. There was something in what he called the 'gay and brilliant colours of the East' which appealed to him. Years ago, in Italy, his father had urged the utility, from a political point of view, of visiting Syria and Egypt. Now that Richard's eye was fixed on that elusive Under-Secretaryship of Foreign Affairs, a closer personal knowledge of those Eastern countries which were endangering the peace of the West and involving France and England in recurring crises could certainly do his prospects no harm. It was satisfactory to be able to write the phrase: 'I have spent the last two or three months in Greece and Turkey' in a long political letter from Smyrna to Sir Robert Peel.

During the eighteen-thirties the career of Mahomet Ali, the Albanian Pasha of Egypt appointed by the Sultan Mahmoud II, had threatened the integrity of the Turkish Empire and consequently the whole topheavy structure of Western European peace. In London and in Paris in the winter of 1840–41 Milnes had witnessed the political tensions to which events in Turkey and Egypt had subjected Anglo-French relations. This was the time at which Mrs. Grote had told him no one would speak to him in Paris, and at which even Montalembert had said that the English were behaving perfidiously. Having experienced the perimeter effects of these Eastern conflicts, he was now to have the chance of viewing the actual arenas in which they had taken place.

Influenced by his French sympathies, by his early dislike of Palmerston and perhaps by his innate contrariness, Milnes had backed Mahomet Ali at a time when almost everyone in England, of either party, was in favour of the Porte. 'Mr. Monckton Milnes . . . is one of the very few members of Parliament who took a right view of the Oriental question, and did justice to Mahomet Ali's Government during Lord Palmerston's persecution' ran one of the notes of introduction he took with him to Cairo; and one object of his journey was to interview the old Pasha himself, for which purpose he had been given a note to Boghas Bey from Dr. John Bowring, the Eastern linguist and traveller, who was then a fellow-member of Parliament. But in spite of all his admirable political intentions, the chief result of his journey was literary. Peel did not relent because an aspirant to office had spent a month on the Bosphorus or had a chat with Mahomet Ali through an interpreter; and the most noticeable product of the winter's junketings was Milnes' last, and in some ways his best, volume of poems, published in 1844 under the title *Palm Leaves*.[1]

> Eastward roll the orbs of heaven,
> Westward tend the thoughts of men.
>
> Let the poet, nature-driven,
> Wander Eastward now and then.

were the verses on the fly-leaf of the book. He had studiously prepared himself for the eastern journey by a very wide reading of English, French and German authorities on the Moslem world. He had read, and made excerpts from, an English translation of the Koran. He had pored over Urquhart's *Spirit of the East*. In his portmanteau were packed the volumes of Lamartine's *Voyage en Orient*, the only book, he said, which treated Eastern religion 'respectfully.' In his pocket he carried a copy of Goethe's imaginative poems on eastern ways, the *Oest-Westliche Divan*.

II

In the preface to *Palm Leaves* (a book which he dedicated to Guizot as a gesture of Anglo-French amity) Monckton Milnes explains that two considerations prevented his writing a book of travel experiences in prose rather than verse. One was his utter lack of knowledge of the Eastern languages. The other was his distaste for adding to the body of Eastern travels, journeys and tours, which were already, in his view, too numerous. An Eastern journey undertaken for curiosity and pleasure, not for trade or duty, was by this time becoming a little less unusual, a little less eccentric and adventurous than in earlier periods. All the same, it was still rated enterprising. The two great classics of Eastern travel which the early Victorian world produced, Kinglake's *Eothen* and Eliot Warburton's *The Crescent and the Cross*, had not yet been published; like *Palm Leaves* they came out in 1844. We have seen that

---

[1] *Palm Leaves*, by Richard Monckton Milnes (London: Edward Moxon, Dover Street, 1844).

Kinglake and Warburton were both of them friends, and Cambridge contemporaries, of Monckton Milnes. Kinglake, whose book has been compared to Sterne's *Sentimental Journey*, had made his tour as far back as 1835, when Lady Hester Stanhope was still alive. He had travelled in the company of Lord Pollington, son and heir of the Milnes' Yorkshire neighbour Lord Mexborough. Warburton, on the other hand, was travelling at the same moment as Milnes. His book, which was dedicated to Milnes, is more comprehensive, less subjective and superficial than Kinglake's, but in its own way equally entertaining. Neither book killed the sales of the other, and both of them achieved immense popularity and went into many editions. Whereas Milnes set off via Venice and Athens to Constantinople, Warburton took the long sea route to Cairo from Southampton on a ship Calcutta-bound. He wrote sadly from Dublin in October 1842 of the 'savage tricks' fate always played him; he would have liked travelling with Milnes above all things, but he could not get off in time. He looked forward, though without confidence, to meeting Milnes in Egypt.

Milnes' conclusions about the Moslem world were unconventional and caused his readers some surprise. He set them out bluntly in the prefatory note to *Palm Leaves*, but indeed they informed and infused every poem in the book. Westernisation had produced little but 'unmixed evil' in the East. We had taught the Moslems to drink and had ruined their natural taste in dress. Eastern women seemed to be in as good a position as those of the West (except for their lack of education), and the harem was a harmless convention confined to the richest class. Our ideas of 'Eastern domesticity,' he declared, were taken from the ballet and so coloured by ferocity and vice that 'what is really commonplace becomes paradoxical.' The 'Frankish' attitude to Mohammedanism he found deplorable. Just as years ago in Rome he had been sincerely receptive to Roman Catholicism, so he was now profoundly impressed by the teaching of Mahomet. A first day in a Mohammedan country he thought was like returning at one leap to the old dispensation—'mankind standing, without mediation, without sympathy, alone, beneath the will of God. There the whole of life goes on in the distinct presence of the Invisible.' Here once more we are reminded of Milnes' uncanny lack of prejudice and preconceptions. He was practically incapable of being surprised or shocked. He was prepared to sympathise with or at any rate to try to understand everything which came his way.

Milnes' views on the East, especially his attitude of apparently condoning polygamy and the harem, did, however, disturb and shock his contemporaries. His first biographer suggests that this reaction was the origin for the many tales of his dissipations and adventures in the East at one time current in London. Sir Thomas Wemyss Reid, who succeeded in watering down the character of Monckton Milnes, presenting him to the public of the eighteen-nineties as a voluble bore who had known Tennyson and been interested in reformatories, is at pains to point out in his biography that Milnes had no 'adventures' in the East at all. Since Milnes was thirty-two, full-blooded and sensual, we may suppose—or, at least, hope—that he did indulge in some such experiments as those described by Flaubert in the travel journal of his own eastern voyage in 1850. One experience, indeed, Milnes did share with Gustave Flaubert and Maxime du Camp; for though he did not see Kuchiouk Hanem at Esne, he did see the bee-dance in the house of Saphia Zougairah there, and spend the evening in the company of the dancing girls. 'Very corrupt and writhing, extremely voluptuous' Flaubert noted of 'la petite Sophie' Zougairah, a small woman with a large nose, black eyes and a necklace of clanking coins. 'A strapping woman' noted Milnes of Têté, one of the voluptuous dancers he watched by the glow of oil-lamps in Saphia's room.

Written evidence of 'adventures,' if it ever exists, is normally destroyed. An ambiguous note from one of Sir Stratford Canning's less resigned attachés has survived, directing Milnes to go to an Italian 'at the Bookbinders, just below the Dancing Dervishes on your way to the Tower of Galata' if he wants to procure 'a Turkish damsel' for 200 piastres. This note may well be a joke. It may, on the other hand, have been kindly meant. A line in the journal of his Nile voyage records that he had been offered, for a modest sum, a twelve-year-old girl at a village near the First Cataract. Milnes' curiosity about Eastern morality was unflagging. His commonplace book for the period is filled with stories of Turkish immorality which the different residents, consuls and travellers had told him. Most of these tales centre round the execution of boy favourites by the Pasha or his Beys. They are jotted down without comment, though once, after referring to the suicide of a young English officer named d'Arcy who had been assaulted by a Turkish soldier, Milnes added the two words—'male Lucretia.' Later on, in London, Thackeray did some of his funny drawings in a copy of *Palm Leaves*. These represented Milnes' Eastern pleasures, and the volume was subsequently presented to Miss Harriet Martineau.

The reign of Queen Victoria was a period in which libertine activity was carefully covered over and concealed—from a sense of privacy rather than from hypocrisy. It was well-known that Milnes was a sensualist, but not a hypocrite, and he seems, too, to have suspected that there are disadvantages to a sensitive man in leading a too-indulgent life. 'It is one of the worst parts of gross and strong pleasures,' he had written a few months before his journey abroad, 'that they seem by their very nature to destroy the power of enjoying the finer and simpler sources of delight.'

III

Although he had at first toyed with a plan for reaching Constantinople by steamboat from Vienna (a city he had never visited), Milnes had at last decided on a leisurely journey through Italy and Greece. It was just ten years since he had been in Greece. Meanwhile, the thoughtless, jocular undergraduate had become a Member of Parliament and a man of the world. The poet had tried to be a politician; and was still trying hard. In aim and in assurance, as well as in physical appearance (he was thicker and heavier to look at these days), Milnes had changed in ten years. But Greece had not.

> Ten years ago I deemed that if once more
> I trod on Grecian soil, 'twould be to find
> The presence of a great informing mind
> That should the glorious past somewise restore;
> And now I cry with disappointment sore,
> 'Is it for this that Greece has striven and pined?'

Milnes had expected to find 'progress' and he had found none. In letters written some weeks later from Smyrna to Charles MacCarthy (on remote Turks Island) and to Peel, he enlarged upon the shock he had received. The young Bavarian princeling, Otho, had landed in Greece in January 1833 to be the first king of a brand-new kingdom. He and his Council of Regency had depended upon their Bavarian soldiery to civilise the Greeks; the soldiery had failed. Greece was as primitive, as filled with bandits and as backward politically as it had ever been. Milnes was told that the king had wasted all his money on building a palace like 'a great stucco barrack' under Hymettus. The palace had been designed by his father and might have looked 'massive and imposing' in Bavaria, but was an atrocious disfigurement of Athens. The 'pretty, dressy' queen did nothing but dance, and the young king tried irresolutely to imitate Louis-Philippe. The regime, Milnes realised, was a failure.

But though Greece was politically disappointing, the landscape and the clear, rich light which revealed it were fully as miraculous as before. In the first week of October Milnes visited Delphi by moonlight, and then rode on over the plateau of Helicon from

Lebadea, paradoxically avoiding by choice the only good, modern carriage road in the peninsula:

> The solitudes of Helicon
> Are rife with gay and scented flowers,
> Shining the marble rocks upon
> Or 'mid the valley's oaken bowers.

His power of rhyme had never been equal to his power of observation, but he responded as eagerly, as readily as ever to natural beauty.

In the Greek capital he struck up an acquaintanceship with the English minister, the middle-aged admiral Sir Edmund Lyons, whose thick, grey-white hair and 'eager, half-melancholy manner' reminded everyone who saw him of Lord Nelson. Lyons was a humorous man, and he sent Milnes on his way with a note to the captain of the *Vanguard,* then in those waters, saying that Milnes appeared to him to be 'a clever fellow and to know the world.' Still writing occasional verse, Milnes passed amongst the Greek islands and on towards the Bosphorus, putting in at Delos on the way:

> Though Syra's rock was passed at morn,
> The wind so faintly arched the sail,
> That ere to Delos we were borne,
> The autumn day began to fail,
> And only in Diana's smiles
> We reached the bay between the isles.

IV

'You are late for Constantinople,' Sir Stratford Canning [1] wrote in a letter of welcome, from the Embassy 'palace,' a wooden villa at Buyukdhéré on the shores of the Bosphorus, not far from its junction with the Euxine Sea; 'but we shall be happy to do what little is in our power to make your visit agreeable to yourself.' It seems that Milnes had lingered too long on the mountain road from Lebadea, for when he reached Constantinople in the last days of October the Bosphorus was shrouded in mist.

I have been watching from the *wooded* heights of Pera to see if the sun will ever again be able to pierce this everlasting mist [one

---

[1] Sir Stratford Canning (1786–1880) better known by his later title of Lord Stratford de Redcliffe, the 'Great Elchi,' was ambassador to the Porte from 1842 until 1858, when he resigned.

of his new friends wrote a few days later], and have come to the
conclusion that tho' he may be a considerable tall time about it,
still we may escape being *fogged* to death.

He was 'late for Constantinople' indeed.

The Bosphorus wears the most animated appearance early in
June, when the trees are in full foliage, and every leaf is redolent
of life, ere the heats have withered the herbage, and when a light
southerly wind is wafting hundreds of vessels up the straits towards
the Black Sea. . . . But to be seen in all its beauty it should be
looked upon by moonlight.

In the year 1842 the range of readable, let alone informative or
thorough, English 'travel books upon European Turkey and the
Bosphorus was limited. It was in fact practically limited to the
three books of Miss Julia Pardoe, from whose volume, *The Beauties
of the Bosphorus*, published in 1840, this extract comes. Miss Pardoe
was a young Yorkshire lady who suffered from consumption and
had accordingly travelled with her father to Constantinople in 1835
(the contemporary cure for the disease being to put the infected
patient into as warm, dank and relaxing a climate as possible).
In Constantinople, Miss Pardoe had not wasted her time. She
had acquired and now purveyed in a stilted prose style a knowledge
of Turkey unrivalled by any Englishwoman since Lady Mary
Wortley Montagu. Miss Pardoe's third book, which Milnes had
certainly studied, is in the shape of an album, but it is in fact a very
long, diligent and scholarly piece of work. The chief beauty of
the volume lies in the fine, feathery steel engravings after the drawings of the topographical draughtsman and traveller Bartlett. It
was upon these drawings and upon Miss Pardoe's rapturous descriptive prose that early Victorian England relied for an interpretation
of that Turkish world which was soon so tragically to affect English
life and politics. The Bartlett-Pardoe interpretation was a most
beguiling and a most romantic one. Plate after plate shows
some new aspect of the glassy Bosphorus in a gentle sunlit
haze or lying under what Miss Pardoe termed the 'deep, purple,
star-encrusted sky of evening.' Roman aqueducts, minarets,
castles, cypresses, ruined palaces, cascading willow-trees are all
components of these lovely views, while Turkish figures loll upon
the ground or lean with a poetic melancholy upon some tombstone
or against the pier of a decaying bridge. It is doubtful whether
the plates are, in fact, inferior to the reality; and the service which
Miss Pardoe rendered the English and the Turks alike should be
respectfully remembered. The Turks did not greatly care for her
book, for some odd reason, and the Foreign Minister of the young

Sultan had a few sharp words to say about Miss Pardoe during a dinner which he gave to Richard Monckton Milnes. 'Miss Pardoe,' said Sumet Effendi, presumably in French, 'came here pure, went away pure and probably will always remain pure. But she is a great liar.' All the same, *The Beauties of the Bosphorus* gives us the best idea we can now get of Constantinople as it must have seemed to Richard Milnes in 1842.

Milnes was at first almost as much disappointed with Constantinople as he had been with the reforms of King Otho in Greece. In spite of the manifold beauties of the Golden Horn, this did not seem to him to be the authentic East. Constantinople gave him the impression that the Turks were 'only encamped in Europe,' and he told MacCarthy that nothing but an odd dress or two warned you that you were not in some French or Italian town. There was not only no intercourse between the Europeans and the Orientals, but the Turks were never mentioned in conversation, and no allusion was made to their existence at all. When he had dined with Sumet Effendi, the European community had been astounded. They talked of him 'as if I had banqueted at the Zoological Gardens.' But he was prepared to run the gauntlet of their disapproval, and he enjoyed the sugar and flowers, the jellied calves' feet and half-boiled fish, and the strong liqueurs his Turkish hosts gave him. Several English writers besides Miss Pardoe came up for comment during the dinner. He was told that Urquhart and Alison and other authorities in whom he had placed some faith 'knew no more about the Turks than anyone else.'

From our point of view, perhaps from his own too, the most interesting contact Milnes made in Constantinople was the friendship he formed—or continued, for they must have known each other in London—with the English ambassador, Sir Stratford Canning, who had been re-appointed to his old Embassy in January of that year. Sir Stratford was already beginning to exert upon Turkish affairs that imperious influence which made him for nearly two decades the dominating European figure in the Near East—the Great Elchi. He combined a quite unparalleled power of work with a very quick and violent temper. He exhausted all of his attachés in turn, cursed and cherished them, and got the best work out of each. He was infinitely exacting and could often be exasperating as well, thinking nothing of working thirty hours at a stretch, but expecting his subordinates to work in the same way. He had, besides all this, a delicate poetic sensibility and a very whimsical, acute humour. He welcomed Milnes warmly, and was genuinely sorry to see him go. They could do anything but lodge him, he explained, for since a great fire at Pera had demolished the European embassies, the English and French ambassadors had established themselves with their staffs at Buyukdhéré, near the Euxine Sea. Buyukdhéré was a very picturesque village on the shores of the Bosphorus, with a great expanse of bright green meadowland behind it and the solemn aqueduct of Baghtche-keui visible in the distance. Warburton, who stayed there in the following year, was charmed by the pretty effect of green verandahs and red-tiled roofs. He describes the little quay at which men-of-war of the different European nations were moored, flags fluttering from their sterns. From Buyukdhéré you could see the Black Sea through a long vista of high cliffs crowned by fortresses, while scudding caiques crossing the bay from Therapia gave a quick animation to the scene. The English occupied a small ramshackle log-house, called a Palace for form's sake, and containing a marble hall. The French Embassy was in a superior building with a fine garden.

The embassy offered Milnes a room in a 'hovel of an inn' at Buyukdhéré or a more comfortable alternative at the hotel in Therapia. The attachés were anxious that he should enjoy himself and see as much of the Bosphorus as he could. The ambassador's private secretary, Robert Curzon, later Lord Zouche, a young scholar and traveller who had been to Mount Athos and was whispered to prefer rambling about the Stamboul bazaars to copying 'even the most exciting' of Sir Stratford Canning's despatches, would take him riding and arrange things for him to do. Curzon was soon on jovial terms with Milnes and some of his notes end a trifle enigmatically—'hoping you are none the worse for the little, little birds' for example. The French ambassador, Baron Bourqueney, who had known Milnes in London, 'evinced an affectionate sympathy which would get him stoned in Paris' and constantly asked him to dine with members of the French colony. As usual, he got on with French people as well as, if not better than, with the English. Lady Canning twitted him on 'the temptations of *La Colonie Française*' and also on his dining with the Turkish Foreign Minister. As a parting gift he gave her a copy of a volume of his poems, and she assured him how much pleasure his company had given them. 'We are all sorry to lose you,' wrote Sir Stratford amiably in mid-November, as Milnes got ready to leave for Smyrna. He added that Milnes was a very lucky man, as he had intended sending him a copy of his own ode on Greece, but had not had time to look for it. Milnes embarked in an Austrian steamer, taking with him some dispatches from Canning for delivery en route. 'You see,' Sir Stratford told him, 'that I have full confidence in your zeal, notwithstanding my French colleague's hospitable attempts to tamper with it, and in your exactness notwithstanding the inspirations of the Muse.'

And indeed he had not been without inspiration on the Bosphorus, for he had composed that descriptive poem on Scutari, *The Greek at Constantinople*, which became famous in the next decade, when he added some stanzas to it in honour of the dead of the Crimean War:

> The cypresses of Scutari
>   In stern magnificence look down
> On the bright lake and stream of sea
>   And glittering theatre of town:
> Above the throng of rich kiosks,
>   Above the towers in triple tire,
> Above the domes of loftiest mosques,
>   These pinnacles of death aspire.
>
> It is a wilderness of tombs—
>   Where white and gold and brilliant hue
> Contrast with Nature's gravest glooms,
>   As these again with heaven's pure blue:
>
> .   .   .   .   .   .
>
> From this funereal forest's edge
>   I gave my sight full range below,
> Reclining on a grassy ledge,
>   Itself a grave or seeming so:
> And that huge city flaunting bright,
>   That crowded port and busy shore,
> With roofs and minarets steeped in light,
>   Seemed but a gaudy tomb the more.

Spending a few days in the port of Smyrna, which was still as Parisian and unoriental as when Chateaubriand had passed through it forty years before, he continued his journey across the Eastern Mediterranean to Alexandria and Cairo. It was too late in the season, he now had to admit, to visit Syria.

V

Always accompanied by his valet, Frederic, Milnes proceeded from Smyrna to the island of Syra in the Cyclades by a French ship. At Syra he transhipped from the *Tancrède* to the *Scamandre* and continued on to Alexandria, which he reached in the first days of December 1842.

At that time a traveller's first impressions of Egypt were invariably unpleasant. You boarded a canal boat at Alexandria in the afternoon of the day you had arrived. The boat threaded its way through melancholy and desolate swamps to enter the Nile as night was falling. The next day's sun rose upon dark mud banks where dead buffaloes, half-eaten by vultures, lay rotting in the slime. After some hours the boat would emerge from the Rosetta branch of the Nile and the bankside scenery became more strictly pic-turesque—clumps of palms, mosques, villages, patches of greenery and desert sand. The following morning the boat lay off Boulac, the port of Old Cairo, and now the rising sun revealed the range of the Mokattam Mountains in the distance. All Cairo was before you like a dream, a sea of minarets and palm-tree tops, with the domes of mosques like great gilt or turquoise bubbles protruding above the houses. Through groves of sycamores and fig-trees you could glimpse the mud ramparts, with their defensive towers. A wide avenue of olives and sycamores, marble fountains gleaming in their shades, led on to the gates of the city. Along this avenue a bewildering procession hustled and thronged—camels with black slave-boys perched on their backs, women swathed in white veils, fat merchants with long pipes, laden donkeys, water-carriers, Armenians, Arabs. Within the city walls you entered a labyrinth, a dreadful tangle, of filthy lanes and alley-ways. The best streets were under twelve feet wide; the verandahs of the houses jutted out overhead, and all that you could notice of the sky was a 'ser-pentine seam of blue.' Lean dogs grovelled and snarled in the gutters; donkeys (the best mode of travel over the unpaved streets) thudded by, their footfalls almost noiseless on the soft earth. Verminous beggars covered with sores leered up into your face, their eyes suppurating. Everybody pushed and jostled you, 'un-less,' said Warburton,[1] 'they recognise you as an Englishman—one of that race whom they think the devil can't frighten or teach manners to.'

As a matter of fact, there were hardly any English in Cairo at this moment. The French were still the predominant Europeans in Egypt, but English travellers recorded that the Egyptians seemed to expect England to come in strength and take part in Egyptian affairs within the next few years. Apart from Mr. Walne the Consul and Mr. Lane, the Egyptologist, to both of whom Milnes carried letters, the English in Egypt that winter comprised a handful of forty or fifty stray visitors. J. F. Lewis, the English painter of oriental water-colours, was then working there, and up the Nile there were twenty boats of English people—two or three to

[1] Upon whose description of Cairo in *The Crescent and the Cross* this passage is based.

each boat. The English consul used the word 'influx' to describe to Milnes the presence of some forty of his compatriots in the whole length and breadth of Egypt. He advised Milnes to engage a Nile boat at once, if he wanted to get a good one, and arranged for him to see a number of the mosques. Milnes had taken rooms in the new Hôtel d'Orient, in the Esbekeyeh, then ringed by a tree-shaded canal and a row of elaborate, mud-coloured houses with delicately carved façades. The Orient was a comfortable hotel, though some of its windows overlooked a cemetery through which wild dogs flitted like ghouls. Beyond the cemetery you could see gardens and kiosks, some tufted palm-trees, the glittering Nile, and then, beyond all this, the reddish-grey desert and the clear and well-known outlines of the Pyramids, so far away that they looked like toys. After ten days of sight-seeing and an inconclusive interview with Mahomet Ali, Milnes chartered a boat named the *Zuleika*, took on a captain and a crew of thirteen Arabs (clad in loose cotton trousers, blue shirts and red tarbooshes), a cook, a Nubian boy and an Italian dragoman called Agostino. He bought furniture, wine, stores, and glasses and plates, and set off, two days after Christmas, on the long journey up the Nile. Like every other Nile traveller, he had found a companion with whom to share the dangers and expenses of the voyage.

Stopping at Syra on his way from Greece to Constantinople the previous October, Milnes had run into a couple of his compatriots. One of these was an impetuous boy of nineteen from Nottingham-shire, who had matriculated at Milnes' old college, Trinity, Cambridge, in 1839. Instead of taking a degree, this young gentleman had impulsively embarked upon a journey to the East. His name was Mansfield Parkyns; a name then quite unknown, but which created a sensation in England ten years later, when Parkyns published, in 1853, his two-volume *Life in Abyssinia*, dedicated on Milnes' advice to Lord Palmerston. This book, which one of Milnes' friends described on its appearance as 'the most successful attempt of a man to reduce himself to the savage state on record,' is a literal account of several years spent in the remote parts of Abyssinia. Parkyns had lived there like a native. He had survived, and indeed enjoyed, his adventures by submitting himself to the customs of the country. Much in the book annoyed and shocked its readers. It is written in a brisk, detached and distinctly combative style. It opens with an attack on English people for criticising Africans for cruelty, and alleges that the English criminal law and the day-to-day customs of English sportsmen were quite as brutal as anything known in Abyssinia. Parkyns then explained that his bird specimens, which had travelled safely

through Abyssinia and Egypt in unaccompanied crates, had been
rifled at the London docks; English people were thus more dishonest
than 'the niggers.' He then went on to describe some of his own
habits in Abyssinia. He said he did not mind what he ate. He
had eaten everything under the sun. He was used to spitting out
the cockroaches which he found in his food on board Arab ships in
the Red Sea. He had never worn shoes in Abyssinia, growing an
extra skin upon his feet instead. For years he had dispensed with
any headgear, substituting 'a little butter' when he could find it.
He was proud of the fact that at the end of his adventures he not
only looked but smelt like an Arab, and was recognised as such
by astute pack-animals—camels, donkeys—which usually resented
the approach of a European. He cheerfully confessed to taking
part in many raids and feuds, to having killed some of the Baria and
other brigands, and to a belief in 'justifiable homicide.' Physically
Mansfield Parkyns was a very muscular young man, who had been
a pugilist at Cambridge. He was headlong and eccentric and
facetious, but he knew exactly what he wanted.

It was this untamed personality that Milnes had selected to be
his companion for two or three months in the cabin of a small
river-boat on the wide solitudes of the River Nile.

VI

'*List of luxuries to take up the Nile*' Milnes wrote out in his scrabbly
handwriting at the top of a blank page of a notebook. The luxuries
included recipes for 'making everything that can be made of
mutton, pigeons, chickens, eggs and rice,' some extra panes of glass
in case those in the cabin broke, a pair of black spectacles, a draught-
board, a stuffed pack-saddle, chisels for removing hieroglyphics
from temple walls, and 'a small camp-stool for a boy to carry behind
you when you go out walking, there being no stones or places to sit
and rest on.' Parkyns, who had been ill since reaching Cairo,
seems to have been more concerned with taking enough fire-arms,
some of which he later lent to an occupant of an English boat they
met up river: 'young Short of the Engineers' who was in the *Lotus*,
and whose face seemed to Milnes to bear a close resemblance to the
sculptures of the Egyptian kings.

In build the *Zuleika* was similar to the other Nile boats: some
50 feet long, with a tall curved mast amidships and another at the
bow, from which sprang spars with lateen sails. When the wind
dropped, as it did constantly and suddenly, the boat could be rowed
by the crew or pulled by them on a tow-rope from the banks. In

the bows was a small charcoal oven, with a fireplace on which
coffee was usually steaming and bubbling, and in the stern a sleeping
cabin, open in front and described by Warburton as 'not unlike
the boxes at Vauxhall Gardens.' The Nile boats hoisted two flags
—the flag of the country to which the travellers belonged and a
private flag adopted for the voyage and registered at all the Cairo
hotels so that Europeans could learn who was 'up' the river and
what flags to look out for. The flag of the *Zuleika* was white, with
a blue cross on it. Mr. and Lady Louisa Tenison, in the *Osiris*,
sported a pink flag with a white cross. Captain Stopford, Mr. Grey
and Mr. Ellice in the *Dromedary* had a parti-coloured flag of red
and white. Sir Thomas Phillips, who was accompanied in the
Phillippa by the painter Richard Dadd, had a white flag with a
green cross. The four gentlemen in the *Cheops* had a blue flag
with a white pyramid in the centre of it; and so on. Although there
were in all some twenty boats up river that December, you could
never count on finding anybody you were looking for. The boats
sometimes passed each other swiftly in the moonlight, when the
English travellers (tired of smoking and talking under the richly
starlit sky, bored perhaps by the atmosphere of 'monastic retirement' on the Nile at night) would be sleeping quietly in their cabins,
dreaming of the House of Commons or Pall Mall. Only the *rais*
and one or two of the crew kept watch as the boat slid onwards
from Esne to Edfou by the light of the Egyptian moon. They would
chant some lulling and probably obscene Arabic love-song as they
managed the white sails bulging to the gentle, sand-laden western
wind.

Milnes and Parkyns went down to their boat at Old Cairo in the
evening of 27 December. The *Zuleika* glided off and away past
the palaces and congested water-front of the city, beneath a
vermilion sky. Gradually the crimson would change to rose-
colour and then to yellow. The yellow melted into green, and
then, through white, to a rich and deep dark blue. To their
right the pyramids of Sakkara cut sharp grey triangles against the
horizon. At the base of the pyramids you could still see the tufts
of palm trees which Flaubert likened to nettles at the foot of graves.

Enormous sails fall from the long yards, like wide unfolding
wings [writes Eliot Warburton of a similar departure], the union
jack floats from the poop, and our private flag from the lofty spars;
the pyramids of Gizeh on our right, the distant minarets of Cairo on
our left, slowly recede. . . . The crew gather about the fire . . .
and discuss, in a whisper, the appearance of the pale stranger, who
reclines on a pile of Persian carpets as contentedly as if he had been
born and bred under the shadow of the palm.

It is hard to judge, at this distance of time, how much the pale strangers on the *Zuleika's* pile of Persian carpets really enjoyed their long and uneventful voyage. Although from time to time they passed another English boat and dined or smoked a pipe with a compatriot, Milnes and Parkyns inevitably spent most of each day together. Milnes had taken a stock of appropriate books with him—Wilkinson's *Hand-book*, Lane's *Modern Egypt*, the works of Champollion, the Frenchman who had done as much as Lane or Belzoni to unearth ancient Egypt, Mangin's *History of Mahomet Ali*, the travel journal of Prince Puckler Muskau. He was prepared to be impressed or interested by all he saw, and he made little tentative sketches of sculptures and reliefs, deciphered hieroglyphics, or noted down how 'full and proud' the face of Cleopatra in the temple at Dendera seemed—'not unlike Mrs. Fitzroy's.' Finding the 'character and sensations of an Egyptian winter . . . very *autumnal* to our English feelings and perceptions' he recorded each change of climate, each veering of the capricious wind. He began again to write verse:

> How happy in that cool, bright air to glide
> By Esne, Edfou, Ombos! each in turn,
> A pleasure and to other joys a guide;—
> Labourless motion,—yet enough to earn
> Syene's roseate cliffs, Egypt's romantic bourn.

Or:

> When you have lain for weeks together
> On such a noble river's breast,
> And learnt its face in every weather,
> And loved its motions and its rest,—
>
> 'Tis hard at some appointed place
> To check your course and turn your prow,
> And objects for themselves retrace
> You passed with added hope just now.

In spite of the weather, which was often very chilly, in spite of occasional headaches, Milnes could not fail to respond to the beauties of the Nile banks—with their sharp contrasts between green cultivated sward and gritty desert wastes; between pretty palm-shaded villages and great raw, purplish cliffs of rock; between majestic tombs and temples and their dusty satellite settlements of Arabs squealing for baksheesh and pressing forward as guides. The reactions of Mansfield Parkyns were more workaday. He belonged

to a younger and more matter-of-fact generation, less steeped in
Byronism and altogether less emotional. In one of Flaubert's
letters from the East he makes the important distinction between
the Orient of Byron—'the Orient of the curved sword, the Albanian
costume, and the grilled window looking on the blue sea'—and the
'baked Orient' of the bedouin and the desert, the depths of Africa,
the crocodile, the camel, the giraffe. Young Parkyns was of the same
practical stuff as Burton, Stanley, Livingstone: men with the high
Victorian conception of discovery and empire. Though Milnes
laughed at Parkyns' jokes and at his spirit of adventure, his point of
view remained consciously romantic. Parkyns told him that he
attributed the solidity of the ancient architecture they were seeing
to the Egyptians' vast consumption of beer (quoting Herodotus),
and when he turned to parodying Milnes' verse he produced this
kind of thing:

> All day drifted down,
> Wind quite contrary;
> Dined in my dressing-gown
> And sculled when it was airy;
> Smoked a new pipe-stick,
> Which almost made me sick.

He also specialised in working-class imitations that are reminiscent
of Dickens—calling the Nile 'that werry beneficent river,' for
instance, or 'I likes a noice drop of good beer'—and sang his own
improvised versions of Tom Moore's songs:

> The Minstrel boy to the war is gone,
> In the Milishay you'll find him,
> A huge blunt sword he has girded on,
> And his bottom goes behind him.

Although Milnes preferred the company of high-spirited eccentrics
to any other (not excluding that of Cabinet Ministers), Parkyns'
effervescent humour must frequently have been a trial. Parkyns
himself, who began by treating his companion with deference,
always addressing him as 'Mr. Milnes,' ended the two-month
journey with feelings of the greatest affection for him. He remained
a lifelong admirer of Milnes; and for some years after the Egyptian
visit the postbag would bring to Pall Mall or to Fryston vivacious,
descriptive letters headed Jidda, Ahdooah or New Dongola, and
signed 'Good-bye, God bless you, and sometimes think on your
old friend (born 16th Feb 1823) Mansfield Parkyns.'

VII

The early weeks of the voyage passed monotonously. At first they kept up with the *Lotus*, another English boat, and dined or breakfasted with its occupants every two or three days. Milnes' dislike of being alone—which as he aged became notorious—was already a well-rooted characteristic. He was essentially gregarious, and on the upper reaches of the Nile at sunset he missed the gaiety and the gossip of Bath House. Yet, aesthetically, he was touched by the multitudinous beauties of Egypt at sunset—the 'wonderful brightness of the lights before sunset under the clouds,' the silver ladders of the sun's rays sloping down across Mount Hagar Salam. Sometimes with Parkyns, sometimes alone, he would wander along the river's bank or out into the desert in the evening. Agostino, the dragoman, did his best to entertain them, and the crew, with their sing-songs and their odd habit of scarifying themselves with a red-hot iron and rubbing salt into the wound (a cure for a cough), were interesting to watch. Lounging on cushions under the shade of the awning, they would gaze at the birds upon the banks as they went by. The yellow Nile water rippled and susurrated round the *Zuleika's* prow, the river was alive with curious, dimly-seen fish, small clouds of gnats buzzed on the decks; while on the river-banks and on the spits of sand that jut out into the water were gathered 'snow-white pelicans, purple Nile geese, herons, ibis, lapwings'; turtle-doves, birds of paradise, hoopoes and swallows swerved and fluttered overhead. Sometimes they would shoot listlessly, and unsuccessfully, at birds and crocodiles. Sometimes they would pass a string of prisoners, wooden handcuffs on their wrists. Sometimes a slave-ship, laden with sad-eyed negroes from far up the river, floated mournfully by. Once they saw a fleet of rafts made of earthen vessels from Keneh, strapped together and bobbing merrily down towards Cairo. On some evenings the villagers or their own crew would indulge them with the sight of a 'bacchanalian dance.' And there were always the temples to be visited, reached by scrambling over fallen pillars and through doorways half-blocked with sand; and then, inside, the dark, cool, formidable and cavernous halls and chambers, where the torchlight glimmered on columns of colossal girth and on the towering hawk-headed gods of the ancient Egyptians looming evilly in the twilight, far above their heads.

In the last days of January the *Zuleika* approached Luxor, and the travellers came across a whole congregation of English boats. After a scene termed in Milnes' diary a 'great dispute and agitation of mind as to whether we should go beyond the cataracts' the boat was turned round, and began floating down on the fast current towards Cairo and London and home. Near the solemn cluster of tombs, temples and monuments that marks the site of ancient Thebes they loitered for a week, making expeditions to the ruins, while Milnes wrote verse. The dispute and agitation had doubtless had its origin in Parkyns' visions of pressing on into Upper Egypt. His sense of adventure was merely whetted by the Nile nights, whereas Milnes said he had 'to return to his parliamentary duties.' He had also, perhaps, had quite enough of the Nile.

> But life is full of limits [he wrote after
>   the dispute], heed not,
> One more or less—the forward track
> May often give you what you need not
> While wisdom waits on turning back.

Parkyns was still too young for wisdom of that kind.

However, in early February they were still lingering in the vicinity of Karnak, the size and splendour of which impressed Milnes more each time he saw it. After bathing in the Nile in the evening they would stroll out together towards those massive ruins, with the camels feeding on the pasture in the setting sun. Milnes (a stocky figure in a turban) clambered up the front pylon of the great temple to look at the sunset from its summit. Once they were entertained to a lunch of rice and chicken inside the temple by an Effendi, and for several days running Milnes would sit drowsily reading Dante at the foot of one of the vast lotus-pillars. Back on board the *Zuleika* he copied passages out:

> E chi podere, grazia, onore e fama,
> Teme di perder, perch'altri sormonti,
> Onde s'attrista si che'l contrario ama.[1]

Against this verse he wrote two words: '*my danger.*'

They used to visit Karnak by night as well, though it was rather bleak: 'Karnak by moonlight too chilly to be agreeable, and so cold as we came home as to make one fear the consequences,' Milnes noted of one evening on which he had conducted Lady Louisa Tenison, her husband and their friend George Thomson to the temple. The Tenisons and Mr. Thomson had dined with Milnes and Parkyns on the river bank. Lady Louisa, an enthusiastic female traveller who later wrote a book on her experiences

---

[1] 'There is he who is afraid he will lose power, favour, honour and fame because another is exalted; and for this reason he grows melancholy and loves the opposites of these things' (*Purgatorio*, Canto XVII).

in Spain, adored Egypt; she would even smoke 'the graceful nargileh,' or water-pipe, after each meal. Eliot Warburton, who came across the Tenisons a few days later, was startled by the dark tan of Lady Louisa's aristocratic skin. She might have passed for Cleopatra in a tableau, he thought, 'but,' he added fatuously, 'but for the ivory white forehead that indicated its proud claim to Norman blood.' Mr. Tenison and Mr. Thomson had grown long beards and wore turbans, after the habit of Europeans up the Nile. Milnes made this moonlight expedition a number of times over, and on each occasion the effect seemed to him finer. He went, too, to see the Tombs of the Kings, the Colossi and the Memnomnia at night, standing beneath tall obelisks stained by the droppings of vultures, with 'the moon shedding a light like a conflagration before she rose.'

Meanwhile, as they lingered at Karnak, Milnes' devoted friend Eliot Warburton had reached Cairo, hired a boat named *The Lethe*, and set off on the first stage of the journey which was to bring him fame as author of *The Crescent and the Cross*. In the first edition of this book he described how eagerly he scanned the river night and morning for a sight of the *Zuleika's* blue and white flag. For many days he was disappointed. Then, one morning in February, he was wakened at dawn by the cry 'Bindera Ingeeleez!' Peering out from the cabin, he caught a glimpse of a red ensign fluttering behind a group of palm trees at the river's bend. In a few moments more the English boat bore swiftly down upon them, and Warburton saw with a throb of delight that high on her tall spars floated a white flag with a blue cross, clearly visible in the crystalline air of the dawn. A shot brought the *Zuleika* to, and she was soon moored astern the *Lethe*. Warburton jumped aboard, and entering the cabin found Milnes sleeping: 'he was not a little surprised to see, standing by his bedside, one whom he believed to be three thousand miles away.' Their servants pitched a tent upon the shore, and Warburton gave Milnes a bundle of English papers and reviews which he had brought out for him from home. Warburton said that he recollected few more pleasurable hours than those they 'past in the shadow of the tent, looking out upon that strange wild scenery, with the Arabian hills and all their wonder and the Nile.' The crews of the two boats danced and sang upon the desert shore, while Milnes, Warburton and Parkyns 'laughed as much in an hour as Upper Egypt had done in a year.' But like Milnes (who recorded simply 'spent the day together—a sad pleasure'), Warburton was affected by melancholy at the transitory nature of their meeting. When he returned months later to Cairo, long after Milnes was back in England, Warburton was hurt to find that his friend had left him a packet of reviews but no smallest letter or note in his own hand. Parkyns too suffered later from this apparent indifference of Milnes'; his letters from Abyssinia usually begin and end with a reproach.

At evening the two friends parted. The crew of the *Zuleika* got out their oars and their boat was soon skimming downstream towards Siout. Warburton, cursing the ill-luck which had delayed his own arrival in Egypt by so many weeks, strained his eyes to follow the *Zuleika* as she sped away, her red ensign glimmering through the twilight. 'We could long catch glimpses of the watch-fires on their deck,' he wrote, 'and hear snatches of their wild Arab song.' [1]

VIII

Back in Cairo, Milnes found a collection of English letters waiting for him, and was soon immersed in London news. The Berrys were flourishing. Lady Holland was being very hospitable. Peel's difficulties were increasing. Lord Melbourne still had to be lifted into his carriage and have his food cut up for him. Dick Gascoyne had been found dead in his bed. Lord John Russell had produced a book. Tom Acland had had a row with *The Post*. Mrs. Trollope was going about London praising Milnes' poetry with the result (wrote Colville) that 'people go no more to Murrays to ask for Childe Harold, but stop by the way at Moxon's, I need not say for what.' Lord Leicester was definitely going to marry Miss White-head, and Bear Ellice was suspected of being engaged. It had all begun again. The world was waiting to envelop him once more.

While Parkyns was making final arrangements to rush across the desert to Suez on a dromedary (which kicked him off one night by the shore of the Red Sea), Milnes took a passage on a French ship to Malta and began a leisurely and civilised homeward journey via Rome and Paris. He was held up in Malta by a quarantine, but reached Rome in time for Holy Week. Here he revisited his old haunts (including the English College, now in the able charge of Dr. Baggs) and renewed his friendship with Rio, who tried to tempt him to go up to Urbino, where he was gathering material for *L'Art Chrétien*. But, difficult as it was to leave Italy in spring-time, Milnes posted up from Marseilles to Paris and spent a week or two seeing his French friends.

Paris was still, and inevitably, anti-English; though Milnes found

---

[1] In later editions of this amusing book this and other personal incidents were cut out. *Eothen*, on the other hand, remained as quirky and anecdotal as when it first appeared.

Guizot and Mérimée, Lamartine, Tocqueville and George Sand (whom he thought *très rangée*, busy with her new book) as personally amiable as ever. One day in May he went out to Neuilly to have an audience with the King of the French. Louis-Philippe discussed with him the new cause of Anglo-French diplomatic friction—the Spanish marriages.[1] If England would not have a Bourbon consort for the Queen of Spain, the King feared the appearance of a German one: 'Have you not had enough with the kings of Greece and Portugal?' Louis-Philippe must have been well aware of the pro-Prussian tendencies already evident in London; of the assiduity of Milnes' friend the Chevalier Bunsen as Prussian Minister, of the Queen's sympathies and the Prince Consort's convictions, of the attitude of many educated English people, who still looked down on France as a defeated nation, the home of a decadent culture it amused them to patronise. But Louis-Philippe was always pre-pared to flatter an English member of Parliament. In December 1842 he had succeeded in making a fool of Disraeli during his visit to Paris, and now he turned his attention and his charm on Monck-ton Milnes. 'Remember that whenever you come to France,' he said to Milnes in his perfect English, 'you will always be welcome here—that you will always be received with regard and with confidence.' Most of Milnes' Parisian friends regarded their monarch with distaste: 'Le roi gouverne par la peur,' Tocqueville remarked to Milnes in this spring of 1843: 'non qu'il en inspire pour lui, mais qu'il en fait naître aux autres.'

Milnes got back to London at the end of May. One of the first of his friends to welcome him warmly was Carlyle. 'In good hour hast thou returned,' he wrote. 'The impatience of the public was fast mounting towards anxiety. Everybody said: "We cannot want our Milnes!"'

---

[1] *The Spanish Marriages.* This question, which finally broke the entente between France and England and was a contributory cause of the downfall of Louis-Philippe in 1848, centred round the marriage of Isabella II and her younger sister. Louis-Philippe's ambition to renew the old marriage-alliance between French and Spanish Bourbons was strongly opposed by England. He tried to get round this situation by arranging for Isabella to marry her cousin, who was known to be incapable of having children, while her younger sister married Louis-Philippe's son, the Duc de Montpensier (1846). The 'Spanish Marriages' became an outstanding international issue of the middle 'forties.

I

The summer of 1843 opened damp and chilly. With 'the sensation of Egyptian light and warmth' still on him, Milnes complained that the shivering English June was making Fleet Ditch of his intellect. The rugs, pipes and oriental carpets which he had shipped from Smyrna had never arrived. His mother was ill; his father was talking of shutting up Fryston for economy; and every way he looked something depressing met his eye. Like most long journeys, his expedition into the Moslem world had had the effect of making the familiar seem odd. Now he was back he saw London in a new perspective.

Physically there were few real differences between the London of 1842 and that of 1843. Trafalgar Square, begun under Barry's directions in 1840, was still completing; the Houses of Parliament were now beginning to rise, white, elaborate and Perpendicular beside the Thames [1]; Pugin had completed St. George's pro-Cathedral, Southwark; the Bank of England was lit by gas. But Milnes perceived subtler signs of change.

The gradual pauperisation of the upper classes is distinct and tangible [he wrote to MacCarthy two or three days after he had got back, with his valet, to Pall Mall]. I never saw so many houses to let. Barouches are turning into flies, chariots into broughams. There are fewer balls, and it is getting rather respectable than not, to have little money to spend. As long as they were rich the aristocracy preached up the indispensableness of wealth, and now they are getting poor they will declaim against the vulgar ostentation of it. Although the declination will pervade the whole rank of landed proprietors, and small ones such as ourselves are the first to feel it, I cannot help thinking the general social effect will be a good one, and that we may get something in compensation for luxury which nobody enjoyed and pleasure which left everybody discontented.

Although, as it turned out, the railway boom of 1844–45 helped Mr. Pemberton Milnes (and many other country squires) to stave

————————

[1] 'The new Houses of Parliament seem to me like a magnificent fender,' said young John Ruskin to Milnes in 1846.

off impoverishment to a later generation, the heyday of the landed classes, both financially and politically, was drawing to its close. Already enlightened members of the aristocracy—Lord Ashley, for example—came forward in their new role of protectors of the working people against the exploitation of the manufacturers and the middle class. In *Past and Present*, published in the spring of 1843, Carlyle was declaring the old aristocracy to be both unworthy and dispossessed. Its place would be taken by an industrial élite of able men pledged to serve and to command; men of the calibre of those northern manufacturers who were pillars of the Anti-Corn Law League. Unlike most people, who thought European civilisation was slowly breaking up, Carlyle foretold that the period of convulsion would soon be followed by a regime of order. *Past and Present* had a big sale, though not all of Carlyle's admirers liked the book. 'Toujours la même et toujours naïve' was Milnes' verdict on it. He thought it could be very dangerous; he added wittily, 'if turned into the vernacular.' Carlyle had been 'unjust and insulting' to everyone who was trying to remedy the current discontents, and though Milnes might privately be tiring of Sir Robert Peel (whose reply to an account of Milnes' recent conversations with the King of the French at Neuilly had been cold and unencouraging), he did not care to see his party's leader pilloried as Sir Jabez Windbag by Carlyle.[1]

The position of Peel's Ministry, rickety when Milnes had left England in August 1842, was really most unenviable by the summer of 1843. The power of the Anti-Corn-Law League was growing swiftly, and even *The Times* now had to admit 'the League is a Fact.' Although the League had not united with the Chartists, they were as one in opposition to the Government. The Prime Minister's popularity in the country had fallen mercurially in two years. In the autumn of 1842 he was being burned in effigy in more than one provincial town north of London. There had been convincing rumours that Drayton itself had been sacked and set on fire. Peel was blamed on all sides for 'personal responsibility' for the high prices of corn and the near-famine conditions of industrial England, taunted in the House of Commons yet told he was abandoning his principles, universally criticised for the disillusioning 'do-nothing policy' revealed in his declarations to the House, the most recent of which had been in January 1843. A more horrible and more dramatic incident had occurred that

---

[1] This criticism of *Past and Present* was unconsciously copied from a letter from Miss Martineau to Milnes, written in 1843. Milnes' friends sometimes teased him for making use of other people's opinions without acknowledgement. Such a constant talker expressed so many opinions each day that they could hardly all be his own.

January (as Milnes and Parkyns floated tranquilly upon the Nile):
the Prime Minister's private secretary, Edward Drummond, had
been shot dead one evening outside a bank at Charing Cross, the
victim of an insane attack intended for Peel himself. From
Staffordshire and the North came perpetual reports of the workers'
use of their new weapon, the strike. Greville noted in his diary
that never in his whole lifetime had he seen England in so grave
a condition. Revolution or some form of uprising was openly
discussed. Peel's firmness of character alone held his Ministry
together. Only two years before he had seemed to Milnes as
well-established and as popular as William Pitt or Sir Robert
Walpole.

Abroad the Ministry seemed little more successful than at home.
The country had become involved in activities such as the First
Opium War and the annexation of Scinde, which even to jingoistic
contemporaries did not seem quite necessary or quite right.
Although Aberdeen was trying hard to undo the damage of his
predecessor, Palmerston, and to construct a working friendship
with France, the *entente* was not cordial. Oddly enough, it was
Milnes who introduced a more personal note into the Anglo-
French understanding. At Neuilly he had asked Louis-Philippe
why he did not invite the English Queen and her Consort to visit
France. The King had seemed surprised, then intrigued, then full
of questions. He finally acted upon Milnes' suggestion, and in the
autumn of 1843 the English royal family paid a visit to Château
d'Eu, where Aberdeen and Guizot informally discussed the Spanish
marriage question. But by next year, when the return visit of the
French court to England was expected, all sorts of things had gone
wrong: the Tahiti affair, Tangier, the familiar cry that the Mediterranean was becoming a 'French lake.' Relations were so strained
that it needed all Guizot's tact and Aberdeen's determination to get
Louis-Philippe to England in October 1844. Amongst the English
tributes presented to the French king on this visit was a basket of
late fruit from Fryston Hall.

II

Both before he had left for the East and after his return, Monckton
Milnes was known to be an active supporter of Lord Ashley in his
various campaigns to improve factory and mining conditions.
Sadler's famous child labour report of 1843, which showed that
women and small children were used as draught-animals in the
mines, crawling on hands and knees dragging trucks, a chain passed
between their legs and attached to a belt round the waist, had

profoundly shocked everyone in England. Even so no early Victorian parliament took stringent or systematic action on it. The First Factory Act was mild and negative, merely forbidding women to work underground and stating that children should not be sent into the mines below the age of ten. These provisions took many years to make operative, since the whole question of inspecting mines to see that orders were carried out was extremely complicated. It was only in the worst mines and mills that these appalling slave conditions existed; but life in all the industrial cities and villages was brutish and diseased. In 1844 Manchester was described by Friedrich Engels as a city in which 350,000 human beings were herded together in mildewing, putrescent hovels, shrouded in an atmosphere thick with coal-dust. Enlightened men such as Lord Ashley and Charles Dickens tried to stir up public feeling against these conditions, aided by a few enterprising women like Miss Burdett-Coutts. The Queen herself was known to be 'grave and sorrowful' about the factory children, making the Prince read Chadwick's reports aloud to her in the evenings. Popular poets took up the cause with an effort at ruthless realism that was new. Hood's *Song of the Shirt* swept the country when it appeared in *Punch* at Christmas 1843, and behind the painted sun-blinds of Wimpole Street Miss Elizabeth Barrett was penning her *Cry of the Children*, a lengthy work inspired by the child labour report. Miss Barrett's poem moved many people to tears. Milnes copied it out when he first heard it that same year:

> But the young, young children, O my brothers!
>   They are weeping bitterly,
> They are weeping in the playtime of the others
>   In the country of the Free.
>
>   .   .   .
>
> For all day we drag our burden tiring,
>   Through the coal-dark underground—
> Or all day we drive the wheels of iron,
>   In the factories round and round.

This was verse with a purpose, and contrasted somewhat with Milnes' Morland-like vignette of poor children in his *Poetry of the People* published in 1839:

> . . . the People's honest child,
> The field-flower of the open sky,
> Ready to live while winds are wild,
> Nor, when they soften, loth to die.

Wordsworthian sentimentality was no longer applicable to the realities of life in these later stages of the Industrial Revolution.

In all public philanthropic activities Milnes was from now on prominent. By 1844 he was taking a leading place on the platforms of London meetings for the amelioration of working-class conditions; and at this epoch he introduced the first of his bills to establish juvenile reformatories and try to stem at its source the flood of vice and crime. His reformatory schemes, which later became law, were at this time discussed by most people as the vagaries of an idealist and a poet. There was little general support for the belief of Milnes and Lord Ashley that environment was in itself a cause of crime. Although Milnes never loved the West Riding, this industrialised countryside was in his blood and bones. His family, which had begun as mill-owners in Wakefield, had blossomed into country gentry, and this gave him a traditional interest both in factory and country labourers' conditions. Each view from the windows of Fryston Hall reminded him of his responsibilities: the plumes of factory smoke smudging the horizon, the dour mining villages a few miles from the gates of the park, the coal-barges passing slowly, slowly on the oily waters of the River Aire, the smutty cypresses in the garden and the rhododendron shrubberies dark with dust. His goodness of heart, hitherto confined within the wide circle of his friends, now ranged out in a genuine concern for the English poor. In his support of Factory Bills and Education Bills he ran counter to the opinions of most of his constituents. The dissenters of Pontefract seemed to him 'bitter and fanatical' on these questions. He found that by giving his aid to Lord Ashley he was risking his seat in Parliament. He continued to give Lord Ashley his aid.

The Pontefract burghers were not alone in their dislike of Milnes' new activities. Opposition came also from his friends and from one in particular—a loquacious, able, invalid lady who was on some matters one of the clearest thinkers of her day. 'What *do* you mean about your living on the earnings of the poor?' Miss Harriet Martineau wrote to him in the summer of 1843. 'Are you jesting, or do you take me for a dunce? You pay wages, I suppose. . . ?' Immobile on her sofa in a furnished lodging at Tynemouth, awaiting death in the company of her mother, her ear-trumpet, a pyramid of books, and a good many friends and admirers, the authoress of *Deerbrook* and *Society in America* was as trenchant as before her illness. She differed from Milnes and Lord Ashley on almost all the philanthropic theories they professed. She particularly disliked Lord Ashley's Ten Hour Bill for limiting the working time of women and young persons in factories. She accused him of being 'a well-meaning mischief-doer.' She was a manufacturer's daughter, she wrote to Milnes, and so she *knew*

Lord Ashley to be misled. His statements were 'profoundly untrue.' He had no experience of mill-life, and his descriptions of it in his great speeches to the House were about as authentic as 'the descriptions of high life in the novels of the silver fork school, or as if I were to present Life in China.' She pointed out that Lord Ashley passed over the infinitely more wretched and degraded existence of the peasants and the country workers. If he concerned himself with them (and after all, they were more his responsibility) he would do much better. How utterly misguided Milnes was to become entangled with this 'hasty patch-work' legislation. She had herself seen factory conditions in the United States:

seen the women and girls at Lowell and Waltham—fresh and brisk —dancing in the winter evenings, and walking in the summer— playing on the piano, attending Emerson's lectures, reading and writing while working in the mills 70 hours per week.

The evils affecting the country were town, not mill, evils, she wrote. And the way to cure these was to provide cheaper food, by repealing the Corn Laws. Why did not Mr. Milnes follow Charles Buller and Lord Howick and agitate, like them, for repeal? It seemed absurd to Miss Martineau that he should be so excitable about factories and mines and yet seem to adopt the conventional attitude of the Tory landowners over repeal. The reason parents sent their children into slavery was because there was not enough to eat, and each child came to be callously regarded as a breadwinner from the age of four or five: 'no Act of Parliament—no kind or amount of express legislation—would protect the children against their natural guardians.'

A republican and an agnostic, Miss Martineau was at this period looking forward hopefully to the religious conflict which she thought imminent. England would once more be 'knee-deep in blood' she wrote in 1844. To her thinking the parson was the

evil genius of English life: sadly apt . . . to stay the hand of the noblemen and others,—seeing 'no occasion' for village libraries, —or for a playground to the school,—or for making the school-room above 6 ft. in height or more than 14 ft. square—or for paying the master more than L25 or the mistress than L15—while the butler is paid—how much more?—and L1000 is given for a rare plant.

In the coming civil war between the High Church and the Dissenters, she and Milnes would be on different sides:

but certainly [she wrote] it was never any particular agreement in Opinion that brought us acquainted; and it will not be any disagreement that will alienate us. Besides [she added in one of her not infrequent references to her own expected death], the dispute cannot have gone very far before I go to find a solution elsewhere.

For Miss Martineau had been told by her doctors that she was doomed to die at any moment, and she had made her plans accordingly. In fact, owing to a sensational cure which she attributed to mesmerism, she lived until the age of seventy-four, dying in 1876 in the Lake District, not many years before Lord Houghton.

Milnes, who must at times have been amused by Harriet Martineau's solemnity and lack of humour, took her seriously on the whole. He dedicated a poem entitled *Christian Endurance* [1] to her. This compliment gratified her, coming from 'so young a man.' Like other friends whom she had convinced that she was dying, Milnes kindly made a journey to Tynemouth to visit her as she lay looking out at the glittering northern sea, the yellow hayfields in the sunshine and the wind-blown sycamores down by the harbour. He arrived with a stack of books and sat by her couch shouting into the ear-trumpet about politics or Lamennais' last book or Comte's philosophy, while she did her wool-work and gazed out to sea. Miss Martineau at this time was just past forty, eminent and satisfied to be so, laughed at by some people but receiving homage from a very great many more. In appearance she was plump and even 'motherly-looking,' with brown hair dressed very flat and low on her forehead, and an eager eye that tried to interpret what people were saying from the expression on their faces and the movements of their lips. Her admiration for Milnes' poetry was very sincere. Its moral tone appealed to her, and she often kept a volume of his poems open on her desk when she was writing. After his visit she felt that she had wasted her opportunities, by being too

---

[1] *Christian Endurance. To H.M.* appeared as one of a series of *Arabian Legends* in *Palm Leaves* (1844):

> Mortal! that standest on a point of time,
>   With an eternity on either hand,
> Thou hast one duty above all sublime,
>   Where thou art placed serenely there to stand:
>
> To stand undaunted by the threatening death,
>   Or harder circumstance of living doom,
> Nor less untempted by the odorous breath
>   Of Hope that rises even from the tomb.

There are seven further stanzas. Miss Martineau told Milnes she was 'very deeply indebted . . . you little know how deeply' to him for these verses; but before the publication of *Palm Leaves* she was mystified to find that a manuscript copy of the lines had come into the possession of Mrs. Butler (Fanny Kemble the actress). 'I have been wanting to tell you . . . that *I* have not made them common,' she wrote post-haste to the poet, '& how they got abroad I know not. I shd as soon think of praying in the street-window as giving abroad those lines.' (MS. letter from Tynemouth, June 22nd, 1844(?).)

reticent to question him about his experiences. His poems seemed to her deeply autobiographical, and she was puzzled that this laughing, kindly being should have the knowledge of evil which she detected in his verse. How had he come by his sympathy with so many kinds and degrees of suffering?

I am surprised in my turn [she wrote] . . . not on account of any kind of knowledge or ignorance of your life—but from your temper and air. It would seem as if it were well to see and know and keenly feel the mystery of Evil and its extent, if it does no more harm than it seems to have done to you.

Unlike his London or House of Commons friends, Miss Martineau had persuaded herself that Milnes' influence in the House was growing from session to session. How clever of him, she said, to overcome his chief disadvantage: 'a want of acquaintance with ordinary affairs and with ordinary ways of thinking of them.'

Whatever Miss Martineau might suppose, Milnes knew that his career was not progressing. He had returned from Egypt to find that Gladstone, his precise contemporary, had become a member of the Cabinet at the age of thirty-three and with only a few more years of parliamentary experience than Milnes' own. The violence of the Pontefract electors over education, over the Irish question and over the factory bills distressed him. Extremes in politics had always been distasteful to him, though in life and in relationships he remained emotional and erratic. He wrote to MacCarthy that as a moderate protectionist he could please neither party—

via media vilissima, and somehow or other I never *can* get out of it . . . from having lived with all sorts of people and seen good in all, the broad black lines of judgement that people usually draw seem to me false and foolish, and I think my finer ones just as distinct, though no-one can see them but myself.

He became extremely discouraged, talked of giving up his rooms in Pall Mall, and declared that he was going on

piano, piano, expecting daily less of the world—and getting less too. I am contracting my acquaintance [he continued in an access of despair], losing my desire of knowing and liking everybody, and becoming like other people, having got little good out of my originality.

In this mood he set off for Wales to stay with his caustic old ex-tutor, Thirlwall, now Bishop of St. Davids, at the Palace, Abergwili, and with the Stewarts at Cardiff Castle. While in Wales he wrote a long letter asking Gladstone for advice.

III

It was now nearly fifteen years since that December day of 1829 when a merry deputation of Trinity men had driven through the snow to Oxford to defend the poetry of Shelley against that of Byron in the Union. Writing of the occasion to his mother, Milnes had observed that the Oxford man who '*took*' him most had been the youngest Gladstone of Liverpool—'I am sure a very superior person.' That first acquaintance had moved on with the years into friendship, and ever since then Gladstone had been a cordial or (as he signed himself) an 'attached friend' to Milnes. He was now proving himself a very superior person indeed,[1] and though Peel objected to his habit of publishing tracts and articles in the reviews, he had been chosen by the Prime Minister to be President of the Board of Trade. In the records of Milnes' long friendship with W. E. Gladstone there is no trace of that envy, that 'insane vanity' which Disraeli attributed to him, and which he declared made 'Dicky' most unamiable. On the contrary, Milnes seems to have relished Gladstone's success; and he was always treated by Gladstone with affection and respect.

The letter which Milnes wrote to Gladstone from Carclow, Penrhyn, in October 1843, was, briefly, a confidential application for a post just fallen vacant at the Paris Embassy. He told Gladstone that he found his present position in the House 'most uncomfortable' and that he was 'stranded on an uneasy insignificance.' He proposed, should the post in Paris be available, to apply to Peel for it, to give up his seat in Parliament, and retire, at least temporarily, to France. He explained that he did not wish to abandon public life altogether, but that he saw no future for himself in the House of Commons. He said he felt too loyal to Peel to throw in his lot with the Young Englanders, who were led by Disraeli and animated by intense dislike for the Prime Minister, and yet he seemed to be doing no good by 'officially obtruding my support on a Government (thank God) too strong to want it.' He felt he had more experience of Continental affairs than most young Englishmen of his age, he wrote, and so seemed justified in applying for the Paris post vacated by Henry Bulwer, who was going to Madrid.

The background of this letter was a little more complicated than

---

[1] Gladstone's moral tone was already well established at the age of thirty-three. Milnes recorded a scrap of conversation between Abraham Hayward and Mrs. Norton at this time: 'Hayward saying "that Gladstone from his Puritanism could not understand a great deal of men and things"—Mrs. Norton: "And do you think that all your worldly knowledge enables you to understand anything so pure and good as Gladstone?"'

its frank tone suggests. Disraeli was already at work preparing to
deal his hammer-blows at Peel's administration. He was inspired
by ambition, but also by a bitter hatred for Sir Robert Peel.
This hatred was apparently based upon Peel's refusal to give him
office when he had applied for it in 1841; a fact only revealed after
Disraeli's death, from a note found among Peel's private papers.
Unlike Milnes, who went about everywhere complaining of Peel's
neglect, Disraeli had suppressed this private incident and took a
public stand against Peel on party and patriotic grounds. Disraeli's hatred of Peel may also have been influenced by the fact
(recorded only by Milnes) that Peel had guffawed with laughter
over the failure of his first speech in 1837. Milnes Disraeli treated
with outward cordiality but inward contempt; and one of his chief
henchmen in the Young England movement, George Smythe, later
Lord Strangford, was fast becoming Milnes' bitterest enemy.
The original of Disraeli's *Coningsby*, George Smythe, was nine
years younger than Milnes, and was becoming a rival to him
in his knowledge of Continental affairs. He and Disraeli laughed
openly when Milnes (who had 'no rural taste or accomplish-
ment') appeared in the House during the Corn Law debates
dressed in a squire's cutaway green coat with basket buttons.
'See Dicky!' whispered Smythe. 'Protection looking up!' This
undercurrent of ridicule was exactly what Milnes (who was very
sensitive) disliked most, and it was this rather than any sense of
loyalty to the august and chilly Peel that kept him from plunging
into the Young England movement. According to Disraeli, Milnes
was distressed to find in 1844 that the author of *Coningsby* (a book
filled with real people) had not introduced him as a character into
that novel. If Disraeli is to be believed, 'Dicky' came to him 'with
great earnestness—tears in his eyes—I had never appreciated him
and all that sort of thing.' He reminded Disraeli that he had
sometimes voted with the Young England group and should thus
by rights have figured with them in the novel. The result of this
conversation came three years later, when Disraeli paid Milnes the
doubtful compliment of depicting him in *Tancred* as the eccentric
Mr. Vavasour—'a social favourite; a poet, and a real poet, quite
a troubadour, as well as a member of Parliament; travelled, sweet-
tempered and good-hearted; very amusing and very clever.' It
was not a wholly flattering portrait.

In applying for the Paris secretaryship Milnes was also influenced
by his love of France, his intimacy with men such as Guizot and
Tocqueville, the friendly way in which the King of the French had
treated him that spring, and a general vague dissatisfaction with
English ways. Perhaps, too, he thought of the gay if hardworking

lives of the attachés of Sir Stratford Canning at Constantinople;
their knowledge of what was really going on all over Europe, the
secret despatches, the embassy dinners, the early-morning rides
round Buyukdhéré to watch the sun break through the autumn mists
across the Golden Horn. An embassy life might have suited his
talents and his temperament to perfection.

Gladstone did not think so. In a letter of eight pages he
told Milnes, first, that he believed the post at Paris already filled.
He went on to hope that

you will *not* . . . carry your half-matured intention into effect
[and to emphasise that there was] nothing in the character of your
Parliamentary position which should make your friends rejoice in
your being removed from it.

All independent-minded men must be 'uneasy' in such times,
Gladstone went on, and he was convinced Milnes should not
'remove' himself altogether from English life. But the pivot of
Gladstone's argument was really a moral issue which he
detected, or created, in Milnes' mind. It appeared to him, he
wrote, that Milnes was chiefly influenced by 'a repulsive rather
than an attractive force' in wishing to leave England and the
House of Commons. Gladstone was not a man to admit the validity
of such a motive. To wish to do something else merely from distaste for what you were at present doing seemed to him weak,
almost immoral. To men like Gladstone (and there were then
many persons of his mind in England) pleasure was not a legitimate consideration in any personal decision. The fact that Milnes
was not happy in the House of Commons and might be happier in
the Paris Embassy was of no consequence to Gladstone, who
clearly felt it should also have been of no consequence to Milnes.

Gladstone put the case so strongly that Milnes succumbed to his
arguments and replied that he would stay where he was. The
chief reason, he frankly admitted, was the uncertainty as to whether
Bulwer's position was still vacant; he did not wish to make the
blunder of asking Peel for something which would have to be refused.
He said that Gladstone's letter had strongly suggested to him that
he might be performing 'almost unconsciously, a humble duty
in remaining in the House of Commons at the present moment,'
that he might be 'exercising some infinitesimal influence for
good' which he 'ought not to abandon on mere grounds of personal
discontent.'

And so he stayed on in the House of Commons, facing the
ridicule of the Young Englanders, the calm, deliberate neglect
of Sir Robert Peel. He spent the autumn of that year at Fryston

and at Bawtry, with his parents. He hated walking in the country, and spent most of his time indoors working up *Palm Leaves* for the press. He said he found his poetry less spontaneous than 'in the fair old times of Italy and Greece'; 'more plastically correct . . . (but) . . . less true and genial.' On the other hand, he thought that his prose style had improved.

IV

Milnes wrote an article on *Coningsby* in *Hood's Magazine*[1] for June 1844. This article, though complimentary in tone, was rather more critical than most of the other notices of this wildly popular book had been. It was written, too, over the signature 'Real England,' and maintained that while *Coningsby* was a good book it could not be called a great one. The characters were not created, Milnes said, but copied straight from life; they were essentially ephemeral, and the book seemed to him, as it seems to posterity, artificial, smart and lacking in real quality. He probably agreed, in fact, with his friend Lady Harriet Baring, who said that the people in *Coningsby* seemed like 'the envelopes of men,' not real men at all. Disraeli amiably thanked him for the review, but added that Mrs. Disraeli was ready with some 'puissant arguments' against it. Although neither Milnes nor Disraeli ever had any sincere regard for each other, they remained on perfectly polite, familiar terms. Milnes would call on the Disraelis in the evening, or dine with them, or go to one of Mrs. Disraeli's drums at the big house at the corner of Grosvenor Gate which had belonged to her first husband, Wyndham Lewis, and had been left her for her lifetime. In the autumn of 1844 (but at the invitation of Milnes' father rather than at his own), Benjamin Disraeli and Mary Anne came to stay at Fryston for some days. Disraeli was at this time thirty-nine, while his wife was fifty-two. They had been married for five years, but the discrepancy in their ages was very noticeable, and was emphasised by Mrs. Disraeli's girlish clothes and simpering behaviour, which caused a certain amusement wherever they went. Fryston was no exception.

Under Mr. Milnes' directions great preparations had been made for their entertainment, for Mr. Milnes affected an unbounded

---

[1] *Hood's Magazine* had been established in January 1844 by the dying poet Thomas Hood, who had retired from the editorship of the *New Monthly Magazine* at the end of 1843. The undertaking proved too much for him, and he broke down completely at Christmas 1844 and died the following May. Milnes, who helped the journalist F. O. Ward get a pension for Hood, also aided him by writing unpaid articles for *Hood's Magazine* and whipping up other people to do so.

admiration for Disraeli (who attributed this to the old man's wish to 'vex' Dicky). The Galways had been persuaded to lend their chef from Serlby to take care of the kitchen, the regular Fryston cook being relegated to the position of a mere assistant. The food was described by one of the guests as 'sumptuous'—turtle soup, salmon, woodcocks, snipe, dishes of truffles, champagne. Eighteen or twenty other guests were staying in the house or passed through it while the Disraelis were there: the Galways, the Milnes Gaskells, Mr. Slingsby Duncombe and his beautiful but 'under-jawed' and ill-born wife, young Gathorne-Hardy, and so on. Also amongst the party was Lady Elizabeth Spencer-Stanhope, with two of her children. Lady Elizabeth Spencer-Stanhope was nearly fifty. She was the daughter of old Mr. George Coke of Holkham, who had been made first Earl of Leicester in the new creation, and who had been the friend and perforce the host of many royal dukes in earlier reigns. His daughter was a rich woman, accustomed to the ritualistic and well-regulated luxury of life at Holkham. She was witty and wrote excellent, lively letters; but she was also in a very strict sense Victorian. Her attitude to homely, easy-going Fryston was one of pert and rather over-bred curiosity. The atmosphere that Carlyle had found idle and oppressive, Thackeray charming and 'like a tavern,' seemed to Lady Elizabeth Spencer-Stanhope merely eccentric. 'Everyone is very queer here,' she wrote of another visit to the Milneses; and though she had to admit she was very much amused by the way people came and went and did just as they pleased, she was secretly a little irked by it all.

I do not think you could have stood this house [she wrote to her husband]. Last night, from excessive fatigue, what with the heating and late hours, poor Mr. Duncombe actually could not be roused by the butler from a deep sleep into which he had fallen on the sofa, at nearly 2 o'clock in the morning, during which I believe Lord Galway blacked his face.

She had known Mrs. Milnes for many years, remembering her as a handsome young woman dressed in the plumed turban and flat straight brocade robes fashionable under the Regency; she found her now an ill, elderly lady, who relied on her sister-in-law Louisa and her daughter Harriette to help her with a houseful of guests. Old Mr. Milnes was hospitable and charming. Richard she liked too, calling him in the London way 'Cool of the Evening,' and listening to his descriptions of Thebes and to his singing of sentimental songs. On one night of the Disraelis' visit charades were acted, with characters from *Martin Chuzzlewit*, published the year before. Richard Milnes distinguished himself in the part of Mrs. Sarah Gamp.

Lady Elizabeth had been prepared to dislike Mr. and Mrs. Disraeli, but she was won over by Disraeli the first evening. His soft voice and half-foreign manner, the way he asked her if she drank champagne or helped her to dress her truffles was most disarming. Next morning she found she liked Mrs. Disraeli too; in spite of her wearing a wreath and a lace dress over pink satin, looped up on either side. Mary Anne seemed so really devoted to 'her D'Izzy' and so off-hand and spontaneous that it was not easy to resist her. And then she specially entertained Lady Elizabeth, who adored gossip, by telling her the inner story of the rows of Lytton Bulwer and his wife and of how she had vainly tried to mediate between them.

The reasons for which Lady Elizabeth Spencer-Stanhope felt uneasy at Fryston were just those for which Richard's real friends particularly liked the place. Several factors combined to make up the Fryston atmosphere at this period. There was Mr. Milnes' own breezy and quirky hospitality. There was his wife's tolerant gaiety and attitude of *dolce far niente*. There was Harriette Galway's needle-pointed wit. There was Richard's dislike of country things, his originality of mind, his love of paradox, and his habit of strewing the house with new books. The wander-years in Italy had left indelible marks upon each member of this Yorkshire family individually and upon all of them collectively as well. They liked to sit up till any hour past midnight, to breakfast at eleven and have luncheon at one. They left their guests to their own devices, and so long as they were amused and amusing and did not seem overtly uncomfortable, the Milneses supposed that all was well. Lady Elizabeth stayed again at Fryston nearly ten years later, when Mrs. Milnes was dead. On this occasion, too, she complained of the heat of the rooms, of Lady Galway's indifference to time, and of her custom of sitting up to watch the whist till two in the morning instead of leading the ladies to their bedrooms. To Lady Elizabeth the bedrooms seemed as topsy-turvy as ever, and the tone of the household as lackadaisical. The candlesticks on her mantelpiece wore garlands of dusty artificial flowers with tarnished leaves of gold and silver paper, pathetic relics of some long-past festivity. There was no water in her jug when she wished to dress for dinner, and when she rang the bell to ask for some 'one of the housemaids answered it *en chemise.*' [1]

---

[1] Details from *The Letter-Bags of Lady Elizabeth Spencer-Stanhope*, ed. A. M. W. Stirling (2 vols., 1913). The visit is also mentioned in Lord Cranbrook's Memoir of his father, Gathorne Gathorne-Hardy, first Earl of Cranbrook (1814–1906).

V

The small water-colour drawing (by an amateur hand) which forms the frontispiece to this book shows us a group of the Milnes family and their neighbours, standing amongst the red-leather chairs upon the stone-flagged floor of the library at Fryston in the year 1844. Richard Milnes is in the foreground, a pouter-pigeon figure, stocky, self-satisfied, his hands deep in his pockets, one knee on a chair. You may fancy it is he who is talking. His sister Harriette, in a lace cap, her husband Lord Galway, and Lord Morpeth and one or two other men are also present; but the most significant feature of the drawing is the attitude and expression of Richard's father. If Richard resembles a pouter-pigeon, Mr. Milnes is looking like a startled but inquisitive crane. His grey head tilted forward, he seems to be listening with a certain wry or cynical attention to his son's discourse. His attitude accords exactly with the description which Disraeli gives of him at one of Richard's Pall Mall breakfasts at about this time: the 'Shandean squire' standing upright by the fireplace, watching the company and 'astonished at the scene, not accustomed to in Yorkshire.' From being an annoyance, Richard had become a puzzle, almost a pastime, to his father, whose affection for his son, though genuine, was always exceedingly detached.

It was all very well for Mr. Milnes to have fed Richard's political ambitions and pushed him into a career for which he was in no way suited. He had himself withdrawn from politics when very young and singularly sought after, and for the rest of his life he had been doing much as he pleased, within a framework straitened by moderate poverty. He was leading just the sort of life he liked, his time comfortably divided between his two houses at Bawtry and at Fryston, his son-in-law's mansion at Serlby, and places like Kippax which belonged to old neighbours who were mostly his cousins as well. His life was marred only by anxiety about his wife's health, by his own recurrent headaches and bouts of depression (legacies of the Malvern accident of five years before), by such events as the death of his agent or such slight inconveniences as the non-arrival of post-horses to take him in his carriage from the West Riding to Nottinghamshire or vice versa. His interests were local country interests. His chief amusement was piquet, varied by a little mild literary activity (re-reading Milton, for instance). His chief excitement (apart from rare expeditions to London) was the repainting of the Fryston hothouses or the 'burnishing' of the Hall and garden at Bawtry, where he would superintend the cleaning of the lake. He wrote frequently to Richard, usually on business or politics, but sending accounts of the 'great breadth of corn, dead ripe' which he had seen from the Great North Road, or of the health of people in Pontefract, or of the rotten wood the railwaymen were using for some new viaduct. His letters contained, too, the usual caustic commentaries on Richard's political news: 'You say Peel made a bad speech—it reads better than any speech in the debate'; or some crisp expression of a difference of opinion beginning ' wonder you did not put this . . .' or 'What *did* you mean by . . .' When Richard began writing for the *Edinburgh Review* Mr. Milnes would scrutinise the published articles:

The punctuation is in several places faulty [he wrote of his son's *Germany and Erfurt*, which appeared in the *Edinburgh* for April 1850]. You always write for an instructed class (perhaps this may be a fault too in *speaking*) & I doubt if one reader in a hundred ever saw 'Hegemony' in print—or knew what 'mora' is.

He would send lists of what he called 'small corrigenda': when Richard had used the phrase 'balance the plain reasonableness,' for instance, his father commented: 'you *balance probabilities*—not reasonableness—and *plain reasonableness*!!' As the Corn Law agitation reached new heights, the differences of opinion between father and son increased.

All Mr. Milnes' energies were not absorbed by this halcyon country existence. Throughout the decade of the eighteen-forties he was deeply and successfully engaged in trying to recoup his family's fortunes by means of the railway boom. 1845 was the peak year of the railway speculation which had seized upon the whole nation in much the same way as the eighteenth-century South Sea Bubble. In November 1845 *The Times* newspaper, which was striving to expose the railway scandals, published an analysis showing that over 1,200 railway lines had been projected by private companies and that the total capital investment required from members of the public amounted to £500,000,000. A great number of these lines were competing with each other; many of them were unnecessary; several of them were impracticable; a few were outright swindles. Greville noted in his diary for this year how wild the speculation had become, how unsafe yet how wholly irresistible. The attention of members of Parliament was soon distracted by service on one or other of the numberless railway investigation committees set up (in the temporary wooden sheds used as committee rooms at Westminster) to try and protect the public and save the country from transport chaos, and from what Richard Monckton Milnes called 'the confused net of iron' which

was being spread all across the English counties. Milnes himself
served on one of these committees:

The extent of railroad speculation has been perfectly awful [he
wrote in June 1845], and the loss will be proportionate. The lobbies
of the House of Commons have been like an Exchange, with carrier
pigeons going off to the City with the decisions and turns of Committees. Mine has now sat six weeks.

Three months before this he had published an article [1] pointing
out the aesthetic merits of the French and Italian railroad projects,
which were being built with English labour and English capital,
but were designed by foreigners and with a view to the landscape:

the one from Rouen to Paris [he wrote] keeps crossing the Seine
like a huge snake lying over its course, and exhibits a series of
continuous pleasant rural pictures such as we hardly know of on
any English line.

He suggested, too, that when the whole continent was made
'permeable' to English travellers, the political effects might be
considerable:

when . . . we are all well jolted together in the same train, the
entente cordiale will perhaps be closer than it is now. No longer
will the English carriage roll through the plains of Touraine and
Auvergne in all its solitary pomposity, with the lady's maid indignant
at not stopping regularly for tea at four o'clock in a housekeeper's
room, and the courier as pretentious as an Eastern dragoman:
no longer will the steamer descend the Rhone with the light freight
of one English family, taking the boat to themselves to avoid the
annoyance of continental contact.

But English people in 1845 did not like being told home truths
any more than they do today. Milnes' views were dismissed as
just one more example of his love of paradox. Railway construction,
unplanned, unchecked, went fast ahead.

The Milnes' estates at Bawtry and Fryston, at Fishlake and
Thorne, lay right across the routes of at least seven of the projected
railways. With the companies directing six of these Mr. Milnes
concluded very satisfactory negotiations. The seventh company,
that of the Great or Direct Northern, which had absorbed the
original London-and-York project, proved tougher to deal with;
but even so Mr. Milnes netted a round sum of £100,000 in a few
years. The most spectacular personality in the railway boom was
George Hudson, the 'Railway King.' Hudson was a Yorkshire
farmer's son whose extraordinary enterprise had swept him from

---

[1] This railroad article was published in *Hood's Magazine* (March 1845).

the position of apprentice to a York draper to that of a millionaire railway magnate, a Member of Parliament, and builder of two vast and lavish houses in Albert Gate, Hyde Park. Richard Milnes and his father both liked Hudson; and for many years after the crash which ended his career they remembered him and tried to help his impoverished wife and family. Though ready to laugh at the accents and education of the railway magnates and their wives,[1] the Milneses, like most other land-owning families in England, were only too ready to profit by these new phenomena. Indeed, the land-owning class showed itself, in these years, quite as astute at money-making as any of the hard-headed new rich. Mr. Milnes always suspected the railway companies of trying to get the better of him. He liked to prolong and complicate negotiations until he had screwed out the last penny for his land. He would confront the company promoters with a mixture of efficient financial sense and well-bred charm which was most disarming. After a deal with George Hudson involving tens of thousands of pounds, he added a postscript to a letter to Richard: 'I said to H.,' he wrote, 'that whatever it is, it must be *guineas*, as I mean to give the shillings to my wife. He said "by all means."'

Although they had an unusual chance to make big sums of money, the landowners' position during these negotiations remained a little delicate. On the one hand, as much land as possible should be sold to the railways as expensively as possible, before the bubble burst and values dropped (a process which began in 1847). On the other hand, the line must not pass too close to one's own house or ruin the appearance of one's estate. Together with his daughter's husband, Galway, Mr. Milnes became a positive authority on engineering in these years. He would decide where stations should go, whether a line ought to take a high or a low bank, how a plantation or a willow-bed could be saved, a lodge moved, or a tunnel dug under the village of Brotherton. At one moment the best course for a new line seemed to him to be slap through the middle of Byram, his neighbours' house across the Aire, at another a deviation behind Ferry Fryston church seemed most desirable. Although his advice was not always taken by the railway companies, it amused him to give it; and in these days Fryston rang with talk of viaducts and deviations, loops and halts, the merits of the Sheffield-and-Manchester as against the Leeds-and-Bradford. He

---

[1] E.g. 'My father has let Bawtry to a railway director, whose wife promises to take great care of the furniture, declaring that "'er 'ome is 'er 'obby"' (Milnes to MacCarthy, Sept. 29th, 1848). The rise of the Hudsons also caused comment: 'Mrs. Hudson saying she had no trouble about her dress. "I say to my maid—dress me for six—dress me for ten—dress me for forty—& it always comes right."' (Commonplace book, 1844–45.)

would make sketch-maps on little scraps of paper or count up the number of passengers on some new express train to show that in the end the passenger traffic could never pay. Born into the easy coaching world of the late eighteenth century, he showed a remarkable adaptability in assimilating the conditions of the new steam age. Mrs. Milnes was less enthusiastic about the railroads. She wrote to ask Richard never to cross the line at a level-crossing, citing the recent Brighton accident in which a 'young person' had been knocked down by an engine (the severed head being afterwards found inside her bonnet beside the track). A female cottager at Castleford had cried out against the railways as Mr. Milnes was passing by: 'Oh, the railroad, the horrid railroad, do promise me, Mr. Milnes, that you will stop it.' In Ferrybridge the five coaching inns were already on the decline as wheeled traffic on the Great North Road fell off. Of fifty pair of post-horses only three were left by the end of the decade, and one of the three postboys (so Mr. Milnes said) had hanged himself. All over England the iron web was spinning. For the first time movement from one end of the country to the other was becoming quick and easy for the rich and possible for the poor.

Richard Milnes was less violently interested in all these developments than his father, though he said he did not mind serving in the stuffy sheds of the railway committees, since it gave him the feeling of being 'an infinitesimal wheel in this world-machine of ours.' This was rather an insincere statement, since he did not ever like to think of himself as an infinitesimal wheel, nor had he any taste or genius for high finance. More and more, as he grew older, his affinities with creative artists were becoming evident. Less and less did he conform to anybody's idea of a responsible man of affairs. A letter written to him from Marseilles in May 1847 emphasises the real ambiguity of his position at this time. It is written by Saville Morton, a philandering painter and newspaper correspondent with whom Milnes had made friends as they cantered through the chestnut-shaded valleys of the Pyrenees in 1838.[1] In May 1847 Morton was just returning from Turkey and

---

[1] Saville Morton, who was a particular friend of Tennyson, Thackeray and Edward FitzGerald, and to a lesser degree of Milnes himself, is a figure of great interest about whom little has survived. He matriculated at Trinity College, Cambridge, in 1830, but did not meet Milnes until the Pyrenees journey of 1838 ('he said you were sunshine to him' wrote Morton's mother to Milnes after Saville's death). Morton led a wandering life as painter, journalist and lover. His mistresses included Lola Montes, and he was finally murdered by a jealous husband, Elliot Bower, who was also a newspaper correspondent, in Paris in the autumn of 1852. As interesting as this dramatic end to his career is the fact that FitzGerald greatly admired his letters and wished to get them published. FitzGerald's opinion is strongly confirmed by the survival of five long descriptive

Syria. Sitting in a hot Marseilles hotel-room he wrote Milnes an extended rhapsody on his own experiences.

But what are all these strange touches and wild transitions of travel to you [he concluded], you poor civilised creature, who are chain'd to Irish Poor Law Committees, and live among newspapers and railways, scarcely filching an hour of the 24 to rhyme a sonnet? Ah! what a depth of pity I feel for you, while you are struggling through that London world . . . snatching at fame through the hurly-burly like a drowning man trying to get a gasp of air—born an artist and doom'd a politician—framed to expatiate in Edens, and condemn'd to be jostled at soirées.

In the past Morton's attitude had been rather more deferential than this. He ended the letter with apologies for his 'impertinence' in speaking his own mind.

VI

But Milnes continued to be jostled at soirées. It was by his own choice. In the face of the frank criticisms of the most intelligent and attached of his friends—Thomas Carlyle, Stafford O'Brien, Saville Morton, Warburton, MacCarthy for example—he persisted in leading, while in London, a life crammed with acquaintances. He might feel moody at times, but the wish to see a very great many people each day quickly reasserted itself. He was getting on towards the age of forty, and the shape and habits of his life were beginning to set.

Disraeli's sketch of Milnes in *Tancred* is biassed, but it is instructive. When the young hero of the book, enamoured of the gambler Lady Bertie and Bellairs, gives a river party for her on his yacht, *The Basilisk*, Milnes comes aboard as one of the guests.

Mr. Vavasour, who was there [we read], went to all his evening parties; to the assembly by the wife of a minister in Carlton Terrace; to a rout by the wife of the leader of Opposition in Whitehall; to a literary soirée in Westminster, and a brace of balls in Portman

letters from Morton to Milnes (which, together with a sketch of Morton and some letters from his mother and sisters, religious fanatics resident at Torquay, will be published in due course). All the available information upon Saville Morton has been skilfully summarised by Dr. Gordon N. Ray in the first volume of his superb edition of *The Letters and Private Papers of W. M. Thackeray* (Oxford University Press, 1945). Dr. Ray suggests that some 'fragmentary letters from Morton to FitzGerald' might if published 'prove unexpectedly enlightening.' After Morton's murder his papers and poems were entrusted to Milnes by Mrs. Morton, but they were returned by him to the family and may not have survived. Morton is certainly an unrecognised English letter-writer of some consequence. See also Terhune's *Life of Edward FitzGerald* (Oxford University Press, 1947).

and Belgrave Squares; and told them all that they were none of them to be compared to the party of the morning, to which, it must be owned, he had greatly contributed by his good humour and merry wit.

In the ominous phrase 'it must be owned' Disraeli's real attitude to Milnes lies revealed.

Milnes' first appearance in *Tancred* is at the select little dinner-party given by Sidonia, the Jewish banker, at which the other guests are Coningsby (George Smythe), his wife, Lord and Lady Marney, Lord Henry Sidney and Tancred himself. Milnes arrives late from a division in the House, and is described as a troubadour and a member of Parliament in the passage already quoted. Disraeli goes on to assert the renown of Milnes' breakfasts:

Whatever your creed, class or country, one might almost add your character, you were a welcome guest at his matutinal meal, provided you were celebrated. That qualification, however, was rigidly enforced. . . . Vavasour liked to be the Amphitryon of a cluster of personal enemies. He prided himself on figuring as the social medium by which rival reputations became acquainted, and paid each other in his presence the compliments which veiled their ineffable disgust. . . . A real philosopher, alike from his genial disposition and from the influence of his rich and various information, Vavasour moved amid the strife sympathising with every one. . . . He liked to know everybody who was known, and to see everything which ought to be seen. He also was of opinion that everybody who was known ought to know him; and that the spectacle, however splendid or exciting, was not quite perfect without his presence. His life was a gyration of energetic curiosity; an insatiable whirl of social celebrity. There was not a congregation of sages and philosophers in any part of Europe which he did not attend as a brother. He was present at the camp of Kalisch in his yeomanry uniform, and assisted at the festivals of Barcelona in an Andalusian jacket. He was everywhere and at everything; he had gone down in a diving-bell and gone up in a balloon. As for his acquaintances, he was welcomed in every land; his universal sympathies seemed omnipotent. Emperor and king, jacobin and carbonaro, alike cherished him. He was the steward of Polish balls and the vindicator of Russian humanity; he dined with Louis Philippe and gave dinners to Louis Blanc.

The food and wine Sidonia offered his guests were so good that at first they talked little. There was no general conversation save 'a burst now and then from the ringing voice of Mrs. Coningsby crossing a lance with her habitual opponent, Mr. Vavasour, who however generally withdrew from the skirmish when a fresh dish was handed to him.' But when the conversation does become general, Milnes' part in it, and the attitude of his friends towards him, is of a certain subtle interest. Mrs. Coningsby suddenly announces that the Queen is to give a costume ball, and that she has herself been told the period it is to cover. Some of them hope it will be confined within the bracket of a distinct age, others hope it will not:

'. . . What can be finer [said Mr. Vavasour] than to represent the spirit of an age?'

'And Mr. Vavasour to perform the principal part,' said Mrs. Coningsby. 'I know exactly what he means. He wants to dance the Polka as Petrarch, and find a Laura in every partner.'

'You have no poetical feeling,' said Mr. Vavasour, waving his hand. 'I have often told you so.'

'You will easily find Lauras, Mr. Vavasour, if you often write such beautiful verses as I have been reading to-day,' said Lady Marney.

'You, on the contrary,' said Mr. Vavasour, bowing, 'have a great deal of poetic feeling, Lady Marney—I have always said so.'

When Mrs. Coningsby admitted that the ball was to be a question of gentlemen in wigs ('Mr. Vavasour, you will not be able to crown yourself with a laurel wreath') and ladies in powder, Vavasour 'pondered somewhat dolefully on the anti-poetic spirit of the age.' Later, during a discussion of Maynooth, Vavasour upholds the value of public opinion:

'What do you mean by public opinion?' said Tancred.

'The opinion of the reflecting majority,' said Vavasour.

'Those who don't read your poems,' said Coningsby.

'Boy, boy!' said Vavasour, who could endure raillery from one he had been at college with, but who was not over-pleased at Coningsby selecting the present occasion to claim his franchise, when a new man was present like Lord Montacute on whom Vavasour naturally wished to produce an impression.

On the publication of *Tancred* Milnes wrote to the new editor of the *Edinburgh Review*, Professor Empson, offering an article upon the novel. Empson and Lord Jeffreys tentatively accepted; and the result was an analysis of Disraeli's writing so able and so ruthless that Milnes' son, the late Lord Crewe, used to attribute to this article alone Disraeli's manifest dislike of Milnes. It maintained that Disraeli degraded his function as a novelist by condescending to 'draw mimicries of individuals composing the most vapid and limited of all classes of the community—namely that which is conventionally called the highest,' and asserted that all he achieved was to give 'a superficial portrait of what the man appeared to superficial people, and the reality of him rests unknown or misinterpreted just as before.' With this criticism in mind, it is still useful to linger for a moment over the conversation at Sidonia's dinner-party.

This conversation contains a number of sly digs at Milnes. His love of food; his wish to make an impression; his solemnity over his position as a Member of Parliament; his impersonation of Chaucer at the State Fancy Ball of 1842; his habit of publishing his occasional poetry in the morning newspapers (for it was in a newspaper that Sybil Marney would have seen his verse that day); and his inclusion among the literary lights of the new age in R. H. Horne's two-volume illustrated symposium *A New Spirit of the Age*, published in 1844. Disraeli's own novels reveal with a searchlight clarity that he was himself utterly devoid of any aesthetic sense. Milnes' position as a poet, which was distinct and justified, seemed to him a trifle ludicrous. But by 1844 it was a position which could not be ignored.

It was in this year that Milnes published his final volumes of poems, *Palm Leaves*, the results of his Eastern journey, dedicated to Guizot, and *Poems Legendary and Historical*, dedicated to Gladstone, a collection of verses which had mostly appeared already in the magazines. In the same year Moxon republished two former volumes of Monckton Milnes' verse: *Poems of Many Years*, which re-emerged from the press with a new inscription to the Conversazione Society (i.e. the Apostles), and *Memorials of Many Scenes*. According to Miss Martineau these new editions were much needed. She wrote to Milnes in February 1844 from Tynemouth that her 'bad morning hour' had gone by 'unawares' while she was reading his *Poetry for the People*:

You know it was out of print [wrote Miss Martineau] when you sent me the rest. I have got it from a London library, & it shoves my business aside, as you see. I wish you cd. see how delectably dirty & broken backed this copy is. It almost requires gloves and scissors to turn over with. I am more glad of this than you wd be; for you are more in the way of knowing than I am where your writings penetrate, & how far they spread. It is a perpetual surprise to me that I do not hear more of them,—though evidence of their acceptableness does reach me. To me they are, more than ever, miraculous in their sympathy & insight—& perfectly fresh & new, though treating of matters as old as Man.

VII

Soon after these words of Miss Martineau's were written, there appeared in London R. H. Horne's *A New Spirit of the Age*, in which she was dealt with in a manner she greatly disliked, while

Milnes was allotted high praise. *A New Spirit of the Age* was com-
piled in imitation of Hazlitt's *Spirit of the Age* and consisted of
twenty-five essays in which more than forty living persons were
candidly discussed, a large percentage of them being novelists: it
included every contemporary of any apparent literary consequence,
and was received with anger and petulance on all sides. The two
volumes were not the unaided work of R. H. Horne.[1] His chief
assistant had been Robert Bell, but he had also received much advice
and some actual essays from Miss Elizabeth Barrett, whom he had
not yet met, and with whom he corresponded through their mutual
friend Miss Mary Russell Mitford. Miss Barrett's part in the *New
Spirit* was kept a deadly secret; it was not till after his own return
from Australia (in 1869) that Horne confessed to Milnes that she had
collaborated with him over the book, contributing especially to the
notices of Milnes himself, Hartley Coleridge, Landor, Tennyson and
Carlyle. A year or two before this, Horne and his unseen friend had
formed another project, *Chaucer's Poems Modernised* (published in
1841), in which they had tried to involve Monckton Milnes. 'I am
very much pleased,' wrote Horne to Milnes, 'to find you have com-
menced practising what Miss Barrett very finely calls "the art of
smoothing the locks of the Father Poet's sublime grey hair."' The
fact that Elizabeth Barrett took a main part in the assessment of
Milnes' poetry for the *New Spirit* gives it an especial interest.

Richard Monckton Milnes and Hartley Coleridge is the title of the
essay in question. 'The poetry of Richard Monckton Milnes,' it
begins, 'has met with considerable praise in many quarters, yet
hardly as much as it deserves; and it has met with peculiar dispraise,
more than it deserves, either in kind or degree.' Mr. Milnes had
been accused, the writer said, 'of a want of the divine fire of imagination and passion . . . of merely thinking what he thinks.' Admitting that Milnes did not appear to possess 'the least *dramatic* passion'
and that there was no impulse, energy, nor momentum in his
lines, Miss Barrett claimed that he was a poet of 'inherent
beauty,' not of passion: 'It is as a lyric and elegiac poet (in the
ancient sense of elegy) with a temperament rather elegiac than lyric,
that Mr. Monckton Milnes takes his place among the distinguished
writers of his age and century.' She considered him a 'specifically
Christian' poet:

His poetry is even ecclesiastical sometimes; and the author of
'One Tract More,' and his tendency towards a decorative religion,
are to be recognised in the haste with which he lights a taper before

---

[1] Richard Hengist Horne (1803–84) was author of several tragedies and of
the epic *Orion*. He went to Australia in 1852, returned in 1869, and was granted
a Civil List pension in 1874. Miss Barrett's letters to him were published in 1877.

a picture, or bends beneath a 'Papal benediction.' . . . With every susceptibility of sense and fancy [she continued] he would often write pictorially if he did not nearly always write analytically. . . . His poems, for the most part, are what is called 'occasional,' —their motive-impulse arising from without. He perceives and responds rather than creates.

She quoted extracts from Milnes' poems to support her estimate, including the beautiful lines from *Leucas*:

> But when in clearer unison
> That marvellous concord still went on;
> And gently as a blossom grows
> A frame of syllables uprose.

Taken as a contemporary verdict the closing paragraph is also worth consideration:

The general estimate of Richard Monckton Milnes is a thinking feeling man, worshipping and loving as a man should . . . and singing the songs of his own soul and heart, in a clear sweet serenity which does not want depth, none the less faithfully and nobly, that he looks occasionally from the harp-strings to the music-book. His 'Lay of the Humble,' 'Long Ago,' and other names of melodies, strike upon the memory as softly and deeply as a note of the melodies themselves—while (apart from these lyrics) he has written some of the fullest and finest sonnets, not merely in our age, but of our literature. [1]

[1] The essay on Milnes and Hartley Coleridge is to be found at page 187 of the *World's Classics* edition of *A New Spirit of the Age* (Oxford, 1907). The original 1844 edition was in two volumes, illustrated with engravings.

Chapter Ten

1844   *1845*

I

'Our poet Monckton Milnes—one of the *young England* set—has been to Berlin,' wrote Anna Jameson to her dear friend, Ottilie von Goethe,[1] in February 1845. 'He says he went to decide for himself whether the King of Prussia was or was not a humbug, and I am anxious to know whether he has made up his mind on the subject.' Milnes, who had not been in Germany since 1834 (when, incidentally, he had escorted Mrs. Jameson to tea with Auerbach in Dresden), had first thought of the visit to Berlin seven or eight months after his return from Egypt. The novelty of being back in England had begun to rub off, and on Gladstone's advice he had given up his idea of applying for a job at the Paris Embassy. In a letter to MacCarthy of January 1844 (in which he repeated the humbug joke he had made to Mrs. Jameson) he spoke of going to Berlin for six weeks; but by April he found himself 'too hampered with business private and public' to get even as far as Paris for Easter. He wrote to Guizot to explain how busy he was as 'an aide-de-camp of Ashley's' over the Ten Hour Bill. Milnes' first biographer takes the year 1844 as marking the 'beginning of his serious political career.' It would be wiser to take it as marking the end of his serious poetical one.

Although Milnes was still officially a Peelite until 1846 and was never (with all deference to Mrs. Jameson) a real Young Englander or follower of Disraeli, he was swiftly developing a dislike of Peel almost as strong as Disraeli's own. 'Sir Robert Peel,' he told Guizot in an access of patriotic discretion in April 1844, 'is in great vigour and good spirits'; but at the same moment he was writing to his father that

Peel is absolutely indefensible. He is asking from his party all the blind confidence the country gentlemen placed in Mr. Pitt,

[1] The letters of Anna Jameson (1794–1860; authoress of *Sacred and Legendary Art* and other books on painting very popular in their day) to Goethe's daughter-in-law, Ottilie von Pogwisch (1796–1872), were edited by G. H. Needler and published (Oxford University Press) in 1939. The two hundred and eighteen letters of Mrs. Jameson in this volume are of a certain interest, though the value of the edition is much vitiated by numerous unexplained excisions.

all the affectionate devotion Mr. Canning won from all his friends,
and all the adherence Lord John and the Whigs get from their
'family compact,' without himself fulfilling any one of the engage-
ments on his side.

'. . . Peel, as a leader, is done for,' he wrote in another letter
to Fryston a few weeks later; '. . . he has forfeited the only kind
of confidence left him, viz., that in his practical management of
affairs.' 'I never saw him more haughty and uncompromising,'
he wrote of Peel again about this time. House of Commons
business and various personal factors, such as the birth of his sister's
boy, kept him in England until December 1844. Meanwhile he
found time to write his first article for the *Edinburgh Review*.

The articles in the *Edinburgh*, a quarterly then more than forty
years old, were of course anonymous, but their authorship was very
soon known all over London. The *Edinburgh* was specifically and
notoriously Whig. Milnes' decision to write for it was thus another
step towards the Whig fold, to which by temperament and outlook
he belonged. The articles were lengthy—20,000 words or so—
and, in accordance with the tradition set by Francis Jeffrey,
the first editor, and carried on by his successor, Macvey Napier,
they had to be not only intelligent, knowledgeable and easy to read,
but sharp and malicious as well. Milnes' first article, which appeared in the *Edinburgh* for April 1844, fulfilled most of the editor's
requirements. In substance it was a very long attack upon a
popular new French book on Russia, which had been written by
the Marquis de Custine. Custine was a French nobleman who had
travelled through Russia in 1839, been graciously received at the
Imperial Court and shown anything he wanted to see, and who
had then, on his return to Paris, published a four-volume onslaught
on the Russian Government, its tyranny, bigotry, persecutions and
system of police-spies. Although writing for a Liberal and thus
anti-Czarist paper, Milnes took the view that Custine was both
dishonest and unreliable; his book was 'not, as it professes to be, a
picture of Russia in 1839, but a portrait of the author with a Musco-
vite background.' The author, Milnes suggested, had misunderstood Russia from first to last, since he had treated it as though it
were a Western country, whereas it is in reality 'an advanced post
of the East.' Milnes' article was exceedingly clever, but also level-
headed and sensible. On his return from Prussia he published a
series of four authoritative and enlightened articles on Germany in
the *Edinburgh*.[1] The first of the articles on Germany, *The Political*

---

[1] The four German articles are: *The Political State of Prussia* (January 1846);
Reflections on the Political State of Germany (April 1849); *Germany and Erfurt* (April
1850); and *The Menace of War in Germany* (January 1851).

State of Prussia, was based on the judgements he formed at Berlin in the winter of 1844–5.

II

It was not until December of 1844 that Milnes became free enough to set out for Berlin. He travelled through Hanover, Brunswick and Magdeburg in mid-winter, reaching Berlin in the second week of the month. At Brunswick, he found he could indulge that taste for the picturesque which had infused his *Poems Legendary and Historical*.

I like the town of Brunswick [he noted]; the curious gabled houses in the broad streets—the handsome palace with the people passing freely through its gardens and by its windows—the tame crows pecking about in the quiet spaces and the strange old churches with their two towers united by a huge gloria window. Of the princes, too, in the Cathedral vault eight have fallen in brave battle —few royal houses, if any, can say as much.

He passed, too, the 'Porta Westphalica' (the break in the hills through which the Weser forces its way near the battlefield of Minden), and at Magdeburg he was shown over the fortifications and the citadel by a Prussian lieutenant.

Berlin itself was still a severely classical city, with smooth white eighteenth-century churches, the Dom, the wide, trim streets through which the hired droshkies rattled; and the vista of the Brandenburg Arch through the lines of stripped and wintry linden trees. Milnes noticed that in this icy, often fog-bound city the window-frames of the houses were coated with green moss, while the carriage-horses standing in the streets wore leopard-skins to protect them from the cold. Berlin society struck him at once as stiff and *gênant*. He quickly understood that the scholars and 'learned people' were the best company in a rather oppressive community which placed an exaggerated emphasis on birth and etiquette. Berlin society was impoverished, and the only amusing dinner-parties were those given by the foreign diplomats—the French ambassador, for instance, who had one hundred and eighty candles in his dining-room, or the English ambassador, Lord Westmorland, who was aided by his intelligent and influential wife. The interiors of the Berlin houses, heated by huge stoves, were ugly and encumbered. 'The decline of natural taste here is frightful,' a Prussian acquaintance said to Milnes; 'ten years ago the forms of decoration were simple and classical—e.g. in the palace of Prince Albert; now everything is monstrous and unartistic.' In 1844 Berlin and the whole Prussian kingdom was ruled by an absolute monarchy.

The country was gagged by an iron censorship. Trials were conducted without juries. There was no true freedom of religion, and the king's pet form of evangelical pietism was steadily gaining ground. It was not an atmosphere in which Milnes or any other liberal-minded Englishman could feel at home.

In 1844 Prussia was still one of a great number of small German states. The Czar's policy, after the collapse of the conference system set up at the Congress of Vienna in 1815, had been to prevent any union or federation in Germany, for this would aggrandise either Austria or Prussia. By 1840 liberalism, influenced by French and Swiss refugees, by the writings of young journalists like Karl Marx and by the teaching of Hegel, was seeping in all directions through the German states. As the 'forties went on political unrest broke out in many places: in Saxony and Baden, in Hesse-Cassel, Bavaria, Nassau and Hanover. The whole network of little kings, princelings and grand-dukes felt threatened, for the avowed aim of German liberalism was a federation of all the German states under a central government. In Prussia itself the late king, Frederick William III, had promised to grant his country a constitution; as reactionary as Metternich in Austria, he had failed to honour his word, but had, by a purely personal popularity, got away with it in his lifetime. The accession of his son, Frederick William IV, in 1840 (just four years before Milnes' visit) had roused popular and liberal hopes; for he was a man of noble character and lofty ideals, with a misty medieval and romantic conception of kingship. These hopes were disappointed.

In spite of some slight initial relaxation of the throttling censorship on printed books and newspapers, Frederick William IV soon showed that he was as opposed to liberal principles as he professed himself to be to strict bureaucracy. He was a scrupulous man, but he lived in a perpetual dilemma. 'The King of Prussia always reminds me of the Emperor Galba,' one of Milnes' new friends in Berlin said to him. 'He would be the best and even the greatest of men were he not a King, or even were he a Constitutional one.' The king was encircled by advisers and relations who were determined he should never grant Prussia a constitution. At the head of the anti-constitutional party stood his brother and heir, the Prince of Prussia, known to history as the Emperor William I. Milnes was told that the Prince of Prussia had threatened to leave the kingdom with his family if the king showed signs of giving way to the demands of the liberals; and, though the troubles of 1848 did finally result in the granting of a half-hearted kind of constitution in 1850, Prince William's point of view was not really at variance with the king's own most secret instincts. But Frederick William IV, who earnestly affected the sciences as well as the arts and kept the septuagenarian Alexander von Humboldt in Berlin (with a seat opposite his own at the royal table every day), was open to the influence of favourites. Almost his greatest favourite was Hans Christian von Bunsen, Milnes' old friend from Roman days, who had been Prussian Minister in London since 1841.

The Chevalier Bunsen was known to be urging the king to draw up and grant a constitution to his kingdom; and though he himself told Lady Westmorland [1] that he had only spoken of a constitution at the king's express wish, Bunsen was regarded as a dangerous enemy by Prince William and the reactionaries of the Court of Berlin. Humboldt, even, particularly disliked Bunsen, chiefly for his pietism; for, as Milnes wrote (in *Fraser's Magazine* in 1860),

by a singular fatality Bunsen was looked upon in this country with much suspicion and ill-will, as a latitudinarian and neologist, while he was abused and persecuted as an evangelical fanatic on the banks of the Spree.

When Richard Milnes set off for Berlin he was perhaps blithely unaware of the general hostility to Bunsen of the Prussian court. It was largely on Bunsen's advice that he had gone to look at Prussia, and he arrived armed with letters from the Prussian diplomat. 'I have a notion,' he wrote to MacCarthy, 'I shall find the King what the Yorkshiremen call "a little soft," but very good. Bunsen is in higher favour than ever.' In point of fact Milnes had no opportunity of finding out whether Frederick William IV was soft or hard. Bunsen's enemies had made up their minds that this genial and inquisitive English gentleman was a secret emissary to the king, and they set to work to prevent Milnes having any conversation with Frederick William IV.

The anti-Bunsenites have been quite successful—one way or the other—in preventing the King from having any talk with me [Milnes wrote to Fryston]. As I have done all that was civil, and Lord Westmoreland always shown his good-will to me, I cannot care about this politically or socially: . . . and I am not sorry that I am now left to speak or write whatever I please, without any fear of a charge of Custinism.

III

Milnes' Berlin notebook contains a stock of those acid political jokes then, as always, current in the Prussian capital: barbed jokes against King Frederick William and his government, inevitable in

---

[1] See *The Correspondence of Priscilla Countess of Westmorland* (1813–1870), edited by Lady R. Weigall (John Murray, 1909).

an absolutist state. He garnered, too, a good deal of rather trivial gossip, though on the whole he cared little for the genteel world of Berlin, observing with detachment its childish obsession with precedence, and with the writing of notes in French, still the language of polite society. He had really come over to find out about Prussian politics and to get to know the intellectual life of Berlin. For this knowledge he relied chiefly on three rather elderly personages: two of them men of immense distinction, the third a woman of considerable notoriety. The first of these persons was Alexander von Humboldt, then seventy-five and working daily at his *Cosmos*—a scholar with a world-wide reputation who enjoyed the ostentatious favour of the Prussian king, but who was all the time committing to a secret diary and to private letters to a close friend the most scathing criticism of the king, his entourage and his methods of government. 'In what condition do I leave the world,' he wrote despairingly in 1853, 'I who remember 1789 and have shared in its emotions?' These letters were addressed to the second of Milnes' new acquaintances: Karl August Varnhagen von Ense, the eminent historian, biographer and diplomat, widower of the Jewess Rahel. The third person was the editor (or, most people said, the author) of the volume *Goethes Briefwechsel mit einem Kinde*, Elisabeth von Arnim.

Baron Humboldt, as Milnes called him, received the stranger with a graceful dignity. 'Moi, qui suis le père éternel de tous les voyageurs,' he said to him. Humboldt's suavity was such that when, years afterwards, his correspondence with Varnhagen was published by the latter's niece, Milnes was as much astonished at its tone as the Prussian court itself. He described Humboldt's relationship with the king as he had seen it in Berlin this winter:

it was the fair and honourable interchange of the highest social station and the noblest mental powers; the patronage was on both sides. Who suspected the deep discontent that lay on the bottom of that old man's heart? Who believed that he was seeking refuge from that courtly splendour, and even from that royal friendship, in secret satire. . . ?[1]

But, however good a face he put upon his life at Berlin, Humboldt was depressing, even mystifying about German politics. Varnhagen had told Milnes that it was his personal belief that Germany was not meant to be one single state any more than Greece had been; Baron Humboldt went further and suggested that even

---

[1] From Milnes' review of the Varnhagen-Humboldt correspondence, published as *Alexander von Humboldt at the Court of Berlin* in *Fraser's Magazine* for November 1860, and substantially reprinted in Lord Houghton's *Monographs, Social and Personal*, 1873.

Prussia was not properly a country at all. 'Le royaume de Prusse,' he told Milnes, 'est comme un mauvais rêve. C'est formé des lambeaux des peuples: la nationalité Prusse est absolument fictive.' 'All the Liberalism and Constitutionalism of Prussia is as its two sides,' he added, leaving the plump English member of Parliament to hurry back in a droshky to the Hôtel de Rome, where he committed these somewhat baffling statements to his stout little day-book. 'The learned people,' Milnes wrote wistfully to his father, '. . . are simple and unpedantic and very good company; they are, however, too busy to have much time to give to mere talk.'

Milnes had better luck with Varnhagen von Ense, with whom he established an easy, informative friendship rather like the friendship with Monsieur Guizot. Varnhagen was ten years younger than Humboldt, and of his many claims to fame the most interesting to Milnes were that he had been married to Rahel and had been a friend of Madame de Staël. Rahel, who had died in 1833 and was, anyway, a good deal older than her husband, had made for herself a European reputation as the centre of a brilliant intellectual circle first in Vienna and later in Berlin. Her husband had written her biography, thus confirming and prolonging her reputation. In Berlin Milnes found an amiable French lady who tried to dissipate for him most of his illusions about Rahel. Rahel, this woman told him, was a very plain and large-boned Lesbian, who kept a common, low-class woman friend, and was always treated by her husband with a signal rudeness, even in society. She was, Madame de Samier admitted, an excellent conversationalist and had great charm of countenance which lit up when she spoke. At Vienna people had used her house 'for all kinds of purposes' and her receptions had been called 'der Thé-Levi.' 'She always gave me the idea,' this lady concluded irrelevantly, 'of the Good Samaritan.' None the less, some time after the Berlin visit, Milnes went so far as to ask the widowed Varnhagen for a letter of Rahel's for his autograph collection.

Three years after Rahel's death, Varnhagen von Ense was travelling by steamboat up the Rhine from Rotterdam. During this eight-day journey he formed a deep and serious friendship with a young Englishwoman, Miss Charlotte Williams-Wynn, aged twenty-nine, who was journeying with her parents towards Wiesbaden. His friendship with Miss Wynn was continued in a correspondence, which, interrupted by occasional meetings, was carried on until Varnhagen's death in 1858. In the earlier stages of this twenty-year friendship Miss Wynn's friends (Milnes amongst them) assumed that she would succeed Rahel as Baroness Ense;

but by the time of Milnes' Berlin visit this was no longer thought likely.[1] It was through Miss Wynn, whose sister had married Milnes' cousin, that he first came into touch with Varnhagen von Ense. Charlotte Wynn had sent the German historian a copy of *Palm Leaves* when it appeared in the spring of 1844. The author's character, she wrote, came out more clearly in this eastern volume than in any of his previous works.

The evident admiration he] feels for Mohammedanism [she added] shocks many. Last year they said he was to become a Roman Catholic, now it is to be a Mohammedan, and one is just as likely as the other. My opinion is simply that he is sufficiently a poet to see the beauty that is to be found in all.

Later she passed on a message from Milnes about his *Edinburgh* article on Custine, which he hoped Varnhagen would read. When Milnes had written to MacCarthy of his projected Berlin journey he had told him that one of his reasons for going to Prussia was to 'see a good deal of Varnhagen,' who had promised him 'much intellectual hospitality.'

Milnes called on Varnhagen the day after his arrival in Berlin, bustling round to his house in the Mauerstrasse with another volume of his own poetry under his arm. Varnhagen was out. When he in turn called on Milnes, Milnes was out. This Cox-and-Box procedure was ended on Sunday, 15 December, when Varnhagen noted in his diary that Herr Milnes had stayed two hours and entertained him with a 'splendid' description of O'Connell's magnetic personality. This visit was followed by many others, always long, often filled with 'exciting' conversation or with the slow, delicious examination of Varnhagen's famous collection of autographs and

---

[1] '. . . there seems no more chance of her becoming Madame v. Ense,' wrote Milnes to MacCarthy, 30 May 1843. Charlotte Williams-Wynn (1807–1869) was the eldest of the five daughters of the politician Charles Watkin Williams-Wynn, of Wynnstay, Denbighshire. Rated by contemporaries as a very distinguished woman (she has her own notice in the *D.N.B.*), Miss Wynn was connected with the Milnes family through the marriage of one of her sisters to a Milnes Gaskell. She liked Richard Milnes, though his gay manner baffled her: 'He has really great gifts and high power,' she wrote to Varnhagen in 1843, 'and a temper such as I never saw before, but there is a want of earnestness and a love of paradox in his conversation which vexes me, for I see there is something behind if he would but give it me. . . . He is just now wild on the idea of founding an institution of Sisters of Mercy like your Prussian one, and was civil enough to say that he thought I was particularly suited to be one; and I shocked him at once by declaring that I had no idea of joining it. . . . "We are all so selfish in these days; there is such a want of self-devotion" was his speech.' The *Memorials of Charlotte Williams-Wynn* (from which this extract comes) were edited by her sister, Mrs. Lindesey, for private circulation, but published in 1877 (Longmans, Green). These, and Miss Wynn's letters to Milnes amongst the Houghton Papers, show her to have been thoughtful, pious and high-minded, lively but humourless.

historical documents. On one or two occasions Varnhagen notes
that he was unable to resist attacking Bunsen, who he said was an
arch-hypocrite both in London and Berlin. Milnes defended his
old friend, but he could never dispel Varnhagen's prejudice against
the Chevalier. These lively argumentative evenings in the
Mauerstrasse formed the basis of an intellectual friendship which
Milnes and Varnhagen sustained by letter for the remainder of the
German's life. Twenty-three of Milnes' letters to Varnhagen,
covering the years 1844 to 1854, have survived, and have been well
edited and published.[1] Most of Varnhagen's letters to Milnes,
written in a handwriting of almost incredible neatness, also exist.
Milnes' letters are typically full of amusing political and literary
gossip. He would buy and send to Varnhagen the autographs of
famous Englishmen:

Byron is to be had occasionally, but is dear; Pitt and Gibbon
are very rare [he would write; or] I enclose you a note from
Dr. Pusey, one from Mrs. Shelley (the authoress of *Frankenstein*)
enclosing a portion of the Ms. of one of her husband's poems,
and an autograph of Mr. Hume.

He sent him, too, autographs of Keats, Brougham and Mackintosh
and one 'of a name so odiously famous that it is better that it
should be merged in a large collection like yours than in one like
mine, where it would be prominent' (against this sentence Varnhagen annotated: 'Marquis de Sade'). It was probably the sight
of Varnhagen's documents this winter that stimulated Milnes himself to extend his own rather haphazard collection of autographs.
By the end of his life the Fryston collection was as famous in England
as Varnhagen's in Germany. Milnes specialised in English literary
manuscripts and holographs and in documents concerned with the
French Revolution and the English Civil War. There was also
the assortment of murderers' and criminals' signatures and con-
fessions, documents signed by the public hangman, and, ultimately,
some complete manuscripts in the handwriting of the 'odiously
famous' Marquis de Sade.

From Varnhagen's comments on his second, and last, meeting
with Milnes five years later it is clear that he had judged him
a little volatile and unserious in 1844.

Herr Monckton Milnes . . . came from Dresden yesterday
[Varnhagen noted in his *Tageblättern* in September 1850]. He
seems older and more earnest than before and makes a better

---

[1] By Dr. Walther Fischer of Dresden: *Die Briefe Richard Monckton Milnes ersten
Baron Houghton an Varnhagen von Ense* (1844–1854) (Heidelberg, Carl Winters
Universitatsbuchhandlung, 1922).

impression. He speaks German more fluently. Otherwise he is quite an Englishman, aims at gentility, and at all high spheres of living including that of the mind.

On this occasion Milnes was filled with a passionate admiration for Austria and the Austrian army; and told Varnhagen that the English had but two pleasures on Sunday: brandy and going to church.

We have had a visit from Herr Milnes [Varnhagen wrote to London, to his friend Amely Bolte [1]] and have been very much pleased with it. He seems much more in earnest, without the fountain of his humour and his ready laughter being dried up.

IV

Milnes' ready laughter (described as 'Falstaffian' by Henry Adams, junior) was much noticed in Berlin. 'I know you are of a melancholy temperament because you laugh so much and in such a way,' declared the third of his new friends, Bettina von Arnim. Elisabeth von Arnim—known throughout Berlin quite simply as 'Bettina'—was the same age as Varnhagen. She was the daughter of an intimate friend of Goethe's youth, Maximiliane Brentano, and having often heard her mother speak of Goethe she had rushed to Weimar in 1807, when he was sixty, declared she had fallen in love with him, and poured out an unbridled enthusiasm at his feet. On a later visit to Weimar she had a violent scene with his wife and was forbidden the house. Later on she married the poet and novelist Ludwig von Arnim, and was left a widow in 1831. In 1835, shortly after Goethe's death, she published a sensational volume entitled *Goethe's Letters to a Child*. A notorious eccentric, Bettina's word was questioned by everybody, and at the time of Milnes' visit few people really believed that Goethe had written any of the *Letters to a Child*; later research has proved, however, that the volume was at least based on authentic material. George Lewes, who was among those who dismissed Bettina's claims to intimacy with Goethe, wrote of her in his great biography published in 1855 (while Bettina was still alive) as

this strange figure who fills a larger space in the literary history of the nineteenth century than any other German woman. . . . She is one of those phantasts to whom everything seems permitted. More elf than woman, yet with flashes of genius which light up in

---

[1] Amely Bolte (1817–1891) was a friend and copious correspondent of Varnhagen's, keeping him informed of the activities of the German colony in London, where she was working as a German teacher.

splendour whole chapters of nonsense, she defies criticism and puts every verdict at fault. If you are grave with her, people shrug their shoulders, and saying 'she is a Brentano' consider all settled. 'At the point where the folly of others ceases, the folly of the Brentanos begins' runs the proverb in Germany. [1]

Bettina was now established with her daughters in a house in the Zelten, to the north of the Tiergarten and not far from the banks of the Spree; there she entertained. She was one of the only beings in that censor-ridden capital to whom free speech was permitted. The King of Prussia extended to Bettina the same sort of tolerance which Goethe had once shown her. This indulgence she repaid with abuse. Milnes was told that she had written to the King that she would have no objection to coming to his court, if he were there alone; but that he was surrounded 'mit solchen abgesmachten Wesen, solchen Excrementen der Natur, das man konnte nicht mit sie in Gesellschaft treten wenn man nicht vom Jugen aus gewöhrt war.' Bettina was as outspoken to everyone else. When the English ambassadress, Lady Westmorland, complained to her one day that there was 'no nature about Berlin,' Bettina swiftly answered that that did not vex her at all, since 'there was only one object in nature she enjoyed looking at, and she must have it well and clearly before her, and that was a naked man.'

Milnes cherished a religious veneration for Goethe, and anyone who had known or seen him shared in the reflected light. On his first visit as a youth to Ireland, when he had suddenly turned up to stay with the de Veres at Curragh Chase, Aubrey de Vere had been struck by his knowledge of German literature and philosophy, but above all by his passion for Goethe, whose minor poems he pronounced 'the perfection of art.' *Palm Leaves* had contained translations of poems in Goethe's *Oest-Westliches Divan* (a book which, as we have seen, he took with him to the East). As an old man, at Fryston, in 1879, Lord Houghton stumped into the room in which Wemyss Reid was sitting, a piece of paper in his hand. He explained that he had been making out a list of all the celebrities he had known, but that the greatest name was missing: '"Goethe," he said; "and I was actually at Weimar when he was living and never went to see him. I can never forgive myself."' Thackeray had told him his own audience with Goethe was like a visit to the dentist ('If Goethe is a God, I'm sure I'd rather go to the other place,' he had added); but to Milnes Goethe and anyone who had known him (Frau Schopenhauer, whom Milnes had met in 1832, Bettina von Arnim now) were almost equally sacrosanct. He formed an ideal audience for Bettina.

[1] Pp. 360–5 of vol. ii of Lewes' *Goethe* (ed. of 1855) deal with Bettina's claims.

You don't understand Goethe's religion [she would say to him]. He would to the very last stoop to pick up a piece of bread thrown on the floor, and would place it carefully on the table . . . he would select with the greatest care the best of two copies of a print to place in the Grand Duke's collection, and keep the other himself, and he would respect the true intelligence of the meanest man as much as his own.

Bettina did not only rely on reminiscence of the great dead to beguile her new friend. She was a woman of volcanic vivacity and she seems to have enjoyed ragging Milnes. 'You write about the beating of your own heart, so it never really beats—you old bachelor, you,' she cried to him, perhaps a little disingenuously; for Frau von Arnim had three unmarried daughters in the house in the Zelten. In 1849 Milnes' journalist friend, Saville Morton, was in Berlin, and, armed with letters from Milnes, he made great friends with Bettina. He described to Milnes an afternoon he had spent in her house. Someone had written from London to Frau von Arnim to say that Milnes used to pace his room in Pall Mall talking of Bettina and all her ways. 'He never says a word about *us*,' chimed in the sprightly sisters, Gisel and Armengarde; 'he only talks about Mama, does Mr. Milnes.' Morton, who seems to have had in his pocket a letter from Milnes warning him against the sisters, replied that he could show them a proof to the contrary. 'Yes?' they shrieked. 'Did he speak to you about us? What did he say? Come quick—well, you shall bring us his letter. Is he married? Why doesn't he get married?' A distinguished English husband— a poet and member of Parliament—might well have proved very acceptable to Armengarde von Arnim or to her sister Gisel, a girl whose 'still droop' and 'crystal' soul won Morton's experienced, almost professional admiration. 'O thou soft-eyed musing Muse, Gisel,' he wrote, 'I love thee best of all the three that sing about the golden tree.'

'But I am most in love with Bettina,' Morton told Milnes, in a long description of that lady which will serve to give us some idea of what Milnes endured in her house.

I got from her yesterday morning [wrote Morton] this immortal note : 'Come when you are alive : come for to see another beautiful girl of mine.' . . . Bettina's first word was : 'Our house is full of cholera' while she stood by the little round tea-table assiduously buttering slices of white and brown bread. . . . 'But how are you?' Bettina disdains reply to an enquiry about her health. . . . The vigor of this little old woman is one of the most triumphant answers I know to that disagreeable theory which makes disease the condition of genius. . . . I find [he continued] that the amount of favour which I possess with her depends entirely on something accidental in the mood : and I cannot always jump with her humour, which is so swift, nimble and changeful. What she requires is that one should be in a *state* to understand her, and supply the second voice of the conversational duet by some internal process of sympathy while she pursues a rapid darting monologue : which written down would seem to be spoken by some spirit. Sometimes she climbs the steepest ladder of the crudded rack of metaphysicks, and runs upon the platforms of the wind. Hers is a spirit beautiful and swift. . . . She is the soul of honour. The ear of the finest judge in music which she tries the voice of Sountag, the sensibility of the iodated silver plate to the music of flight, are *gross* types of the inviolable instinct of right, which wraps her being as with some subtle and strong membrane, at once an armour and an instrument, which tests all sentiments with instantaneous accuracy and repels all but what are pure and noble. I am astonished at this woman [Morton concluded], so frail yet so strong : like one of the Berlin buckles or brooches of iron, of more faery texture than the silver filigree of Genoa, yet you may dash it against the pavement and jump upon it without harming or displacing one of the thin bright wires of its magical steel woof. . . . [1]

This was in 1849. When Milnes himself revisited Berlin in 1850, he found Bettina as outrageous and amusing as ever. It was a rather different Berlin, a city which had undergone the 1848 revolt; and Bettina had set up two rooms for receiving—one for her democratic friends, Milnes noted, the other 'for Prince Adalbert and the genteel world.'

V

As well as visiting Humboldt, Varnhagen and Elisabeth von Arnim and dining off *jambon d'ours* or willow-partridges at a variety of foreign embassies and legations, and dancing at such houses as Princess Radziwill's, Milnes seems to have spent a good deal of time in the Berlin Gallery. The Palmerstons, who had been lately to Berlin (and to whom Milnes had begun to pay an assiduous attention), had advised him to make the acquaintance of the German art-historian, Dr. Waagen, at the Gallery:

and Cornelius [Lady Palmerston had added in her note from Broadlands], the great Fresco painter who was just putting up a beautiful work when we were there. Berlin is a charming place [she went on], and I liked it very much, and the Number of beautiful buildings and Palaces there and at Potsdam will I am sure surprize you as they did me.

[1] MS. letter of Morton to Milnes, dated 'Berlin, Hôtel de Russie, July 21.' Dr. Fischer finds mentions of Morton in Varnhagen's diaries from April to September 1849, when he seems to have returned to Paris.

Milnes was quite prepared to appreciate the pictures, sculpture and architecture in Berlin. In the summer or autumn preceding his journey to Prussia he had been studying (and making extracts from) the first volumes of John Ruskin. It may have been this reading of Ruskin that had developed his interest in works of art; for from now on his notebooks contain comments on pictures and sculpture. Hitherto he seems to have approached painting along strictly personal lines: collecting stories of Wilkie or Haydon or some anecdote of the Prince Consort's ingratitude to Landseer's brother. His youthful years in Italy had left him with a good grounding in Italian painting and architecture. He had, too, a very quick and natural response to beauty. But his attitude to pictures (and in this instance at least Milnes is typical of his generation and class) was a thoroughly literary attitude. It was always 'subjects' that he noted. 'Subjects in the Berlin Gallery' which impressed him included a crucifixion with Christ nailed to the apple-tree of original sin; an assumption of the Magdalen hidden in her own hair; the combination of religious and genre work in 'the Dutch sacred painters.' He admired too the 'paradasaical' foliage in the background of the great Van Dyck, and the painted Italian busts of wood, and the 'fine collection of porcelain sculpture' by the della Robbias, Sansovino and Mino da Fiesole; as well as the Etruscan and Roman pottery.

The drapery of one of the Muses in the B.G. is of incomparable beauty [he noted]. There are the double folds of a very thin over a very thick drapery—she is placed against one of the red pillars; there is also a capital Muse in the round room, with her right hand inside her robe.

But he was also capable of admiring the paintings at Dresden of the Danish painter Friedrichs and he really preferred in pictures the sort of subjects he used to choose for his own poems. 'Affecting little picture in the collection of Mr. Wagner the Swedish consul' (for instance) 'of the mother sleeping from overfatigue by the sick child who remains weariedly wakeful.' The shadow of Wordsworth lay over him still.

During the Berlin visit another of Milnes' social characteristics was in evidence. This was his talent for charming the very young and winning their enthusiastic loyalty. His darting mind and fluid opinions, his eager, easy manner had an irresistible appeal to young people; and in an age in which youth was not in itself rated either a merit or a virtue, Milnes took extraordinary trouble to listen to, advise and help the young. In Milnes' affection for his friends of any generation there was a strain of unusual

tenderness and a gentle sensibility which made him irresistibly
lovable to those who knew him well. Fitzroy and O'Brien at
Cambridge, Charles MacCarthy in the English College at Rome, in
London Carlyle, Buller, Mrs. Norton; the Guizot family and
Tocqueville in France; Parkyns on the River Nile or Saville Morton
in the Pyrenees—each of these people had submitted in turn
to Milnes' powerful, flickering charm. 'My love knows no more
of forgetfulness than children do of death' he wrote in a mood of
introspection (a sentence quoted by Sir Thomas Wemyss Reid);
and it is the echo of this phrase that we catch in an account of Milnes
sent to his first biographer by George von Bunsen, the Chevalier's
son. George Bunsen first met Milnes on this visit to Berlin. The
young man was then nineteen. A letter from his English mother
had warned him of Milnes' arrival, but he seems to have approached
the Englishman with some diffidence. He was astonished by his
welcome and by the strength of Milnes' affection.

From whatever side I try to contemplate the fact [wrote George
von Bunsen] it must remain mysterious to me how it ever came to
pass that his acquaintance with a lad of nineteen . . . ripened
within a few months into an intimacy which the blindest could
have seen must endure. His friendship was all tenderness. Its
reality came upon me like a revelation, in that look of sadness which
refused to disappear from his countenance, even in his joyfullest
sallies of wit and humour, during the hours I spent with him at the
Hôtel de Rome, on the eve of his departure from Berlin.

But the friendship did endure, surpassing in strength and ease
Milnes' more deferential affection for George Bunsen's father (with
whom he had never felt utterly at home).

After the first encounters at Berlin [the younger Bunsen continued in the memorandum he sent to Reid] I found nothing in his
behaviour towards me but a true friend's love, nothing but pleasure
in seeing himself, not, of course, understood, yet guessed at by one
so much younger, nothing but a total unrestraint in giving rein to
that humour of which he has remained to the last . . . one of the
most brilliant representatives ever known. During forty years
there never was a falling-off in Milnes' affection. [1]

George Bunsen did not realise what a welcome change his youth
must have seemed to Milnes, jaded from the studies of Baron
Humboldt and Varnhagen and the whimsical but memory-laden
atmosphere of the von Arnim salon. We may recall too (but without malice) Disraeli's picture of Milnes setting out to captivate the
young Tancred at Sidonia's dinner-table.

[1] Memorandum by George von Bunsen, printed *in extenso* by Reid, vol. ii,
pp. 67-8, and presumably written about 1889.

VI

The chief result of Milnes' Berlin winter was exactly what he had intended: he returned to London in February 1845 knowing a good deal more about the Prussian scene than most other Englishmen of his acquaintance or of either party. His article on what he had observed, entitled *The Political State of Prussia*, was written in the autumn of 1845, but did not appear in the *Edinburgh* until January 1846, and in a greatly shortened form. Milnes wrote to Varnhagen that the article had caused him much 'trouble and vexation.' It was, in fact, a singularly perspicacious article, for it prophesied the imminence in Prussia of the revolution which occurred in 1848. He was perfectly polite about King Frederick William, but he openly declared his disapproval of the king's system of rule:

Royal authority [he wrote] is no longer an object of reverence, and the laws themselves, being considered in no higher light than as the expression of the royal will, are gradually losing their salutary influence. . . . Prussia, unconstitutioned, will soon become a country ruled by suspicion and submitting with disgust, and at last sullenness will burst into rage, and political rights be forcibly wrung from the hand that withheld them. The people will enter on the task of self-government without gratitude to their sovereign—without distrust of themselves—without reverence, as without humility.

Amongst his Berlin acquaintances the article was ill-received. Baron Humboldt at first declared to Varnhagen von Ense that what Milnes thought of the king, 'who had shown him no personal civilities,' interested him little; but when he came to read the article and found Milnes criticising the dominant influence of Kant's thought in Prussia and suggesting a kind of American federation for the German states, he became, to use his own word, 'indignant.' He accused Milnes of knowing nothing but a string of German names and all the street-corner gossip of the capital. Humboldt was wrong, for what Milnes predicted came to pass.

Milnes' new knowledge of Prussia confirmed him in his old predilection for German company, and in Berlin in 1844, as at Bonn in 1830, he found that Germans liked him. 'Is it possible that an Englishman can be so lovable?' one of his new Berlin friends had exclaimed after Milnes had left the room. In the years following his Berlin sojourn he was always ready to welcome and anxious to help any German who came to England with a letter from one of his Berlin friends. Thus in the summer of 1846 he entertained the famous one-eyed woman writer, Gräfin Ida Hahn-Hahn, who had made the cardinal mistake of bringing to England a male companion and protector, Oberst Bystram.

I fear Countess Hahn cannot have liked her visit to England . . . [Milnes wrote in a letter to Varnhagen, explaining how awkward the position of Bystram seemed to 'our conventional morality']. At first [he continued] he was called her cousin, then her secret husband, then her guardian, then I don't know what. . . . If she had been handsomer, we might have permitted it. . . .

He did not tell Varnhagen that Samuel Rogers had called Countess Hahn and Bystram 'the ugliest pair of adulterers he had ever had in his house' or that Lady Harriet Baring had said: 'Madame Hahn-Hahn's teeth quivered like the diamonds our grandmothers used to wear on their heads.' The authoress of *Sibylla* was quite unaware of anything odd in her behaviour, and enquired why George Sand was not received in London. After Berlin, English life seemed to her as invigorating as a 'bath of steel.'

London exceeds every imagination and every expectation [wrote the Countess Hahn to her friend Berta von Marenholtz]; I expected to find a gigantic town and found a world . . . I spent five of the most tumultuous weeks of my life there, whirling like an atom through this universe of diamonds and mud.

Milnes later wrote a review for the *Athenaeum* of the novel *Diogena* (an ill-concealed caricature of Countess Hahn by her rival, the Jewess Fanny Lewald). In this review he came down heavily upon the Gräfin's theory of love, describing it as 'a state of continual paroxysm and ecstasy—a chronic fit of bridal rapture, or of the delirium of a first happy love in its first happy moment.' When Countess Hahn produced an answer to Frau Lewald in the form of another novel, *Levin* (published in 1848), Milnes dismissed it as 'a libel on human nature.' A later work of Fanny Lewald's, *Prince Louis-Ferdinand*, dedicated against his wishes to Varnhagen, and containing a portrait of the dead Rahel, was also fiercely criticised in the *Athenaeum* by Milnes, who always objected to 'the cooking-up of dead characters' in novels. *Prince Louis-Ferdinand* had been sent to him by Fanny Lewald's friend Amely Bolte. Fraülein Bolte had indicated that Fanny Lewald expected Milnes to give the book a good review; the result was that he published a slashing three-column attack, or (as he called it to Varnhagen) 'a contradictory paragraph in the *Athenaeum*.'

When Fanny Lewald herself came to London, in May 1850, she met Milnes at breakfast with Bunsen, and found him stout, intelligent and good-tempered, his 'open face shadowed by brown hair.' Wise enough to treat him as 'one of the first living lyric poets in England,' she soon found herself breakfasting at 26 Pall Mall.

The thing was laughable to me [wrote little Amely Bolte to Varnhagen]; I found myself last Friday at the breakfast table—the Lewald at his left, I at his right—Milnes between these two emancipated women, about whom he had lately made so rude a fuss.

Other people at this breakfast were Mrs. Carlyle and Miss Jewsbury and a dozen men, including Bishop Thirlwall, Mr. Russell ('the future Duke of Bedford,' Fraülein Bolte pointed out) and Thackeray. But Fanny Lewald's visit to London ended badly; she had a fierce row with Amely Bolte, slandered her to her English friends, and left for Edinburgh without even saying good-bye. 'The Lewald . . . is not used to having a place in society,' Fraülein Bolte scribbled in a fury to Varnhagen,

either in London or anywhere else . . . Milnes bothered no more about her. Bunsen only invited her with several Germans. Aristocratic people she did not see, but could I help that? Enough of this. One must thrust away unpleasant memories.

More solid than his hospitality to these German literary ladies was the cordial and sensible welcome Milnes gave to many of the German refugees flooding into England in the years 1845–1850. He got a job in Huth's bank for the banished and penniless poet Ferdinand Freiligrath, and when he lost this position through the idiotic indiscretion of Amely Bolte, Milnes gave him money. Another poet, Moritz Hartmann, who fled from Vienna in 1848, arrived in England in the spring of 1850 and was warmly welcomed by Milnes. Under the influence of the insidious Fraülein Bolte Hartmann ascribed Milnes' friendliness to the fact that he had successfully translated part of *Palm Leaves*; this charge, so typical of the refugee mentality, may be dismissed.

Herr Milnes [wrote Hartmann] is, besides, a very good and well-meaning man, who possesses the high courtesy which comes from an educated and humane spirit, and is, for an Englishman, exceptional for his lack of prejudice.

Lothar Bucher and Gustav von Struver, the one a refugee from Berlin who became English correspondent of the *Berliner-National-zeitung*, the other a German republican agitator, seem also to have received kindnesses at 26 Pall Mall. The position of the foreign political refugees in London after 1848 was very precarious and offers no real parallel with the status of foreign refugees in London in our day.

I cannot hope that (Bucher) will find his position among us very pleasant [Milnes warned Varnhagen in a letter of 2 April 1850]. Few among us talk German, but he will learn English and get over

16 225

that difficulty. A more serious one remains—the character of a political refugee. The Reaction which has indulged itself on the continent in hanging and shooting and flogging and banishing, here exhibits itself, especially in the higher circles, in a horror of political agitators of all kinds, and is as indiscriminate in its judgement as public prejudice is wont to be. . . . I remember a woman who had left her husband, talking to me one day of her position, said 'Ah! the exclusion is nothing to bear—it is the *inclusion* which is so terrible!'[1]

[1] The woman, no doubt, was Mrs. Norton. This letter, as well as the details on Lewald, Freiligrath, Hartmann, etc., are taken from Dr. Fischer's scholarly pamphlet.

Chapter Eleven

I

Milnes was now thirty-five. He was still the jovial if reluctant witness of the public successes of other men of his own age. Some of these successes were political and some of them were literary. A few of them—Disraeli's in particular—were both at once, and doubly hard to bear. Milnes must sometimes have thought of the lines from Dante's *Purgatorio* which he had copied out into his commonplace book in Egypt, in the shadow of the pillars of Karnak, three years before.

Even in Berlin it had not proved possible to get away from praise of Disraeli. 'Everybody here from the Princess of Prussia downwards,' Milnes wrote to him, 'is reading and talking *Coningsby*'; and when he got back to London from Berlin he found that *Eothen*, the travel-book of his old friend and fellow-Apostle, A. W. Kinglake, was having a success almost as great as that of *Coningsby*. 'I want so much to hear you speak of *Eothen*,' Mrs. Procter had written to Milnes in the autumn of 1844, when the book was still quite new. 'It seems to me the most brilliant book of travels that ever was written. *It is so true.*' In the winter of 1844 to 1845 the book was generally recognised as being very brilliant indeed, and there was great rejoicing among Kinglake's little group of intimate friends— the Duff Gordons, 'Carrie' Norton and Thackeray. Like *Coningsby*, *Eothen* was also popular abroad. One of Lord Houghton's best stories of his visit to Paris during the 1848 Revolution was of how he had been to call on Lamartine in the hectic days of June, and, finding him writing decrees without stopping to eat or sleep, he had waited importunately in his ante-room. On the table lay an open book, face downwards. With his usual impertinent curiosity, Milnes picked the book up. It was a copy of *Eothen*, open at the account of Kinglake's interview with Lady Hester Stanhope during which she had spoken of Alphonse de Lamartine.[1]

In the *Palm Leaves* introduction Milnes had explained why he did not care to write a travel book of his Eastern journey and why he preferred to publish his scattered impressions in verse. But as

[1] This story is recorded by Janet Ross, the daughter of Lucie Duff Gordon, in *The Fourth Generation* (Constable, 1912), p. 42.

the fame of Kinglake's volume spread, surpassing and then engulfing he modest 'saloon celebrity' of Milnes' own little volume of poems, he felt that here was another missed opportunity. When he had first mentioned *Eothen* to MacCarthy, listing it in his bulletin of the new books of the autumn of 1844, he had labelled it 'a charming Voltairean volume on the East'; but writing to him again in the spring of the next year from Serlby (where he was attending the cold March christening of his nephew, the Galways' son and heir), he added that Kinglake had had 'an immense success. I now rather wish,' he confessed, 'I had written his book, which I could have done—at least nearly.' A month later the Reverend William Brookfield, the snobbish husband of Thackeray's Egeria, was bracketing Milnes and Kinglake together as some of the 'few remarkables' at an evening party of Mrs. Procter's: 'Kinglake—Milnes—Lady Chatterton' wrote Mr. Brookfield to his mother '—and several of a somewhat smaller fry of literature.'[1] Kinglake's was a quick, deserved, and rather enviable reputation. His book had made his name overnight.

Coincident with the acclamation of *Eothen* in London clubs and drawing-rooms there had appeared, in the *Quarterly Review* for December 1844, an article on *Palm Leaves* which seemed to Milnes' friends to constitute a personal attack on him. The article was called *The Rights of Women*[2]; the first book listed in the heading was *Palm Leaves*, followed by *The Englishwoman in Egypt* (the work of Mrs. Poole, the sister of the Egyptologist E. W. Lane), *The Women of England*, and *The Wives of England* by Mrs. Ellis, and two works of Mrs. Anna Jameson—*Characteristics of Women: Moral, Poetical and Historical* and *The Romance of Biography, or Memoirs of Women loved and celebrated by Poets*. It was not a very distinguished company for Monckton Milnes; and the point of the article was to defend the English ideal of womanhood against Milnes' alleged praise of the harem system in *Palm Leaves*, chiefly by proving that Milnes did not know what he was writing about. The article was skilful and bantering, and although quite unspiteful it made great game of Monckton Milnes. 'The meek pilgrim of Pontefract,' the 'bard as blind as Homer' was accused of 'omnicredulity,' of misconceiving the position of Eastern women, and of mistaking for 'tranquil delights' the 'noisy realities' of harem life—which the reviewer suggested was about as tranquil as an English schoolroom full of grandchildren. Although Milnes was called 'an able polemical writer' and 'a grave and thoughtful poet,' he was also termed 'a man

---

[1] Letter of W. Brookfield to his mother April 1845, printed in C. & F. Brookfield's *Mrs. Brookfield and her Circle* (1905).
[2] *The Quarterly Review*, vol. lxxv, No. cxlix, p. 94.

of the world primely favoured and sought in the Faubourg St. Germain as well as at home in May Fair,' and told he was 'accustomed to the double and simultaneous duties of defending and opposing the Government.' As 'the first publishing Englishman' to gain access to an Eastern harem, he was next asked whether he had got in under false pretences. 'The Society of Friends will naturally be curious to know by what ingenious stratagem the member for Pontefract has baffled the vigilant jealousy of a thousand years.' Had he adopted the traditional disguise of a female perfume-seller?

. . . . did Mr. Milnes thus disguised make his way to the women's apartments, entreating them 'just try his only true and genuine Kalydor for the People,' or his pots of modest 'blushing Paste *à la jeune Angleterre*,' and imploring them too 'to beware of the unprincipled persons who imitate his inimitable and refreshing Essence *à la fraîcheur du soir?*'

When Milnes got back to England in February 1845 people were still reading and talking about the article. For it was no secret that the author of it was the successful Kinglake himself.

Milnes' reaction to the review is not known, but he is unlikely to have been greatly amused. He had known Kinglake for nearly twenty years—indeed, it was Milnes and Sunderland who had ensured his election to the Apostles at Cambridge. He sent Kinglake a message through their mutual friend, Mrs. Procter: 'I will do all you ask about Mr. Kinglake,' she replied, in a letter of February 1845. 'He told me that having some misgivings upon the subject he shewed the Article to Mr. Eliot Warburton, who could see *nothing objectionable*—May I review *his* next book!' Warburton himself had written hurriedly from Dublin, to say how distressed and repentant Kinglake felt.

I have just had the most pained letter from a man who reviewed you in the last Quarterly [he told Milnes] on finding, he says, that his article was considered an attack on you, and that his unlucky pen seemed to have a curse on it, for his heartfelt praise was considered irony, while his bantering was taken to express real bitterness. [Warburton considered that] the fair impression derivable from the article is on the whole tributary to your fame . . . if I knew nothing of you—except what is apparent in this Review— I should picture to myself a combination of Beckford, Sheridan and Alfred Tennyson.

This was perhaps too Irish an interpretation of Kinglake's article, but though it did Milnes' reputation as a poet little good, the review was soon forgotten. Milnes accepted Kinglake's explanations, and they remained friends.

II

A less conventional ex-Apostle than Kinglake had fallen into bad financial trouble by the year 1845. Alfred Tennyson, whose work was still known only in a limited circle, had lost a great deal of money in a foolish wood-carving speculation. He was suddenly penniless as well as melancholy: 'I have drunk one of those most bitter draughts out of the cup of life, which go near to make men hate the world they move in,' he told a friend of his about this time.[1] Although he was young and strong, Tennyson's friends were sensible enough to try to get a Civil List pension for him. Carlyle is said to have put Milnes up to asking the Prime Minister for this pension, which was a yearly sum of £200. At the same moment Peel was approached for a similar stipend for the old Irish dramatist and actor James Sheridan Knowles. Knowing nothing of the work of either writer, he turned for advice to Milnes,[2] who sent him (or, in another version of the story, read him aloud) *Ulysses* and *Locksley Hall*, telling Peel that if the pension was to be awarded as a charitable gift and for services rendered, it should go to Sheridan Knowles; if 'in the interests of English literature and of the English nation' it should be given to Alfred Tennyson. Peel gave the pension to Tennyson,[3] who was grateful but reluctant. 'Something in the word "pension" sticks in my gizzard,' he wrote to Rawnsley.[4] 'I feel the least possible bit Miss Martineau-ish about it,' he added —in reference to Miss Martineau's recent ostentatious refusal of a pension on the grounds that she 'should be robbing the people who did not make laws for themselves'—a decision which flung her back again upon the charitable support of her immediate friends.

Carlyle's appeal to Milnes over the Tennyson pension is in itself a pointer to the position which he was slowly acquiring. He was not a first-class poet. It was perfectly clear to everyone else that he would never be an eminent politician. But his literary flair and his warmth of heart, together with his innumerable good-humoured contacts in the world of power and fashion, made of

[1] Quotations from Hallam Tennyson's *Tennyson, a Memoir* (1897).
[2] In the third volume of *Sir Robert Peel from His Private Papers* the editor, C. S. Parker, declares that Lord Tennyson's story 'does less than justice to Peel' (*op. cit.*, pp. 439–442) and shows that it was Henry Hallam who first wrote to Peel on this subject, in a letter dated 11 February 1845. In this letter, however, Hallam refers the Prime Minister to such judges of poetry as Rogers and Henry Taylor, but he adds 'I could easily mention some others—for example Mr. Milnes, whose judgement in poetry deserves considerable regard.' On 15 February Peel replied that he had read some of Tennyson's work and had 'formed *a very high estimate* of his powers.' It seems unlikely that Lord Houghton concocted the story of Peel's seeking his advice; Peel consulted him between 12 and 15 February.
[3] Sheridan Knowles was given a pension in 1848.
[4] Hallam Tennyson, *op. cit.*

him a sort of liaison figure between this world and that other struggling, vital, passionate and improvident universe of creative genius and talent. It was a unique position. It became the real *raison d'être* of his middle years and his old age; and by it he performed countless services to English literature in a period when his sharpness of perception, his lack of sentimentality, snobbishness and prejudice were excessively rare. A story told by Gosse in his *Life of Coventry Patmore*, though inexact in detail, well exemplifies this aspect of Milnes' activities. Gosse relates that after a dinner at Mrs. Procter's house in 1846 Milnes said to her: 'And who is your lean young friend with the frayed coat-cuffs?' 'Oh, Mr. Milnes,' Mrs. Procter replied, 'you wouldn't talk in that way if you knew how clever he is and how unfortunate. Have you read his poems?' Gosse states that Milnes then took the poems away in his pocket and wrote to Mrs. Procter the next day:

If your young friend would like a post in the Library of the British Museum, it shall be obtained for him, if only to induce you to forget what must have seemed my heartless flippancy. His book is the work of a true poet, and we must see that he never lacks butter for his bread.

Milnes wrote to Panizzi at the British Museum, and in November 1846 Patmore received an appointment in the Library; but his benefactor's kindness did not stop there, for Milnes afterwards lent him money, employed him in the preparation of the *Life of Keats*, and stood godfather to his elder son, who was christened Milnes Patmore.[1]

Mrs. Procter, who had already twice mentioned Patmore and his poetry in letters to Milnes in 1844,[2] cherished all her life a rather wistful affection for Monckton Milnes. 'You give to all,' she wrote, in terms which from someone less sincere would seem a trifle unctuous, 'beautiful thoughts and happy hours to the rich, and money and pity to the poor—I really felt this so much that I only asked you when all others failed.' Anne Procter, the wife of Bryan Waller Procter (who wrote poetry under the name of Barry Cornwall) and stepdaughter of Basil Montagu, the editor of Bacon, was ten years older than Milnes. She had married in 1824, when Milnes was still a boy at Thorne, and her husband now held a comfortable position as Commissioner of Lunacy. Until 1843 she lived in St. John's Wood, but in that year she moved down into Harley Street and in 1853 to Weymouth Street. In each of these

---

[1] Patmore's second volume of poems, *Tamerton Church Tower* (1853), was dedicated to Milnes.

[2] Though Milnes may not actually have met the young poet until 1846.

little houses she attracted a small, unfashionable circle of literary
people, which included Milnes, Thackeray, the Brookfields, Kinglake (who called Mrs. Procter 'Our Lady of Bitterness') and others.
Mrs. Brookfield apart, Mrs. Procter was the woman to whom
Thackeray wrote most constantly. Sometime in the eighteen-
fifties this intimate friendship cooled, and Mrs. Procter complained
to Milnes about Thackeray's behaviour. She thought Thackeray
altered by success:

Mr. Thackeray has for many months entirely absented himself
from our house. This he has a perfect right to do—but he has
no right to tell every gossiping acquaintance that *Mrs. Procter
never speaks to him, but to say something galling*—(I think I could
recall to his memory some words that were not so). I never wished
or intended to vex him—but when old friends begin to take any
view but a kind one of what one says it is better to part. One
outlives a love—why not friendship? If any one rejoiced at
Thackeray's success I am sure I did—and was as proud of him
as if he had been my son. I thought it was foolish his leaving
Punch about Lord Palmerston—I think so still—but I should have
been wiser had I not told him so—but like his other friends sneered
at him behind his back.

On the other hand, the friendship between Milnes and Mrs. Procter
never fell off: 'you are exactly what you were when I first knew
you,' she once wrote to him; 'believe me that what is *real* remains;
and that fifty years of town life will do you no harm.' Mrs. Procter
admired his poetry as fervently as Harriet Martineau herself. She
was always urging him to print or to reprint poems she had liked—
The Song of the Railroads, for instance:

> When speed and joy go hand in hand,
>   And loves are side by side,
> We are the sunbeams of the land
>   On which the angels glide;
> The husband to his anxious wife,
>   The friend to friendly care,
> The lover to his life of life,
>   On burning wings we bear.
>
>   ·   ·   ·   ·
>
> A few short words writ overnight
>   Hundreds of miles are borne,
> And scatter sorrow or delight
>   Far, ere the morrow morn.

Or his ode on the departure of the Austrian dancer, Fanny Elssler,
for New York:

See, the triumphant waves upbuoy
Your image, plumed with hope and joy:—
Let it be borne, now mountain-high,
A star fresh added to the sky,—
Now sunk within that central deep
Where memories of Atlantis sleep;
Yet, ever floating safe in grace,
As when upon the earth's still face
Your steps in gay caprices light,
Like cataract spray from Alpine height;—
Till, to our gaze confused and blent
With the red-golden Occident,
The lessening outline fades away,
And we can only look and pray
That all our brothers oversea
May love you, prize you, just as We.

You must print the lines to Fanny Elssler [she wrote in 1844],
they are charming. Nothing was ever happier, the lines beginning
'See, the triumphant waves upbuoy' are some of your best. If
you cannot write lines to a dancer who can? who dare? The days
are evil indeed if a man of your character cannot venture on such
a subject. . . .

She also gave him unsolicited advice: 'The only way to treat the
world,' she told him, 'is to trample on it.' It was perhaps to help
Milnes in this process that she embroidered him a pair of slippers
while she was in Italy in 1841: 'They are almost worthy of being
worn by a Poet,' she said, 'for they have seen Florence and Venice.'

In his help to poor writers Milnes was as much guided by his
own kind instincts as by the wish to enrich English literature.
During 1844 and 1845 he gave a great deal of aid to Thomas Hood,
contributing free articles to *Hood's Magazine* and getting his
friends to do so too. When Hood finally died, in May of 1845,
Milnes gave his widow advice about the funeral (held, at his
instigation, in the new cemetery at Kensal Green) and helped
with a subscription for Hood's family. In the previous year he
had also taken trouble to get a civil service job for the nephew of
the poet Thomas Campbell, towards whom he felt a kind of family
responsibility. Thomas Campbell's sister had been governess to
Richard Milnes' aunts, and through this connection Milnes had
known Campbell since the year 1830—when he had sent the old
man Tennyson's first volume of poems, which Campbell had
pronounced the work of an 'elegant, original, delightful young
poet.' Milnes' sympathy with Hood is easy to understand; for
the pathos and the humanitarian aim of such pieces as *The Song*

of the Shirt would have moved him very much. About Campbell, though, he had no illusions. During the funeral service in the Jerusalem Chamber at Westminster, in July 1844, Milnes had to be hushed by people standing near him: he was loudly murmuring that Campbell's poems were only ballads, and in a letter written just after Campbell's burial in the Poets' Corner, he wrote:

He has got the Poets' Corner cheap: '*le coin retiré des rêveurs de l'empire*' holds few men who have not done more. What would the *Pleasures of Hope* be, written now? *Hohenlinden* and *Ye Mariners of England* are very good, but not better than *Sir John Moore* by some Irish parson who sleeps quietly amidst his bogs.

In this and many other utterances of Milnes' late youth we are again reminded that he was not, in any commonly accepted sense, Victorian. In contrast with the stiff, accepted views and the pasty sentimentality of many of his most intelligent contemporaries, Milnes' own volatile opinions seem free and even anarchic.

It is in keeping with his general attitude that Milnes should have been one of the first of Robert Browning's acquaintances to write and congratulate him on his elopement with Elizabeth Barrett from her father's house in Wimpole Street in September 1846. Browning replied to this note in March 1847, from Pisa:

. . . very pleasantly your voice sounded in the few words of it as I read them here under the grim Campanella, the top of which, with the real honest balconies in these parts, will just hit the roof of this huge old Collegio Ferdinando, 'where Bartolo,' of crabbed memory, 'once taught,' as the inscription states.

He went on to ask Milnes' help. He thought it likely that England would soon send a mission to Pio Nono, and he wished to be secretary to it.

One gets excited—at least here on the spot—[he explained] by this tiptoe strained expectation of poor Italy, and yet, if I had not known you, I believe I should have looked on with the other by-standers. It is hateful to ask, but I ask nothing; indeed, rather I concede a very sincere promise to go on bookmaking (as my wife shall) to the end of our natural life.

Since no envoy was then sent to Pio Nono by the English Government, it is plain that nothing came of this application. But the fact that Browning made it at all serves to show the quality of the person who now turned confidently and affectionately to Monckton Milnes for help.

II

While Milnes' worth as a critic and as an authority on literary questions was now generally recognised, his political career was not going any better than before his visit to Berlin. In the spring of 1845 it received a very severe jolt. For this jolt he had only himself to blame.

The Irish religious debates in the House of Commons had begun in February 1844. By the time Milnes got back from Prussia in February 1845 the agitation over the Maynooth Grant had become nation-wide and by May of that year the country was in what he himself termed 'a state of religious tumult—worse I fancy than anything during the Catholic Emancipation squabble.' The origin of the trouble was Sir Robert Peel's just and logical proposal to increase the state grant to the Royal Catholic College of Maynooth and to contribute a further lump sum of £30,000 towards rebuilding the squalid and penurious barracks in which the Irish Roman Catholic clergy were educated. It was a reasonable proposition. Seven-eighths of the population of Ireland were Catholic. The conditions at Maynooth were scandalous. The principle that the Government should contribute to the education of the Irish Catholic clergy had already been conceded when the Royal College was founded in 1795; all Peel wanted was to make this contribution a decent and a useful one. But the result of his proposals (over which Gladstone resigned from the Cabinet, though he later voted for the Bill) was to throw the whole country into an uproar. Hostile petitions poured into the new Houses of Parliament from every quarter in England. In Richard Milnes' own constituency of Pontefract the majority of the electors were either Dissenters— as his own immediate forebears had been—or at any rate rigid Protestants. He was implored and he was ordered to vote against the Bill by his constituents, but in fact he voted for it, a noble and quixotic action which much diminished his popularity at Pontefract and nearly cost him his seat in the election of 1847 when he scraped in by a mere nineteen votes.

My constituents have been especially savage [he wrote in May 1845]. The whole electoral body, headed by parsons (from Episcopal to Ranter), raged against me for six weeks, pledging themselves never to support me again, and ending by asking me to resign.

The day following the passage of the Maynooth Bill through the Commons Milnes wrote to the Mayor of Pontefract to explain his action. In this letter, which he begged the Mayor to show around the town, Milnes pointed out that the Bill emanated from the Duke of Wellington and Sir Robert Peel and was supported by Lord Stanley and Sir James Graham; had Peel been defeated he would have given up office to a party pledged to great changes in the Protestant Establishment of Ireland. No public man sharing in the government of a mixed Protestant and Catholic country could act solely on his own convictions, Milnes added; and in any case the Maynooth Grant could not injure the Protestant religion in any way.

Protestantism [wrote Milnes in a passage of special pleading] is the reformation of the Roman Church: that reformation was brought about by the printing press, by intellectual light, by diffused information: if I give the Irish priests more opportunity of this, can I be said to be encouraging Popery?

He asked the people of Pontefract to look on these questions from 'an *Irish*, not an *English*, point of view' and to recognise that

Ireland is there, and we can't get rid of her, without ruining the Empire; she is governed by Roman Catholic priests whom we *cannot* convert and *must* not persecute; she compels us to keep up an immense army in time of peace and prevents us going safely to war.

This letter did little good, for to the Yorkshire dissenters Milnes' name was already tarnished by his connection with the Tractarians as well perhaps as by his long residence in Italy. Popular ignorance and prejudice were always as distasteful to him as were ordinary English conventions or royalty-worship; and all through his life he stood out against them whenever he got the chance, and without calculating the consequences. This was not the road to success in politics.

Not content with having alienated his constituents upon the Irish question, Milnes next published a little book *The Real Union of England and Ireland* [1] which annoyed most of his fellow Tories as well. On the book's title-page he printed a characteristic quotation from old Landor: 'Folly hath often the same results as Wisdom, but Wisdom would not engage in her schoolroom so expensive an assistant as Calamity.' He was very pleased with this 'libretto,' in which he called on the Tories to do justice to Ireland by endowing the Catholic Church. He told his sister that he thought it the best thing he had ever written in prose, and his father that he had been very glad to put in print opinions which he could not voice in any other form. Bishop Thirlwall, who had been his tutor at

---

[1] *The Real Union of England and Ireland*, by R. Monckton Milnes, Esq. (London: John Ollivier, 59 Pall Mall, 1845), 87 pp., 12mo.

Trinity, wrote to him that the fault of the book was that of all his writing—'. . . excessive candour. If you go on this way saying everything you believe, how can you expect people to suppose you sincere?' *The Real Union*, though turgid, over-polished and rhetorical in style (forming a contrast to the well-knit *Edinburgh* articles he had begun to write), is a valiant if rather ungainly attack on accepted English ideas of the Irish problem.

Where else [the author asked] has the Roman Catholic Church, the champion of civil order and submission to authority throughout Europe, been perverted into an engine of tumult and protector of rebellion?

But the public which Milnes' booklet reached was not very receptive to clever arguments. English people did not like being told by a compatriot that they had 'persecuted' the Irish; they were not grateful to Milnes for pointing out the 'devoted character' of the Irish priesthood, nor were they ready to agree with him that 'the hope of still Anglicanising the Roman Catholics of Ireland can hardly rest in one instructed mind.' *The Real Union of England and Ireland* did quite considerable harm to what was left of Monckton Milnes' political prospects. His closest friends would not have been surprised by the book or by the moment he had chosen to publish it. When someone asserted in 1846 that Milnes had accepted a Colonial appointment, Lady Harriet Baring cried out, 'I hope not—we shall have no one to show us what we ought not to do and say!'

Milnes' earnest, emotional interest in Ireland, first awakened by his friendship with Stafford O'Brien at Trinity in 1829, had been confirmed by his two idyllic visits to that island in his youth—when he had seen Lady Morgan in all her chattering glory in Kildare Street, and visited the old Knight of Kerry, and driven up unannounced that summer's evening to the de Veres' house at Curragh Chase, and ridden to the Giants' Causeway with Eliot Warburton in open cars. He was thus deeply concerned at the onset of the Irish potato famine in August 1846. The famine, which started some six weeks after the Whig victory, had been foreseen by Peel the year before; but he was now out of office, and the Whig Government at first mishandled a horrible situation. The peasantry of Ireland were soon dying in their thousands, and though generous relief was sent by private people from all over England, the rate of deaths from starvation and 'famine-fever' mounted week by week. In November 1846 [1] Richard Milnes crossed over to Dublin (where

---

[1] Reid ignores this visit to Ireland, and its duration is not known. Milnes was at Bessborough on 11 November 1846 and at Headfort on 6 December.

he stayed with the new Lieutenant-Governor, Lord Bessborough, at Viceregal Lodge) and made a short tour of the famine areas. It was perhaps inevitable that this visit involved a short tour of the larger country houses also—to the Headforts at Headfort, to the Duke of Leinster, to Lord Mayo, to the Kenmares and to Lord Bessborough's own house at Bessborough. He saw, too, his friends Warburton and O'Brien, who were hard at work on Relief Committees; and as he moved about the country he heard varying accounts of the behaviour of the landlords: how some had 'given up all hope of rest' and sold all their horses ('passionate for hunting as the fellows here are'), while others, such as Lord Bandon and Lord Bantry, were displaying a callous apathy to their tenants' suffering and had become 'objects of execration' in the countryside. In spite of the hideous condition of the peasantry, life in the big houses went on undisturbed: at Headfort—where, he told his mother, he had 'a bedroom as big as the drawing-room at Bawtry, with one of the windows mended by a bit of newspaper'—there were charades in the evenings, and at Bessborough the company hunted all day and acted *tableaux vivants* and Sheridan's *St. Patrick's Day* (with an impromptu prologue written by Milnes) at night.[1] But on his way to the Kenmares' at Killarney, Milnes made a detour through the terrible famine districts of the south and west:

I arrived last night from Skibbereen [he wrote to his father from Killarney], and the excursion answered completely, as far as giving one a specimen of the worst destitution in Ireland. There was no exaggeration in the priest's words to me—'there will be no violence, for the poor creatures have made up their minds to die,' and that was the look that hundreds of them have. The famine-fever is carrying them off fast and that is the best prospect they have, for not only is sufficient food unattainable, but their clothing is all pawned and they have no means to redeem it with—I have some pawn-tickets for the meerest articles of necessary life. For miles around the country looks abandoned by human life.

In 1847 Milnes was asked to write something for *The Irish Bazaar*. He produced the following lines:

> The Woes of Ireland are too deep for verse:
> The Muse has many sorrows of her own,
> Griefs she may well to sympathy rehearse,
> Pains she may soften by her gentle tone.

---

[1] The frivolity of the Dublin season during the Irish famine was such that even the death of the Lord Lieutenant, Lord Bessborough, in May 1847 could not quell it. 'It was sad to hear the ladies wishing him dead that the gaieties might recommence, and the younger A.D.C.s fearing not to be "clear" in time for the Derby!' wrote Eliot Warburton to Milnes from Castle Armagh.

But the stark death in hunger and sharp cold,
The slow exhaustion of our mortal clay,
Are not for her to touch—she can but fold
Her mantle o'er her head and weep and pray.

When he got back to Yorkshire, Milnes, with other members of
his family, sent cheques to the priest at Skibbereen and to the
distributing agents at Bantry and at Mallow. 'We hate the Irish
for their poverty and their piety, their idleness and their imagination,' he noted down about this time. The sight of suffering always
affected Milnes acutely; it was no doubt of Ireland that he was
thinking when he wrote down a second and more serious reflection
in the same notebook; he felt ashamed, he said, at not sharing in
the evil of the world: 'I feel as if it was base to lie upon a grassy
slope lapped in the sunset overlooking a fair plain, on which a bloody
battle was taking place and the tumult of which just reached me
on the evening air.'

III

To Frenchmen the answer to the Irish problem seemed simple:
there was nothing to be done about it at all. The clotted arguments
of Milnes' *Real Union* would not have influenced any French
mind. 'I wonder every political writer in England does not
see how irresoluble is the question of Ireland,' said Tocqueville
to Milnes in the autumn of 1845. Tocqueville was in favour of
expediency and laissez-faire: 'leave it to time and the modifications
of the moment to do all they can.' He also drew an unpleasing
parallel between English behaviour in Ireland and French action
in Algiers.

In the last week of September 1845—just six months after the
Maynooth Bill and the appearance of his little book—Richard
Monckton Milnes set off for his first visit to Alexis de Tocqueville
and his English wife, Marie, in their early Renaissance château
on the Cherbourg peninsula. On the way he made a detour to
see Rouen (the new spire on the Cathedral looked to him like the
scaffolding round a factory chimney), Caen with its two great
abbeys, and the Cathedral at Bayeux, where he found decoration
in the nave that seemed 'Egyptian.' Unlike Mr. and Mrs. Grote,
who shipped their open carriage to Dieppe when they visited the
Tocquevilles in July 1846, Milnes travelled in cheap and uncomfortable 'old-fashioned diligences'—vehicles like the *Hirondelle*
which Madame Bovary would take to Rouen. He was angered by
the way the horses were made to gallop uphill. 'La mère des
chevaux n'est pas morte,' the post-boy pertly retorted when his

English passenger scolded him for ill-treating his animals. Milnes thought it an analogy with the famous saying of the great Condé.

The weather at Tocqueville was dull and grey, but not cold. It was a splendid apple year, and they would walk to the nearby coast through lanes and orchards laden with the fruit. The sinister potato disease had just appeared in Normandy, but (Milnes told his mother) the food at the château was so good you did not notice the absence of potatoes. The house, which was of grey stone, with a seignorial *colombière*, was very neatly kept: 'it shows it has an English mistress.' There were no flowers about, because Tocqueville had an antipathy to them: shuddering as if he were near some reptile when he saw a bowl of roses—and 'if they touched him, shrinking as from touching a caterpillar.' Madame de Tocqueville could not even wear an artificial flower in her bonnet.

The Château de Tocqueville had been built in the reign of Louis the Twelfth and had come to Alexis de Tocqueville, who was not an eldest son, by a family arrangement. He had reconstructed the house with money he made by *Democracy in America*—the first time, he said, that democracy had been used to build a château. Milnes was much impressed by the steadfast, traditional way of life of the Cotentin peasantry: the grave farm-labourers, who drank cider and sour milk, slept in their kitchens, married in middle age, and went regularly to mass and the sacraments. There was only one villager at Tocqueville who did not go to church, but got drunk and read Voltaire instead. Life in the heart of Normandy formed a singular contrast to life in the smoky, industrialised West Riding, where each horizon was ugly with the slag-heaps of nineteenth-century progress. Until Alexis de Tocqueville's improvements, there had been no road up to the château at all, and he remembered his grandmother being carried by retainers in her litter. To visit the Château de Tocqueville was to take a step backward into the reign of Louis Quinze.

Although this part of the Cotentin gave you the feeling that the French Revolution had passed it by, the events of 1789 were constantly discussed. Tocqueville had acquired an unrivalled knowledge of the politics of that not then remote period—the French Revolution seemed to Milnes and his contemporaries about as distant in time as the Boer War does to us—and he entertained his guests with stories of it: of how, for instance, his own grandfather, stumbling on the way to the scaffold, had murmured, 'C'est un mauvais augure. Si j'étais Romain je retournerais.' A fine service of Sèvres had been buried in the garden at Tocqueville during the Revolution, but nobody now knew where it lay. From Tocqueville and his friends the Beaumonts, who were also in the house, Milnes heard long panegyrics on life in France before the Revolution.

It is difficult to comprehend the depth and unselfish earnestness of the loyal feeling of France in the old time [Tocqueville said to him]. The King was to them their country, their home, their property, everything. I have never seen anything like it, except the way in which some old Canadian nuns spoke of George the Fourth.

Tocqueville would discuss current French politics as well as those of the Revolution. He disliked Guizot and distrusted the king. He believed that when Louis-Philippe should stand revealed to posterity by his memoirs and letters ('a large mass of which will come to light') it would be found that the political task he had accomplished had been in reality a very easy one and that 'his great art has been to evoke and make use of all the mean and vicious parts of the national character, as Napoleon did of all the spirited and chivalrous.' He admitted that the king was 'doux et brave —ce sont deux vertus qu'on ne peut pas le contester,' but he professed dislike for the way Louis-Philippe was 'always crying and beating his heart like a drum' and humming the Marseillaise. Tocqueville talked, too, of many other things: of Lamartine's facility, of Chateaubriand's descriptions of America, of the indignity of wearing the *Ordre de Juillet*, of the glass of wine which Thiers sometimes had brought to him in the Tribune. In English politics he especially admired Sir Robert Peel—for his stoicism. In spite of this Milnes felt he had much in common with Tocqueville—including his hatred of being laughed at in the Chamber. 'May it not be the necessary function of men like Peel and Guizot to disseminate, as it were, into the practical life of passing moments the great integral thoughts of better men like Tocqueville and myself?': he posed this question in his notebook while at Tocqueville.

He stayed with the Tocquevilles some ten days in all, returning to England in mid-October. Before he left Normandy he witnessed a 'beautiful fair' at Sainte Gabrielle, and admired the 'white caps of the women—hedges red with berries—green trees—and bright blue sea.' He came back to England refreshed.

When he got back Milnes found that Monsieur Thiers, whom he had known slightly in Paris in 1840, had come to London. Charles Greville, in his diary, records going down to The Grange purposely to meet Thiers, who stayed with the Ashburtons, as well as with Lord Lansdowne at Bowood.

He was very agreeable and very loquacious, talking with a great appearance of abandon on every subject [Greville wrote],

politicks general and particular, and his own History, which he was
ready to discuss, and to defend against all objections and criticisms
with great good humour. [1]

Milnes was evidently a member of the party at The Grange, for he
recorded many of Thiers' Napoleonic anecdotes, together with a
few comments by old Lord Ashburton. Last time he had seen
Thiers, in 1840, the French leader had been going about saying
that he would make Lord Palmerston cost more to England than
any Minister had ever cost any nation before. Thiers was now in a
more pacific if still rather anti-English mood, and had a very friendly
interview with Palmerston before he left. It had become clear
to everyone in the French Government, and so to its opponents
(of whom Thiers was the head), that Peel's administration was
moribund, that a Whig cabinet must come in, and that Palmerston,
the enemy of Louis-Philippe, would certainly be Foreign Secretary
and perhaps Prime Minister.[2] It was thus very agitating to Louis-
Philippe and Guizot to find Thiers making friends with Palmerston;
and even the latter's goodwill visit to Paris at Easter 1846 did little
to dispel their anxiety. To Milnes and the Ashburtons Thiers
openly ridiculed both Guizot and the King. He said he had told
Louis-Philippe that he should not do his own diplomacy: 'I said
to the King—when a lawyer has a suit he does not manage it himself, when a doctor is ill he sends for another doctor.' Thiers
constantly praised Napoleon, and told the company at The Grange
that they had no conception of 'how deeply grounded in France
are the institutions of the Empire'—a remark some of them had
cause to remember ten years later.

Thiers had a particular dislike of Tocqueville and also of Lamartine. 'M. Lamartine s'est grisé de la vanité à manière de faire
peine,' he told Milnes, '—et votre ami Tocqueville de même.'
Tocqueville, according to Thiers, was the most envious and most
odious man in the Chamber; and what was worse, a theorist.
'Je déteste messieurs les istes—"économistes," "Tocquevillistes,"
etc., etc.,' he said. But altogether this short, squat Provençal, with
wire-framed spectacles and a wheezing voice 'like the sighing of the
wind through a keyhole,' [3] made a good impression in London.
Milnes, who had been warned by Tocqueville that Thiers had a

---

[1] *The Greville Memoirs 1814–1860*, ed. Strachey and Fulford (Macmillan, 1938),
vol. v, p. 233.

[2] It was during this winter that the 'Palmerston House' set were intriguing at
Windsor to overcome the Queen's prejudice against Palmerston, in the hope of
getting him the Premiership of a Whig government in 1846. See Bell's *Lord
Palmerston* (Longmans, 1936), vol. i, chapter xvi.

[3] Description by J. A. Roebuck, the radical M.P. (1801–1879), in a letter to
his wife of February 1852, recording a breakfast with Monckton Milnes (*Life and
Letters of J. A. Roebuck*, edited by R. E. Leader, Edward Arnold, 1897, p. 250).

dual personality,[1] did not take everything he said very seriously, and wrote jocularly to Guizot of 'the friendly professions (M. Thiers) lavished on all of us during his visit to England.' After Thiers' death in 1877, John Morley, then editor of the *Fortnightly*, asked Lord Houghton to write an obituary article on him for that paper. Lord Houghton refused: 'Thiers will be talked and written about, and have become a bore by the time your next number is out, so I would not write about him if I could.' He said his own letters from Thiers had been lost, and were not in any case as interesting as those from Guizot. He repeated to Morley [2] a saying of Lord Granville, who had been ambassador in Paris from 1824 to 1841:

All French politicians lie, but with distinctions. Comte Molé lies to keep up the dignity of his country and his own; Thiers lies *de gaieté de cœur*—it is natural to him; M. Guizot only lies when the condition of the State requires it.

IV

When Milnes returned to Westminster from Normandy the question of Corn Law Repeal was reaching its final crisis. The heavy rains of the later summer all over England—'the rains that rained away the Corn Laws'—had helped Peel to force his Cabinet's hand and to persuade Ministers pledged to Protection that the only course was a total repeal of the laws controlling the price of foreign grain. The Queen and the Prince were said to be strongly for repeal ('Lord Melbourne told me he had never seen the Queen so interested in any public measure—she is believed to be "Total and immediate"' Milnes wrote to his father). Only the fierce and powerful Protectionist faction of the Tory party—led by Disraeli's marionette, Lord George Bentinck, and supported throughout the counties by old-fashioned squires like Robert Pemberton Milnes— were still stonily opposed to it, and as anxious as the Whigs themselves to bring Peel down. On 3 December 1845 Lord Aberdeen privately informed the editor of *The Times* that the Cabinet had decided on Repeal. On 4 December *The Times* published this information. On 6 December Peel resigned, resuming office on the twentieth after the failure of Lord John Russell and the Whigs to form a Government.

The Times leakage was then, and for many decades afterwards, attributed to the action of Milnes' friend Caroline Norton, who was alleged to have charmed the secret out of Sidney Herbert and sold

---

[1] 'There are two distinct men in M. Thiers—the one coarse, clever, imprudent, *gamin*, the other cunning, *réfléchi*, with a taste for art and with tact and nicety quite marvellous': Commonplace book, 1845–6.
[2] Letter dated from Fryston, 14 September 1877, quoted by Reid, vol. ii, p. 366.

it to Delane of *The Times* for £1,300; this mythical story inspired Meredith to write *Diana of the Crossways*. Milnes noted the Norton rumour at the time it was first current, together with two other versions of the leakage—one attributing the indiscretion to Lady Wharncliffe, who was said to have opened one of her husband's despatch boxes when he was ill,[1] the other relating that the Duke of Wellington had spoken of the Cabinet decision to Lord Fitzroy Somerset in the presence of two or three clerks. In any case, Peel's reconstituted cabinet was determined on Repeal. The Speech from the Throne on 22 January 1846 left no doubt that the Corn Laws were doomed. The Corn Bill was presented; it passed its final stages on 15 May. On 26 May the Tory Government fell, and was replaced by the first Whig administration for five years, under the leadership of Lord John Russell.

In the general hubbub of the Corn Law repeal days in the House of Commons—with the Tory party split into hostile groups— sudden reputations flared up and died. Unexpected members of the House had an ephemeral success. Stafford O'Brien, particularly, came forward as a brilliant supporter of the Protection interest—making clever, sentimental and telling speeches, and shedding what Milnes called 'his glitter and grace' over 'the dull sobriety' of the country party. But Milnes' part in the debates was undistinguished and unimportant. His opinions on the Corn Laws had changed and wobbled for months. From being a 'moderate protectionist' he had become (he told his father in March 1845) a supporter of the towns against the country interest, but at the height of the Corn Law debates he wrote again to tell Mr. Milnes that he could not unconditionally support Peel: 'I am not under the faintest shadow of a pledge to Pomfret,' he wrote, 'and even if I were I had better eat my words now at the general banquet than live on that food for the rest of my life.'

Peel has behaved to his party as Washington did to the old horse that had borne him through all his battles—sold him [he wrote to MacCarthy. . . .]. He is acting with a rash courage and singleness of object unlike his whole life, making probabilities futile and calculations impossible.

In the end, after further hesitations, he voted for Repeal. But when Peel's administration fell at the end of May 1845, Milnes chose a quick way out of the dilemma in which he, like most moderate Tories, then found himself. Lacking the sense of personal

---

[1] James Stuart-Wortley-Mackenzie, 1st Baron Wharncliffe (1776–1845), Lord President of the Council since 1841, died of 'suppressed gout and apoplexy' at Wharncliffe House, Curzon Street, on 19 December of that year.

devotion to Sir Robert Peel which inspired some members of the Tory party to remain Peelites, unwilling to become a follower of Disraeli and Bentinck, Milnes gave what he at first called his 'independent support' to the new Government. He wrote a letter to his constituents explaining how he had come to take this decision. The letter received much favourable newspaper publicity. Some months later he confirmed his new political allegiance by relinquishing his membership of the Carlton Club. Milnes had not in any way affected the repeal of the Corn Laws, but the repeal had drastically affected Milnes. It had made him turn Whig.

In the spiteful memorandum on Milnes' character which Disraeli wrote in the 'sixties he described Milnes' behaviour during the Corn Law days.[1] According to his analysis, envy was a chief component in Milnes' character; and the new and powerful position of Disraeli in 1846 (so different from the old, romantic Young England period of a few years back) had aroused this envy to the full. Disraeli represents Milnes as strutting about saying, 'It is impossible that I and Sidney Herbert can be led by Disraeli':

No one expected Sidney Herbert would be led by me [Disraeli explains]. He was a member of Sir Robert Peel's Cabinet, which had been mainly if not entirely destroyed by my efforts. Milnes was one of the most insignificant members of the House of Commons; but he gratified his vanity by classing in his own talk himself with S. Herbert. When he found Peel was flung in a ditch [Disraeli's amiable note continues] he changed his politics, and took to Palmerston, whom, as well as Lady Palmerston, he toadied with a flagrant perseverance that made everyone smile.

It is no part of the duty of a biographer to exonerate his subject from the charges of those who knew him when he was alive. But it is relevant to note that other factors as well as thwarted ambition led Milnes to leave the Tory party in 1846. It is also just to remember that he had never been in any way indebted to Sir Robert Peel. By character and temperament, as well as by a family tradition which his father had broken, Milnes was inclined to Liberalism. Most of his friends were Liberals—and he saw a good deal of the more earnest, thoughtful radicals, like Mr. and Mrs. Grote and Sir William Molesworth. Richard Milnes did not like or understand English country life, and to him the point of view of the squires was anachronistic and remote. He reacted, too, against his father's active faith in Protection.[2] But more powerful than

---

[1] Moneypenny and Buckle, vol. iii, p. 51.

[2] The Corn Law row had stimulated Mr. Milnes into political activity in the spring of 1846, when he delivered 'a brilliant Philippic' against Repeal when supporting the Protectionist candidate for the West Riding, whom his son opposed.

any factor in Milnes' ultimate decision to leave the Tory party was his touchy and almost morbid dislike of Peel.

The days of Milnes' earliest enthusiasm for Peel were dead and gone. In the late eighteen-thirties he had told Carlyle 'with great seriousness, "Peel was a man of real talent," a great man.'[1] This was the period when Milnes would be asked to dine with the Peels in Whitehall Gardens in a room hung with the famous pictures Sir Robert had collected; and when he would listen reverently to Peel's reminiscences and opinions. But this had been at a time when the Tories were still in Opposition, and when Peel was presumably sizing up the value of the new followers brought him by the election of 1837. 'The kindly intercourse with which he honoured me when in Opposition has, probably of necessity, been so remitted of late years that it would be impertinent in me to approach him on any footing of intimacy,' Milnes wrote to Gladstone in January 1846. To Milnes, indeed, Peel seemed increasingly chilly and neglectful. They were not exactly complementary characters, and Peel's manner was very far from winning. Few people could conjure up more than an awe-struck admiration for his grave and noble mind. The Queen (Milnes heard) used towards Peel 'quite the manner of a woman in love with a man'; the Duke of Wellington cried at his death; the Prince Consort felt as though he had lost a second father; but these were people who had been in daily personal contact with Peel and who had seen him at work. The less important Tory members of Parliament had little chance to develop any personal devotion to him. He took no trouble to placate those whom he disappointed; and he clearly found such a variable character as that of Richard Monckton Milnes —now thrusting and flippant, now poetical and moody—almost incomprehensible. He would have remembered, too, that Milnes' first appearance in London had been as a poet; and Peel had a notorious distaste for political men who put their names to so much as a published pamphlet, let alone to several neat volumes of sentimental verse. Milnes' apparent confusion of aim, his ill-success at speaking in the House, his love of gossip and his seeming indiscretion were quite sufficient to make Peel judge him not suitable for office—just as they served to obscure his real and lucid intelligence and his wide acquaintance with foreign politicians' affairs.

While he had never directly applied for a place in Peel's administration (as Disraeli and others had done in 1841), Milnes had obviously expected one. This had been the motive behind the long, assiduous letters to Peel from Paris or from Smyrna. Peel's

[1] Letter from Carlyle of 2 December 1841.

replies to these letters were brief, polite and entirely non-committal, and he had passed over every opportunity of giving Milnes even some minor job—the last occasion being a vacancy on the Board of Control in 1845. The courteous but lofty way in which he treated Milnes or answered his letters was desperately annoying. It is well exemplified in a letter of Peel's written in January 1842 and apparently in reply to Milnes' hint that his father should be made a baronet on the occasion of the birth of the Prince of Wales.[1] Peel's reply ended: 'You will quite understand me, that it is from the unfeigned respect I have for the talents of your father that I advise him to retain the distinction of not being a Baronet.' It was an explicit letter.

By 1846 Peel's snubbing process had begun to exasperate Monckton Milnes. Nothing he did made the slightest impression upon the porcelain-like surface of Peel's Olympian neglect. And so Milnes, who had as few hatreds as Carlyle had many—'learn to hate at least two-thirds of the human race' was Carlyle's most recent advice to him—Milnes began to foster a real hatred—a hatred of Peel. 'I am sorry you have chosen Sir R. Peel for your antipathy,' remarked the forthright Mrs. Grote; 'but I am so glad you have learned to hate somebody at last, that I willingly give him up to you.' Even now, Milnes did not hate easily: 'I only wish I liked or reverenced the man himself,' he wrote to MacCarthy during the Corn Law debates; 'but I cannot do it, though I try very hard, and write and speak in puff of him.' This was in March 1846; and when Milnes said 'speak in puff of him' he already meant 'speak publicly in puff of him.' For long now, amongst his friends, he had abandoned all pretended reverence for Peel. In his notebooks he had begun to assemble a quantity of derogatory comments on Sir Robert: some of them petty and absurd. For instance, Macaulay had told him that Peel could not pronounce the 'h' in words like 'adhere' and 'inhabitant'; someone else that he sat at whist with his legs tucked under his chair ('result of a bourgeois education'); Milnes himself discovered to his infinite amusement that Peel's hair was of the shade which Rosalind in *As You Like It* calls 'the dissembling colour.' He began making *mots* of his own against the Prime Minister: 'Peel has not belief enough in him to be a humbug—he is not even a hypocrite of sincerity.' Milnes had

---

[1] Letter dated 19 January 1842, printed in Parker's *Sir Robert Peel from his private papers* (John Murray, 1899), vol. iii, p. 431. Peel was more sparing of honours than any previous Prime Minister: creating only six peerages in five years and offering three baronetages in the same period. 'I do not intend to advise her Majesty to create any Baronets on account of the birth of the Prince,' he wrote to Lord de Grey in November 1841. 'There would not be a simple squire in the land if the fever for honours were not checked.'

become, in fact, a victim to pique. 'You abuse Peel like a woman,' said Lady Harriet Baring; 'you become *Miss* Milnes.'

This was Milnes' frame of mind at the beginning of January 1846. He was at Bawtry, waiting for the opening of the Repeal session of Parliament, and he was still a Tory in name. His peace of mind at Bawtry was suddenly shattered by the news that the one appointment for which he languished above all others—the Under-Secretaryship for Foreign Affairs—had been vacated by Lord Canning who had held it since 1841. On getting this news Milnes wrote immediately to Gladstone pressing his case in a long, earnest and not wholly judicious letter. He explained how well equipped he was to be Under-Secretary. He stressed his valiant public support of Peel: 'I have now for near nine years earnestly, conscientiously, and independently, in and out of the House of Commons, with voice and with pen, supported Sir Robert Peel and his policy.' He next declared that if Sir Robert and Lord Aberdeen conferred the office 'on any other member of Parliament of lower standing' than himself, 'he would be compelled to take it as an intimation of their opinion' of his 'inability to share the public service in any department.' He would prepare himself, he added ominously, 'to act on that belief.'

Of all the moral difficulties I have encountered in my intercourse with the world [he continued], I have suffered far the most from the problem of reconciling that self-respect, without which public life is disgraceful, and that desire of effecting some practical good in one's generation, without which it is useless, with an entire freedom from selfish motives; and knowing with what subtlety evil influences work upon the spirit, I own I dread the effect that a sense of personal injustice may have on my decision of questions likely soon to be brought before every member of Parliament, and to the consideration of which I had hoped to bring a mind untouched by bitter feelings.

Gladstone would have read this passage of Milnes' letter in the scrupulous sense in which it was written. To-day it reads almost like a threat. Cumbersome and hastily drafted, the letter was an unpersuasive document. Gladstone's reply, on the other hand, was a model of terse discretion.

My dear Milnes [he wrote from the Colonial Office on 16 January], Your letter reached me in due course. Even if I remained silent, I am sure you would not believe I could be indifferent to its contents, but it can do no harm that I should send one line to assure you for the present that they interest me deeply and that I have not been inattentive to the suggestion which you made to me. . . . I send you [Gladstone added in a post-script] a note I have received from Peel.

Peel's note, in which he seems to have referred to Milnes as 'a candidate for office,' has not survived.

When Mrs. Grote had congratulated Milnes on hating somebody at last, she had overlooked the fact that there was one individual whom he had openly and always loathed. This person was the Young England hero, George Smythe, the original of Coningsby. Smythe seemed in some ways a more youthful and more handsome as well as a more successful version of Monckton Milnes himself. He was already Milnes' rival in his knowledge of European affairs, and he had Disraeli at his back. Then, too, Smythe had had a long and famous novel written round his character [1]; while Milnes had been left out of *Coningsby* altogether, and was only to be popped into *Tancred* to provide comic relief. Moreover, George Smythe enjoyed insulting Monckton Milnes. When a new member of Parliament, Beresford Hope, had made a very bad speech in March 1842, Milnes came up to George Smythe (the story is, of course, Disraeli's) [2] and said ('with his queer face of solemn depreciation and conceit'): 'Why don't you interfere to prevent him speaking, Smythe?' 'Why, I don't interfere to prevent you speaking, Milnes,' was Smythe's uncharming repartee. 'Even Milnes' impudence,' Disraeli annotates, 'was floored.'

We may thus picture Milnes' feelings when he discovered, just five days after he had written to Gladstone, that the Under-Secretaryship for Foreign Affairs—the post for which he had worked and read and travelled—had been given to George Smythe. He wrote off to Gladstone in a mood of scathing resignation:

No ingenuity could have made the blow more provoking from the hands of the man to whom I have shown the most public respect, through those of the one for whom I entertain the most private dislike. But in morals, as in physics, if well used, the bitter braces. [3]

The shock of Smythe's appointment completely and finally alienated Monckton Milnes from Peel, though he voted for his old leader over the Corn Laws that spring. But there was no real disloyalty in the haste with which he joined the Liberal Party; for of all the many members of the House who were gratified to see Peel 'flung

---

[1] Smythe had even made himself a small literary reputation by the publication in 1844 of his *Historic Fancies*, a miscellaneous collection of poems and essays on historical subjects.

[2] Letter of Disraeli to his wife, 10 March 1842; Moneypenny, vol. ii, p. 129.

[3] These letters to Gladstone are taken from Reid, since I have not had access to the originals. Reid's transcription and punctuation of MS. letters were not invariably accurate.

in a ditch' none can have been more quietly jubilant than Richard
Monckton Milnes.

Disraeli has left one more acid description of Milnes in these
Corn Law days: an account of a breakfast party, in June 1846,
at 26 Pall Mall at which Disraeli and Cobden and Suleiman Pasha
and Prince Louis Napoleon found themselves as ill-assorted guests.

Went late [Disraeli noted] (Half past eleven perhaps) as his
breakfasts were 10 o'clockers, but kept up at the House. All the
breakfast eaten: that nothing, as I never eat in public at that time.
Some coffee on a disordered table; M. M. murmured something
about a cutlet, not visible, which I did not notice. Strange scene.
. . . They were fighting the battle of Konieh like Corporal Trim.
'Voilà la cavalerie,' said Suleiman, and he placed a spoon.
'L'infanterie est là,' and he moved a coffee-cup etc. etc.; d'Orsay
standing behind him and affecting immense interest in order to
make the breakfast go off well. A round table; at the fireplace
Milnes' father . . . Cobden there: a whitefaced man whom I did
not know, who turned out to be Kinglake, then the author of
Eothen which I had not read, and never have; and other celebrities.

Disraeli thought Louis Napoleon mad, while Cobden judged him
'a weak fellow but mild and amiable'; d'Orsay, Cobden wrote in
his journal, was 'a fleshy, animal-looking creature.' [1] Probably
this was not one of Milnes' most successful meals.

V

Except for his trip to Ireland in the early winter, Milnes spent
the whole of the year 1846 at home, held in England by acute anxiety
about his mother. Mrs. Milnes' health had begun to decline
soon after the family's return from Italy in 1836, though she put as
good a face on it as she could. Ten raw West Riding winters had
now done their worst. She suffered terrible paroxysms of coughing,
but she resolutely refused to go to Torquay or some other southern
resort; saying in a stoical, old-fashioned way that she could never
think of putting her husband to leaving his home. Like Mr. Milnes,
she divided her time between Fryston, Bawtry and Serlby, moving
as and when her husband told her. Richard wrote to her frequently, sending her the pieces of gossip he judged she would most
like. She would reply, on writing paper with a blood-red border,
telling him village stories, or about the 'gentlemanly' new curate
Mr. Aldred, commenting on the new magazine, *Punch*, for which
Richard had sent her a subscription, or on the last volume of the

---

[1] *The Life of Richard Cobden,* by John Morley (Chapman & Hall, 1881), vol. i,
p. 386.

serial *Dombey and Son* ('I like Dickens so much more in the ludicrous than the pathetic') or recommending some 'odd and interesting' French book. She would have liked to see Richard married, and suggested that if her husband were given a barony this might help—'I am certain no girls like to marry without the prospect of a title.'

In 1846 Mrs. Milnes let herself be taken to Brighton for the summer; but while there she caught the English cholera, and returned to Yorkshire worse than before. The winter of 1846 to 1847 was an exceptionally severe one throughout England. Even in the south the snow lay long upon the fields, and the ponds everywhere were frozen hard for many weeks. In the West Riding the cold was ferocious. Mrs. Milnes' cough did not improve. In January it was clear that she was likely to die, though in March she could still write to Richard, with her old gaiety, 'I am very weak and say with Queen Catherine "my legs like loaded branches."' On the first of May she died at Serlby, the house from which she had been married and in which much of her childhood had been spent.

To Richard (who was himself ill with gout and suffering from low spirits) his mother's death was a hammer-blow. He had always had far more in common with her than with his father, and it was from her that he inherited his flamboyance and his power of enthusiasm, as well as his easy, level good-humour. 'It is good moral instruction to examine yourself after the death of one you have loved and test your duty by the feelings you then experience,' he wrote down on the day of his mother's death. It was the first time he had had to watch anyone die.

Providence [he wrote in his notebook, just below this last sentiment] seems to have surrounded Death with so much pain and so many circumstances of horror and repugnance to prevent men from loving it too well and embracing it too eagerly as a refuge from the vicissitudes and vacancy of Life.

Chapter Twelve

I

After seeing his mother's coffin lodged in the Monckton vault at Serlby, Richard Milnes returned sorrowfully to London by train, travelling in the high, upholstered railway carriage above the English fields and past the fresh green spinneys of mid-May. Back in Pall Mall he was soon at work on a long exposition of Palmerston's policy in Portugal and of the recent Allied intervention in the Portuguese civil war. This speech he delivered in the House in the second week of June.

Milnes was temperamentally incapable of remaining sad for long. 'The best thing for you,' Thomas Carlyle had said to him one day in 1846, 'would be to be cast for some weeks, perhaps years, on a shoal of black despair.' 'I am not sure of that' (Milnes records that he answered), 'I should probably drown myself.' 'No,' cried Lady Harriet Baring, who was in the room at the time; 'you might throw yourself in the water, but you would float, you know.' It was not only to Milnes' spiritual buoyancy that Lady Harriet referred. The self-indulgence which was a weakening and important factor in Milnes' character (and which he did little to curb) was by now affecting his stocky figure as well as his joints. The gout, which had come on him very early in his life, might be attributed to his heredity. His growing corpulence could not. One of the old Berry sisters wrote to a friend in India in the autumn of 1847 that Monckton Milnes was 'grown too fat to be a poet.' W. E. Forster, who met him for the first time in the summer of this same year, described him as 'well-fed and fattening.' 'A pleasant, companionable little man,' wrote Forster (who afterwards became one of Milnes' most devoted intimates), ' . . . with some small remnant of poetry about his eyes and nowhere else.' As an old man Milnes was almost notoriously ugly; and already, at the age of thirty-eight, his appearance began to lack charm. 'Mr. Milnes is lively and pleasant, but he is plain and common-looking,' wrote Fanny Allen to her niece in December 1847.[1] By the early eighteen-fifties Milnes had become 'rather stout, and rather

---

[1] Letter to Elizabeth Wedgwood, 26 December 1847, published in *A Century of Family Letters*, edited H. Lichfield (1915), vol. i, p. 113.

Monckton Milnes at the B^h Association
Sketched by Caroline Smith

RICHARD MONCKTON MILNES, CIRCA 1848

reddish in the face, and with a mouth that looks as if he had lost his upper teeth.'[1] He was now taking less care about his clothes:

You forget [he wrote in 1845 to his sister Harriette, who had remonstrated with him on the dull colour of his waistcoats] the forcible lines of a great Poet on the subject of your note.

> Learn, that if naturally stout,
> Light waistcoats make you seem stouter,
> And, if at all inclining *out*,
> You then become an out-and-outer.

but I have plenty of light waistcoats &, if any consolation to you, I can tell you that Colvile told me at the Buccleughs, that 'he had never seen me so well got up before.' I quite agree with you how few people look fresh in London—but it is owing as much to the unwholesome complexions they get from the way of life as to the blacks in the air & the dirt in the streets.

Monckton Milnes had never been handsome, but as he approached forty he had to rely more and more upon his personality—the agile mind, the bounding conversation, the winning manner, the shining good nature—to attract the needed quota of new friends.

In June 1847 Parliament was dissolved and there was an election, although no very definite issue lay before the country.

We approach our dissolution with great equanimity [Milnes had written comfortably to Varnhagen von Ense on 19 June]; there will be a good many contests but they will be mostly of a local and personal nature. . . . The Protestant (or rather anti-Catholic) spirit will be almost the only public element, and a placard has already been circulated in my borough, stating that I intend 'to give the Pope a seat in the British Parliament.'

But the election did not pass off so smoothly as he hoped. The No-Popery cry, which defeated Lord John Manners at Liverpool, was loudly raised at Pontefract by the dissenters. For the first time Milnes found himself facing a closely contested election. His dabbling in Puseyism, the tolerance towards it which he had shown in *One Tract More*, had enraged his more narrow-minded constituents. 'Protestants, keep awake!' ran little posters pasted up all over Pontefract town; 'don't be duped by Mr. Milnes.' His support of Maynooth and Repeal had also alienated many Pontefract voters, and when the poll closed at four o'clock on July 30 it was found that Mr. Monckton Milnes had only just got in

---

[1] Description from a letter of the Hon. Mrs. Edward Twistleton, a young Bostonian who was visiting London for the first time with her English husband. Her letters were published by John Murray in 1928.

by nineteen votes.   His father, who was too ill and depressed to take an active part in the election campaign, told him that one of the Fryston characters, Miss Richardson, had begged him not to press her to vote for his son.   'His life hangs on a thread,' Mr. Milnes told her, referring to his son's thin chance of getting in; 'I only wish,' replied the strange old lady, 'that it hung on a rope.'

A few days before the dissolution, Milnes had intervened in the debate on Portugal with his long and authoritative speech.   It was the second big speech on foreign policy which he made in that year, for in March he had delivered (and had printed as a pamphlet) an attack upon the suppression of the Free State of Cracow by the Emperor of Austria.   His reputation in the House did not stand high, since he was no orator, and probably these two speeches did not get the attention which they certainly deserved.   His defence of Palmerston's doctrine that England had a right of 'interfering in foreign countries in cases of emergency' was logical and well-argued, while his analysis of the diplomatic exchanges between London, Paris and Madrid leading up to the Allied intervention in aid of Queen Maria II of Portugal in May 1846 seemed convincing.   But though his speech bristled with quotations from the dispatches quoted in the Blue Book just laid upon the table of the House (and which Milnes brandished in his hand as he spoke), it contained certain errors of interpretation, even certain errors of fact; for he implied that England had been backward in helping Portugal when Costa Cabral, Count Thomar, the Portuguese statesman (then acting as Portuguese ambassador to Spain) had first invoked the aid of the countries which had signed the Quadruple Alliance of 1834.[1]   This misconception elicited a letter to Milnes from Henry Bulwer, the British minister at Madrid.

I see in a report that I have just got a speech of yours in Parliament [Bulwer wrote from Madrid on 25 June] that you seem to think that in spite of a declaration made by me to Ct Thomar, we did nothing here, and he did everything in the late negociations.   I have not seen what papers are published but the facts are directly the reverse from this.

[1] The Quadruple Alliance of April 1834 pledged the Governments of Great Britain, France, Portugal and Spain to support with effectual aid the Legitimist causes in both countries of the Peninsula.   The 'civil war' or insurrection on which Milnes was speaking had broken out in April 1846, twelve years after the signature of the Alliance; it was chiefly caused by the unpopularity of Costa Cabral, then head of Queen Maria da Gloria's government.   The situation was aggravated by the return of Marshal Saldanha in July 1846 and his establishment at the head of a new Cabinet.   In May 1847 the Allies, who had hitherto tried mediation, intervened actively, and a British squadron held the mouth of the Douro.   The civil war ended in June of the same year with the Convention of Gramido.

He explained what trouble he had had in checking the Spaniards' desire to intervene on their own, and in an anti-liberal sense, in the Portuguese insurrection, and that he had had to use strong language to keep the Spanish Government from acting in a head-long way and outside the terms of the Quadruple Alliance. He had said everything possible to them, short of menacing war.

. . . It is a false calculation [he continued] to imagine that such a menace would necessarily have been attended to—Spaniards and Portuguese run a-muck and do not attend to such representations altho' common sense wd tell them to do so. . . . The menace of war therefore wd probably have been war, that is to say a war against the queen of Portugal & the Queen of Spain two independent sovereigns, because they made an arrangement suitable to their interests. Such a war would have been an European anomaly. . . . However [he ended], all I wish to rectify was the assertion of yours which I just noticed with respect to which I wish my own credit & that of my Govt here to stand well with an old friend and acquaintance. Come [he added as an afterthought] and see us here this autumn.

These words caught Milnes' eye.

Henry Bulwer signed himself Milnes' 'very affectionately and truly.' He was eight years Milnes' senior. They had first made friends in that winter of 1840 which Milnes had spent investigating the salons of Paris while Bulwer was acting at the British Embassy as Chargé d'Affaires for Lord Granville. Henry Lytton Bulwer was an elder brother of the novelist Edward Bulwer Lytton. Like Monckton Milnes, he had travelled in Greece as a young man, had been brought up to admire Byron, had lived in Constantinople, had served as a member of Parliament, and was immensely fond of the French. He had an intimate knowledge of Parisian society, and had written in the eighteen-thirties a sort of survey of French life in two volumes called *France, Social, Literary, Political.* Since November 1843 he had been British Minister at the Court of Isabella II, where his great diplomatic skill and his consciously languid air had earned him a good many fierce enemies as well as friends. His conversational powers were famous, while his 'high-bred manner,' his 'sweetness of disposition,' his acute sense of humour and his radical views were exactly what Milnes would most like. He was subject to racking headaches and in appearance he was pale and delicate. 'Sir H. Bulwer,' Milnes noted in his commonplace book, 'looks like a faded Velasquez.'

The temptation to see Madrid in Bulwer's company was a great one, and there was no reason for Milnes to resist it. Moreover, the project coincided with something Palmerston had lately said to him

—Palmerston, with whom it was so important to stand well and whose 'cocky common sense' Milnes was now loudly declaring that he much admired.   He decided to go to Spain.[1]

II

My present project [Milnes wrote to Charles MacCarthy, now settled unhappily in Ceylon] is to leave England the beginning of September, pass a few days at Lisbon, run over Andalusia and spend a month with Bulwer at Madrid. . . . I may make this an agreeable and instructive tour.

I am going to Spain out of no vague locomotiveness [he told another friend on 27 August], but from a suggestion of Palmerston's that I should be much better able to understand the complicated politics of the Peninsula if I would go and look at them myself, which I thought true enough.   I really dislike tossing and moving about except for the after-thought it gives me.   I have too a great dislike of burdening myself with details of matters, the foundation of which I do not thoroughly comprehend : I am naturally critical and thus cannot build my views with any comfort to myself on the authority of others. . . . If I have one talent it is that of seeing what I *don't* know, & the immensity of this district often appals me.

I got here yesterday in time to see Palmerston [he scribbled to his father in a note from Pall Mall], who was very communicative about Spain & glad I was going there : it is impossible to conceive a greater imbroglio. . . . I think I shall go to the Ashburtons on Friday & only come up to town for the day before I sail. . . . Palmerston said he had written to Seymour & Bulwer authorising them to trust me with perfect confidence on political matters.

Milnes found Lord Palmerston very talkative about Spain. He told him he was certain that Queen Isabella's new favourite, Serrano, was in the pay of Louis-Philippe.   Since the French coup of the double marriage of the Queen of Spain and her sister in October 1846, Lord Palmerston was inclined to suspect the French king and Guizot of an almost diabolical capacity for intrigue.   The Spanish marriage question had agitated the French and English Governments for five years—England being determined that the Queen of Spain should not marry a son of Louis-Philippe, while France refused to countenance a Coburg match.   When Milnes, on his way back from Cairo, had been to see Louis-Philippe at Neuilly in May 1843, the king of the French had chatted to him about the marriages and had asked him why the English seemed to want a German king in Spain.   At the Château d'Eu meeting

---

[1] 'Dicky Milnes . . . always Palmerston's Lacquey' wrote Greville two years later (8 August 1849).   Elsewhere he calls Milnes one of Palmerston's 'devils' and 'the laughing-stock of the House' (Greville, ed. *cit.* vol. vi).

in 1845 Queen Victoria and Lord Aberdeen had pledged England to agree to the marriage of Queen Isabella with a descendant of Philip V and not to give their support to any other candidate; while Louis-Philippe and Guizot were understood to have promised that she should not marry one of the French king's sons, and that if her sister the Infanta Fernanda Louisa did so it should only be after Isabella's own marriage and the birth of an heir to the throne. Owing largely to Palmerston's mismanagement of negotiations which Bulwer could have handled successfully on his own, Guizot and Louis-Philippe assumed that the Foreign Office was now going back on Aberdeen's promise and was planning a Coburg marriage. Seizing on this flimsy pretext they quickly and secretly arranged that Queen Isabella should marry her impotent cousin, Don Francis d'Assiz, while her sister married the Duc de Montpensier on the same day but not at the same hour. By this plot they alienated England, infuriated the English court, the Whigs and the Tories, and wrecked the *entente cordiale*. Queen Victoria's Government had been the only one in Europe to enter into cordial relations with the Orleans regime. In their new isolation Guizot and the king turned to Austria, and in an effort to win Metternich's friendship supported the cause of reaction in Switzerland, thus strengthening the hand of the Liberal opposition inside France. The breaking of the *entente cordiale* by the Spanish marriage intrigue was thus a directly contributory cause of the fall of the Orleans monarchy in February 1848. But in the autumn of 1847 few things seemed more unlikely than the collapse of Louis-Philippe's house of cards. The danger of French predominance in Spain seemed a very real one to Palmerston at the time of Richard Monckton Milnes' visit to Madrid.

A letter to Milnes from Charles de Montalembert, written in December 1847, reflects the French attitude to Palmerston's policy, and though ultramontane in tone, suggests how far the breach between England and France had gone: feelings were once more as embittered as during the Near Eastern tension of 1840.

I have not the slightest idea of what *we* (as you say) are now doing in Spain [Montalembert wrote in English from La Roche en Bressy in the Côte d'Or], but I know enough of Spain to laugh at the idea of its being a *province* of anybody's. But admitting that *we* have behaved there as bad (sic) as we could can anything in our behaviour be compared with *yours* in Greece, and particularly in Switzerland! Alas! my dear friend, for the honour and the morality of England. . . . You know what an Anglomane I am, but I confess I am positively *disgusted* at English policy on the continent—how such a nation can allow itself to be governed by such a man as Lord Palmerston is more than I can conceive.

18   257

Many people in England, from the Queen and Prince Albert downwards, shared Montalembert's distrust of Palmerston's activities during his five-year tenure of the Foreign Office from June 1846 till December 1851. A letter from Milnes' Cambridge contemporary, the journalist G. S. Venables, dating from the same epoch as Montalembert's, epitomises the general complaints against Palmerston: selfish and unprincipled at home, rash and undignified abroad, going by no rule except to bring things into such a state as to make himself of importance, drafting 'vulgar, impertinent and ill-written' dispatches. 'What an immense superiority both intellectual and moral your friend Guizot shows,' wrote Venables. Milnes' own enthusiasm for Palmerston, which endured until October 1860, was not at all chilled by such attacks.

The first plan for the Spanish journey had been that Mr. Milnes should accompany his son; but Richard had quickly 'given up all hope' of this, and his father remained at Fryston sunk in ill-health and melancholy. Richard's own spirits had revived by August. It was an exceptional and balmy summer, and as he flitted from country-house to country-house the prospect of the Spanish journey glowed before him.

What a wonderful day for Engd. Sunday was [he wrote to Lord Galway in August]. I past it under Burnham Beeches with Mrs. Grote, who had tumbled down stairs the day before but recovered on my presence. We had Chas. Buller & Roebuck & were as merry as became philosophers.

With the coming of the railway into this part of Buckinghamshire three years before, the sylvan glades in which the hollow, ancient Burnham Beeches stood were now less of a rural solitude than when the Grotes had bought their house there in 1838; but it was still leafy and quiet. In this decade, the eighteen-forties, Mrs. Grote was one of Milnes' dearest and most humorous friends—a heavy, stately, blue-eyed woman of between fifty and sixty with a very sharp wit, a good literary style and a social conscience. Some people laughed at her but she laughed at herself before they could, and maintained with intimate friends like Monckton Milnes and Charles Buller an astringent, bantering relationship which they found very refreshing.

From Burnham Beeches Milnes went north to Fryston to say good-bye to his father, came down to London to engage a Spanish servant and then retired to the Barings at the Bay House, Alverstoke, to await the date of his departure. It was windy weather and he was no sailor, so he went out to sea in Lord Ashburton's yacht 'as a sort of practice.' The Barings told him they had heard that his bribery at Pontefract was 'frightful,' and that he had been detected going around in a blouse with a yellow handkerchie giving out handfuls of sovereigns. John Wilson Croker was also staying in the house and would talk of nothing but the Duchesse de Praslin's murder (which had occurred in Paris a fortnight before) and of Peel's wonderful memory. Sir Walter Scott's son-in-law, Lockhart, was there too, and spoke of joining Milnes in Spain by the next packet.

On 7 September Milnes set sail in the *Madrid*, and reached Lisbon on the 13th. His fellow-passengers included the intrepid traveller Lady Emmeline Stuart-Wortley and the old Miguelite general Povoas, who was returning to Portugal from exile. Milnes was sea-sick for three days.

III

'Lockhart did not come out, but Potocki (Dietrichstein's brother-in-law) did & a very pleasant accomplished fellow he is,' Milnes wrote on mourning notepaper from Cadiz. 'Very *facile à vivre*, which is *the* quality of a travelling companion,' he told his father in another letter. Alfred Potocki was the brother of the heiress Countess Potocka who had married the Austrian ambassador in London, Count Moritz von Dietrichstein. An attaché at his brother-in-law's Embassy, he was popular in English society and a particular friend of Henry Greville. Potocki was in every way a typical specimen of the Polish aristocracy: devout, sensual and reactionary, proud of his family, interested in etiquette and with the attitude to women of a professional libertine. His grandfather had shot himself with the silver knob off a sugar-basin, 'taking his own portrait just before the act,' Milnes wrote. On shipboard in the Bay of Biscay, on horseback in the Spanish mountains, in cafés and at tables d'hôte, in royal palaces, libraries and cathedrals, in the Prado, at the bull-fight or the Opera, Milnes would listen to Count Potocki's low and melancholy voice relating family histories, anecdotes of the London Embassy, or, more often than anything else, discussing sex in all its varied aspects. During Milnes' first year in London society he had observed that so soon as two or three men were left alone together the talk 'always turns to bawdy or religion.' Count Potocki's talk was not religious. 'The greatest part of the virtue of London women,' he told his companion, 'consists of London houses, London servants and London hours.' He said that he had asked a doctor why English women 'have no busts' and was told it was because they drank so much tea. He warned Milnes that any marriage was doomed so soon as the

husband awakened in his wife 'sensations of sensuality and desire';
and told him that the Circassians had no 'commerce' with women
in summer, 'but allow themselves the other passion as taking so
much less strength out of them.'

Milnes' first impression of Lisbon was one of noise—the noise of
windmills and of carts, 'the first like immense Aeolian harps out
of tune, the others like a hundred doors creaking at once.' 'Like
Stamboul in its beauty, brightness and bursting vegetation,' he
wrote in his notebook, 'like Pera in its dirt, its dogs and its declivi-
ties.' He found the breadth and sweep of the Tagus astounding,
more of a strait than a river, and was candidly glad to discover
that there was little sight-seeing, 'for the ups and downs of the
town are very trying.' He dined with the British Minister, Sir
Hamilton Seymour, who had been Minister in Florence in the
far-off days of Milnes' Italian youth; and with Sir Charles Napier,
then in charge of the British squadron in the Tagus. Sir Hamilton
arranged for his visitor to be presented at Court, at 'a very gay
and showy levée.' Milnes thought the Coburg husband of Queen
Maria da Gloria handsome and the queen herself 'a dull, good
woman,' 'an ugly likeness of Lady Caroline Lascelles, and . . .
well spoken of by almost all parties.' The king declared that
Mr. Milnes' conversation was so interesting that he must see him
again—'which is a bore,' Milnes commented. The queen's
manners were less good. Watching her at a soirée in her palace
at Cintra, Milnes observed that after speaking to a very few persons
Queen Maria da Gloria stalked to an armchair at the end of the
long Swan Room and sat absolutely alone for nearly two hours,
'occasionally giving tremendous yawns.' Marshal Saldanha
thanked Milnes for his speech in the House of Commons and paid
him the compliment of telling him that he was the Englishman who
knew most about the matter. After dining again with Sir Charles
Napier, Milnes and Potocki set sail for Cadiz in the *Jupiter* on
24 September. They reached Spanish soil, after a rough passage,
the next night.

IV

Travel in Spain was still, in theory, dangerous as well as uncomfortable. English visitors were regaled with lurid anecdotes of
robbery and murder which must have reminded Milnes of his journeys
in Greece fifteen years before. The small number of Englishmen
who had at this time any real knowledge of the Peninsula had
mostly gained it under military conditions: old men who had
fought there with Wellington, younger men who had volunteered

for the British Auxiliary Legion in the Carlist Wars. Several of the latter had published books, such as Captain Alexander Ball's *A Personal Narrative of Seven Years in Spain* [1]; and some of Milnes' Cambridge contemporaries had, as very young men, become impassioned for the Spanish exiles' cause. In his *Life of John Sterling* Carlyle has described the effect of that Spanish enthusiasm on these inflammable young minds. Sterling did not personally take part in Torrijos' foredoomed expedition to Spain in 1830, but at least one of Milnes' most intimate Cambridge friends, Richard Chenevix Trench, had done so. Though his interest in Spain was chiefly of a political nature, Milnes had read the Spanish works of George Borrow—the *Gypsies in Spain,* which had appeared in 1841, and *The Bible in Spain,* published in 1843; while for topographical and architectural information he relied on Richard Ford's *Handbook,* which Murrays had issued in 1845, and also probably on Ford's more discursive *Gatherings from Spain* (1846). Although the most portable of English books on Spain, Ford did not please every traveller.

Bye-the-bye, I am a little out of conceit with Ford [wrote Lord Canning, who reached Madrid a week or two before Monckton Milnes [2]]. It is a charming book to be read at leisure in one's room, but his quotations and illustrations (sometimes rather far-fetched) get in the way and provoke one when one is in a hurry for a fact.

But Milnes did not rely exclusively on English interpretations of the Spanish scene. Just as he had gone to Constantinople in 1842 with Lamartine's *Voyage en Orient* in his portmanteau, so he now took with him Théophile Gautier's *Voyage en Espagne.* Gautier's little book, which gave an account of his visit to Spain in 1840, had achieved an immense and deserved success. It was a witty and a very personal book, and it suddenly revealed Spain to the Romantics, setting a fashion in France which was fostered by Milnes' acquaintance Prosper Mérimée, who published *Carmen* in 1845 and his *Histoire de don Pèdre Ier* in 1848. Milnes was amused by the candour and perverseness of many of Gautier's judgements. He copied out the well-known passage upon the atmosphere of the Escorial:

Je conseille aux gens qui ont la fatuité de prétendre qu'ils s'ennuient, d'aller passer trois ou quatre jours à l'Escurial; ils

---

[1] J. Chappell, London, 1846. Captain Ball had been an officer under de Lacy Evans in the British Legion.

[2] Lord Canning to Lord Malmesbury, Madrid, 21 October 1847, quoted at length in the latter's *Memoirs of an Ex-Minister* (Longmans, Green, 1884), vol. i, p. 199.

apprendront là ce que c'est que le véritable ennui, et ils s'amuseront tout le reste de leur vie en pensant qu'ils pourraient être à l'Escurial et qu'ils n'y sont pas.

But Milnes was seldom subject to ennui. As soon as he and Potocki had looked round Cadiz—which Milnes called 'a cleaner and more oriental Venice'—and had got their mail from the English consul, Mr. Brackenbury, they set off for Seville to see the cathedral and the pictures of Murillo, a painter whom both Richard and his father much admired. Seville too seemed oriental, as they wandered by night along the steep, dim streets and peered through the grills of private houses at the gaily-lighted, flower-filled courtyards in which fountains sparkled. The porticos were furnished and the walls hung with pictures and engravings, just as if each courtyard was itself a room. Writing to his father from Seville on 2 October, Milnes explained that in politics he had so far seen only the Moderados (who were Conservative and anti-English). In consequence he had heard nothing but abuse of Palmerston and of Bulwer, who was accused 'of everything that goes wrong in the country, including the frailty of the Queen.' He had sent Bulwer a note from Cadiz, and he now got a reply to say that the end of October would be a good time for him and Potocki to make their way north to Madrid. 'Don't believe a word you hear till you get at this laboratory of lies,' added Bulwer, 'out of which you shall distil the truth.'

Milnes had written from Cadiz to another friend in Madrid—Saville Morton, now representing his newspaper, the *Daily News*, in the Spanish capital. 'Your note from Cadiz was hardly a surprise,' Morton wrote in welcome on 29 September;

I made you out already in a letter from Lisbon, although cruelly disfigured under the title of Barckton-Bills, as one of two illustrious Englishmen of letters who arrived in the same steamer with old Povoas. . . . I am horribly tied by the leg, but it will be a relief to shake hands with you. If I could only get somebody to do the D-Nd letters while you are here and ride about with you to La Granja, the Escurial, Aranjuez &c—But there is no help for it, I remember at this moment a blazing ride we took at Rome through the Ghetto to St. Paul's & round by the Appian—returning quite calcined. . . . Bullwig is not going away as the Spanish papers say. It is to be hoped that he will dine you better than he has me. . . . O your tour, your tour in Andalusia! it would be a delight beyond dreams to me to ride the most rickety mule, to sprawl anights in the most wicked venta if I only had 2 clear months ahead to ramble about with you.

At Seville Milnes was mildly surprised to hear the wife of the
Captain-General of the city discussing the technique and accomplishments of the great matador Redonda 'just as an English lady
wd talk of Jenny Lind.' Her husband told the travellers that he
had always disliked bull-fighting until, forced to go to it regularly
in his official capacity, he had come to admire and understand it in
all its details—a psychological fact to which Mérimée and a host
of other converts to the bull-ring all bear witness. Count Potocki
suggested that the English in Spain would soon be organising 'an
anti-bull-fight association,' more especially since the Animals'
Friends Society in England had already taken the matter up.
Neither he nor Milnes went to a bullfight until they reached Madrid,
where they saw a matador's neck broken.

After three sweltering days in Seville the travellers returned to
Cadiz and steamed down to Gibraltar. Here they dined at the
Cottage with Sir Robert Wilson, who had been governor since
1842, met Duke Bernard of Saxe-Weimar and his son on their way
to winter with the Queen Dowager in Madeira, saw Lady Emmeline
Stuart-Wortley again, and had a talk (of which Milnes unfortunately
kept no record) with Théophile Gautier. Gautier was no lover of
Gibraltar. In his *Voyage* he had written of the promenades 'ou
l'on voit des calèches et des cavaliers absolument comme à Hyde-
Park. Il n'y manque que la statue d'Achille-Wellington. Heur-
eusement les Anglais n'ont pu ni salir la mer ni noircir le ciel.'
Milnes' days at Gibraltar were spent in riding with the Governor's
aides-de-camps, in inspecting galleries, fortifications, and the con-
vict settlement, and in other pastimes equally characteristic of life
in an English colony. From Gibraltar he went to Tangiers, where
he found an inn kept by two elderly spinsters from Elgin, and then
crossed over to Malaga preparatory to setting off for Granada,
Cordova, Toledo and Madrid. Before leaving Malaga he and
Potocki attended a ball on board the French war brig, *Agile*,
which lay in port there. For these festivities the *Agile* had been
gaily decorated: the mainmast was disguised as a palm-tree; the
capstan had become one immense nosegay; the ship's sides were
fringed with aloes; wreaths of cypress mixed with flowers hung
everywhere. 'Pretty manners of the sailor-lads' (Milnes noted)
'handing the things round.'

Milnes and Potocki had heard that to travel by the diligence to
Granada was almost insufferably uncomfortable. One of the
passengers told them he had had to tie an air-cushion on top of his
head to save his skull from being cracked by the jolting on the
Spanish roads. So they set out on horseback, riding to Velez
through the rich warm land of sugar-canes and autumn vineyards—

'the grapes hanging from the trees'—and on to Granada the next day. Here they stayed a week, sight-seeing in the city and riding in the country round it, wandering for five hours through the Alhambra and watching the sun set over the Sierra Nevada at night. From Granada they were forced to take the diligence to Jaen and Cordova, bumping along a 'fine rich road' with miles of olive-groves on either hand in the company of an armless American dwarf who used his toes for fingers and who spent the journey abusing Spain for not 'going a-head.' From Cordova, where they passed a day looking at Moorish architecture, Milnes and his friend set off for Toledo in a coupé with two Spanish travelling companions. The mules drawing the coupé 'knocked up' outside Andujar, and the travellers had to walk into the town in the midday heat and shut themselves up for a siesta while waiting for the diligence to reach the town. When the public diligence arrived at Andujar, Milnes climbed up into it and sank back on the centre seat: a crowd of women standing by cried out 'Eh! che grand papa!' as they watched this plump foreigner make himself comfortable. On 24 September they crossed the Sierra Morena and came down into a landscape that flowed in gentle waves to the horizon and was tinted with the yellow of a myriad saffron flowers. They reached Toledo in the twilight of that day. On the 29th they were at the gates of Madrid: the domed and steepled city loomed before them in the cold, clear autumn evening, a white town with no suburbs, rising on an eminence from the golden stubble of the wide wheat-fields, behind it the high and massy outlines of the Guadarama stained by snow.

When they had scrambled down from the diligence and made their way through crowded streets to the little Fonda de Paris, where Bulwer's secretary had booked them rooms, Milnes was a trifle disappointed. Madrid was neither so grand nor so romantic as he had hoped. 'The first appearance of Madrid,' he scrawled into his notebook, 'is that of the 2nd-rate quarters of Paris.'

V

Henry Bulwer had just driven out of Madrid for three days' rest in the country when Milnes and Potocki arrived. He left a note explaining that he was 'literally used up with business and talking' and that he had instructed his exhausted private secretary, Mr. Fenton, to look after them. 'When I come you & Potocki will I hope dine with me whenever you have nothing better to do & consider my house & its master yours,' he wrote courteously. As usual, Milnes was quite capable of looking after himself. He faced

Madrid society unabashed, and he had not been more than a few hours in the Spanish capital before he was at work establishing contacts. He dined out on the night of his arrival, and even managed to catch a glimpse of Queen Isabella and her minister Narvaez before going back to his hotel. The next day was spent in leaving cards and letters of introduction. In the evening he dined with Saville Morton and Potocki, and the following afternoon they all went to a bullfight, dined together and saw the ballet. And so it went on, the same life of immense sociability which was Milnes' habit in London and which he had tasted in Paris, in Berlin, in Athens and Constantinople and Cairo, in Dublin and Edinburgh, Rome, Florence and Milan, in Venice, in Naples, in Berne. There were dinners at embassies, dinners with Spaniards, musical soirées, hours passed lounging and talking in curtained opera-boxes, visits to the theatre, the bullring, the ballet, the picture galleries, the Escurial, rendezvous at the Palace to watch the king and queen, followed by a curious-looking dwarf, proceed in all their panoply to mass. He was particularly well received in Progressista circles in Madrid, for the members of this pro-British political party were convinced (as were their enemies the Moderados also) that this self-confident, quick-witted English member of Parliament, who seemed to know everyone in London, had come out to Spain on a special secret mission from Lord Palmerston: an emissary sent to redress the diplomatic balance dislocated by the Spanish Marriages storm. 'Un personage diplomatico ingles con una mision delicada,' declared at least one Madrid newspaper, and Milnes was treated accordingly. A letter from Saville Morton dated 28 November 1847 shows how successfully and how quickly Milnes had tunnelled his way into the hieratic structure of Madrid society. Morton had been sacked by his employers, with no good reason; he was writing to ask Milnes, then on his way back to England, to try to find out from the *Daily News* office why this had happened.

I am certainly in a much better position to serve them now than before you came [he wrote]: for I had no means whatever of extending my acquaintance with persons who could be of any use to me, before you came. I am disposed to attribute what little attention Bulwer show'd to me in inviting me to dinner &c, which he did for the first time shortly before your arrival, arose simply from hearing that I knew you.

I remember sometimes with pleasure those sittings of mine with you at the little Fonda de Paris while you were putting on your white waistcoat to dine out [Morton wrote some weeks later]: and our dark walks to your amphitryons.

Potocki having left for London after one week in Madrid, Milnes remained alone there until the end of November: '. . . not much alone, however,' he told his sister Harriette, 'for I have Bulwer's house and that of the resident Rothschild to dine at whenever I choose, and have got to know some of the best men.' Some of Milnes' amphitryons occupied him so much that even Bulwer lost sight of him: 'Yr Palm Leaves [1] have consoled me for your absence' the British minister wrote in a note sent round to the Fonda de Paris.

They brought peace to my soul. Yr Tancred is invisible. Where is it? Where are you? I expected you at breakfast, at dinner—& still I expect you. What siren has beguiled you— The Montijo! Pauvre enfant! [2]

Although living in temporary lodgings (his new house was not ready till the end of the year), Henry Bulwer entertained a great deal, maintaining the tradition of English hospitality established by Lord Clarendon, who, as Mr. George Villiers, had been Minister to Spain ten years before. Bulwer received on Tuesdays and on Fridays, but he also had at least two or three distinguished Spaniards to meals every day of the week.

From my long residence in Spain [he writes in his *Life of Lord Palmerston* [3]], my acquaintance with the language and the principal persons of almost all classes in the country, I had a certain influence, and, as is usual in these countries, that influence was much exaggerated. . . .

He was of immense value to Milnes in elucidating the tortuous and emotional politics of Spain—'the only country' (as he told him that the Duke of Wellington had said) 'in which two and two do not make four.' Bulwer explained that Spain was 'in a continual conflict between ancient manners & modern ideas & the old manners in the end get the best of it.' The resemblance between the Spaniards and the Turks, whom both he and Milnes had studied at Constantinople, was always before him: 'the same good manners, clever talk and seeming calmness—the same vindictiveness, blood-thirstiness, treachery & incapacity to work.' He told Milnes that

[1] Milnes had given a volume of his poems to Bulwer, who afterwards said that it was this book he was reading as he raced across France after Narvaez had told him to leave Spain in the spring of 1848, passing the Spanish Government's messenger on the road and reaching London before him. 'Fugitive pieces, I suppose,' said Lord Douro when Milnes repeated this story to him.

[2] Milnes did, in fact, go to several of Madame de Montijo's receptions, where he saw the queen, danced on 'thick, dirty carpets,' and admired the 'real Spanish beauty' of Madame de Montijo's daughter Eugenia.

[3] Bulwer's unfinished *Life of Lord Palmerston* was published after his death, edited by Evelyn Ashley, in 1874. It does not go beyond the year 1847.

as long as you could gratify a Spaniard's vanity or his revenge you could get any amount of activity out of him—'but not a moment longer'; and that of all the Spaniards he had had to do with he hardly knew one 'who did not talk like a man of sense and who did not act like a perfect fool.' He related for his guest's benefit the whole complex story of the Spanish Marriage intrigues, adding that the Queen Mother's husband, the Duke of Rijavarez, had told him 'over and over again' that they knew Don Francisco to be impotent. In his perpetual war with the successive French ambassadors, de Bresson and the Duc de Glucksburg, Bulwer had found himself much handicapped by a lack of money with which to pay the newspapers of Madrid: 'I should much like a *few* decorations to distribute here,' he told Milnes wistfully; 'I could make *five* go a great way.' Milnes listened carefully to all these various scraps of information, regretting perhaps that he had let Gladstone dissuade him from entering diplomacy, and making notes in his hotel room of facts to repeat to Lord Palmerston and of stories for the London clubs. But Bulwer's conversation was not all complaint: like Morton, he regaled his guest with scurrilous tales of the queen's infidelities, though deprecating the opposition stories that she went incognita to brothels, 'having any number of men.' For all his affectation of languor Bulwer loved his busy existence in Madrid. He told Milnes that he found his enjoyment of life increasing with his years, that he had 'ten times the pleasure now he had when he was young.' 'After taking opium,' he remarked to him on another occasion, 'one feels as if one's soul was being rubbed down with silk.' He enjoyed Milnes' presence in Madrid, and when he himself got back to London in April 1848, dismissed by Narvaez for having presented an unusually impertinent note to the Spanish Government from Palmerston, he found Milnes one of his strongest supporters during a tiresome and critical moment of his career. Milnes' speech in his favour in the House of Commons debate upon his conduct earned Bulwer's warmest gratitude.

I have once or twice in my life been a bitter enemy, tho' it is agt the grain [Bulwer wrote to him in June 1850 from Washington, where he had just been appointed]; but I have at all events been ever a constant friend, and *never* shall I forget your cordial & kind support of me at a moment when I feel that I deserved the support of friends, but was anything but certain, considering I stood in need of such support, to obtain it. *Ainsi va le monde.*

VI

Count Potocki (whose political views were, of course, the precise opposite of Milnes' liberal and uncrystallised opinions) had given a very poor account of Spain on his return to London. He told Henry Greville that he had been much struck by the 'total demoralisation' of the whole of that country, and that nobody outside Madrid cared anything for politics. But Spain and particularly Madrid, with its ceaseless intrigues and its formal gaiety, had caught Milnes' wandering fancy; and, in an unusual spurt of activity, he wrote enthusiastic letters to various of his friends. 'Why do you say I should like Spain and its Anarchies?' Thomas Carlyle replied sourly to one of these lighthearted missives:

Anarchy, and all ruin, of greasy begging friars or other such lost cattle, is utterly hateful to me: but putrid superstition, damnable by God and detestable to man, must be cleared away out of this creation;—and it is no wonder the *scavenging* makes a pretty mess at times! As for me, I had rather save my boots and *nose*, and be out of all that, till it be abated somewhat.

England was at this moment agitated by the Bill to admit professing Jews to Parliament, occasioned by Rothschild's election for the City of London. Indeed, it was an anxiety to be home in time to vote in favour of this Bill that made Milnes leave Madrid on 28 November. Henry Bulwer had scoffed at the Bill, and now called England 'Jewsland'; while Carlyle fiercely attacked the measure.

A Jew is bad [he wrote to Milnes, in the letter of December 1847, already quoted], but what is a Sham-Jew, a Quack-Jew? And how can a real Jew, by possibility, try to be a Senator, or even Citizen, of any country, except his own wretched Palestine, whither all his thoughts and steps and efforts tend?

When Milnes arrived at the Hotel Meurice, after travelling as quickly as he could by way of Burgos, San Sebastian, Bordeaux and Poitiers, he found a very characteristic letter from his father awaiting him. 'I am not sorry you are missing this session—particularly the Jew bill,' Mr. Milnes had written, unaware that Richard planned to reach London in time to vote upon this issue.

I don't think Mr. Rothschild's dinners should be set off against the strong tho' silly prejudice at Pontefract, & then there is such plausible reason of absence—They think you are at Madrid, I having written to that effect a fortnight ago to 'Emma Knight' who applied for a subscription to a girls school. I told her you had seen a man kill'd at a Bullfight which I dare say has gone the rounds of every house at Pont. We heard that Dr. Buchanan *knows* you are on an important secret mission—You can get at the embassy or the newsrooms a file of the Times, the commercial leaders of which you should get up. Think of C. Wood's statement on Friday, of 60 millions being sunk in railways within the last year

& a half. . . . How I wish for the first time that Peel was in—to have to bear the brunt of bringing us to this pass, & the responsibility of getting us out of it . . . don't let Meurice's bill be more than you can help . . . Louisa & Caroline are both laid up with colds & fever. I keep tolerable but feel low &'palpitating till after luncheon. Augusta Bland comes here for three nights this week otherwise we see nobody. . . . I wish you would have a French conversation master for an hour in a morning to correct your slips & give you the turn of the Paris phrases.

Neither ill-health nor his quiet, vegetative life in Nottinghamshire and in Yorkshire had done much to mellow Mr. Milnes.

The Paris Embassy had changed hands since Monckton Milnes' last visit there. He now found it in the charge of Lord Normanby, who was carrying on a personal feud with Guizot which did much to envenom the already bitter Anglo-French relations. Lord Normanby thought Guizot had insulted his honour during the Spanish Marriage trouble. He had in his turn gone out of his way to insult Guizot by recalling an invitation for Lady Normanby's ball which had been already sent to the French Foreign Minister. The grand and rather pompous English marquess was no match verbally for Guizot: 'Je prétends seulement parler mieux le Français que Lord Normanby ne le comprend,' he said mischievously to Monckton Milnes, who dined with him the day after his arrival in Paris.

Je ne vous pardonnerais pas de passer à Paris sans me voir [Guizot had written in reply to the note Milnes had sent round from the Meurice to the Affaires Etrangères]. Voulez-vous venir dîner avec moi, aujourd'hui même, en famille? . . . C'est à cette heure là que j'aurais le plus de loisir pour causer avec vous.

After dinner Guizot took him on, inevitably, to Princess Lieven's. Both Guizot and 'the Lieven' were still deeply disturbed by the collapse of the *entente cordiale* and the new isolation of France, though Guizot naturally tried to put a good face on it, and told Milnes that he was determined to 'defend the rights' of the Duchesse de Montpensier to the Spanish throne should this become necessary. He criticised the Whig Government, declaring that what he called 'Sir Robert Peel's destruction of the Tory party' had been 'entre les plus grands chagrins de ma vie' and pointing out to Milnes that all the Pretenders of Europe were now congregated in England under Whig auspices. 'It is natural,' said Milnes, 'that they should take refuge in the freest country.' 'Do you think, then,' Guizot answered, 'that it was out of pure hospitality that Louis Quatorze received the Stuarts?'

The evening following his dinner with the Guizots was passed by Milnes at the palace of Saint Cloud. Although Tocqueville repeated to him that the King of the French had said: 'La colère de la Reine d'Angleterre ne m'empêchera pas de mener mon fiacre,' Milnes found Louis-Philippe in a mood of reflection and regret. He explained that the great object of his life had been the union between France and England. It was now 'suspended by temporary passions.' 'I suffered much at it,' he said, 'but I have got over it now and trust to time.' As anxious as ever to make a good impression on any stray member of the English Parliament, the king spoke nobly of Algeria (which France had just conquered), saying he hoped it would become a great independent kingdom: 'till then it must remain our India.' He declared that he would resist the partition of Switzerland since 'white men can no longer be sold or given away—& even black men must cease to be so treated'; and said sadly that many of his subjects held to a political system which tended inescapably towards war: 'When the National Guard met me with cries of "vive la Pologne,"' he said, 'they little thought it was an European war they were asking for.' But though melancholy in tone, the king's conversation seemed full of confidence. 'There is no fear for the internal welfare of France or the peace of Europe,' he said, 'as long as we have a good Chamber. But a Chamber with bad dispositions can ruin everything.' Milnes drove back from Saint Cloud to the Rue de la Paix with the king's cordial invitation to return ringing in his ears. But on his next visit to Paris, only two months later, Milnes did not tell his hired coachman to take him to Saint Cloud. He had already had his interview with the king of the French—at Claremont.

During his ten days in Paris this December of 1847 Milnes hurried about seeing his old and his new friends—Monsieur and Madame Thiers, Madame Marliani, Madame Lenormand, Madame de Circourt in the Rue des Saussayes, Gautier, the Nathaniel Rothschilds, Victor Cousin, Mignet, Alexis de Tocqueville. Only one of all these persons seemed aware of the imminent fate of the July monarchy. That person was Tocqueville. He told Milnes that he was convinced that the king had lost his delicate sense of the public conscience of France. Surrounded by 'une véritable adulation,' Louis-Philippe was now at length losing his judgement. 'En France,' said Tocqueville, 'nous passons d'un état de léthargie aux crises nerveuses—qui sont beaucoup plus dangereuses.'

Milnes dutifully recorded Tocqueville's solemn warning, but it is questionable if he understood what Tocqueville meant or realised that when he next returned to Paris the delicate fabric of the Orleans monarchy would have disintegrated and all its chief personnel—the heavy, ageing, subtle king, the royal princes and princesses, his friend Guizot himself—would have been whirled away across the Channel, like dead leaves in the wind. Nor, when he paid his *visite de congé* at the Hotel Talleyrand, could he have imagined that the next thing that he would hear about Princess Lieven would be her flight from Paris, 'with her diamonds in her bustle,' and her ignominious arrival at the Clarendon in Davies Street.

Chapter Thirteen

1848

I

New Year's Day 1848 found Milnes staying at Woburn Abbey. His admission on familiar terms to this great stronghold of the Whigs (as well as to other big 'ministerial houses') was one result of his switch in politics. Milnes was rated a very agreeable person to have in a country house. He had always been good at charades and amateur theatricals, and on this occasion he composed a long rhymed epilogue to be spoken after a ballet, *Les Arbres Célestes*, performed in the miniature theatre at Woburn. This epilogue, full of rhymes and quips, was spoken when the dancing had finished and just before the pulling back of a curtain revealed a glittering Christmas tree 'with the Lights and Gifts all over and round it.' In his verses, afterwards printed as a broadsheet,[1] Milnes speculated upon the nature of the 'wondrous tree' (a Germanic innovation in Victorian England). He began by explaining what 'the Tree is—not!':

> It is not the Royal Oak,
> Out of which Prince Charlie spoke;
> It is not the sacred Bay,
> Worn by Tennyson to-day;
> It is not the Palm which Gough
> And Hardinge lately carried off;
> Nor the Statesman's hardy Laurel,
> For which Peel and Russell quarrel;
> 'Tis no Eastern Cedar, seen
> By Warburton or Lamartine;
> Nor the Cypress, such as weeps
> Where forlorn 'Protection' sleeps;
> Nor the burst of Orange-spray
> Such as you'll all wear some day.

The last remark was addressed 'To the Young Ladies.' Other asides were aimed at 'The Ministers' and at 'Lord John,' and contained bright political innuendoes.

---

[1] *Woburn Abbey Theatre, Epilogue written by Richard Monckton Milnes, spoken at the end of the ballet of 'Les Arbres Célestes.'* 1 *January* 1849. The date, correct in the proof, was misprinted in the finished broadsheet.

Joking apart [wrote Richard's father from Bawtry] I half fear
it is not of advantage to be much mix'd up with these 'Mimes'—
however pleasurable for the time. Would Ld John for instance
think better of you for *serious* business?—Don't think me hyper-
critical. I remember at Milan a rebuke was sent from Vienna to
Genl. Walmaden for acting at Madame Somieloff's & the reason
given that it would lower him in public respect.

From Woburn he proceeded in the first week of January to the
more intimate and cosy atmosphere of the Bay House, Alverstoke.
The company at the Bay House included old 'Bear' Ellice, the
Henry Taylors, the Buller brothers and Carlyle. Carlyle, who
packed up and left after ten dyspeptic days and sleepless nights,
complained to his wife of 'the idleness, the folly, the cackling and the
noise' at the Bay House, and noted in his journal that Milnes, 'fresh
from Spain,' was 'full of sophistries and socialities as usual.' [1] Milnes
liked the gossip and the laughter which Lady Harriet encouraged
in her houses. It amused him to hear her describe how she now
spoke '*at* her maid through her parrot' (the maid retorting in the
same way) or when she declared that 'women continually moving
about like Lady Morgan had better be put on castors at once.'
Lolling in the great material luxury with which his hostess encircled
herself and her guests, Milnes was able to acclimatise himself once
more to English life. The autumn in Spain, though sometimes
cold, had been soft and brilliant with a little rain: 'I love the
tender ill-humour of an autumn day,' Saville Morton had said in
Madrid, adding on another occasion: 'with this sky one feels
enclosed in a sapphire.' Even the comfort of Lady Harriet's house
could not make the Hampshire sea-coast seem sapphire-like in
early January; amongst the squat and wind-swept evergreens of
Alverstoke, Milnes must have sympathised with a remark he overheard and noted down about this time: 'English scenery is all dark
green set in black.'

It was Carlyle's third visit to Alverstoke, and he hated it even
more than usual, committing to his journal comments upon the
English aristocracy and their 'gracefully idle' way of life. He
found Milnes by far the easiest person to get on with in this circle.
In his conversations with him in the library of this comfortable,
well-heated house (while the wind howled across the pebbly beaches
and the sea between Hampshire and the Isle of Wight was whipped
into foam), Carlyle broached the subject that was uppermost in his
thought—aristocracy.

[1] *Thomas Carlyle, A History of His Life in London* (1834–81), by J. A. Froude
(Longmans, 1884), vol. i, pp. 417, 422, etc.

The English aristocracy [he remarked to Milnes] just now are to me a most tragic spectacle. Wonderful how they undertake that suicidal enterprise of theirs, how they endure their vacant existence. I always think of the sublime ennui of the Halls of Eblis—of men with burning fire for hearts in their bosoms, who will stand no pity or advice in any way, but suffer on. Yet these men assimilate greatness better than any other Englishmen: they are not the Chinese jugglers of the middle class, and they alone can now save us from the absolute anarchy of the bottomless pit.

In Milnes Carlyle found more than a ready and intelligent listener: he found a man with a similar point of view. That spirit of contradiction, that quirky integrity which had made Milnes differ from all of his contemporaries at Cambridge and keep to his own whimsical opinions when he first embarked on London life, was still at work within him. Milnes adored society, conversation, novelty, gossip, the pace of Victorian London: 'I wonder whether you will feel the whirl of London as I do,' he had once written to his sister; 'it is like infinite wheels ever in one's ears'; but he was no more deceived over the real value of any aristocratic society than Carlyle himself. Many of his notebooks consist of stories showing the idiocy of what were then called 'the fine people': Lady Exeter repeating that she never read books as 'she liked to have her mornings to herself'; Lord Stanley's aunt asking whether if a man gave birth to a child ('a thing I know to be impossible') it would inherit; Lord Tankerville saying 'I like a rainy Sunday. The people can't come out and enjoy themselves. I hate the people'; 'Lady Clanricarde taking no cognisance of her family or household—no servant allowed to speak to her on business—no child to enter the room unless sent for—her whole time spent in getting up conversation and dress.' The conclusion which Milnes drew from these innumerable tales and anecdotes, and from his own twelve years' observation of the antics of the rich and great, was a political conclusion: 'We never,' he wrote in his 1848 notebook, 'calculate among the democratic influences, as we should do, the effect of the stupidity and helplessness of our present aristocracy.'

Linked with Milnes' progressive distrust of aristocratic government there was a growing passion for democracy. He romanticised democracy.

It is inevitable [he wrote] that as the world becomes democratized, politics will less & less occupy & deserve the employment & attention of first-rate men: all *great* work will be & in fact is done by the community itself. . . . Not but that the men of letters & thought will be more than ever the indirect rulers of the world:

through the masses, they will really move the political system &
have the uses of power.

He regarded the introduction of the income tax as a major step
towards the goal of equality: 'Peel is the founder of Communism
in England,' he wrote.   'The income tax in time of peace is the
thin end of the wedge, which only wants circumstances to drive it
on.'   Although well acquainted with Louis Blanc, Milnes did not
believe in socialism:

Democracy [he wrote on this subject] should tend to the complete enfranchisement & freest responsible action of the individual
man, but socialism steps in with the State for a tyrant and . . . you
have all the old social evils back again.

There was one more effect of Milnes' now considerable experience
of English and foreign aristocracy and government: he became a
Republican.

It is since I have seen the governors of mankind, and what they
are in comparison with the governed, that I have become Republican [he noted secretly in his day-book]; now that the superiorities
of distance have vanished, how can I do otherwise than acknowledge
that humanity is nearly a plane?

'Why should a royal will be better than a popular one?' he asked
himself on another page.   'The facility one King has in getting
another to help him to do violent things is a strong argument against
monarchies.'   We have already seen that Milnes was utterly devoid
of any sycophantic reverence for English royalty.   In his commonplace books the Queen and Prince Albert fare as badly as Lady
Exeter or Lord Tankerville.   Queen Victoria emerges from those
crowded pages as absurd, prejudiced, spartan, unintelligent and
inconsiderate; Prince Albert as able, pettish and quick to take
offence.   The reaction of the English court to the events of 1848
thoroughly amused Milnes and Carlyle.   'There's the poor little
Queen looking out into the world,' Carlyle said to him, after the
February revolution, 'like a small canary prying into a thunder-
storm.'

II

The letters which Mr. Pemberton Milnes had addressed to his
son in Spain in the autumn of 1847 had been charged with acrid
criticism of the Whig Government, attacks upon Sir Robert Peel,
and grim predictions for the future.   The same views were at that
moment being expressed in Tory country houses throughout the
length and breadth of England.   To the die-hard Tories it seemed

that Great Britain was toppling on the verge of ruin, chiefly owing to the mortal blow dealt at their party by the Corn Law Repeal of 1846. In point of fact, the Year of Revolutions and the Chartist threat culminating in the Kennington Common fiasco of April 1848 gave English Toryism new life and also new blood.

Under ordinary circumstances [wrote Bulwer in his notes for the *Life of Palmerston*] the downfall of Louis Philippe, and any movement that had overcome the monstrous despotism . . . in Spain, would have been hailed with satisfaction; but a sudden change had taken place in the public opinion in England, especially amongst the higher classes in London, where the dread of an insurrection had completely changed the ordinary tone of opinion.

But in the weeks before the February Revolution and the climax of the Chartist movement, the Tories could not foresee this swing of public opinion to the Right. It was not only Mr. Milnes' generation that was affecting despair. Writing to Richard Monckton Milnes from Belvoir Castle (in a letter dated 26 November 1847 and dispatched to him at the Meurice in Paris), Lord John Manners took up the same line. John Manners, who was nine years younger than Richard Milnes and had been defeated in the 1847 election on religious grounds, began by thanking 'Dicky' for

remembering the discarded politician, & sending me so agreeable an account of the mad Usurper at Madrid. . . . Your Essay on the causes of our distress is beyond my feeble intelligence [he continued] —all I know is that our Colonies are on the verge of Rebellion, our Mills are closed, the Irish starving, the Usurpers gaining millions, the Revenue falling, trade dished, Commerce ruined, & Credit annihilated—You may compare these facts with Peels, Woods, Cardwells and Cobdens predictions, & draw any inference you please.

Milnes was unlikely to draw the same inference from any set of facts as Lord John Manners. He was on affectionate terms with Manners, but he did not take him seriously as a person. 'There is an impotent purity about John Manners,' he remarked in 1848, 'that is almost pathetic.' Manners had been heart and soul in the Young England movement while Monckton Milnes had never done more than hover inquisitively round the group. 'When I was young,' Milnes once said, 'I could idealise everything, even Toryism': but he had never been able to idealise it with the romantic, the almost religious fervour of John Manners and George Smythe. In one sense, he was not young enough when Disraeli's movement had been at its height. Even if he had really liked Disraeli, Milnes could never have submitted to his leadership, still less addressed him in George Smythe's adulatory

terms as 'dear Cid and Captain.' Towards another member
of the Young England Group, his old friend Stafford O'Brien (who
now called himself Augustus Stafford), Milnes' attitude had
become ambivalent: 'You and Mr. Stafford go about like Luttrell
and Rogers,' said Lady Harriet Baring, 'always together and
always hating one another.' For Lord George Bentinck, whom
Disraeli had produced like a rabbit from a hat during the Repeal
debates of 1846, setting him up as nominal leader of the Country
or Protectionist Party in the House, Milnes felt a lukewarm contempt. '(He) had a marvellous memory, but so had the learned
pig,' he wrote to his friend MacCarthy after Bentinck's death in
the autumn of 'forty-eight; 'and I never saw in him a scintilla
of statesmanship.' Milnes still treated Benjamin Disraeli himself with grudging admiration, though declaring total mistrust
of all his motives: 'Dizzy believes the world to be governed by
men. I believe it to be governed by God.' But his sour feeling
for Disraeli was as nothing compared to Milnes' absolute loath-
ing for Disraeli's ex-lieutenant, young George Smythe. When,
in 1846, Smythe, spoiled, dissolute, enthusiastic, but almost
divinely handsome, had accepted from Peel the office of Under-
Secretary for Foreign Affairs for which Milnes pined, he had
alienated himself politically from Disraeli and Young England,
whose ranks were closed against Repeal. For a brief moment
Milnes saw Smythe as enviable and successful; but the young
man's character (a rather unstable affair, inherited from his
violent and beautiful Irish mother and made worse by the pam-
pering which Lord Strangford moodily lavished on his son) had
not borne the burden of office for long. Smythe had retired,
a public failure, to Italy. Although re-elected as a Peelite Tory
in 1847, he signed on in the spring of the next year as one of the
staff of the *Morning Chronicle*. This newspaper, the organ of the
Peelites, printed his brilliant articles on foreign politics for the next
two years, but Smythe seems to have used his position as a popular
political journalist to ventilate old prejudices and pay off old scores.
He kept a sharp and jaundiced eye upon the activities of all his
enemies, including his best enemy, Dicky Milnes.

Though personalities as well as principles had driven Monckton
Milnes out of the Tory party, he had few illusions about political
parties, anyway. 'A party,' he wrote in 1848, 'is never really
grateful to you except when you sympathise with its abuses or
defend its errors.' On his return from Spain he completed his
divorce from Conservatism. 'I am going to break off the last
link of Peelery, the Carlton Club, and mean to pass an observant,
undemonstrative session,' he told Charles MacCarthy in a letter

of December 1847. Milnes' letters to MacCarthy, which were
rare but regular, inevitably present a simplified version of his
life. Writing to his friend in Ceylon once every two or three
months, he tended to give him a well-edited, almost a public
account of what he did and thought. Without being self-conscious
or wishing to posture, he made his own actions seem swifter and
nobler than they often were in fact. The decision to leave the
Carlton Club had not come easily, nor had he taken this step
unaided.

Milnes could not readily exclude himself from any circle. Yet
even he realised that to become a Russellite Whig and to remain
a member of the Carlton Club would look a little too much like
running with the hare and hunting with the hounds. In his
dilemma he consulted his friend and precise contemporary in age
Sir John Hanmer, a poet who had sat in the House of Commons
since 1832, and who had now gone over—'bag and baggage,'
as John Manners called it—to the Whigs. 'I was in town for
a few evenings and took my seat with the supporters of this government, which I avowedly number myself among,' Hanmer replied
to Milnes' letter, in December 1847.

I have consequently taken my name out of the Carlton and since
you are so kind as to allow me to think my doings may have any
relation to yours, I recommend you strongly to do the same. . . .
Act then my dear Milnes according to your convictions like a true
man . . . never mind yourself but act upon your honest opinion.
In many respects it must be more easy and even agreeable to you
to take the course you are taking than it is to me, you know most of
the Whigs, I know very few of them.

An officious letter from Eliot Warburton warned Milnes that his
'secession to the Johnian faction' had excited great interest. It
had been the topic of the day at Lord Clarendon's dinner-table.
'I hope,' wrote Warburton, 'that now you are actually committed
to a principle, you will do justice to your high talents and to your
future.'

And in a curious way the fall of Louis-Philippe and the consequent
rise to brief power of Lamartine in 1848 and of Alexis de Tocqueville in 1849 gave Milnes a little palpitation of fresh hope. Was
this perhaps the dawn of a new age in which poets and idealists
and thinkers were to rule in Europe? Had he—a Liberal, a
Republican, a cosmopolitan—a political future after all?

III

Like every other individual in England, Milnes was much excited
by Louis-Philippe's dramatic flight from Paris to Dieppe in the

last week of February 1848. Unlike most of them, Milnes felt
elation and curiosity rather than alarm. There had never been a
French Republic in his lifetime. He welcomed the downfall of the
Orleans monarchy with nearly as great an enthusiasm as that with
which he had acclaimed its establishment in July 1830, when he
had been a boy of twenty singing German love-songs at Bonn.

As usual, Milnes saw these events in terms of personalities. He
kept the Galways and his father informed of the arrival of each fresh
batch of eminent Orleanist refugees. 'The King and Queen have
arrived at Newhaven in a packet Palmy sent for them,' he wrote to
Harriette, on 3 March, adding that he had already called on the
Guizot children ('the poor things were wonderfully cheerful').
The little Guizots' spinster aunt told Milnes that she had seen the
caps and bonnets of Queen Marie-Amélie being flaunted through
the Paris streets on pikes. 'This is better,' Milnes sensibly remarked, 'than the heads of 'ninety-one.' He begged the Guizot
family to stay at Bawtry for the summer—a kindly suggestion which
originated with Mr. Pemberton Milnes, but implied a certain
scepticism over the Guizots' prospects of a quick return to France.
François Guizot himself reached London a few days later, accompanied from Dover by his elderly mistress, Princess Lieven, whom
Milnes termed 'the Founder of the Republic.' Milnes reacted to
this gathering of distinguished exiles with all the gusto of the *Punch*
cartoonists, but with more sympathy. He began to feel restive in
London. He suggested to Harriette that she should run over with
him to France and spend Easter in revolutionary Paris. We may
fancy that Lord Galway did not think much of this idea.

The King and Queen of the French, frightened, weary and in-
cognito, had stepped ashore at Newhaven on 3 March. They had
travelled under the name of Smith, and Louis-Philippe afterwards
told Milnes that the queen had been so nervous that he had been
obliged to keep crying out: 'Mrs. Smith, on ne prie pas tant en
voyage!' They had readily accepted Queen Victoria's offer of
hospitality, settling themselves, their children and the remnants
of their court at Claremont, the house in which Princess Charlotte
had died. Richard Monckton Milnes' mother had been born at
Claremont. This fact may have added edge to the curiosity with
which he hurried down to see the royal exiles. During his early
weeks in England the Comte de Neuilly (as Louis-Philippe now
called himself) had no money, and he and his family lived at Claremont in a hugger-mugger fashion, without liveried servants or any
attempt at style. Milnes made his first visit to Claremont on
22 March. The king received him graciously, assuring him that
he was glad to see him there or in a cottage. The queen was

more emotional, gesticulating towards her husband and crying out:
'Il méritait un meilleur sort!' while referring to her children as
'Si bons, si dévoués à la France.' The king then recapitulated for
Milnes' benefit some of the events of 22 February, spoke disparag-
ingly of Thiers, declared he had refused to abdicate in favour of
the Duchesse d'Orleans, and said the Duc de Nemours had shown
a 'cold and perfect courage' unlike that of his brothers, who were
'full of passion and sympathy.' This reference to the Duc de
Nemours' behaviour confused Milnes' first biographer, who printed
Milnes' account of his visit to Claremont on 22 March in refutation
of an anecdote to be found in Lord Malmesbury's *Memoirs* under
the date 15 April. Malmesbury records that on 15 April 1848 he
took his wife and her mother Lady Tankerville to pay their respects
at Claremont. They found the king and queen looking well, but
'wretchedly low in spirits,' the king in particular seeming unable to
hold up his head. While they were there Guizot entered the room,
to tell the king that Prince Metternich, who had just fled from
Vienna in the face of threatening crowds, was not expected in
England.[1]

Mr. Monckton-Milnes then arrived [Lord Malmesbury's note
continues] and sat by the King, while Lady Tankerville and I were
talking to the Queen. We saw the King suddenly start up and
exclaim, 'Ah! c'est le dernier coup!' The Queen jumped up and
enquired, 'Qu'est-ce-que-c'est, mon ami? Calmez vous!' to
which he replied by repeating, 'C'est le dernier coup!' It then
appeared that Mr. Monckton-Milnes had informed him public
opinion thought his son the Duc de Nemours had not shown the
courage the occasion required. Why he did so I cannot understand.

Harriette Galway supported Wemyss Reid in denying that this
little incident had ever taken place, for she said she had herself gone
with her brother to Claremont. It seems likely, however, that Lady
Galway had some other interview in mind (Milnes went to Claremont again on 27 May, and no doubt on several subsequent
occasions), for it is unreasonable to suppose that Lord Malmesbury
invented this story when writing in his diary, nor is the indiscretion
at all uncharacteristic of Milnes in certain moods. We may
once more recall Tocqueville's verdict: 'un garçon d'esprit qui
faisait et, ce qui est plus rare, qui disait beaucoup de bêtises.'

Milnes had arranged to leave for Paris on 18 April. The purpose
of his second visit to Claremont was to ask if he could take any

---

[1] Metternich did, however, take refuge in England, landing at Blackwall on
20 April 1848.

letters from the exiled court to Orleanists in France, for on the day
before he sailed General Dumas called in Pall Mall with a message
of thanks from 'S.M. le Comte de Neuilly,' a letter from the ex-king
to be delivered to the Comte de Montalivet (the former *Intendant
Général de la Liste Civile*), and one to the General's wife, Madame
Dumas, who lived in the same quartier as Monsieur de Montalivet.
Louis-Philippe cannot have been very deeply upset by Milnes'
comments on the Duc de Nemours, since he not only entrusted to
him the Montalivet letter (which was unaddressed, and was about
finance), but courteously added a little personal note in his own
spidery hand:

Le comte de Neuilly fait bien des compliments à Monsieur
Milnes [he wrote] & profite de l'offre obligeante qu'il a bien voulu
lui faire pour lui recomander l'incluse bien particulièrement, & en
priant Monsieur Milnes de vouloir bien la faire remettre en mains
propres par une personne sûre.

This rôle of Scarlet Pimpernel was one that Milnes adored.

IV

It was natural that Milnes should want to go to look at Paris in
all its revolutionary turmoil. He could not forgive himself for
having missed the 1830 Revolution, which Augustus Fitzroy and
other Trinity friends had enviably seen. The present Revolution,
too, seemed much more progressive and exciting. The Days of
July had merely produced a middle-class monarchy; February
1848 saw the birth of a free republic, inspired and apparently ruled
by a Romantic poet and orator. When Milnes set out for Paris the
Chartist agitation was still a source of grave anxiety to the Government and the English upper-class. He, of course, had been all for
the Charter. Writing scoffingly to Lord John Manners at Belvoir
in March about the little cockney boys who ran about the streets
throwing stones at clubhouse windows, Disraeli included in his
letter a tart reference to

Dicky Milnes asking questions at five o'clock of Secretaries of
State about the collision between 'the people' and the police in
Trafalgar Square, amid groans and ironic cheers. Dicky dying of
envy of Lamartine, and ready to put himself at the head of the
gamins and break the windows of Buckingham Palace. [1]

Milnes was well aware of this ridicule. He told his family that his
fellow-member for 'Pomfret,' Mr. Martin, and himself were now
known to wags in the House as Le Martin and La Martine.

[1] Moneypenny and Buckle, vol. iii, p. 95.

Although a thin stream of refugees from Europe was flowing steadily into this country, a few enterprising English were already starting out in the opposite direction, bent on seeing revolutionary Paris in these April days. Amongst them was a party of four persons, comprising Milnes' new acquaintance W. E. Forster, the lanky and sententious Bradford Quaker; Forster's friends the Paulets; and Jane Carlyle's talkative confidante from literary Manchester, Miss Geraldine Jewsbury. Milnes already knew Miss Jewsbury. She had been brought to breakfast at Pall Mall by Mrs. Carlyle, and had thought it very dashing that she and 'Jane' should be the only women at the meal. Neither Forster nor Miss Jewsbury had Parisian contacts. They had to be content to elbow their anonymous way through screaming Paris crowds in order to catch a single glimpse of Lamartine (his noble, arrogant profile scarred by a bayonet scratch upon the cheek) as he rode at the head of a troop of horse after the arrest of Barbès on 15 May. Milnes, on the contrary, had known Lamartine (whom he thought vain) for eight or nine years. He penetrated into the very sanctum in which the poet sat wearily signing decrees, he attended the Lamartines' diplomatic soirées, called on them in the evenings if he wished to do so, and listened to Madame de Lamartine's accounts of her husband's superhuman energy in this time of crisis.

Milnes reached Paris on 19 April. He remained there one month. The day after his arrival was the Fête de la Fraternité. He watched a grand parade of 300,000 men, 'a river of bayonets flowing for 13 hours,' followed by illuminations all night. He walked back to the Meurice through the moonlit streets of old Paris, alive with lurching, shadowy figures of armed youths, some streets still blocked by broken barricades. At the review a man standing next him had cried out, 'Ce ne sont que des enfants!' on seeing the beardless faces of the National Guard. 'Il n'y a plus d'enfants,' an angered child replied. Most of Milnes' time in Paris was spent collecting anecdotes and listening to stories, and scampering from one point of vantage to the next. He trotted backwards and forwards from the Hôtel de Ville to the Assemblée, for which he was given a ticket of admission marked *Citoyen Milnis rentier*. He investigated the new revolutionary debating-clubs, such as Barbès' and Blanqui's, low, ill-conditioned rooms guarded by ruffians with lantern-jaws and naked hairy chests, who seemed the reincarnation of the men of 1789. He went to one theatre to hear Rachel sing the *Marseillaise* at the end of her performance, and to another to see Musset acting in his own play. He accompanied Montalembert when he voted and Lenormand when he went to the Hôtel de Justice to make a deposition against two colleagues.

He extracted from Thiers a detailed account of the King's abdication. He talked with everyone of any interest in Paris, from Balzac's Duchesse de Castries to Louis Blanc, from Lord Normanby to Ledru-Rollin, from George Sand to Considérant, the ardent disciple of the dead socialist, Fourier. He found that even the Paris 'women' had become political: 'Tu es paresseux, tu fais le Guizot' one said to him reproachfully when he wanted to go to sleep. He was especially glad to have been present in the Assemblée during the 'Revolution and Counter-Revolution' of 15 May, when an attempt to overthrow the Provisional Government almost succeeded and even Lamartine's silver eloquence was met by furious cries of 'Plus de lyre!' Milnes, watching the invasion of the Chamber by the Paris mob, likened it to the bursting over of a sea.

Meanwhile Milnes' radical friend the English journalist F. O. Ward had struck up a comradely friendship with W. E. Forster; they tramped the streets together, taking part in any political discussions that they found going on. Their curiosity was resented by the Paris mob, and on one occasion they hastily took refuge with cries of 'A bas les Anglais' sounding in their ears. To French people the revolution was either miraculous or horrifying; to none of them was it a trivial spectacle for foreigners to enjoy. Before Monckton Milnes departed on 17 May his own activities had become the subject of some sharp and bitter comments. Relying on their old friendship, Tocqueville determined to let Milnes know what his French friends were saying about him. He took the opportunity of doing so on 21 June, when sending Milnes some paper he had asked for. Writing from the Château de Tocqueville, its owner bluntly stated that he had intended to send Milnes 'une brusque lettre' a few weeks before, but had not found the leisure for it. 'Je ne veux pas cependant terminer celle-ci,' he wrote, 'sans vous faire connaître et vous mettre à même de démentir un bruit qui a couru sur vous et qui a affligé vos amis.' This *bruit* (which originated with persons whom Tocqueville thought trustworthy) referred chiefly to Milnes' behaviour in public during the perilous day 15 May when he was said to have been seen in the Assembly with a smile on his face and overheard to say that the spectacle amused him very much. He was accused of looking on at this scene of violence and revolution as though it were a cock-fight or a play. Tocqueville's letter was couched in courteous, even affectionate terms, but it was stern in tone. He begged Milnes to realise that although he did not himself believe these rumours about him, many other people did so. He did not add that he had himself been a little flabbergasted by Milnes' dinner-party for George Sand.

V

'Dinner at home' runs a note made by Milnes on 3 May 1848,[1]
'G. Sand—Mr & Mrs Conyngham—Tocqueville—Mérimée—de
Vigny—Mignet—Considérant—Ward—Damer—Madame Marliani.' At home was the Meurice. Milnes had also asked his old
friend the ex-abbé Lamennais and David d'Angers to dine, but
they had excused themselves.

Two separate accounts of this dinner-party have survived—one
by Alexis de Tocqueville in his *Souvenirs*,[2] one by Prosper Mérimée
in his letters. Both Tocqueville and Mérimée were taken aback by
the way in which Milnes had jumbled up his guests: was it care-
lessness or was it deliberation? Tocqueville called the composition
of the dinner-party 'fort peu homogène.' This was an under-
statement. Apart from Madame Sand the only other women were
a young English lady of fashion, Mrs. Conyngham (whom it is no
longer possible to identify with certainty), and Madame Carlotta
Marliani, a talkative old woman in a fur bonnet who was the
intimate friend of George Sand and of Madame d'Agoult. There
was also Prosper Mérimée, who arrived late, Considérant the
socialist (who shouted and thumped the table throughout the meal),
and an Englishman, Colonel Dawson Damer, as well as the historian
Mignet, the poet de Vigny, the journalist F. O. Ward, and
Mrs. Conyngham's husband. Tocqueville was very prejudiced
against Madame Sand, whom he had never previously met—
'j'avais peu vécu dans le monde d'aventuriers littéraires qu'elle
frequentait.' Her recent newspaper articles in favour of the
Revolution were repulsive to him. Yet he found he liked her dark
expressive eyes, and that her conversation was instructive and
interesting. But even worse than Milnes' juxtaposition of Tocqueville and Sand was the fact that he had invited the novelist and
Mérimée to the same meal; for, as even Tocqueville knew, they
had had a very short affair in 1833 which had ended in a Stendhalian
fiasco, and they had never met again. Mérimée pretended not to
recognise Madame Sand and asked Colonel Damer who she was.
When he gave Damer a cigar after dinner, the Colonel exasperated
him by walking up and offering it to George Sand. His other
neighbour, Madame Marliani, had spent the meal abusing all
his friends in Spain to his face. Mérimée had seen Milnes in

---

[1] This note in Milnes' commonplace book ends a controversy between George
Sand scholars in France as to the date of this dinner. Owing to a slip of memory
in Tocqueville's *Souvenirs* it was thought to have taken place on 6 June, while
M. Vladimir Karenin in the fourth volume of *George Sand, Sa Vie et Ses Oeuvres*
(Paris, Librairie Plon, 1926) urges 6 May as a more likely date.
[2] *Souvenirs d'Alexis de Tocqueville* (new edition, Gallimard, 1942), pp. 133-4.

Pall Mall, and may have remembered that in London his system of asking personal enemies to meet each other at his table was considered harmless and even original. Parisians, less phlegmatic and by nature more conventional than Londoners, did not appreciate the habit so much. News of the dinner flew across Paris. One of Milnes' newest friends, Madame Mohl, who wrote to him a day or two later to offer him a theatre box which, because of Chateaubriand's illness, Madame Récamier could not use, knew all about it: 'Mérimée came last night and told us of your *états généraux* of a dinner—very piquant.' Tocqueville remarks in his *Souvenirs* that he had never forgotten Milnes' dinner-party. 'L'image des journées de Juin qui suivirent presque aussitôt après, au lieu d'en effacer de mon esprit le souvenir, l'y réveille.'

Like Tocqueville, Mérimée thought Monckton Milnes a singular but somewhat disarming figure: 'Homme d'esprit beaucoup plus vif et fou qu'il n'appartient à un Anglais.' [1] He ascribed Milnes' reputation for being 'quite a character' to the fact that he lolled on the furniture and said a thousand idiotic things.

According to Tocqueville Milnes was 'épris de Madame Sand' throughout his stay in Paris. He had known her slightly for a number of years; on earlier visits to Paris had frequented her apartment in the Place d'Orléans, and had even been told by his friend Monteith in April 1847 that he resembled her: 'George Sand not only in breeches, but actually male.' But on this visit he did not see her again after the dinner of 3 May. In the second week of June she wrote him a very long letter from Nohant, excusing herself for having missed him when he called on her, and giving him her views on French political developments: 'J'ai eu le regret, un jour à Paris, en me réveillant d'une épouvantable migraine,' she wrote, 'd'apprendre que vous étiez venu avec Mr. et Mrs. Coningham pour me voir.' Milnes seems to have suggested that if the reaction became too pronounced George Sand might go to swell the ranks of London exiles.

La réaction n'en est pas encore à ce point qu'on puisse t'envoyer de Paris mon individu inoffensif . . . [she replied, denying that she had been involved in the affair of 15 May]. Il est vrai aussi qu'une *fausse Sand* s'est montrée ce jour là, qu'elle haranguait la *manifestation* dans un style qui n'était pas le mien, et qu'elle avait bu beaucoup trop de bierre, ce qui n'est pas dans mes habitudes. On m'a montré cette héroïne en me disant que c'était moi à quoi j'ai répondu que je ne croyais vraiment pas que ce fût moi.

[1] Mérimée's opinion of Milnes is given in letters to Madame de Boigne and Madame de Montijo, now printed in M. Maurice Parturier's satisfying edition of the *Correspondance Générale de Prosper Mérimée* (Le Divan, Paris, 1946), vol. 5.

Although she had welcomed the February Revolution, and had written stirring articles upon it during March and April 1848, Madame Sand had now abandoned politics. She told Milnes not to believe it if he heard she was any longer involved in them: she had neither taste nor capacity for 'cette vilaine chose.'

Je comprends trop ce qu'il y a au fond de cela pour y prendre de l'intérêt. Aussi je ne serai jamais de ceux qui crient aux armes, mais si je me trouvais derrière une barricade, comme je sais que les bourjeois sont toujours de l'autre côté, je ne passerais pas de l'autre côté. On pourrait bien me trouver le lendemain parmi les morts mais je n'aurais point conspiré pour cela. Voilà toute la politique que je comprends. Elle est simple et radicale.

She told him that the French countryside was settling back into peace, at any rate the countryside round Nohant:

Mais dans les petites villes on renchérit sur les haines personelles qui ont si fort gâtés notre beau et généreux Paris de Février. Je suis heureuse d'être aux champs. . . . On n'y fait rien, on n'y sert à rien, mais enfin on ressentirait un reproche d'être étendu sous l'ombrage et d'écouter chanter les rossignols quand Paris souffre et combat. J'y retournerai donc au premier coup de fusil, signal que je ne desire pas comme vous pouvez bien croire. Adieu, Adieu, mon cher Anglais . . . Tout à vous, George Sand.

During his next visit to Paris, in April 1849, Madame Sand was in the country. But Carlotta Marliani tore off for him the bottom of a letter she had received from Nohant: 'Dites à *Milnes* mille tendresses pour moi,' Madame Sand had written, adding without enthusiasm, 'je l'aime beaucoup.'

Mr. Milnes affected some relief at Richard's safe return to London.

I am glad you are again a British denizen [he wrote], not that I thought they would ever *mean* to kill you, but a chance shot might have hit you, as it did Lord Blantyre. . . . I should have enjoyed with you the contrast of a French and English mob—they seem to have no notion of using their hands & arms as we do (the great use by the bye of making boys fight at schools) & can do nothing without pistols or bayonets. I have seen Frenchmen fight & they slapp'd each others' faces (their hands open) and then tore each other's hair.

VI

While Milnes was in Paris another famous refugee from Continental Liberalism came to London. Metternich, 'the Chevalier of the Holy Alliance,' the Prince of the Peace of 1815, had disembarked at Blackwall on 20 April, accompanied by his arrogant third wife. It was more than distasteful to the Metternichs to seek sanctuary in Palmerstonian England. Princess Mélanie Metternich, convinced that the English revelled in every disaster on the Continent, regarded the whole nation with a gloomy suspicion which neither the manifold courtesies of the Tory aristocracy nor the more servile attentions of Disraeli were able to dissipate. The Vienna insurrection had been a bad jolt to her nerves and the very sight of an English radical alarmed her. Milnes' speech on the suppression of the Free State of Cracow had aroused more notice in Vienna than in London. To Princess Metternich he seemed a powerful and a sinister figure—'one of the most advanced democrats in England, and that is saying a good deal.' [1] When he came to talk with 'Clement' (who was old and very deaf) about Hungary, the Princess was persuaded he had been put up to it by Hungarian dissidents. Milnes, on his side, was impishly inquisitive about the Metternichs: 'I sat with old Metternich two hours on Sunday,' he wrote to Lord Galway, 'he talked all the time—very prosy— I liked his insolent wife.' When the Metternichs left London for Brighton, Milnes pretended that they had been driven out of their rented house in Eaton Square by the daughters of their next-door neighbour, Lord Minto. He said that these young women had spent all day playing 'Pio Nono' and 'Mourir pour la Patrie' on every imaginable instrument as loudly as they could.

By the end of 1848 even the Metternichs need not have worried about the general English attitude to the European revolts. Although Lord Palmerston remained at the Foreign Office, his policies were commanding less support than ever among the educated classes in England, Whig as well as Tory. Few influential Englishmen were still enthusing over those transient insurrections, but amongst these few was Richard Monckton Milnes. Exasperated by the timidity with which his compatriots had watched the surge and ebb of Continental Liberalism, Milnes settled down to write his last political pamphlet, a seventy-page production cast in the form of a letter: *The Events of 1848 especially in their relation to Great Britain—A Letter to the Marquis of Lansdowne by Richard Monckton Milnes, M.P.* This pamphlet, which was executed in Milnes' most grandiose and authoritative manner, surveyed the state of Europe during 1848, heavily criticised English apathy, pleaded for England's support for liberal movements everywhere, and paid a burning tribute to Charles Buller, who had died suddenly in November 1848. Milnes distributed his

[1] See Princess Mélanie Metternich's journal, printed in vol. 8 of de Klinkowstroem's *Mémoires, Documents et Ecrits Divers laissés par le Prince de Metternich, Chancelier de Cour et d'Etat* (Librairie Plon, Paris, 1884).

Letter broadcast amongst his acquaintances and friends. It met with a varying reception. Lord Lansdowne himself, the old and powerful Whig nobleman now nearing seventy, owner of Bowood, with its great park and its Italian pictures, and of Lansdowne House in Berkeley Square, expressed an amiable surprise to find his name screening Milnes' outburst.

If I have accidentally in any degree provoked its publication [he wrote politely], I am sure the publick is indebted to me, far more than a mere speech on these important questions, as a more striking & rapid glance at European affairs, as respects the past, the present & (as far as the great unknown can be dealt with) the future I have certainly not yet seen.

Mr. Milnes senior sent his usual list of grammatical mistakes: 'on p. 10 two words I never saw in print'; or 'p. 18—*sodden* ruins—what are *sodden* ruins?'; or 'use of material violence—what a cumbrous expression!' Lord Brougham wrote that there was not one word in the whole pamphlet with which he could not concur. Lord Jeffrey sent from Edinburgh a letter of exuberant and overwhelming praise. Carlyle told Miss Williams-Wynn that it was the 'greatest thing' Milnes had yet done—'earnest and grave,—written in a large, tolerant, kindhearted spirit and as far as I can see, says all that is to be said on *that matter*.' Guizot, of course, disagreed profoundly with it. On the whole, admiration for Milnes' humane and liberal attitude was general, and shared even by friends like Gladstone and Henry Reeve who did not sympathise with the arguments of the pamphlet and attributed Milnes' 'bias' to his admiration for Palmerston. Henry Bulwer thought it had 'some remarkably graceful as well as powerful passages in it.' Miss Mary Berry, Mrs. Grote and Lady Davy much admired it, and poor Lady Blessington, on the verge of bankruptcy and with only two more months to live, found the time and energy to write Milnes the last note he got from her hand: 'It proves that *Poets* can shine in Politics' wrote Lady Blessington, 'as well as in their own Craft, and does you great Credit. How can you hope to be forgiven for thus excelling in so many different ways?' The Whig newspapers gave considerable space to reviewing the pamphlet. Whether it met with approval or abuse, *The Events of* 1848 made a great deal more stir in London than anything Milnes had written before. On 22 February 1849, the *Morning Chronicle* printed a leading article upon the pamphlet. The author of this article was officially anonymous, but he was not particularly difficult to identify.

After the levity of Lord Palmerston's characteristic defence of his own peculiar foreign policy [George Smythe's leader began], there was wanting nothing more than a pamphlet in its eulogy from Mr. Monckton Milnes. The professional jester has a prescriptive claim to break his bulrush (after the danger has passed away) where the lance of the knight had been ruefully shivered. Or, to use a metaphor more germane to both performers, if the venerable Harlequin has escaped cleverly and nimbly through 'a plain and well-noted trap' there remains a Pantaloon (as Mr. Rogers tells us in the notes of his noble poem, *an Italian character*) . . . Immethodic, absurd and illogical as is this pamphlet of Mr. Milnes, it is occasionally, and by involuntary glimpses, so unwittingly true, that it is not without a purpose that we propose to gibbet him, in front of every country of which he has written with universal ignorance and omniscient pretensions.

Milnes' habit of noting down conversations was turned to ridicule. He was accused of having been 'a boy-Boswell' at Cambridge, and of having 'become (unsuccessfully) Boswell to Lord Melbourne, Boswell to Sir Robert Peel (until his fall) and Boswell to Lord John Russell'; he was called 'a would-be employé,' a candidate for inclusion in Thackeray's *Book of Snobs*, and an *ami terrible* of the Foreign Office. Eleven quotations from this pamphlet were scornfully vivisected. 'Indeed,' the article ended, 'there is only one observation of Mr. Milnes (at p. 58) in which we can entirely agree, when he speaks of long years of repose, indolence, flattery, assentation, and folly—"fattening men for destruction."' Even by the journalistic standards of that day it was a vitriolic onslaught.

Milnes' first reaction was to dispatch a letter to the *Morning Chronicle* by hand, pointing out that four of the quotations in his article had been falsified and another four badly garbled. This letter, which was printed next day, produced a short note from George Smythe admitting his authorship of the attack. Milnes' next step was uncharacteristic and already at that epoch very quaint: he challenged Smythe to a duel. It is most unlikely that he took this decision on his own initiative, and without seeking a good deal of advice—turning for it, perhaps, to some foreigner or to a member of an older generation for whom eighteenth-century and Regency conceptions of honour still held good. All that we know is that Warburton was engaged as Milnes' second, while a Captain Darell was briefed to act in the same capacity for George Smythe. An undated note from Smythe, apparently sent to Milnes' room in some country house in which they were both staying—'out of regard for Hope, pray, keep as secret as possible our difference in this house'—accused Milnes of making an incorrect statement in a letter. On 24 April, more than two months after the publication of the offensive article, Warburton and Darell signed a paper at the Army and Navy Club declaring themselves satisfied that the affair was terminated with honour to both sides. Wemyss Reid records that Lord Houghton used to tell him how annoyed Warburton had been to find there was to be no duel after all. It is impossible to establish exactly what did happen or how Milnes, who was pacific, genial and unable to shoot straight owing to an astigmatism, became entangled in this very improbable affair. It seems strange, too, that a challenge to a duel should drag on without any decision for eight or nine weeks. It seems stranger that Milnes should have maintained a comparative silence about the course and conclusion of the quarrel. Yet what can he have had to conceal?

On 1 April 1849—in the very midst of the row with George Smythe—Milnes left suddenly for Paris. He drove to Folkestone with d'Orsay and crossed with him to Boulogne, where they lunched off 'excellent cotelettes panées' and proceeded to Paris the next day. For those who find a melancholy fascination in the collapse of the Gore House establishment it is of interest to learn that Milnes accompanied 'Cupid' on his surreptitious departure from London. It is evident that Milnes, fond of the Count and of Lady Blessington, ever ready to help anyone in distress, helped to smuggle d'Orsay out of the country that Sunday morning before the new writ could be served. D'Orsay, who was besieged by creditors, is alleged to have left Gore House with his valet, a portmanteau and a jewelled umbrella at three o'clock in the morning of 1 April. It would have been typical of Milnes to shelter him at 26 Pall Mall until later that morning, and then to drive with him to the coast. In Paris he saw him installed at the Elysée as 'a sort of Chamberlain to the President.' Milnes, too, was welcomed by Louis Napoleon, whom he had often entertained in London, and whom in ten years more he learned to hate.

The mood of Paris had changed in the year since Milnes had been there. 'Notre beau Paris de Février' which George Sand had mourned was a city of the past.

VII

By the end of the eighteen-forties Milnes' ambitions as a poet had withered away. His interest in the poetry of others flourished still. In 1846 he had seriously told Panizzi that young Coventry Patmore might 'really come to a Chatterton's fate' if he was not given employment at the British Museum; he was even more ready to attack English apathy over poets than over foreign revolutionaries. *A Letter to the Marquis of Lansdowne* was not the only protest that Milnes made against the public's prejudices at this time, for it is in this light that his single celebrated and enduring work must be regarded—*The Life, Letters and Literary Remains of John Keats*, which Moxon published in the summer of 1848.

The two neat volumes of this first available biography of Keats were modestly described as 'Edited by Richard Monckton Milnes.' They contained sixty-seven of Keats' poems, together with as many of his letters as Milnes could lay his hands on. The poems and the letters were riveted together by a framework of simple narrative prose, into which Milnes had inlaid the anecdotes and recollections he had picked up from John Keats' surviving friends. His stock source for the chronology of the poet's life was the unprinted memoir[1] by Charles Armitage Brown, which had been left in Milnes' care in 1841 when its author and his son Carlino had emigrated to New Zealand. Milnes had been assembling Keats material for many years[2] and Moxon had advertised the book early in 1845, though he did not sign an agreement purchasing the Keats copyrights from Keats' first publisher, Taylor, until September of that year.[3] The delay in the appearance of the *Life and Letters* was not solely due to Milnes' indolence but to certain external factors as well—the quarrel, for instance, between Brown and George Keats, the poet's brother who lived in the United States. This quarrel had prevented Brown from getting access to a major collection of John Keats' letters and poems; and it was only in 1845 that John Jeffrey, the American second husband of George Keats' widow, sent Milnes transcripts of the papers in his wife's possession.[4] Then Keats' early friend, John Hamilton Reynolds, had been touchy and difficult at first, refusing to allow publication of any of Keats' letters to himself. Reynolds was finally won over by a letter from Milnes, and wrote 'all the papers I possess—all the information I can render—whatever I can do to aid your kind and judiciously intended work—are at your service.' By the time Milnes embarked for Spain, in September 1847, Reynolds had become restless at the long delay.

Dear Rich [ran a letter from Mr. Pemberton Milnes to his son, dated 14 September and addressed to Lisbon], There are only

---

[1] The memoir was published by the Oxford University Press in 1937. It was then in the possession of Lord Crewe, but now forms part of the Keats collections in the Houghton Library of Harvard University.

[2] The material used by Milnes for this work is now in the Houghton Library of Harvard University. This important collection of Keatsiana has lately been published in *The Keats Circle: Letters and Papers* 1816–1878 (Harvard University Press, 1949) under the expert editorship of Professor Hyder E. Rollins, author of the study, *Keats' Reputation in America to* 1848.

[3] Rollins, *op. cit.*   [4] Rollins, *op. cit.*

two letters for you at Bawtry—one from the Horse Guards refusing to exchange Wharlton into another regiment—the other signed J. H. Reynolds & only this—'My dear Sir—Elections over—Autumnal quiet on—what of Keats? Yours faithfully JHR.'

There was a brevity about the note that Mr. Milnes would have relished, but he can otherwise have cared little for the progress of Richard's work on Keats. He would certainly not have understood or even wished to understand that the issue of his son's book of Keats' manuscripts was not only far more important than the letter on *The Events of* 1848 but even, in the long view, more important than any of those political events themselves.

Two volumes of Keats' verse had been re-issued in 1841. They had aroused so little interest that both Rossetti and Holman Hunt, youths who discovered his poetry in that decade, thought that they had come upon an entirely unknown poet. 'No other copies of his work than those published in his lifetime had yet appeared,' Hunt wrote of the year 1848 in *Pre-Raphaelitism and the Pre-Raphaelite Brotherhood*.[1] 'These were in mill-board covers and I had found mine in book-bins labelled "this lot 4d."' In the 1848 Academy Hunt had exhibited a picture—*The Eve of St. Agnes*—with a subject taken from Keats, and when Milnes' book appeared that summer both he and his new friend Rossetti seized it eagerly, reading it all through an August day upon the Thames as they floated down the summer water to Greenwich and the Isle of Dogs. Few young men of their generation had even heard of John Keats; to a limited public the appearance of Milnes' volumes was almost as revolutionary as Bridges' publication of Gerard Manley Hopkins in our own century. The taut and eager face of Keats, gazing with impassioned eyes from the engraved frontispiece of Milnes' first volume,[2] is now as familiar to us, as much a part of our lives as the strange, egg-shell countenance of Shakespeare from the First Folio. In 1848 in England that face was still unknown.

The genesis of Milnes' biography lay far back in his Cambridge period. To write it was to pay an obligation to his lost youth—to those now distant days when Arthur Hallam had come bounding back from Pisa with a copy of Shelley's *Adonais* under his arm, when he and Milnes and the Tennyson brothers would read and discuss and worship the poetry of John Keats. Later, in Rome, Milnes' admiration for Keats had been strengthened and confirmed by his friendship with Severn, whom he had commissioned to copy the head of Keats for Harriette. In the summer of 1831 he had

---

[1] Two vols., 1905.
[2] Joseph Severn had lent Milnes a portrait of Keats for this engraving.

been laid up with malaria at Landor's villa at Fiesole, and had there made friends with Charles Armitage Brown. When Brown left for New Zealand he sent Milnes his Keats papers, with the request that he should publish a book of them as soon as he could. Brown did not make the choice of Milnes suddenly or idly, for he told Severn that in his opinion Milnes was better able to make a selection for publication than any man he knew. Severn, who painted Milnes in London in 1847,[1] was as anxious for the book to be published as were Brown and Reynolds, but though he volunteered to help he did not wish Milnes to print any part of Brown's memoir of Keats.

While you are sitting [he wrote, after expostulating with Milnes for missing some appointment] I could tell you some of the many interesting things *not* in Brown's life of Keats and also explain my serious objections to its being published in any way. As I was in doubt & did not like that my individual opinion should influence you I have consulted Dilke, who more than confirms it—I have lots of beautiful things about Keats which may inspire you to begin.

Severn, like Charles Dilke, Charles Cowden Clarke, Reynolds, Haslam and other of Keats' surviving friends supplied Milnes with a great quantity of reminiscence. The usual jealousies cropped up—Severn, for instance, declaring that Brown had never been as intimate with Keats as he pretended. Benjamin Haydon also sent information, and some faulty transcripts of sonnets; his last letter, containing further recollections, was written four weeks before he cut his throat. Help of another sort (no doubt well-paid, for Milnes was always generous) was given him by the impoverished young Patmore, who acted as amanuensis during the compilation of the work. In those days Coventry Patmore was rather shocked by Keats: 'Keats' poems collectively are, I should say, a very *splendid* piece of paganism. *I have a volume of Keats' manuscript letters by me.* They do not increase my attachment to him.'[2]

Patmore was not alone in being shocked by Keats' paganism, and some people were anxious to attribute Keats' beliefs to his biographer.

I hope Mrs. Nightingale does not bother her daughter to accept of Monckton Milnes [wrote a gossiping female in February 1849[3]]. He is not worthy of her. Have you seen his life of Keats?

---

[1] This portrait is probably that now at Madeley Manor, Staffordshire.
[2] Letter to H. S. Sutton, dated 26 February, 1847, kindly communicated to me by the poet's great-grandson, Mr. Derek Patmore.
[3] Fanny Allen to her niece Emma Darwin in *A Century of Family Letters*, already cited.

T. Macaulay says he never knew what religion he was of till he read his book. He expects to find an altar to Jupiter somewhere in his house.

As a biographer, indeed, Milnes was singularly forthright, for though he omitted a few personal references—notably any references to Fanny Brawne—he did not conceal anything about Keats' life. The object for which he wrote the book was simple and very characteristic. He defined it in the preface:

I saw how grievously (Keats) was misapprehended [he wrote], even by many who wished to see in him only what was best. I perceived that many, who heartily admired his poetry, looked on it as the product of a wayward, erratic genius, self-indulgent in conceits, disrespectful of the rules and limitations of Art, not only unlearned but careless of knowledge, not only exaggerated but despising proportion. I knew that his moral disposition was assumed to be weak, gluttonous of sensual excitement, querulous of severe judgement, fantastical in its tastes and lackadaisical in its sentiments. He was all but universally believed to have been killed by a stupid, savage article in a review, and to the compassion generated by his untoward fate he was held to owe a certain personal interest, which his poetic reputation hardly justified.

Milnes' reward was the eager, emotional gratitude of Keats' friends, who wrote to him one after another to thank and to congratulate him. In other quarters, too, the book served its purpose. It was given high praise in the *Westminster*, the *Quarterly* and other reviews, and was enthusiastically admired by men of letters like Landor, Lord Jeffrey (to whom it was dedicated) and John Forster. But several very intelligent people reacted against it, adopting Macaulay's views or at any rate arriving at not dissimilar conclusions.

Milnes has written this year a book on *Keats* [wrote Carlyle in his journal [1] for December 1848]. This remark to make on it: 'An attempt to make us eat dead dog by exquisite currying and cooking.' [2] Won't eat it. A truly unwise little book. The kind of man Keats was gets ever more horrible to me. Force of hunger for pleasure of every kind, and want of all other force—that is a combination!

Although Milnes had done his best to show that Keats was not the 'unmanly,' weak and self-indulgent character that the few people who had read his poetry still thought him, many readers would

---

[1] Froude, *op. cit.*, vol. i, p. 450.
[2] 'Carlyle of my Life of Keats—"Whatever made Milnes so waste his time—making curry of a dead dog"': Milnes' commonplace book, 1848–9.

have compared *The Life, Letters and Literary Remains of John Keats* with its predecessor by four years, Dean Stanley's *Life of Arnold*, an oddly popular work which became a best-seller, whereas it took three years to exhaust the first edition of Monckton Milnes' *Keats*. Yet all through the 'fifties and 'sixties and 'seventies Keats was more and more widely read and loved in England and America. Severn said that by 1863 his grave in Rome had become a point of pilgrimage for visitors from every part of the world. Much of this strong and steady surge of recognition must be attributed to Milnes' small book.

A good biography reveals almost as much about its writer as about its subject. The very fact that Milnes' *Life of Keats* contained so many of Keats' letters was in itself revealing, for Milnes had a definite theory about biography, which may have been the result of original thought or may have been derived from Mason and Tom Moore. His preface makes the same points that William Mason made when he introduced into English literature the new biographical form of *Life and Letters* with his work on Gray, published in 1774. Milnes seems to have been more conscious of what he was doing than Mason had been, for he began by stating the case against his chosen biographical technique. For this he turned to a turgid passage from William Wordsworth. Wordsworth had declared that, in biography, truth 'is not to be sought without scruple and promulgated for its own sake.'

The general obligation upon which I have insisted [he continued] is especially binding upon those who undertake the biography of *authors*. Assuredly there is no cause why the lives of that class of men should be pried into with diligent curiosity and laid open with the same disregard of reserve which may sometimes be expedient in composing the history of men who have borne an active part in the world.

In a long quotation Milnes reproduced Wordsworth's case for *suppressio veri*, calling it a 'grave warning.' He then set out to explain why he intended to turn his back upon these theories. He said he had not wished to construct a eulogistic monument to Keats, easy though that would have been. He proposed, instead, to let Keats speak for himself and to print as many of his actual words as he was able. It was a bold and typical decision. Had Milnes known Keats as Mason had known Gray, his book would now rank alongside that calm and vivid tribute to eighteenth-century friendship. As it is, Milnes' book remains one of the most readable and impartial biographies in English. Like most of his speeches on foreign affairs, Milnes' *Life of Keats* contained errors, a few of them flagrant. He had, for instance, relied on Mrs. Procter's recollections of Keats' appearance as against those of Keats' real friends. Mrs. Procter, who had scarcely known him, distinctly remembered that Keats' eyes were blue, and his hair auburn; neither statement was true. Then Milnes had confused the ages of the Keats brothers, and had 'killed off' Keats' friend Bailey, who he said had also died in 1821. As a matter of fact, Bailey was alive and resident in Ceylon as an archdeacon. He gravely wrote to rectify the mistake, which caused Milnes' friends some merriment, and inspired one of them to rhyme:

> Dicky Milnes—Dicky Milnes! why what the deuce could ail ye
> When you wrote the life of Keats—to write the death of Bailey—
> The poet sleeps—oh! let him sleep—within the silent tomb-o
> But Parson Bailey lives, and kicks—Archdeacon of Colombo—[1]

Milnes' versions of Keats' letters were not always faultless, but the essential fact about Milnes' book was its warmth, its courage and its objectivity. These were qualities which no errors of detail could impair, and here at last was an achievement Milnes could be proud of, and one which placed future generations in his debt. In a letter to Varnhagen dated August 1848 he told him that he had just

published a life and some remains of a remarkable young poet of the name of Keats, little known even in this country. It is the biography of a mere boy. . . . I cannot expect any reputation for the book, when the merits of the subject of it are so little known.

Yet Milnes' speeches and pamphlets and verse are now utterly forgotten, and it is by virtue of his publication of Keats' poems and letters—by virtue, in fact, of his most disinterested literary action —that Milnes' name survives. Here is a thorough 'Milnesian paradox' indeed.

Milnes received many letters of congratulation from his own friends. He could feel that at least some of the people who read the book in that summer of 1848 had understood what he was trying to do. Wordsworth was not among them. 'What a pity you and Keats did not see more of one another when he expresses himself as he does about you!' Miss Martineau remarked to him at Ambleside.[2] 'Yes,' replied Wordsworth. 'It was so. If I had seen more of him, it might have done him good.'

---

[1] Rollins, *op. cit.*, vol. ii, 259.
[2] Story in commonplace book, 1848-9.

Chapter Fourteen

1849   1851

I

On 19 June 1849 Richard Monckton Milnes turned forty. In his youth he had hoped that by the time he had reached this age he would have forged for himself a fine political reputation. He had not done so. He laughed at the way in which his speeches emptied the House of Commons and allowed his friends to twit him on it, but in 1848 he told Emerson that he now had only one ambition: to make a single telling parliamentary speech. Americans invariably liked and understood Milnes. His kindness and his spontaneity made them feel at home in London, which he himself now called 'the Scornful City.' Emerson found him 'the most goodnatured man in England, made of sugar,' and the profile of Milnes in 1848 which he has left in the pages of his European journal forms a good pendant to Henry Adams' later and more detailed portrait.

Milnes . . . is everywhere and knows everything [Emerson recorded]; has the largest range of acquaintants, from the Chartist to the Lord Chancellor; fat, easy, affable and obliging; a little careless and slovenly in his dress. . . . His good humour is infinite. . . . He is very liberal of his money and sincerely kind and useful to young people of merit. . . . Jane Carlyle testified to his generosity—rare, she said, among people of fashion—with his money. . . . He is one of the most valuable companions in London, too, for the multitude of anecdotes he tells about good people, and at Paris I found him equally acquainted with everybody and a privileged man, with his pockets full of free cards, which admitted him everywhere.

Many people in London, Coventry Patmore amongst them, told Emerson how eagerly helpful Milnes could be. An instructive example of Milnes in this role is provided by the tactful, secret manner in which he tried to help James Anthony Froude after *The Nemesis of Faith* scandal in the early spring of 1849.

A bomb has fallen into the midst of the religious world in the shape of a book called *The Nemesis of Faith* by a brother of

297

Froude, the dead Puseyite [Milnes wrote in May 1849[1]]. It is
a sort of religious, anti-religious Wilhelm Meister, and balances
itself between fact and fiction in an uncomfortable manner, though
with great ability, and has caused the poor man to lose his Fellowship and a college in Van Diemen's Land, and to fall into utter
poverty. We call ourselves a free people, and what slaves of
opinion we are after all!

The Nemesis of Faith, which Froude himself termed 'heterodoxy
flavoured with sentimentalism,' had been published in February
1849, when its author, a fellow of Exeter, was thirty. Its subject
was the sceptic's progress of its hero, Mark Sutherland, through
Tractarianism to Catholicism and then to loss of faith. In orthodox
quarters the book was thought to be blasphemous. On 27 February
a copy of it was publicly burned by Dr. Sewell, the Senior Tutor of
Exeter College, in a scene of theatrical bigotry in the college hall.
Froude resigned his fellowship and accepted nomination as candidate for a post in remote Van Diemen's Land. When it was
announced that his name had been selected from that of sixty-three
other candidates for the job of Headmaster of Hobart Town High
School, the London newspapers, headed by the *Morning Herald*,
published a series of vituperative attacks. Froude was refused the
post. A very few level-headed persons in London—amongst them
Chevalier Bunsen, F. D. Maurice, Dean Stanley and Max Müller
—sympathised with Froude and began to discuss ways of helping
him. Monckton Milnes did more: he at once made a private and
anonymous offer of money sufficient to finance Froude at a German
university, where it was understood he wished to go to study theology.
This offer, to which Bunsen later contributed, was accepted by
Froude with hesitation and gratitude. Although he finally decided
to marry and to work at Manchester rather than to go on someone
else's money to Germany, Milnes' action made a deep impression
on his mind. Many years later Froude found out who his unknown
benefactor had been. He wrote to thank Lord Houghton[2]:

I have long felt it must have been so. Müller kept the secret—
assuring me only that it was not Bunsen—but as I grew to know you
better the conclusion forced itself on me and with it, I hope, a
sense of gratitude toward yourself which could not have been
greater if I had availed myself of your kindness. That offer coming
upon me in the middle of my troubles unlooked for out of the skies,
gave me for the first time some confidence in myself. I was in a

[1] Letter to Mrs. Charles MacCarthy in Ceylon. MacCarthy had married
the daughter of Benjamin Hawes in March 1848 and had returned with her to
his post in Ceylon, an island Milnes romanticised and the MacCarthys loathed.
[2] Undated letter, May 10, no year, from 5 Onslow Gardens.

condition in which if no hand had been held out to me I might have given up and gone to the Devil—I don't know how but there are many roads there and I should have tumbled into one or another of them.

Froude added that he was glad he had not gone to Germany or read theology, but that in 'the other line' of historian which he had chosen he had determined to show his anonymous friend that his confidence had been justified. '. . . It was to you,' he concluded, 'that I owed the first inspiriting thoughts that ever came to me.'

At forty Milnes' intentions were as benevolent as they had been at twenty-five or thirty, but he was now less frivolous and more powerful—and in a better position to give help.

II

Like other liberal-minded Englishmen, Milnes was shocked by the violence of the reactionary movements which broke across Europe in the three years following 1848. He watched Louis Napoleon's crabwise progress towards the imperial throne with great distaste. He abhorred General Oudinot's advance on Rome [1] as 'done with the blindest French vanity and disregard of the feelings of other men.' He feared the suppression of the new Prussian constitution and was appalled by the strength of the reaction throughout Austria and her dominions. Russian pretensions made him foresee a general war: 'Russia, hitherto so quiet, has begun to move,' he told Varnhagen in March 1849, 'and has demanded the passage of the Dardanelles, which is the next thing to the possession of Stamboul. The position is critical.'

In England the reaction merely took the form of a growing hardening of opinion against the liberal refugees from France and Germany who were now succeeding in London the frightened 'reacs' and 'aristos' of the spring of 1848. Milnes himself incurred the usual opprobrium by welcoming Louis Blanc, who had fled to this country in 1849. In the spring of that year Harriette Galway's young brother-in-law had been severely wounded in India, in the Sikh War; and the Moncktons and the Milneses endured a foretaste of that suffering and anxiety which had been unknown to English households since the field of Waterloo, but became general after the outbreak of the Crimean War. In April 1850 the Don Pacifico dispute seemed likely to precipitate an Anglo-French conflict, and Milnes' friend, the French ambassador, Drouyn de

---

[1] General Oudinot, at the head of a French army, stormed Rome on 3 July 1849 and restored Pius IX.

Lhuys, was temporarily withdrawn from London. The coup d'état of December 1851 and the restoration of the French Empire in November 1852 threw English people into a kind of panic. War and invasion formed the current talk. Two years later came the Crimean War.

Meanwhile, under the constant direction of Prince Albert, London had prepared to celebrate the mid-century with an Exhibition befitting the capital of the richest and most powerful country in the world. The Great Exhibition, first projected by the Prince in 1849, was opened by the Queen in May 1851. After much contention about a site, the shimmering Crystal Palace of Paxton began slowly to rise above the plane-trees of Hyde Park. Milnes watched its progress with as much admiration as everyone else. 'The great glass-house is now more beautiful than it will be when full,' he wrote in February 1851, 'for then there will be blinds over a great part, but now it looks quite magical in the setting sun.' The Great Exhibition was intended to be 'a Festival to open the long reign of peace.' In fact, as Justin MacCarthy pointed out in 1880, it almost exactly coincided with the close of the brief peace era that had followed Waterloo: 'from that year, 1851, the world has scarcely seen a week of peace.' The civilised and cosmopolitan Europe reconstructed at the Congress of Vienna had been the background of Milnes' youth. His early memories were of small Italian courts, of English family carriages rolling southwards across the plains of France, of carefree German students on the Rhine boats, of fashionable (but also erudite) international society in Naples or in Rome. The remainder of his life was spent in a world some part of which was always at war, a world in which the new railroads were used to mass troops swiftly, in which passports became necessary to get over the most friendly frontiers, in which many of Europe's greatest cities became hideous and industrialised. He lived to witness the decay of liberalism over much of the Continent, the ruin of France by Napoleon III and that grim concomitant the rise of the Prussian Empire under the direction of Count Bismarck.

In July 1850 Sir Robert Peel was thrown from his horse in the Mall and died from his injuries. In August 1850 Louis-Philippe died peacefully at Claremont. Milnes was moved but rather surprised by the scenes of popular emotion that Peel's death evoked —'the thick, sad crowd night and day about his house; the weeping women rushing out of dark alleys as his body was taken to the railroad.' No doubt he was right in attributing some part of this display to the sudden and sensational nature of Peel's end. He could not resist quoting a remark made by Lord Brougham—'Let every statesman take care to ride like a sack and he may die like a demigod.'

Milnes was never deceived by popular enthusiasm. In August 1849 the Queen's reception in Ireland infuriated him: '. . . idolatrous,' he wrote, 'utterly unworthy of a free, not to say ill-used nation. She will go away with the impression that it is the happiest country in the world.' He was equally exasperated by another aberration of public opinion: the 'Papal Aggression' scare of the autumn of 1850, which his old friend Nicholas Wiseman had inadvertently provoked by the *Letter from the Flaminian Gate* establishing a Roman Catholic hierarchy in Great Britain. Although Milnes voted for the Ecclesiastical Titles Bill (the Government's half-hearted reply to the *Letter*) he declared that the public's feelings over this incident were an anachronism and worthy of the days of Hildebrand. He was amused by the little court the new Cardinal had begun to hold in London, 'where the devotion and prostration of the converts scandalises the old Catholics.'

Milnes still continued his prodigious reading of new books. The first two volumes of Macaulay's *History*, which had come out in the same year as his own *Keats*, were so successful that he inferred that they could not 'be worth much': 'A young officer said to me, "That is what I call a history. We took five copies at our depot."' He seems to have preferred Bulwer's *The Caxtons*—'Without being a good work of Art, it is yet most agreeable and with a certain healthy English tone about it, which makes it a real accession to our popular literature'—and *Alton Locke*, 'a socialist novel written by a clergyman of the name of Kingsley.' 'The literary season has been remarkably stagnant,' he wrote in July 1850. 'An Anglo-German novel "The Initials," two new volumes of Grote's History, and Tennyson's "In Memoriam" are the only books that suggest themselves.' This is Milnes' only known comment upon *In Memoriam*.

Thackeray, whom Milnes had first known well in Paris in 1840, was now no longer an obscure journalist with an insane wife, but a literary lion and a public figure. Milnes observed his admittance to the dinner-tables of the great with some uncertainty: 'I doubt whether he will be much the happier for it, though I think people generally are better for satisfied vanity.' In the autumn of 1849 Charlotte Brontë crept timidly to the metropolis. Thackeray asked Milnes (at very short notice) to dine with her. Milnes had early admired both her fiction and her poetry (he had read the *Poems* of Ellis, Acton and Currer Bell aloud to the Nightingale sisters in 1847), but he was unable or unwilling to go. He did not meet Miss Brontë until he went up and introduced himself to her as a Yorkshireman at one of Thackeray's lectures in 1851.

At the end of the London season of 1850 Milnes made his

customary round of country houses.   In late July he was at Nuneham, the noble Palladian house of George Granville Harcourt in
Oxfordshire.   George Harcourt was considered rather a figure of
fun. 'Such is the oscillation of the South Western railway,' he
solemnly told Milnes, 'that Lady Waldegrave was forced to stand
up all the way from Southampton—not but that Lady Waldegrave
is quite well.'   'It is somewhat imprudent for me to ask Peel to
Nuneham,' he said just before Peel's fatal accident, 'for he is as
much hated in the county as the Pope—not but that the Pope would
come to Nuneham, if he visited England.'   Lord Waldegrave, who
was killed at the battle of the Alma in 1854, and his wife Frances
were among Harcourt's guests, as well as Milnes' friend the Belgian
minister in London, Van de Weyer, and his American wife, Lord
and Lady Granville, Lord and Lady Norreys, and young Lord
Dufferin, Mrs. Norton's dark and beautiful nephew, who cherished
a well-known but hopeless romantic passion for the prettiest of the
Queen's ladies-in-waiting.   Lord Dufferin acted one of Bluebeard's
murdered wives in a charade, *Mr. Bluebeard Discovered*, which the
guests at Nuneham organised one evening, while on another occasion
Milnes and Lady Waldegrave performed in *The Earl and the Duchess*,
a duologue adapted by Milnes from Musset's 'proverbe' *Il faut qu'une
porte soit ouverte ou fermée*, which he had seen in a Paris theatre
during the hectic weeks of April 1848.   The printed version of
The Earl and the Duchess was dedicated by Milnes to Lady Waldegrave.   From Nuneham Milnes returned to an empty August
London and started out with his valet for Marienbad.

III

Marienbad was Milnes' very first experience of a Continental spa.
As he got older and goutier he formed the habit of spending a few
weeks of each year at one or other of the better watering-places of
Germany or France.   In 1882 the anonymous writer of an article
in the paper *Truth* described Lord Houghton's behaviour at some
spa:

At a Continental watering-place where he was staying not very
long ago, the bathers, who had not found out what his position was
in England, were greatly exercised to make out his profession or
calling.   Some guessed from his cheery, intelligent chatter that he
was an eminent lady's doctor.   Others thought he must have been
a successful tradesman who could not throw the cares of business
entirely from his mind.   Others opined that he was a man of science.
Their reason for hazarding this guess was that he was frequently

engaged in making entries in what seemed to be a pocket account-book, and totting them up. Lord Houghton was merely trying to kill time by reckoning the clever men and women with whom he had shaken hands. [1]

At Marienbad in 1850 Milnes was in his element. He made sixty-eight new German friends, and became the moving spirit of the small, haphazard colony of idle or ailing English people of fashion who gathered each morning beneath the linden trees. These persons included the second Marquess of Breadalbane, an elderly free-churchman, who was there with his doctor, and Lady Frances Hope, who was there with her niece. Also staying in the town, though not for his health, was a clever bi-lingual boy of nineteen, George Joachim Goschen, the son of a wealthy Anglo-German merchant and lately the head boy at Rugby, the formidable Dr. Arnold's school. The very young make austere critics. George Goschen noted in his diary [2] that he was 'at first little struck' with 'the poet Monckton Milnes' and 'did not get far with him'; 'he fixes himself easily on to a person and seems to wish to know and to talk to everyone.' But in a few days' time Goschen revised his opinion: 'in the long run amusing, full of anecdote, well-read and conversational,' though the conversation was not 'at all times high-toned.' Milnes gave the boy his poems and asked him to meals. 'Never was before in such noble company still it is impossible to me to feel humble or inferior. Always equal and republican,' wrote Goschen humorously. He found Lady Frances Hope's niece, Alice Lascelles, 'a fair-haired interesting young lady' though 'akin to many dukes.' At one of Milnes' evening parties Goschen counted up the guests: 'one marquis, two counts, one priest, two doctors, one clergyman, two poets, one beef-steak-eater as thin as a poplar, one lubberly boy and one deaf man.' He was not accustomed to the Milnesian atmosphere. One night he arrived to find Milnes dressed as a woman, the interesting Miss Lascelles wearing a moustache and another of his new acquaintances decked out in the character of Pope Joan. 'Very *lustig* indeed,' the boy commented, 'like any other circle, but even a little more *laisser aller*.'

Milnes left Marienbad in September, going to stay at Militsch in Silesia and then travelling homeward by way of Dresden, Berlin and Brussels. In Brussels he met Caroline Norton and her admirer, William Stirling. With them he steamed back to England in the late autumn of the year.

[1] *Truth*, 12 October 1882. This sketch of Lord Houghton formed part of a series of *Anecdotal Photographs* of celebrities.
[2] Hon. Arthur Elliot's *Life of Lord Goschen*, 1831–1907, vol. i (Longmans, 1911).

IV

A week or two before he went to Marienbad, Milnes had written another chatty letter to Mrs. Charles MacCarthy. He thoughtfully filled it with the London gossip likely to divert at Kandy. Wiseman, he wrote, was off to Rome to get his hat. Wordsworth's new poem would be out next week. Henry Taylor's comedy *The Virgin Martyr* had 'hardly survived its birth like the child of the Queen of Spain.' The beautiful Miss Pattle—'Thackeray's idol'—was going to marry Lord Euston. Robert Curzon, whom Milnes had known at Constantinople, was engaged to a Miss Hunter who had been born in Ceylon. 'There are scores of marriages,' Milnes told his friend's wife. 'I shall be left the only bachelor in town.'

At thirty Milnes had gone about London saying he would never marry: 'I never mean to marry, but to hang like a ripe plum over the heads of my nephews and nieces.' Before he was forty he had changed his point of view. His mother was dead; his sister Harriette was now a married woman with a family; Fryston stood empty; he himself had developed a restlessness that was now partly due to loneliness as well as to his old love of society.

I fear you grow sceptical [F. O. Ward wrote to him in April of 1850]. You live in a hurry—you wander restlessly from the enjoyable present—all things touch you, nothing sticks—you are urged on, not as of old by desire tempting before, but by Ennui threatening behind. . . . In your perplexity you drink claret & eat olives. . . . Isn't it all a fine joke? Ah! Milnes, you laugh at me—but behold! 'around your own hat you wear a green willow'!

Amongst Milnes' sophisticated friends the subject of his marriage was taken no more seriously than his political activities. 'Your notion of a wife is evidently a Strasbourg goose whom you will always find by the fireside when you come home from amusing yourself,' said Lady Ashburton. Samuel Rogers told Ruskin [1] that Milnes' failure to marry Miss Coutts provided an exception to the rule that any man could get any woman if he were sufficiently determined. Rogers declared that Milnes had cried out on one occasion, 'If only Miss Coutts was poor!' 'That has been tried before, Mr. Milnes,' someone retorted, 'without the smallest success.' Yet Milnes' remark about Miss Coutts, if made at all, might have been made in good faith. Marriage was still a recognised means of improving a man's fortune, and Milnes, without being cynical, would have wished to marry well; but he could never have made

---

[1] *The Order of Release*, edited by Admiral Sir William James (John Murray, 1947), p. 77.

an entirely worldly marriage. Nor did he wish to marry some pampered or adder-tongued girl. The women he really admired were high-minded, religious, intelligent and cultivated women like Miss Charlotte Williams-Wynn, Miss Coutts, or the sisters Parthenope and Florence Nightingale. Rumour, of course, had linked Milnes' name with a variety of possible wives. It was said he had wished to marry one of the Wyndhams of Petworth; it was known that the Carlisles wanted him to marry their daughter Lady Mary Howard; he was alleged to have proposed to Miss Coutts (like every other bachelor in London) and to have been very 'taken' with some beautiful girl obliquely called in his letters 'the marchesina.' In 1883 he told Jowett that he had once been 'on the point' of marrying Miss Louisa Stuart-Mackenzie, a tiresome woman who became Lord Ashburton's second wife. But from 1844 till 1848 one rumour had persisted about Milnes: he was considered to have fixed his choice upon the younger daughter of a Whig squire from Derbyshire. Her name was Florence Nightingale.

Milnes had first met the Nightingales in 1842, when he was staying with Lord and Lady Palmerston at Broadlands. The family consisted of a father (a rich and educated but not intellectual man, a Liberal who had been at Trinity and had the same background of unitarian forebears as Milnes himself), of a mother who was well-bred and frivolous, and of two daughters—thin-waisted, distinguished-looking girls who had the peculiarity of being named after the Italian towns in which they had been born. In 1842 Florence Nightingale was a grave, demure young woman of twenty-two, with fine arched eyebrows, auburn hair parted in the middle and drawn smoothly back to a braided knot worn high on her head, a strong intelligence, and an expression of reflection, even of melancholy. Unlike Parthenope (who had an aesthetic approach to life, liked flowers and poetry, and lived in what her sister considered a cloud-world of illusion) Florence was early obsessed by a realisation of the miseries of mankind. She already felt a sense of vocation, a conviction of a call from God. When Mrs. Nightingale took her daughters to evening parties she had to remind Florence (but not Parthenope) to take trouble with her clothes, and when the carriage drove up to some lit front-door where the powdered footmen waited and the noise of music and laughter tumbled out into the foggy street, Florence would see only the half-starved faces of the people who stood on the pavements hungrily watching the guests arrive for the ball. Her family's houses, Lea Hurst near the River Derwent in Derbyshire, Embley in the New Forest, oppressed her by their luxury and by the aimlessness of the life they enshrined.   The Nightingales' female friends thought the girls could never hope to find men worthy of them or homes better than that in which they had been brought up.

In these early days none of Florence's intimates or relatives understood that she was called on to improve the world in her generation or that marriage could form no part in her scheme of life.   When it became obvious that Monckton Milnes was captivated by the compelling charm of Florence, her parents were gratified.   Mrs. Nightingale read his speeches and his poetry, arranged for him to take herself and her daughters to the museum or the House, and was enchanted when they found him at the British Association meeting at Oxford in 1847, an occasion on which Milnes gallantly mesmerised Doctor Buckland's tame bear, Tig, so that Florence Nightingale could fondle it.   But more important than the pleasure of the Nightingales at the prospect of acquiring as a son-in-law a fashionable man of letters and Member of Parliament, is the reaction of Miss Nightingale herself.   For it was only after a long and painful struggle that she finally rejected Richard Monckton Milnes.   She reached her ultimate decision in Derbyshire, some time in the summer or autumn of the year 1848.

In a letter written when she was a middle-aged woman, Miss Nightingale referred wistfully to her own refusal of marriage 'with the man whom I adored.'   Although this remark should not be allowed undue weight (Miss Nightingale at times powerfully dramatised her own sentiments) it is certain that when she was young she preferred Milnes to any other man and that she almost married him.

I do not understand it—I am ashamed to understand it [she wrote in her diary in 1849], . . . I know that if I were to see him again, the very thought of doing so quite overcomes me.   I know that since I refused him not one day has passed without my thinking of him, that life is desolate without his sympathy.   And yet, do I want to marry him?   I know that I could not bear his life—that to be nailed to a continuation or an exaggeration of my present life without hope of another would be intolerable to me—that voluntarily to put it out of my power ever to be able to seize the chance of forming for myself a true and rich life would seem to me like suicide.

In another analysis of her feelings written about this time, and published by Sir Edward Cook in 1913, Miss Nightingale considered her intellectual, 'passional' and moral natures in relation to those of Milnes.   She decided that he could satisfy the first two aspects of her character, but not the third, and that she could be content to spend 'a life with him combining our different powers in some great object,' but not to pass her time 'in making society and arranging domestic things.' Milnes' idealism and urge to alleviate life appealed to her. After his death she wrote to Lady Galway:

He had the same voice and manner for a dirty brat as for a duchess—the same desire to give pleasure and good. . . . He had I believe the genius of friendship in philanthropy—not philanthropy—but treating *all* his fellow mortals as if they were his brothers and sisters. In conversation he never allowed his unique power of humour to say an unkind thing.

She said that Milnes had told her father that he seldom subscribed to charities or institutions because he preferred 'to find out individuals and do the best he could for each—(not to give away only money, but time, thought, fellow-feeling with money).' He had once said to her: 'If there is any good in me, it is that I would lay out my life in good service to others.' Although he was not passionately in love with her (he was not capable of passionate love) Florence Nightingale evoked the best part of Milnes' nature. Of all the little mirrors in which we catch a sight of his refracted image, that which Miss Nightingale holds out to us is amongst the clearest. Of all the little beams of light which flicker for a moment on Milnes' elusive, trotting figure, one of the strongest and the purest is that cast by the Lady with the Lamp.

When Miss Nightingale had refused to marry Milnes for the last time (he is said to have made a number of proposals), her parents packed her off to Rome, and in the following year to Egypt. Neither St. Peter's nor the Pyramids made her change her mind. In Italy she studied nursing and in the Valley of the Kings she studied sores. Yet the fact that she did not marry Milnes had made a deeper impression on her life than on his. In 1862, when she had become a personage of international fame, Milnes himself penned the wry epitaph to his old romance. He was staying at Lea Hurst in that autumn, and he was (as usual) writing to MacCarthy:

This is Mr. Nightingale's house in Derbyshire [he wrote] in which fourteen years ago I asked Florence Nightingale to marry me: if she had done so there would have been a heroine the less in the world & certainly not a hero the more.

Much though he learned to admire Miss Nightingale's work (they remained firm friends and collaborators all their lives), Milnes must have known quite well that he had had a providential escape. Miss Nightingale's virtues were public and not domestic virtues. Her inspiration, harnessed to her energy, would have been intolerable at Fryston or at Bawtry. Her special gift, for inspiring her most intimate friends, had proved fatal to several. Milnes needed only to turn his head back to the past year, 1861, to remark the early and exhausted deaths of Arthur Clough and Sidney Herbert. In any case Miss Nightingale was not cut out for marriage. 'People often say to me,' she wrote to her confidante, Madame Mohl, in 1861, 'You don't know what a wife and mother feels. No, I say, I don't and I'm very glad I don't. And *they* don't know what *I feel.*' Looking back from the happy security of his own marriage, Milnes found nothing in Miss Nightingale's refusal that could cause him to repine. For in less than one year after her departure for Italy he realised that he had found someone whom he once described to Tennyson as 'a perfect woman.' She was as idealistic and as elegant as Florence Nightingale. She was gayer, gentler, prettier and more quiet. She was less public-minded and incidentally less rich. Above all else, she had a capacity for a purely personal affection, for concentrating love upon an individual in a way for which Florence Nightingale—with her sweeping anxiety for the reform of the War Office or of the Army in India—had neither the talent nor the time. This young lady, whom Milnes married on 30 June 1851, was Annabel Hungerford Crewe, who lived at Madeley, in Staffordshire.

V

'A pretty place, but with collieries all about' Milnes had written on one of his first visits to Madeley Manor in 1844. While technically in Staffordshire, Madeley was situated close to the Cheshire–Staffordshire border, and lay about a morning's brisk drive in the pony trap from the famous crocketed Elizabethan mansion and the new railway junction of Crewe. Superficially the conditions at Madeley—the sharp tooth of slag that jutted up above the tree-tops, the occasional plumes of factory smoke drawn out along the sky, and the days when the air in the garden seemed to choke you—might have reminded Richard Milnes of his own home in the West Riding; but the scenery at Madeley was far more picturesque and far more rural. Fryston and its gaunt park were by contrast impersonal and bleak.

Madeley was a modest, untidy, black-and-white manor-house which had come into the possession of the Crewes of Crewe by a seventeenth-century marriage, and to which in the very early Regency period a charming modern house with white-plastered walls and a ballroom with a bow end had been tacked on. Over each of the tall french windows on the ground-floor of the new

THE HONOURABLE ANNABEL CREWE

house an oblong basso-relievo with a classical theme was inset. The windows opened on to a plain stone terrace without a balustrading, from which the lawn sloped to an iron fence at the bottom of the garden. On the other side of this fence was a steep meadowland (lush in summer with sheep's-parsley and big buttercups) and a marl-pit pond. At the end of the meadow rose a high, conical hill like a steeple hat, which by a Welsh tradition the family at Madeley called 'the Bryn.' From the high-road to Madeley village you approached the manor-house by a drive which curled through pointed gateposts and between dark, dense shrubberies of rhododendron and old hollies. Behind the shrubberies were the brick stables and carriage-houses and the kitchen garden. In springtime the primroses and bluebells, speckled fritillaries and celandines covered the mossy ground beyond the limits of the Madeley garden, and long pink foxgloves and willowherb and sorrel in their season. On summer afternoons the scent of tea-roses and honeysuckle and syringa and white and purple lilacs hung upon the air, while the gardeners pruned the evergreens, the lopped branches falling with a rustle on the drive. In autumn the woods and paths were spongy with rotting leaves, and toadstools and tree-fungi gleamed in the depths of the Madeley woods.[1]

The owner of Madeley, when Milnes first stayed there, was Mrs. Cunliffe Offley, an old lady who lived there with her niece, Annabel Crewe. Milnes had known both of them slightly in Italy in 1833 and 1834. 'Mrs. Cunliffe' was a widow, only daughter of the first Lord Crewe of Crewe, a Whig politician who was made a baron by George III, but who traced his ancestry back to the middle of the twelfth century. He had married Frances Greville, the beautiful and sprightly Mrs. Crewe to whom Sheridan dedicated *The School for Scandal*, the friend of Burke and Fox and Mrs. Piozzi and of Reynolds, who had painted her portrait three times. She and her husband had two children—a son John, the second Lord Crewe (the subject of Reynolds' *Master Crewe as Henry VIII*), and a girl, Emma, who married a son of Sir Forster Cunliffe and brought him Madeley as her dowry. The second Lord Crewe was a soldier, who got heavily into debt and retired to the Continent. He died in 1835 at his château near Liège, and his title and possessions passed to his son Hungerford, a very tall, bearded, rather weak-minded young man, who spent his life rebuilding and embellishing Crewe Hall with the aid of the architect Ambrose Poynter. Hungerford Lord Crewe had two sisters—Henriette, who had lived abroad with her father, became

---

[1] These details are drawn from Miss Crewe's correspondence with her sister which has happily been preserved.

a Roman Catholic, and on his death settled at Bath; and Annabel, who was brought up by her aunt and uncle Cunliffe at Madeley. Mrs. Cunliffe, who used to tell Milnes how much she had been handicapped by the beauty and brilliance of her mother, was an amiable, religious woman. After her husband's death in 1832 she concentrated all her attention upon her niece Annabel.

Annabel Crewe had been born in 1814, and was just the same age as Milnes' sister Harriette Galway. She was of an elegant appearance, with dark brown hair and light grey eyes, a dimpled face and a smile which Leigh Hunt said was 'like a piece of good news.' Her manner attracted persons as widely different from each other as Nathaniel Hawthorne and Lady Palmerston. 'Quite unaffected, sweet and easy to get on with' Hawthorne wrote of her in his *English Notebooks*, adding (his term of highest praise) that she reminded him of 'the best-mannered American women.' Disraeli called her 'most pleasing' and 'very clever and intelligent.' She was fond of poetry and of gardens, read a good deal, and had become a competent amateur painter of such subjects as scenes from the Waverley novels. She was sensitive and affectionate: the two people she had so far loved most in her life were her aunt Emma and her sister Henriette, her 'Dearest Dear,' to whom she would write almost daily giving every little detail of her life. The third place in her heart was occupied by the house and garden at Madeley—'sweet Madeley,' which she preferred to anywhere else on earth, and for which she longed amidst the heavy chestnut blooms of the London season and in the drawing-room of her aunt's London house in Upper Brook Street.

In London Miss Crewe's closest friend was Milnes' cousin and Varnhagen's correspondent, Charlotte Williams-Wynn. Like Miss Wynn she cared little for general society, would have had no use for the Bath House circle, and went very seldom to balls. Her ideal of life was to live quietly with her aunt at Madeley, reading aloud to her in the high-ceilinged library (where the books were protected with gilt-wire grills), walking in the garden with her cousin Emma Blackburn, picking primroses in the spring or superintending the making of raspberry jam in the summer, helping the sick villagers or embroidering a flag for the Friendly Club, watching to see if the laurustinus would flower in September, or driving herself over in the trap to find out what 'Hungerford' was doing at Crewe. She did not even much care for staying at Crewe, with 'a clatter of folks' making the great Tudor galleries echo, though she was fond of the Greville cousins, who congregated there, and she would sometimes visit at a neighbouring house like Catton or Capesthorne. The life Miss Crewe led

at Madeley corresponded to the life that Richard's father liked
to lead in Yorkshire—a slow, preoccupying country life, peaceful
and vegetative, unchanging and civilised. So long as her aunt
lived Miss Crewe felt no temptation towards any other mode of
life at all.

Mrs. Cunliffe died, after a lingering illness, in February 1850,
and her niece found herself suddenly alone, the owner of the London
house in Upper Brook Street, of some fine Reynoldses and of a
small sum of money which her brother supplemented with an
annual income of two hundred pounds. Throughout the spring
of 1850 Miss Crewe was overwhelmed with grief. She let the
London house and retreated to Madeley, where she busied herself
with the erection of a memorial to her Aunt Emma. 'The
Memorial' became the centre and chief interest of her life in the
sad summer months that followed. It consisted of a piece of land
which she gave in perpetuity to Madeley village for allotments.
On this land she built a cottage for the allotment keeper and an
elaborate stone fountain, which was the visible monument to her
aunt. 'The Memorial' was designed, after many letters and con-
sultations, by the architect Ambrose Poynter, who had built St.
Katharine's chapel and hospital in Regent's Park and had been
employed on the alterations at Crewe. It was a high, elaborate
structure of perpendicular Gothic, with water spouting out of
cast-iron dolphins' mouths, sundials on each side, a central spire
with a ball and a cross upon it, a parapet, and some curved stone
seats on which old people could sit. The details of the monument
were made by Mr. Dean, the London carver, and the whole of it
was constructed of the best Caen stone. Near the memorial there
grew a large oak tree, beneath which Miss Crewe would stand
talking to the workmen as they dug the foundations or poured in
the concrete. She drove down from her house each day with her
dogs, and stood there under the tree, in her long, full skirts and
her shady straw hat, watching the progress of the work. So long
as she lived at Madeley the Memorial, she declared, would be her
'favourite haunt.'

On her aunt's death Miss Crewe had received a great many
consolatory letters, and amongst these one from her 'kind old
friend' Richard Monckton Milnes. In June 1850, before she left
London, they had seen each other, at his request, at the Grafton
Street house of Charlotte Williams-Wynn. He had written to her
again from Marienbad, and this had been followed up by a pointed
invitation to stay at Serlby with Lady Galway, which Miss Crewe
had politely declined. She spent the autumn and winter of 1850
alone at Madeley, having the house repainted, making herself a new

sitting-room upstairs, and trying to forget how forlorn she felt.
In the spring of 1851, the year of the Great Exhibition, she decided
to go up to London and to reopen her aunt's house.

Miss Crewe had not been long in Upper Brook Street before she
detected a lot of 'foolish gossip' about Milnes' intentions with regard
to her. She noticed that he came increasingly often to see her, until
by the end of April they were seeing each other every day. They
met at the dinner-tables of her brother Crewe and of their common
friends; they went with the Dudley Carletons to see a panorama
of the Holy Land; he would hand her into her brougham in
Lincoln's Inn on Sundays, after the fashionable, crowded sermons
of F. D. Maurice; and he kept calling on her and giving her books.
One day Milnes took Miss Crewe and Emma Blackburn for a pre-
view of the Crystal Palace ('MMM in high spirits at our pleasure
and gratitude'), and they admired the sculpture and machinery
which were now filling the great glass conservatory ready for the
official opening on 1 May.

At the end of April Miss Crewe returned to Madeley; Richard
Milnes told her that he was going to stay with the Davenports
at Capesthorne and would like to come over to lunch on St. Mark's
Day. By this time all London thought his attentions 'very marked,'
and Miss Crewe began to realise that she found him the gayest,
kindest, most thoughtful and charming companion in the world.
He asked if he could come to stay for Whitsun, which fell in the
second week of June. He arrived, 'looking very ill and nervous,'
on Whit-Sunday evening, just as Miss Crewe and her cousin were
driving back from afternoon church. They gave him some wine
and water and walked him round the Bryn. Whit-Monday was
wet and the ladies spent the day at their work-frames, while
Richard Milnes read aloud to them 'with his musical voice.' The
ladies thought him increasingly nervous and noticed that he once
referred to Miss Crewe as 'Annabel.'

On the next morning Miss Crewe came down the central staircase at Madeley, from the walls of which the rigid, rectilinear faces
of seventeenth-century Crewes and Offleys stared. As she entered
the sunlit library, Richard Monckton Milnes, who had been sitting
there waiting, abruptly rose from his armchair and asked her
'in his gentle loving tone' to be his wife. When she accepted him,
he told her that he had been wanting to ask this question for the
last two years, but had not known what she felt. Emma Blackburn,
who came suddenly into the library, found them engaged in
animated, happy explanations like those in the closing act of a
Shakespeare comedy. It was agreed that Miss Crewe should write
to her brother and Richard to his father, informing them of the

engagement, at the end of that week.   Meanwhile they read and
laughed and chattered all through the long June day.   The
members of the Madeley Friendly Club, who were proud of their
new band, had arranged to perform in the manor garden that
Tuesday.   When the band had at length shuffled away between
the rhododendrons of the drive, Miss Crewe took Richard Milnes
down to look at the Memorial, which he had not yet seen.

For Milnes, now forty-two, marriage was the last experiment
and natural solution.   He had attained an age when no startling
or volcanic development could be expected of him, even in his
own eyes.   The evident promise of his early youth had blown
away like thistle-down, as Stafford O'Brien had feared it would:
'I think you are near something very glorious, but you will never
reach it.'   The world saw Milnes as a minor poet, a talkative
politician, an endearing companion and a wit.   Those who knew
him most intimately recognised his singular gift for personal friendship, and for gaining and keeping the deep affection of individuals
of every class and kind.   Hitherto, in spite of all his contacts, his
life had been a little lonely; in his marriage with Miss Crewe
he found precisely what he needed.   His wife did not share, and
could not cure, his restless passion for society, but both at Fryston
and at their house in Upper Brook Street she provided him with
the atmosphere of calm, fond domesticity for which in past days
he had often yearned.

If you don't marry and have a family [Milnes had written in
one of his commonplace books] you find that you lose the comfort
of easy, indiscriminating, illogical natural affections just when you
most want it.   Ambitious, lively, loving youth looks almost with
contempt on the parental affection that loves it for itself & not for
its merits, but middle age soon finds it weary work to be for ever
winning fresh affection & ever deserving it & looks back with deep
regret on the lavish love that it neglected or lightly prized.

It was in this mood of ripening wisdom that Milnes embarked
on marriage and on middle age.

INDEX

Index

Buller, Arthur, 21, 156, 273

Buller, Charles, Milnes' collaboration with, 155; their friendship, 157; the Durham Report, 157; death of (1848), 157, 287; Milnes' tribute to, 287; mentioned, 13, 103, 112, 188, 258, 273

Bulwer, Edward Lytton, 103, 301

Bulwer, Henry Lytton, estimate and career of, 255; his *Life of Palmerston* quoted, 266 *and n.*[3], 276; quoted, 288; on *Palm Leaves*, 266 *and n.*[1]; on Jewish Relief Bill, 268; mentioned, 191, 262, 267

Bunsen family, 26, 48

Bunsen, George, cited, 48; Milnes' letter to, on Prince Albert's death, quoted, 122; quoted on Milnes' tenderness in friendship, 222 *and n.*

Bunsen, Chevalier Hans Christian von, appearance and reputation of, 47, 212; Milnes' attitude to, 48, 222; Varnhagen's, 216; mentioned, 182, 298

Burdett-Coutts, Baroness, 186

Burns, Robert, 22

Burton, Isabel, 148; cited, 42, 84 *n.*[1]

Byam family, 80 *n.*[2]

Byng, Poodle, 159

Byron, Lord, influence of, in Cambridge, 21–2; Milnes on Moore's biography of, 23; inter-Union debate on, 24; legend of, 52; Finlay's recollections of, 60; quoted, 62

Bystram, Oberst, 223

Caine, Hall, cited, 70 *n.*[1]

Cairo, 172

Cambridge, balloon ascent over, 14; University: Trinity College, 1; New Court, 11, 13; Milnes at, 1, 6, 12, 292; chapel system and curriculum, 11; wasters at, 11–12; the Apostles, 14 *et seq.*; the Union, 14–15; debate with Oxford, 24; Milnes' leaving, 24

Campbell, Sir Alexander, 50

Campbell, Mrs. Gordon, 106

Campbell, Thomas, 110, 233–4

Canning, Lord, 145 *n.*; quoted, 261 *and n.*[2]

Canning, Sir Stratford, *see* Redcliffe

Capo d'Istria, Conte, 62

Capodistrias, 53, 54, 60

Card, Dr. 23–4

Carlyle, Thomas, Milnes' friendship with, 76, 112–14 *and n.*; their rides together, 119; his welcome to Milnes (1843), 182; warns Milnes against

Mayfair, 161, 202; his estimate of Robert Milnes, 10; his *Chartism*, 152; *Past and Present*, 184 *and n.*; his influence on Charles Buller, 157; his letter to Lady Harriet Baring quoted, 157; visit to Fryston, 139–41; his view of the aristocracy, 159; his estimate of Keats, 294 *and n.*[2]; cited, 261, 288; quoted, 252, 268; on Fryston, 82; on Peel, 101; on Jews, 268; mentioned, 47, 230

Carlyle, Mrs. (Jane), 33, 158, 159, 225, 282; on Milnes, 297

Castle Ashby, 19

Charles X, King, 64

Chartists, 184, 276, 281

Chateaubriand, 285

Chatterton, Lady Georgiana, 154, 228; cited, 89

Church, Gen., 59

Church, Roman, 42

Circourt, Comte and Comtesse Adolphe de, 65–6 *and nn.*, 270

Clanricarde, Lady, 274

Claremont, 270, 279

Clarendon, Lord, 266

Clarke, Charles Cowden, 293

Clough, Arthur, 308

Cobden, Richard, 250

Coleridge, Hartley, 206, 207 *n.*

Coleridge, Mrs. Sara, cited, 50

Colville, James, 116; quoted, 181

Conservative, adoption of a cure, by Tories, 102

Considérant, 283, 284

Constantinople, 162, 164, 167; Milnes' comments on, 169

Conyngham, Mr. and Mrs., 284, 285

Copeland cited, 142 *and n.*[3]

Copyright Bill (1842), 150 *and n.*[2]

Corfu, 56

Cork, Lady (great-aunt), 28 *n.*, 90, 115; her appearance and character, 35–6; her importance, 89; her death, 127

Corn Law Repeal, 243–4; its effect on Pontefract, 253

Cornelius (painter), 220

Cornwall, Barry (Bryan Waller Procter), 231

Corruption, political, 96, 99, 151, 259

Costa Calral, 254 *and n.*

Court fancy balls, 152 *et seq.*–155

Courvoisier, 128, 129

Cousin, Victor, 270

Coutts, Miss, 108, 304–5

Coventry, Lady, 41, 42

Cracow, 254, 287

Cranbrook, Lord (G. Gathorne-Hardy), 195, 196 *n.*

Cratloe, 18, 95

316

Index